DESIGNING
REGENERATIVE CULTURES

Daniel Christian Wahl

Published by Triarchy Press
Axminster, England
   info@triarchypress.net
   www.triarchypress.net

with International Futures Forum
Aberdour, Scotland
   www.internationalfuturesforum.com

Copyright © 2016 Daniel Christian Wahl (some rights reserved)

The right of Daniel Christian Wahl to be identified as the author of this book has been asserted by him under the Copyright, Designs and Patents Act 1988.

This work is licensed under a Creative Commons Attribution – Non Commercial – No Derivs 4.0 International License. For more information, please visit: https://creativecommons.org/licenses/by-nc-nd/4.0/

A catalogue record for this book is available from the British Library.

paperback ISBN: 978-1-909470-77-4

ePub ISBN: 978-1-909470-78-1

pdf ISBN: 978-1-909470-79-8

Cover illustration and custom illustrations: Flavia Gargiulo Rosa
www.flaviagargiulo.com

Printed and bound in Great Britain by TJ International Ltd, Padstow

EARLY REVIEWS OF THE BOOK

"Life on the planet has sustained itself for billions of years by continually regenerating itself. Our modern industrial culture has interfered with these natural processes to the point of causing massive extinctions of species and threatening our very survival. This book is a valuable contribution to the important discussion of the worldview and value system we need to redesign our businesses, economies, and technologies – in fact, our entire culture – so as to make them regenerative rather than destructive."
    Fritjof Capra, author of *The Web of Life*, coauthor of *The Systems View of Life*

"To me as a life-long activist nourished on systems thinking and Buddhist teachings, this is one of the most intellectually exciting and soul stirring books I've read in years. I had the sense of drinking it, with pleasure and surprise, not having known what I'd so thirsted for.

By starting with questions and keeping to questions throughout, Daniel engages the reader, and by example frees her from striving for, or pretending to know, any final answers. This approach – in itself a rare lesson in systems epistemology – invites trust, openness, and a restructuring of the mind.

Among the gifts for which I am especially grateful are these: Conceptual tools for perceiving and experiencing our mutual belonging, and especially what I've come to call the great reciprocity at the heart of the universe. The ways Goethe, Bortoft, Bateson, Maturana, and Varela are brought in, and key insights mediated with economy and clarity. The abundant evidence of the Great Turning, the manifold transition underway to a life-sustaining culture. And, especially valuable to those of an apocalyptic bent like myself, the 'adaptive cycle' of resilient systems, showing that at 'the edge of chaos' comes opportunity for the emergence of greater complexity and intelligence. These are but a few of the ways in which this remarkable book will enrich my thought, my teaching, and my life in this turbulent world of ours."
    Joanna Macy, environmental activist, scholar of Buddhism, general systems theory,
  and deep ecology and author of *World as Lover, World as Self* and numerous other books.

"This book is a treasure for everyone who is looking for a guide to more sustainable living and a roadmap for re-designing our societies, regenerating our communities, cities and societies in harmony with natural systems and our home planet.

Daniel Wahl has deep experience to share and his knowledge in this beautiful book will help all those aspiring to be responsible global citizens working for our common future."
    Hazel Henderson, author and President, Ethical Markets Media, Certified B.
                          Corporation, USA & Brazil

"This is an excellent addition to the literature on ecological design and it will certainly form a keystone in the foundations of the new MA in Ecological Design Thinking at Schumacher College. It not only contains a wealth of ideas on what Dr Wahl has termed 'Designing Regenerative Cultures' but what is probably more important, it provides some stimulating new ways of looking at persistent problems in our contemporary culture and

hence opens up new ways of thinking and acting in the future. Each chapter begins with an important question like, 'Why Nurture Resilience and Whole Systems Health' or 'Why Take a Design-Based Approach' and what follows in each case are suggestions to encourage deeper thinking. This is a very stimulating approach to learning. I am looking forward to using Dr Wahl's book in challenging conversations with colleagues and students."
      Seaton Baxter, Professor in Ecological Design Thinking, Schumacher College, UK

"Worldviews change when existing solutions no longer work and rising problems require new approaches. *Designing Regenerative Cultures* is a lighthouse charting multiple pathways to the restless, impatient, continuing inquiry of our times, and […] gathering, including and transcending scattered parts of the undivided whole. Time may position *Designing Regenerative Cultures* as Daniel's 'meisterstück' and as a must read to all those who are aspiring to be at the forefront of the regenerative (r)evolution."
      May East, Chief International Officer, Gaia Education

"Living in a text-message culture, *Designing Regenerative Cultures* is another kind of text message, an essential textbook for our times, filled with resources, references, practices, methods and pathways, and best of all questions we can each live into, alone and together. Our world has benefitted from the contributions of many authors and visionaries, grassroots activists and social entrepreneurs, modern scientists and wise indigenous elders […] And yet, the single-hero journey of brilliant ones can only carry us so far. There is a deep need and longing for a local and global community of care on all levels in all disciplines. Daniel Wahl takes us there in this comprehensive 'manifesto', offering a wholistic picture of a way and a world we can be for, in lieu of the one that seems so headed for destruction […] Daniel weaves an 'old/new' story helping and I suspect activating, readers to see, respect, learn from and go beyond, as he so clearly has, the great hearts and minds he references throughout. The book contributes to this awakening field as we find ourselves looking through a kaleidoscope of perspectives and teachings - different lenses moving in a spiral together through which to both view and live in our world. It can serve as a foundation for another 'great turn', a directory for next steps worth taking. Many will find inspiration and support to live the way we know we must, to live in the way we know we can if our species is not only to survive, but actually thrive in partnership with all of life."
      Virginia (Gigi) Coyle, co-author of *The Way of Council* and *The Box: Remembering the Gift*; co-creator of the Ojai Foundation, the School of Lost Borders and Beyond Boundaries.

"Daniel Wahl has compiled a great deal of useful information in a masterful synthesis. That alone is a significant accomplishment, but he's given us more than that. *Designing Regenerative Cultures* describes the doorway to a possible, indeed, necessary future. We are not fated to the dystopia in prospect. We have, as he writes, the capacity to design and to organize our societies to protect, enhance, and celebrate life. The blueprint was there all along. The awareness of our possibilities is growing. The art and sciences of ecological design are flourishing. The choice, as always, is ours and that of those who will follow."
      David Orr (environmentalist and Paul Sears Professor of Environmental Studies and Politics at Oberlin College and a James Marsh Professor at the University of Vermont).

Contents

FOREWORD ~ David Orr 11
FOREWORD ~ Graham Leicester 13
INTRODUCTION 15

CHAPTER 1 — Living the Questions: Why change the narrative now? 19

Questioning dangerous ideologies 25
Facing complexity means befriending uncertainty and ambiguity 28
Caring for the Earth is caring for ourselves and our community 31
Wake up to find out that you are the eyes of the world 33
The 'why' will guide the 'what' and the 'how' 36
Spirituality, soul and solitude in nature 38
Sustainability as a learning journey: pilgrims and apprentices 40
Sustainability is not enough; we need regenerative cultures 43

CHAPTER 2 — Why choose transformative over sustaining innovation? 49

The Three Horizons of innovation and culture change 53
Evaluating disruptive innovation in the age of transition 57
Transformative innovation is about deep questioning 60
Sensitivity to scale, uniqueness of place and local culture 62
The transformative power of social innovation 64
Collaborative consumption and peer-to-peer collaboration 66
Facilitating systems innovation and culture change 67

CHAPTER 3 — Why *do* we need to think and act more systemically? 73

Believing is seeing and seeing is believing 76
The whole is more than the sum of its parts 79
From the 'crisis of perception' to the 'systems view of life' 81
Interbeing 85
How can we participate appropriately in complex systems? 87
The IFF World System Model 89
Learning to see nature everywhere 92
Being a process, and seeing in relationships 94

CHAPTER 4 — Why nurture resilience and whole-systems health? ... 97

Rolling back Earth Overshoot Day ... 99
Learning to live within planetary boundaries ... 101
What exactly are resilience and transformative resilience? ... 104
The adaptive cycle as a dynamic map for resilience thinking ... 107
Panarchy: a scale-linking perspective of systemic transformation ... 109
Local and regional community resilience building is going global ... 111
How can we nurture transformative resilience? ... 115
From control and prediction to conscious participation, foresight and anticipation ... 119

CHAPTER 5 — Why take a design-based approach? ... 123

Design education enables cultural transformation ... 124
Design is where theory and practice meet ... 129
Design follows worldview and worldview follows design ... 131
Ethics and design for regenerative cultures ... 132
Aesthetics and design ... 134
Emergence and design ... 136
Designing for positive emergence (a case study) ... 138
Scale-linking, salutogenic design for resilience ... 142
The resurgence of a culture of makers: re-localizing production ... 144
Collective visioning and design conversations change culture ... 147

CHAPTER 6 — How can we learn to better design *as* nature? ... 151

Ecoliteracy: Learning from living systems ... 154
Valuing traditional ecological knowledge and indigenous wisdom ... 157
How does life create conditions conducive to life? ... 163
Biologically inspired innovation ... 166
Green chemistry and material science ... 168
Biologically inspired product design ... 171
Biomimetic architecture ... 175
Nature's whole system optimization informs community design ... 178

Living the questions together creates community 180

Industrial ecology and symbiosis are closing the loops 183

Ecologically informed urban and regional planning... 187

CHAPTER 7 — Why are regenerative cultures rooted in cooperation? 191

Redesigning agriculture for food sovereignty and subsidiarity 196

Regenerative agriculture: effective responses to climate change 199

Learning from and mimicking healthy ecosystems.. 203

Redesigning economics based on ecology.. 209

Creating circular economies 214

Towards a regenerative economy 218

Thriving communities and the solidarity economy 221

Shifting from quantitative to qualitative growth 224

Valuing the commons by cooperatively sharing the gifts of life............................ 226

Earth Law: the enabling constraints of collective living.. 229

Life's collaborative lessons transform business... 231

Co-creating regenerative enterprises... 236

Collaboration and empathy as evolutionary success stories 240

Activism revisited: conscious participation and collective intelligence................ 246

We are coming back to life and this changes everything.. 252

Learning to listen deeply 255

Inner and outer resilience 259

CONCLUSION — Regenerative cultures are about thriving together 263

Acknowledgements.. 271

References.. 275

About the Author... 286

If I had an hour to solve a problem and my life depended on the solution, I would spend the first 55 minutes determining the proper question to ask, for once I know the proper question, I could solve the problem in less than five minutes.

Attributed to Albert Einstein

FOREWORD ~ David Orr

Cultures are not designed from the top down as much as they grow organically from the bottom up. We try to understand the various happenings through the lenses of history, sociology, anthropology and, after the passage of enough time, archaeology. Even if cultures cannot be designed as whole and coherent things, we have acquired a knack for designing parts like the banking system, the educational system or the next high-rise development. The things so created, however, are mostly tailored to the convenience of the existing structures of power and wealth without regard for the other parts or the long term. The resulting incoherence is a source of much befuddlement to scholars.

So, after several millennia of trial, error and happenstance, our future is in jeopardy. We are trending to a world of maybe eleven billion people, divided by ethnicity, religion, income and nationality. We don't much like each other and the prospects for lethal conflicts are many. We are coming apart at the seams as nation-states appear powerless when challenged by drug cartels, cyber criminals and terrorist organizations. We are increasingly networked, interlinked and mutually dependent but often unable to find common purpose and act for the common good. We are caught between the centripetal and centrifugal forces of post-modernity. And the pace of technological change is accelerating, giving us little time – or even inclination – for reflection. Not the least, we are rapidly changing the climate, extinguishing species, acidifying oceans and destroying entire ecologies.

Against this backdrop, Daniel Wahl proposes "designing regenerative cultures". The vision of a designed future is easy to dismiss as yet another utopian scheme with roughly the same chance of success as Marxism or 19th-century Fourierism. The differences, however, are many.

First, in contrast to all previous eras, we know for certain that business as usual will be suicidal. That has been said so often and for so long as to appear trite with the effect of inducing mass narcosis. Unfortunately, it is true and we should pay attention. Second, the scale of our predicament is global; there are no safe places left anywhere on Earth.

Third, as Wahl describes, the ecological design arts broadly are flourishing. They are transforming farming, building, transportation, manufacturing and planning in ways congenial to ecologies and Earth systems. Their common characteristics are the use of nature as a model for design, maximal use of solar energy, preservation of biological and cultural diversity, and full-cost accounting. Ecological design is no longer a distant prospect, it is happening all over the world. It is practical, not theoretical. It has very large political consequences, but is itself non-ideological and neither liberal nor conservative – simply forward. It is also affecting economics, accounting and the behaviour of investors and corporations. But ecological design has yet to change politics and calibrate governance with ecological processes and systems.

Fourth, ecological design transcends the Western experience. It is not synonymous with engineering or science. Rather, it is a compendium of the entire human experience of farming, building, engineering, planning and making. The ancient Javanese farm or the Balinese water system, for example, demonstrated remarkable design skills, which in some ways exceed our own. That is true partly because the design of resource flows of water and materials coincided with cultural and religious norms in ways that we, in our more compartmentalized world, find incomprehensible. Vernacular design, at its best, included humans, animals, land and waters as whole systems ordained by complex religious systems. The flaws were many, but the results were often durable over centuries. The fact is that there is much to learn about whole-systems design from other cultures and in other times.

Fifth, design is a systems revolution which is the art of seeing things whole and regarding our actions together with their likely consequences. Given the complexity of all systems and our inescapable ignorance, a systems perspective requires humility and precaution. It means working at a smaller scale, say, the neighbourhood, the farm, the factory, before generalizing to systems at a larger scale. Changing the scale also changes the system and so on. Thinking in systems over longer periods of time is the revolution of our time. All of our new gadgetry and inventions pale in comparison. We are, as Wahl ably describes, parts of larger wholes, no one and no organization can be an island complete in itself. The upshot is that systems thinking moves us toward enlightened self-interest by which we understand that our wellbeing and human flourishing is collective, not individual; long-term, not short-term.

Sixth, whether acknowledged or not, systems thinking is kin to the core meaning of religion — 'to bind together' in Latin. We, living in a secular culture, tend not to see the connection, but it is nonetheless inescapable. Aldo Leopold's 'land ethic' and the rules of decent behaviour prescribed in each of the Axial religions bear more than a coincidental similarity to the rules of enlightened design. We are our brother's keeper and also that of the bears, whales, birds, soils, trees, lands and waters; and they ours. The entire system is mindful, shot through with consideration.

The word 'regenerative' in the title of this book signifies a commitment to the life processes inherent in ecological design. That, too, is reciprocal, mutual and inescapable. It also carries the command of the writer of Deuteronomy to "choose life" [30:19] Whether from self-interest or duty, the command requires that we comprehend and value life and life processes, become ecologically competent stewards of land, wildlife, soils, waters, and that we care.

Daniel Wahl has compiled a great deal of useful information in a masterful synthesis. That alone is a significant accomplishment, but he's given us more than that. *Designing Regenerative Cultures* describes the doorway to a possible, indeed, necessary future. We are not fated to the dystopia in prospect. We have, as he writes, the capacity to design and to organize our societies to protect, enhance and celebrate life. The blueprint was there all along. The awareness of our possibilities is growing. The art and sciences of ecological design are flourishing. The choice, as always, is ours and that of those who will follow.

David Orr is Paul Sears Distinguished Professor of Environmental Studies and Politics *at Oberlin College and a* James Marsh Professor *at the University of Vermont*

FOREWORD ~ Graham Leicester

This is a book about life and the love of life. It is also a book animated by questions rather than answers.

A moment's reflection on our own lives helps us realise why this must be so. We are reflective creatures, always questioning, always aware that every advance in knowledge expands the scope of our ignorance: why else would 'a little knowledge' be 'a dangerous thing'? We are all living with more or less acknowledged, more or less conscious, always creative doubt.

At one level we have learned to revel in this, to acknowledge inquisitiveness and curiosity as engines of progress – even in those domains, like the sciences, apparently most wedded to certainty. As the philosopher Alfred North Whitehead put it, life itself is "a creative advance into novelty".

Yet at another level we see – and feel – the storm clouds gathering. Daniel Wahl reminds us that, since the early 1970s, humanity has been drawing more from living systems each year than they can effectively regenerate. We have already overshot or are in danger of breaching a number of critical 'planetary boundaries' – the systems that enable life on Earth. This knowledge inevitably makes us anxious and demanding of answers.

The danger is that unless we marry these two conditions, expansive exploration and anxiety to reach a conclusion, both equally present in most of our lives, we risk devoting our energies to finding perfect solutions to the wrong problem.

Don Michael, joint Professor of Planning and Public Policy and of Psychology at the University of Michigan, wrote in his final published essay about "tentative commitment": the need to acknowledge "our vulnerability, our finiteness, our inevitable ignorance" and yet still commit to action, to change, to hope: "because one hopes that one can make a difference in the face of all that stands in the way of making a difference".

This is the spirit of Daniel's book. At every turn it invites us to consider a bigger picture. To see ourselves not as individuals but as living in a pattern of relationship with others; and that pattern of relationship not as separate from but as part of the wider living systems of nature; and these patterns not as stable structures but as constantly evolving, emerging processes that stretch over generations, over aeons, over centuries.

At the same time, he invites us to focus on our own actions, our own lives, the 'tentative commitments' we can make, are making, in the face of the great challenges we face. The reader looking for answers will find them here in abundance: frameworks for grappling with the big picture like the World Systems Model and the Three Horizons, and principles for effective action from diverse disciplines ranging from ecoliteracy to permaculture, biomimicry to mindfulness, all combined in the idea of design as the discipline where theory meets practice. The sages of effective action are all richly present and referenced. Shining examples, including from Daniel's own wide experience, are much in evidence and back up his belief that "a profound cultural transformation is already on its way".

Supporting this cultural renewal means acting both as hospice workers for the dying culture and midwives for the new. This is the practice of 'transformative innovation' and Daniel captures the dual task well in the central question in his book: "How do we keep the lights on, avoid revolution and turmoil, keep children in school and people in work, yet still manage to fundamentally transform the human presence on planet Earth before 'business as usual' leads to run-away climate change, a drastically impoverished biosphere, and the early demise of our species?"

This book expertly maps the territory in which we will find effective responses to that conundrum. But it remains for us to take the first steps on the journey. In much of the literature on transformative change that metaphor plays easily and unconsciously into Joseph Campbell's review of mythic narrative: the hero's journey. That in turn feeds a demand for 'heroic leadership', 'heropreneurship' and other forms of heroic self-sacrifice in pursuit of world-changing goals.

Daniel avoids that trap by offering us an altogether different metaphor for the journey: the pilgrim. The image speaks to the spirit of humility and disciplined commitment that shines through this book. Daniel has chosen to live his own life as "a cultural creative, a transition designer and an evolutionary activist in the co-creation of regenerative cultures". This is not the path of ease and leisure. But it is the pilgrim's journey.

The metaphor sent me back to John Bunyan's spiritual masterpiece of the late 17th century, *Pilgrim's Progress*. It tells the allegorical journey of everyman, in the character of the pilgrim Christian, "from this world to that which is to come". The book provides a metaphorical map, setting out from the "city of destruction" through the "slough of despond" to "the celestial city", and also a set of resources for the journey. This book has something of the same inspirational and practical quality. Perhaps it is no coincidence to find that Daniel's middle name is Christian.

Graham Leicester is Director of International Futures Forum

INTRODUCTION

I don't know about you, but I was disappointed with the way humanity entered the new millennium. I don't mean the last 15 years. In retrospect those years could be summed-up as 'the glass is full'. Half the glass is full of stories of hope and human kindness; and the other half is full of despair about what we are still doing to each other and the Earth. No, I mean the actual start to the millennium.

We had an opportunity as a species, as humanity, to come together and reflect on the story so far, taking stock, listening to what we really want for ourselves, our families, the places and communities we care about. Such a process of deeper listening and asking important questions together might have helped in creating a basis for co-envisioning the future – a future that we would all like to co-create as one human family.

Yes, there was the Millennium Ecosystem Assessment. It gave our species a rather alarming 'fail' in planetary stewardship; and yes, there were the Millennium Development Goals (MDGs) that the United Nations came to agree upon. Let's hope we muster more collective enthusiasm for the new Sustainable Development Goals (SDGs). The most hopeful and thoughtful process that occurred in the run-up to the new millennium, in terms of a meaningful dialogue about humanity's shared values and aspirations, was the creation of the *Earth Charter*. Sadly not many heads of state – and, more importantly, too few of us – took real notice of it or gave it the importance it deserved. By and large we started the 21st century by simply getting on with 'business as usual' rather than initiating a cross-cultural global dialogue on the broader realities of living together on a finite planet, faced with rapidly growing complexity and uncertainty.

I started the 21st century with a commitment to myself. I would do my best to be part of the solution rather than the problem. Initially this led me to enrol in the MSc in Holistic Science at Schumacher College, which led on to gaining a scholarship from the University of Dundee where I wrote my PhD thesis on *Design for Human and Planetary Health* exploring a participatory perspective on complexity and sustainability. In 2006, I visited Professor David Orr, who had been my PhD examiner, at his home in Oberlin, Ohio. I interviewed him about his vision of ecological design as an integrative discipline that could enable the transition to sustainability. In that conversation he planted the seed for this book.

He suggested that in order to successfully co-create a story with enough meaning to guide us through the transition "we will have to decide not just how we make ourselves sustainable, but why we should be sustained. That's a much more difficult thing." In the process we will be confronted with much deeper questions of meaning: "Who are we? What are we? Was our role here on this planet simply to dig up carbon and release it into the atmosphere and then expire? Was that what we were all about?" He added: "If our debate does not go further than the language of neoclassical economics, we are done for! Because you cannot make an economic argument for human survival, you have to make a spiritual argument for human survival. We are worth it, and we are worthy of it in that higher sense."

We need to ask the deeper question of *why* we are worth sustaining. Our answers will inform how we ask the more operational questions and implement tentative answers and solutions. Such deeper questioning will shape *how* we might initiate wise actions that help us to transition towards regenerative cultures. Starting with the *why* will help us to understand our own deeper motivation, purpose and goals. We need to question the beliefs that shape our worldview. Only by starting with the *why* will we inspire people to change their behaviour and to co-create regenerative cultures.

What matters urgently is that we do come together to have conversations about what future we want for humanity. We need to reflect on how we *will* have to change individually and collectively to create this future. By asking such questions together we may come to understand that we *will* have to collaborate as one species and learn to transcend and include our differences if we want a thriving future for all of humanity. We need to ask important questions about *why* and *what if*. We need to rediscover the common ground of human comm*unity*. This will enable us to co-create a future worth living in. We need a collective narrative about *who* we are and *why* we are worth sustaining, a shared story powerful enough to keep us all innovative, creative and collaborative as we question into the *what, how, when* and *where*.

I began the new millennium with a promise to myself to listen more deeply; to listen into why so few people were stepping up to the necessary transformation ahead; to listen into why they were behaving as they were, how they saw the world, why so many of their stories ended with "that's just how it is" or "that's just human nature". I also promised myself that I would pay special attention to the kind of questions we might have to ask ourselves on our long learning journey towards a more sustainable, regenerative and thriving future.

This book is about what I have learned from deep listening and living these questions. It explores how we might *live* our way rather than *know* our way into the future, how we might stop chasing the mirage of certainty and control in a complex and unpredictable world. How can we collaborate in the creation of diverse regenerative cultures adapted to the unique biocultural conditions of place? How can we create conditions conducive to life?

Daniel Christian Wahl
Es Molinar, Majorca
March 2016

(Wherever text is underlined or an obelisk (†) appears, more information is available online at www.triarchypress.net/questions)

CHAPTER 1

Living the Questions: Why change the narrative now?

[…] have patience with everything unresolved in your heart and do try to love the questions themselves as if they were locked rooms or books written in a very foreign language. Don't search for the answers, which could not be given to you now, because you would not be able to live them. The point is to live everything. *Live the questions now*. Perhaps then, someday in the future, you will gradually, without even noticing it, live your way into the answer.

Rainer Maria Rilke (1903)

Our culture is obsessed with quick-fix solutions and immediate answers. Time is at a premium and we don't want to waste it dwelling on questions. The credo is: let's get practical and not waste time with theory or philosophy! But how can you waste time with the '*love of wisdom*'? Is it not wisdom that will help us chart our path into an uncertain and unpredictable future? Do we not desperately need wisdom to respond wisely to the multiple converging crises around us? With wisdom we can see these healing crises as the drivers of a deeper cultural transformation that is already occurring in many places around the world and spreading rapidly, challenging us to let go of outdated mental models and a narrative about who we are that no longer serves us.

Questions, more than answers, are the pathway to collective wisdom

By living and loving the questions more deeply we can rediscover the beauty and abundance around us, find deep meaning in belonging to the universe, deep joy in nurturing relationships with all of life, and deep satisfaction in co-creating a thriving and healthier life for all. Questions, more than answers, are the pathway to collective wisdom. Questions can spark culturally creative conversations that transform how we see ourselves and our relationship to the world. With this in mind, everything changes instantly.

In a culture that demands definitive answers, questions seem to have only a transient significance; their purpose is to lead us to answers. But in the face of constant and rapid change and uncertainty, might not questions rather than answers offer a more appropriate compass? History offers many examples of yesterday's solutions becoming today's problems, so perhaps answers are the transient means to help us ask better questions. Should we not pay more attention to asking the right questions, rather than become obsessed with quick solutions? Equally, in favouring practice over theory, are we not demonstrating how we have become blind to the fact that any practical action is based on our ideas and beliefs about the world whether we are conscious of them or not? The separation of theory and practice is false; they are not opposites but two sides of the same coin. We cannot act wisely without making sense of the world and making sense of the world is in itself a profoundly practical action that informs how we experience reality, how we act, and the relationships we form. Without questioning our worldview and the narrative that has shaped our culture, are we not likely to repeat the same mistakes over and over again?

Virtually every structure and institution around us is in need of innovation, redesign and transformation. At the local, regional, national and global scale we need transformational change in education, governance, industry, transport, infrastructure, energy systems, water management, agriculture and food systems, health systems, as well as social systems. In order to enable transformative innovation to unfold its creative potential we need to redesign the financial and economic system at all scales from local to global. But the most up-stream transformation that has to take place before we set out to 'redesign the human presence on Earth' is to deeply question our way of thinking, our worldview and our value system. Up-stream changes in our mental models, basic beliefs and assumptions about the nature of reality will affect *how, what,* and *why* we design, the needs we perceive, the questions we ask, and hence the solutions or answers we propose.

I believe a profound cultural transformation is already on its way. Humanity is waking up to the complexity of the challenges ahead. A new kind of individual and collective leadership is emerging in business, civil society and governance. After centuries of seeing scarcity and competition everywhere, we are waking up to the abundance that is revealed through collaboration and sharing. In the course of this book we will explore ways in which many people around the world are already working on technological, social, economic and ecological solutions that serve all of humanity and regenerate damaged ecosystems.

On an over-populated planet, facing the threat of run-away climate change and the depletion of many non-renewable resources we currently depend upon, we are increasingly becoming aware of our interdependence. For our species to not just survive, but to thrive, we depend on each other and on the planetary life-support system. While most of our current economic and political systems were designed with a win-lose mindset (zero-sum), we are beginning to understand we will *all* lose in the mid-to-long-term, if we do not maintain and regenerate the healthy functioning of ecosystems, reduce the stark inequity that exists everywhere, and nurture social cohesion and international solidarity through cultures of collaboration.

To move from a zero-sum culture (win-lose) to a non-zero-sum culture (win-win) necessitates widespread collaboration to ensure that nature also wins (win-win-win) and wins first, as she is the provider of the abundance upon which we depend. Only if we collaborate in creating a healthier, diverse, vibrant and bio-productive planet, will we be able to create regenerative cultures where nobody is left behind and everyone wins.

Win-win-win cultures ensure that life can continue to evolve towards increasing diversity, complexity, bio-productivity and resilience. We can think of the three wins of regenerative cultures as individual, collective and planetary wins created through systemic solutions that nurture social, ecological and economic health and wellbeing.

Humanity is beginning to explore the fertile ground of creating win-win-win solutions that drive cultural, ecological and economic regeneration. Innovating win-win-win, integrative, whole-systems design solutions is about creating shared abundance through collaborative advantage. Such innovations optimize the system as a whole, rather than maximizing short-term economic gains for a few to the economic, social and ecological detriment of many.

Climate change is only one of the converging crises requiring a globally coordinated response that is nothing short of civilizational transformation. Humanity is facing unprecedented challenges and unparalleled opportunities. 'Business as usual' is no longer an option. Change and transformation is inevitable.

Humanity is facing important questions: will we be able to steer creatively through this period of cultural transformation? Will we manage to co-create a life-sustaining and regenerative human civilization expressed in a vibrant diversity of locally adapted and globally collaborative cultures? The answers to these questions will remain unknowable for decades, yet they will define the future of humanity and the future of life on Earth. Yes, we need answers and we need to keep experimenting with possible solutions. Both are excellent ways to help us learn from our mistakes and ask better questions. Nevertheless, many of the questions and solutions we are working on are based on erroneous assumptions about our real priorities and true needs. We would do well to follow Einstein's advice and spend more time making sure we are getting the questions right before we rush into offering solutions that will only prolong business as usual, or patch up the symptoms of a system that is based on erroneous assumptions and will continue to fail until we initiate deeper changes by asking deeper questions.

Living the questions more deeply is the cultural guidance system that will help us unleash the power of transformative social and technological innovation in the transition towards regenerative cultures. Questions are invitations to conversations in business boardrooms, community groups and in institutions of governance. Questions are ways to build bridges between these different sectors and between the different disciplines that compartmentalize our knowledge. Questions – and the conversations they spark – can unleash collective intelligence and help us value multiple perspectives. Living the questions, deep listening and learning from diverse ways of knowing – these are all ways to transform consciousness and thereby create cultural and behavioural change. Living the questions more deeply can lead us towards a regenerative culture of equity, sustainability and justice. This book is an invitation to a conversation and a call to live the questions more deeply. It raises many questions; where it offers answers and solutions please understand them as invitations to question their significance in the transition towards regenerative cultures.

A first response to an invitation to 'live the questions' might be: we don't have time for that in the face of the urgency of the climate crisis and many other developments that demand changes *now*. But precisely because of this urgency, we need to take a deeper look at the questions we are asking. Simply doing the wrong thing righter will no longer suffice. We need to question basic assumptions, worldviews and value systems, paying attention to what serves humanity and life and what doesn't.

If the breakdown and need for change that we see around us is the direct result of an inappropriate way of seeing ourselves – the narrative we tell about who we are and the meaning we give to our existence – then cultural transformation has to start a long way up-stream with the way we see and think. We have to change our cultural narrative, and we can do so through culturally creative conversations that are triggered by asking deeper questions. By living the questions, we will begin to see, think and live differently; and by living differently we can bring forth a different world. We are capable of co-creating a regenerative human presence on Earth.

A young species growing up

A new cultural narrative is emerging – one that unites humanity in our interdependence with the wider community of life. This new and ancient story of interbeing with life *and as* life is driving people and communities around the world to create diverse, locally adapted, thriving cultures in global collaboration. Regenerative cultural patterns are beginning to emerge as an "expression of life in the process of transforming itself". Václav Havel saw the need for such a societal transformation when he wrote in *The Power of the Powerless*:

> A genuine, profound and lasting change for the better […] can no longer result from the victory […] of any particular traditional political conception, which can ultimately be only external, that is, a structural or systemic conception. More than ever before, such a change will have to derive from human existence, from the fundamental reconstitution of the position of people in the world, their relationships to each other, and to the universe. If a better economic and political model is to be created, then perhaps […] it must derive from profound existential and moral changes in society. This is not something that can be designed and introduced like a new car. If it is to be more than just a new variation on the old degeneration, it must above all be an expression of life in the process of transforming itself. A better system will not automatically ensure a better life. In fact the opposite is true: only by creating a better life can a better system be developed.
>
> Václav Havel (1985: 30)

Humanity is coming of age and needs a 'new story' that is powerful and meaningful enough to galvanize global collaboration and guide a collective response to the converging crises we are facing. Transformational responses at a personal and collective level take place when we question deeply ingrained ways of being and seeing and in the process begin to reinvent ourselves. In doing so we also change how we participate in shaping culture through our interaction with the world around us.

From a long-term perspective, as a relatively young species on this planet we are collectively undergoing a maturation process which requires us to redefine how we understand our relationship to the rest of life on Earth – facing the choices of either collapse or profound transformation. The basic story we are telling about humanity – who we are, what we are here for and where we are going – no longer serves us as a functional moral compass.

Just as teenagers coming of age must learn not to just demand from family and society but to contribute meaningfully, humanity can no longer continue to draw down the natural capital stores of the Earth. We have to learn to live within the limits of the Earth's bioproductive capacity and use current solar income instead of ancient sunlight (stored in the Earth's crust as oil, gas, and coal) to provide our energy. In stepping from our juvenile – and at times reckless and self-absorbed – phase as a young species into a mature membership of the community of life on Earth we are called to become productive members of this community and to contribute to its health and wellbeing.

Mature community membership means a shift towards a form of enlightened self-interest that goes as far as questioning the notion of a separate and isolated self at its very core. In the fundamentally interconnected and interdependent planetary system we participate in, the best way to care for oneself and those closest to oneself is to start caring more for the benefit of the collective (all life). Metaphorically speaking, we are all in the same boat: our planetary life support system, or in Buckminster Fuller's words: 'spaceship Earth'. The 'them-against-us' thinking that for too long has defined politics between nations, companies and people is profoundly anachronistic.

Humanity as a whole is facing imminent climate chaos and the breakdown of ecosystems functions vital to the survival of our species and many others. We will not find the solutions to these problems by continuing to base our thinking on the same erroneous assumptions about the nature of self and world that created them in the first place. We need a new way of thinking, a new consciousness, a new cultural story; only then will we be able to get the questions right, seeing more clearly what underlying needs have to be met. If we jump into action without deeper questioning, we are likely to treat symptoms rather than causes. This will prolong and deepen the crisis rather than solve it.

Even just subtle differences in word-use affect how we co-create culture. For example, to refer to the natural processes of cleaning water, capturing sunlight and carbon dioxide into biomass, building fertile soils, stopping erosion, or regulating climate as 'ecosystems services' (e.g. Costanza, *et al.*, 2013) is a useful strategy to ensure that these services are included in our economic accounting and recognized as the primary source of value creation in the global economy. On the other hand – implicitly – the words 'ecosystems services' carry a utilitarian attitude towards nature as if these processes were only valuable as long as they provide services to humanity. Using the term 'ecosystems functions' acknowledges that they are vital functions that enable the continued evolution of life as a whole. Worldviews are created and transformed by paying attention to how we shape experiences and reinforce perspectives through the words and metaphors we use.

Humanity is facing the terminal crisis of an outdated worldview. This crisis manifests itself in many different ways, for example as an economic and monetary system that is not fit for purpose on an overpopulated planet with dwindling non-renewable resources. In communities everywhere we can witness social breakdown as a result of rising inequality and the cult of competitive individualism. We are facing a crisis of governance as many of the world's largest economies are no longer defined by national or cultural identity and have become corporations seeking to maximize short-term profit by externalizing collateral damage. We continue to be challenged by a crisis of religious extremism and war, as we tend to pay more attention to our differences rather than our common humanity and common fate on a planet in crisis.

We will have to redefine how we see ourselves and our relationships to each other and to the rest of the community of life on Earth. Only by changing our cultural narrative can we transform our vision of the future, and heal our relationship with life as a whole. Like a fever that peaks and breaks just before the patient begins to recover, the multiple crises don't have to be regarded as something entirely negative. We can reframe them as a "good crisis" (Pigem, 2009) if we heed the clear signs that change and transformation are now inevitable and already on their way and come to see the converging crises as creative challenges to grow up and evolve to planetary consciousness.

Changing the idea of our separateness

I firmly believe that the multiple crises we are facing are symptoms of our pathological habit of understanding and experiencing ourselves as separate from nature, from each other and from the community of life. The same crises are also indications that the healing process is already unfolding. In *Blessed Unrest*, Paul Hawken (2007) described how all over the world tens of thousands, possibly hundreds of thousands, of civil society organizations, community groups, activist networks, entrepreneurs and social innovators are working towards a more just, equitable and sustainable future in which humanity can thrive and culture is a regenerative rather than destructive force. He aptly calls this emerging and growing global movement our planet's immune response.

> [...] we are at a threshold in human existence, a fundamental change in understanding about our relationship to nature and each other. We are moving from a world created by privilege to a world created by community. The current thrust of history is too supple to be labelled, but global themes are emerging in response to cascading ecological crises and human suffering. These ideas include the need for radical social change, the reinvention of market-based economics, the empowerment of women, activism on all levels, and the need for localized economic control. There are insistent calls for autonomy, appeals for a new resource ethic based on the tradition of the commons, demands for the reinstatement of cultural primacy over corporate hegemony, and a rising demand for radical transparency in politics and corporate decision making.
>
> Paul Hawken (2007: 194)

All of these trends are evidence that in a world riddled by multiple converging crises worsening fast, something new and miraculous wants to be born. As Arundhati Roy said so eloquently: "Another world is not only possible, she is already on her way. On quiet days I can hear her breathing." If we take the time to get the questions right, to live the questions more deeply individually and collectively, we will not only be able to hear this new world breathing, we will realize that with each breath we take we are participants in the networks of relationships that are giving birth to this world.

Charles Eisenstein recently provided a lucid exploration of many aspects of the emerging 'new story' we are beginning to tell about ourselves in *The More Beautiful World Our Hearts Know is Possible* (2013). He contrasts the "story of separation" (p.1) that leads us to feel isolated, alienated and insufficient, and thus to compete with each other and to dominate life for our purposes, with the "story of interbeing" (p.15) that acknowledges our relational nature and interdependence.

As the limits of the perspective of separation become more and more evident, and as we find ourselves surrounded by examples of the breakdown, despair and suffering that its cultural dominance is causing, we are beginning to look for viable alternatives, different ways of *being-in-the-world*. We are stepping into the 'story of interbeing'. This story invites us to ask deeper questions: who am I? What makes me come fully alive? What are the deeper needs underlying my perceived needs? What story do I chose to stand in? Who is my community? What is my role? How can I contribute to a more joyful, co-creative, and meaningful world?

> Amid all the doom-laden exhortations to change our ways, let us remember that we are striving to create a more beautiful world, and not sustain, with growing sacrifice, the current one. We are not just seeking to survive. We are not just facing doom; we are facing a glorious possibility. We are offering people not a world of less, not a world of sacrifice, not a world where you are just going to have to enjoy less and suffer more – no, we are offering a world of more beauty, more joy, more connection, more love, more fulfilment, more exuberance, more leisure, more music, more dancing, and more celebration. The most inspiring glimpses you've ever had about what life can be – that is what we are offering.
>
> Charles Eisenstein (2013: 159)

Questioning dangerous ideologies

> Where is the Life we have lost in living?
> Where is the wisdom we have lost in knowledge?
> Where is the knowledge we have lost in information? […]
> What life have you, if you have not life together?
> There is no life that is not in community, […]
> When the Stranger says: "What is the meaning of this city?
> Do you huddle close together because you love each other?"

> What will you answer? "We all dwell together
> to make money from each other"? or "This is a community"?
> Oh my soul, be prepared for the coming of the Stranger.
> Be prepared for him who knows how to ask questions.
>
> T.S. Eliot (1934)

One problem with this idea that nature and culture are separate is that it has predisposed us to create exploitative cultures that degrade ecosystems everywhere. Exploitative and degenerative cultures tend to have economic systems focused around the notions of scarcity and competitive advantage, whereas regenerative cultures understand how collaborative advantage can foster shared abundance.

Our current economic system disrespects planetary boundaries

We have created an increasingly global civilization that is primarily shaped by the rules of an economic system that pays little or no regard to the fundamental processes that maintain the healthy functioning of ecological systems. Our current economic system disrespects planetary boundaries. Conventional economics justifies the over-exploitation of resources in the short term without regard to the long-term effects on vital ecosystems functions upon which all of life depends. The dangerous ideology of neo-classical economics offers economic arguments for the replacement of diversity with monocultures, thereby justifying and structurally embedding competition. This actively drives the erosion of natural resilience which depends on redundancies at multiple scales, in pursuit of 'economics of scale' and 'competitive advantage' in a globalized market. This system has worked well for a few, at the cost of the many and has driven the degradation of communities and ecosystems around the world.

We have come to use the words 'redundant' and 'redundancy' to mean superfluous or unnecessary, yet in living systems redundancies at and across multiple scales are vital, as they decentralize important functions by distributing them across the system as a whole and thereby make the overall system more resilient. It is much harder to disrupt vital functions if they are distributed and decentralized (performed simultaneously at multiple scales and locations) rather than if these functions are performed at one large-scale, centralized facility (which maximizes economies of scale and efficiency but sacrifices resilience and flexibility). We will return to this in Chapters 2 and 4.

Oikos (οἶκος) means 'house' or 'household'. *Logos* (λόγος) means 'that which is said of' or 'the study of'. The role of ecology is thus to provide a deeper understanding of life's household including humanity's participation in it. Combining *oikos* with *nomos* (νόμ-ος) which means 'rule' or 'law' indicates that the role of economy is to establish appropriate rules for the 'management of the household'. Clearly the rules of how to husband the Earth's resources (economy) should be based on a deep understanding of the life-supporting functions of ecosystems and the Earth (ecology). Yet the narrative of scarcity and competition that forms the dogmatic basis of the dominant ideology of economics was established before the science of ecology was invented. An economic system in service to current and future generations will have to be rooted in an ecological understanding of interconnection and interdependence. We have invented an economic system that goes utterly against the basic rules for long-term survival of any living system. The good news is that, since we invented the rules of economics, we can re-invent them!

Ecology is the study of the healthy functioning and the continuous change and adaptation of ecosystems and the biosphere. These dynamics are not open for political discussion and compromise. They are about how life creates conditions that favour life. The economic rules of our current way of managing our household, on the other hand, are 100% made up by us. They can, therefore, just as easily be disregarded on the grounds that they are insufficient and anachronistic. We are free to dismiss them in favour of new economic systems that take the long-term survival of the household and ecological insights as a better basis for sound management than those of the current auto-destructive and structurally dysfunctional system. Contrary to what many economists will have you believe, economics is not a science! *At its current worst, economics has become a dangerous ideology.*

Yet blaming misguided economists will not get us out of this mess. We are all in the same boat. Let us not forget that those who are setting the rules of the system have been directly or indirectly hired by us and are paid by our taxes. We have invited the pipers in, but allowed them to call the tune, and are now dancing to the tune as if it were the only tune possible. But another economics is possible and already being developed and explored under such diverse names as 'new economics'[1], 'steady state economics' (e.g. Daly, 1991), 'the circular economy' (e.g. Boulding, 1966), or 'ecological economics' (e.g. Costanza, 1991). If we stop dancing to the fateful tune of an economics of scarcity and competition and start to collectively hum a different one, we can begin to transform the way we inhabit our common home – planet Earth – in ways that do not damage the health and resilience of the life support system we depend on. We *can* and *must* create economic rules that let us share nature's abundance collaboratively and incentivize business and communities to continuously regenerate the basic resources we depend upon.

We need to initiate culturally creative conversations about what kind of changes to our current economic system are more likely to deliver a thriving and desirable future for our communities and *all of* humanity. We are *all* part of, and participants in, the systems we have helped to co-create (or at the very least quietly consented to maintaining). There is no point in blaming the 'others', a lack of political leadership, greedy corporate executives, inadequate laws and regulations or insufficient education, since we all have contributed, and are contributing, to how things are. All of us, when we spend our money, do our work, educate our children, elect our political representatives and participate in our communities, are making ourselves accomplices in the status quo until we choose to act consciously as 'cultural creatives' (Ray & Anderson, 2000) of a thriving future for current and future generations. Change starts with us! It starts in conversation with our neighbours, colleagues, friends and our communities, by asking deeper questions and being willing to live them:

> Q What kind of world do we want to leave for our children and children's children?

---

[1] Wherever text is underlined, more information is available online at www.triarchypress.net/questions

Q Why are we still at war with each other and with nature?

Q Why do we allow an economic system that no longer serves the long-term survival of our species or the wellbeing of our communities to dictate the way we do business and relate to each other?

Q Why do we let our political leaders convince us that spending large proportions of our national budgets on arms and preparation for war is a necessity, when we know that these funds could provide access to water, education, food and a dignified life for all humanity, thereby disarming the main drivers of war and conflict?

Q How can we meet everyone's basic needs while simultaneously ensuring our common future by protecting biodiversity, stabilizing global climate patterns and creating thriving human cultures that regenerate planetary bioproductivity?

Questions like these invite us to think systemically over longer time scales and to pay attention to relationships and context, rather than rushing for quick answers and silver-bullet solutions. Questions like these are already driving the re-invention of economics, the co-creation of diverse expressions of the new narrative of interbeing, and the transition towards regenerative cultures. By questioning dangerous ideologies that no longer serve us we take the first step towards collectively defining the kind of questions that might help us live into more viable alternatives and help us to create regenerative cultures everywhere. We will take a closer look at this in Chapter 7.

Facing complexity means befriending uncertainty and ambiguity

> May God us keep
> from single vision
> and Newton's Sleep!
>
> William Blake (1802)

Our dominant way of thinking in dualistic opposites makes us blind to the underlying unity. Nature is hardly ever that black or white; mostly we are dealing with shades of grey. The way we tend to try to establish certainty is by defining a particular way of seeing and limiting the boundaries of the system in question. What results is the illusion of certainty. This is a useful technique. Newtonian physics has helped to develop all sorts of useful technologies, even if we have long understood that it is a limited representation of the natural world. As Werner Heisenberg has put it: "What we observe is not nature herself, but nature exposed to our method of questioning".

We would do well to understand that any perspective – no matter what science or philosophy supports it, no matter how transdisciplinary and inclusive it is trying to be, no matter how much research backs it up – any perspective is a limited view of the underlying complexity. In order to befriend uncertainty, we need to let go of our need for prediction and control. Most causality in nature is not linear in the sense that effect follows cause in a linear way. Due to radical interconnectivity, systemic interactions and feedback loops, causality is more often than not circular rather than linear. Effects become causes and causes are the effects of other systems dynamics.

In 2001, while studying for my MSc in holistic science, I had the privilege of being mentored in my understanding of complexity by Professor Brian Goodwin, a founding member of the Santa Fe Institute for Complexity Studies and an international authority in the field. Brian taught me that any system that is constituted of three or more interacting variables is more appropriately described by non-linear mathematics and should be considered a complex dynamic system. One of the defining properties of complex dynamic systems is that they are fundamentally unpredictable and uncontrollable (beyond controlled laboratory conditions). Uncertainty and ambiguity are therefore fundamental characteristics of our lives and the natural world, including human culture, society and our economic systems.

Brian argued that since natural, social or economic systems are best understood as complex dynamic systems, we can finally give up our ill-fated pursuit of ways to predict and control these systems. We are not supposedly 'objective' observers outside these systems, trying to manipulate them more effectively; we are always participants. He suggested that the insights of complexity science invite us to shift our attitude and goal to our appropriate participation in these systems, as subjective, co-creative agents. Our goal should be to better understand the underlying dynamics in order to facilitate the emergence of positive or desirable properties – emerging through the qualities of relationships in the system and the quality of information that flows through the system. We have to befriend uncertainty and ambiguity because they are here to stay.

As the radius of the circle of what is known expands, we become aware of the expanding circumference of our own ignorance. We have to come to grips with the fact that knowledge and information, no matter how detailed, will remain an insufficient and uncertain basis for guiding our path into the future. We will increase our chances of success if we have the wisdom and humility to embrace our own ignorance, celebrate ambiguity and befriend uncertainty. More often than not, certainty is not an option. We are invited to 'live the questions more deeply', to pay attention to the wisdom of many minds and diverse points of view, and to continue the conversation about whether we are still on the appropriate path. We are encouraged into relationship and deeper listening, so that we can stop being at war with ourselves and with the planet.

More than 2,500 years ago, Pericles reminded his fellow Athenians: "We may not be able to predict the future, but we can prepare for it". In our learning journey of human survival and our quest for a thriving regenerative culture, all answers and solutions will at best be partial and temporary. Yet by asking the appropriate guiding questions repeatedly and entering into conversations about our collective future in all the communities we participate in, we may be able to find a set of patterns and guidelines that will help us to create a culture capable of learning and transformative innovation. Living the questions together is an effective way of preparing for an unpredictable future.

This book is my subjective exploration of questions that might help us to chart our path into a more desirable, inclusive, peaceful and sustainable future. It explores how these questions can catalyse the kind of transformative innovation that might help us create regenerative cultures before unintended side-effects lead to the early demise of our species and much diversity of life along with it. One important question to live into whilst acknowledging the limits of our own knowing and whilst befriending uncertainty and ambiguity is:

> Q Which cultural, social, and technological innovations and transformations will help us bring human activity and the planet's life support system into a mutually supporting regenerative relationship rather than an erosive and destructive relationship?

My own practice of *living the questions* has been greatly informed by a wide diversity of thought leaders and practitioners who have mentored and inspired me. Among them are my colleagues at the *International Futures Forum* (IFF). In *Ten Things to do in a Conceptual Emergency*, the IFF's director Graham Leicester and founding member Maureen O'Hara (2009) suggest pathways to finding a transformative response which urge us to ask:

> Q How do we design for transition to a new world?
>
> Q What other worldviews might help to inform a wise response?
>
> Q What can we learn from letting go of the myth of control?
>
> Q What can we learn from re-perceiving the present?
>
> Q What can we learn from trusting our subjective experience more deeply?
>
> Q What can we learn from taking the 'long view'?
>
> Q What would insightful action look like?
>
> Q Which new organizational integrities should we form and support?
>
> Q How can we practise social acupuncture?
>
> Q How do we sustain networks of hope?

The idea of 'organizational integrities' refers to the challenge that the traditional boundaries around organizations are dissolving as we focus more on collaboration (alliances, networks, partnerships, and outsourcing). We are moving from separate organizations and businesses to interconnected ecologies of collaboration that weave businesses and organizations into mutually beneficial partnerships.

The notion of 'social acupuncture' refers to the catalytic transformative effect that well-targeted, small-scale, creatively designed interventions can have, even in large and complex systems. Metaphorically speaking, placing the needle of transformative change in the right place and on the right meridian of cultural meaning-making, can unblock pent-up energy and catalyse transformative social and culture change.

Caring for the Earth is caring for ourselves and our community

To care for the Earth and for life's common future does not require some form of spiritually motivated altruism once we are conscious of the systemic interdependencies that our survival depends upon. The motivation for intelligent and aware people to transform 'business as usual' can simply be a form of enlightened self-interest. Once we start the practice of caring for others (humans and other species) in the same way as we care for ourselves, we begin to realize that the experience of a separate self is a limited perspective and that we are in fact relational beings in a world where everything affects everything else and, as a result, to care for others is to care for ourselves. The word 'individual' reminds us we are undividable from the whole. We are integral participants and expressions of life.

The way to care for ourselves and our families, the way to sustain this and future generations of human beings is *to care for life as a whole*. Whether we draw upon spiritual teachings or a reconnection with the sacred in order to imbue this insight with even deeper meaning for us is our choice, not a requirement. At their very core, all the world's spiritual traditions and sacred texts reflect upon the question of right relationships between self and world. So maybe the way to finally disarm religious fanaticism and separatism could be to revisit these wisdom traditions and explore their common message about how to live in right relationship with each other and the Earth. Our future depends on the health of ecosystems everywhere. The health of the biosphere and the future of humanity are inseparable. More than sixty years ago Albert Einstein saw the challenge ahead:

> A human being is part of the whole – called by us 'universe', a part limited in time and space. He experiences himself, his thoughts and feelings as something separate from the rest – a kind of optical delusion of his consciousness. This delusion is a kind of prison for us, restricting us to our personal desires and to affection for a few persons nearest to us. *Our task must be to free ourselves from this prison by widening our circle of compassion to embrace all living creatures and the whole of nature* […] [italics added]
>
> Albert Einstein (1950)

Einstein understood the limitations we impose on ourselves by our way of thinking, which determines *what* we focus on and *how* we see the world. He asked us to question who we are and our relationships with all of life and the universe as a whole. Einstein invited us to explore a more systemic perspective, holistic thinking and an integrative consciousness that acknowledges our participatory intimacy with the universe, as a fundamentally interconnected and continuously transforming whole manifesting as patterns of energy, matter and consciousness. In this view, matter and consciousness, matter and life, matter and mind, matter and spirit are not separate but intertwined.

We cannot expect our scientific methodology to provide us with irrefutable proof of such claims, as the perspective of being able to prove something based on objective data and research is in itself part of the narrative of separation. We can, however, step into the space between stories and acknowledge multiple ways of knowing, neither dismissing the reductionist scientific perspective nor the participatory holistic perspective. If we are able to suspend judgement from within the dogmatic tendencies of our dominant worldview and open ourselves to experiencing reality in new ways, these are some speculative questions we might want to live into:

> Q   What if consciousness – rather than matter – is primary?
>
> Q   What if our species' most astonishing evolutionary innovation and 'raison d'être' – our saving grace – is that through us the transforming whole (universe) is able to know itself and become conscious of itself?

In *The Passion of the Western Mind*, Richard Tarnas (1996) explored the evolution of our dominant Western worldview and showed that over the last 200 years an alternative perspective has emerged that is based on the "fundamental conviction that the relation of the human mind to the world was ultimately not dualistic but participatory" (p.433). In this perspective "the human mind is ultimately the organ of the world's own process of self-revelation" (p.434).

As T.S. Eliot put it in 'Little Gidding': "We shall not cease from exploration, and the end of all our exploring will be to arrive where we started, and know the place for the first time." So, are we worth sustaining? Life on Earth will continue without us. Yet will it not be a much impoverished place without a species capable of reflecting on the miracle of life's evolution and able to be awestruck by the beauty of this precious planet? We have to be honest with ourselves. Even in dedicating our lives to the creation of regenerative cultures and a more sustainable future, we are not 'saving the planet' or 'saving life on Earth'. Both will continue long after our species meets its almost inevitable fate of extinction. Nevertheless, we don't have to actively accelerate our own demise, as we have done with increasing effort since the industrial revolution.

> Q   Would we not do better to care for all of life and the planetary life support system in ways that ensure that our relatively young species gets its opportunity to live to maturity and wisdom?

Consider all the creativity and beauty we have already been able to express through our diverse cultures and their arts, sciences, literature, music, stories and cultural traditions. Humanity has already created a multitude of reflections of the ultimate in the intimate.

Are you not also curious what our species might be capable of if we "widen our circles of compassion to embrace all living creatures and the whole of nature"?

By caring for the Earth and all of life, we care for ourselves. By embracing our own nature as an expression of nature at large, humanity can become a conscious force of healing. Keeping the limits of our own knowing in mind, we can begin to humbly contribute to the flourishing rather than the impoverishment of life. Overcoming the pain and the isolation of the narrative of separation means learning to love ourselves in order to love life more fully. By co-creating regenerative cultures we are saving our species from an untimely, tragic extinction. Let's give our young species its opportunity to fulfil its wonderful potential! Just imagine the beauty we could co-create. Let's do it for life! Let's do it for beauty! And most of all: let's do it with love, humility, compassion and in gratitude!

Wake up to find out that you are the eyes of the world

The 'Santiago Theory of Cognition' proposed by the Chilean biologists and neuroscientists Humberto Maturana and Francisco Varela offers a scientific way of understanding the process by which living systems engage in 'autopoiesis' (self-creating or self-generating) through entering into relationships that distinguish self from other but without losing their fundamental interconnectedness with their environment.

The act of 'structural coupling' – or relating to other – enables the living system to define itself in relationship to its environment as separate yet connected. Importantly, the environment that is defined by the initial act of distinction of self and other triggers changes in the living system which the system itself specifies as triggers of internal changes. Maturana and Varela argue that this is basically an act of cognition (which does not require a nervous system and is thus possible for all life-forms). Cognition is not a representation of an independently existing world, but rather the act of *bringing forth a world* through the processes of *living as relating*. From this perspective, cognition is the basic process of life.

In *The Tree of Knowledge*, Maturana and Varela suggest that as we are beginning to understand how we know, we have to realize that "the world everyone sees is not *the* world but *a* world which we bring forth with others". The world-as-we-know-it emerges out of the way we relate to each other and the wider natural process. This led Maturana and Varela to the obvious conclusion "that the world will be different only if we live differently" (Maturana & Varela, 1987: 245). In *Biology of Love* Maturana writes:

> Love is our natural condition, and it is the denial of love what *[sic]* requires all our rational efforts, but what for, when life is so much better in love than in aggression? Love needs not to be learned, it can be allowed to be or it can be denied, but needs not to be learned, because it is our biological fundament and the only basis for the conservation of our human beingness as well as our well being.
>
> Humberto Maturana & Gerda Verden-Zoller (1996)

Is our ability to love what makes humanity worth sustaining? We are not the pinnacle of evolution but participants in its processes – conscious participants capable of self-reflection. We are only just beginning to understand consciousness and in the process are becoming aware of our intimate communion and entanglement with all there is. Every living being reflects the whole, the evolving and transforming universe, back onto itself in its own unique way. Some theories of consciousness suggest that only human beings are capable of self-awareness and self-reflection. We are neither aware of any other species writing poetry or composing music to reflect the unifying emotion we call love, nor do we know what the passing of the seasons feels like to a sequoia tree, or how an emperor penguin subjectively experiences the first rays of sunlight after the Antarctic winter. But is there not something worth sustaining in a species that can ask such questions? Love and empathy widen our circles of compassion.

The evolution of consciousness is both a personal journey that we are all capable of experiencing through our lifetimes, and a journey at the collective level. We are on a journey from the 'original participation' of indigenous tribes that perceives everything as alive and meaningful relations, to the 'separation of self and world' (nature and culture) that brought us the Enlightenment and the multiple benefits of science and technology based on analytical reasoning; the next step is towards a new kind of "final participation" – as Owen Barfield called it (1988: 133-134) – which expresses a synthesis of both perspectives. We are part and parcel of nature *and* we have evolved to self-reflective consciousness and free will, which gives us the choice to participate in life's processes in a destructive or a creatively supportive (regenerative) way.

Creating a regenerative culture

There is nothing less at stake than the future of our species, much of the diversity of life, and the continued evolution of consciousness. If we achieve this 'momentous leap' (Graves, 1974) in human self-awareness, what lies ahead of us is the promise of a truly regenerative, collaborative, just, peaceful and equitable human civilization that flourishes and thrives in its diverse cultural and artistic expressions while restoring ecosystems and regenerating resilience locally and globally. The best of our music, art, poetry and technology will be elegant expression of the symbiotic unity of nature and culture. We are capable of reflecting on the 'universe story' as our own story, the story of life evolving. Individually and collectively we are waking up to find out that the world knows and loves itself through our eyes and our hearts. What kind of culture will we create to express this wisdom? Becoming conscious of our *inter*being with the world reminds us of our communion with all life as a reflection of our larger being. As conscious relational beings, love for life is our natural state.

The evolutionary biologist E.O. Wilson (1986), inspired by the psychologist Erich Fromm (1956), suggested that human beings as expressions of the process of life have an innate tendency to be attracted to all living beings. He called this love for life and attraction towards other life forms *biophilia*. The 'deep ecology' movement initiated by the Norwegian philosopher Arne Næss (1988) calls the realization of our own self as a relational reflection of the larger community of life 'our ecological self' and sees in it the basis for responsible action out of enlightened self-interest.

We bring forth a world in relationship to 'other' and without that 'other' – which is a reflection of our larger self – we could not exist. The 'Santiago Theory of Cognition', as we have seen, reframes dualistic categories like self and world as polarities of an interconnected whole which takes form by distinction without separation. As another esteemed mentor and friend of mine, Satish Kumar – editor of *Resurgence* and co-founder of Schumacher College – has put it: "You are, therefore I am" (2002). Or in the words of a Grateful Dead song: "Wake up to find out that you are the eyes of the world!"

In regenerative cultures, personal development and the evolution of consciousness will accelerate. As we cease to be paralyzed by the fear-driven cycle of separation, scarcity and the struggle for control and power, we will begin to unfold the potential of a compassionate, empathic and collaborative culture of creativity and shared abundance, driven by biophilia – our innate love for all of life. The narrative of separation from the rest of life and alienation from nature's wisdom is beginning to give way to a narrative that celebrates our communion with nature as the very essence of our being. Our subjective conscious awareness of the transforming whole (limited as it may be) is an important and valid reflection of that whole getting to know itself *through* all of us and *as* all of us. By living the questions together, we can learn to appreciate multiple perspectives and gain a shared understanding of our participation in that wholeness.

So far, most evidence of the healthy evolution of human consciousness and personal development (e.g. Graves, 1974; Wilber, 2001) indicates that nobody is born with a holistic and planetary consciousness and full awareness of the co-arising of self and world. So all present and past states and stages of consciousness (see Combs, 2002 & 2009) have to be welcome as they form the stepping stones of personal development in individuals, as well as being expressions of the evolution of consciousness of our species.

A regenerative culture will have to facilitate the healthy personal development of a human being from ego-centric, to socio-centric, to species-centric, to bio-centric, and cosmos-centric perspectives of self. This means paying attention to how our culture and education system shape our worldview and value system. We need to encourage life-long learning and personal development through supportive community processes and ongoing dialogue, guided by questions rather than answers. We need to live these questions individually and collectively to co-create a new narrative. As the multiple converging crises we face are creating an accelerated climate of transformation, where change is no longer a possibility to entertain but an inevitable consequence of our collective actions, we are called to switch out of the mindset that created these crises in the first place. In doing so, we undergo a species-level rite of passage that offers us a new and more mature perspective on our intimacy with, and responsibility for, all of life. We are "coming home" (Kelly, 2010).

The creation of diverse, regenerative cultures collaboratively united in a regenerative civilization is the only viable future open to us as we move into the 'planetary era'. Our collective challenge is to create cultures capable of continuous learning in the face of complexity, not-knowing and constant change. We have the creative opportunity to give birth to a human culture that is mature enough to express the insight that life creates conditions conducive to life in all its designs, systems and processes. We *can* co-create a world that works for all of humanity and all of life. We are capable of vibrant and diverse cultural expressions of the profoundly transformative insight that *we are the eyes of the world*.

The 'why' will guide the 'what' and the 'how'

> We are distracted from distraction by distraction,
> filled with fancies and empty of meaning.
>
> T.S. Eliot (1943)

In *Start with Why*, Simon Sinek (2011) explains how Martin Luther King Jr., Mahatma Gandhi and Nelson Mandela were able to drive large-scale cultural changes in a non-violent way. The common thread is that they articulated their vision from the *why*, to the *how*, to the *what*. Inspiring leaders start with what they believe in first, making their worldview and motivation explicit. Sinek suggests that once we are clear about *why*, we can define the values that will guide our behaviour and inform the systems and processes we put into place. The *why* defines the *how* in an action-oriented way. In a nutshell, *why* offers a purpose, cause, or belief; *how* expresses the values that guide our actions and how we aim to manifest the higher purpose in action; and *what* refers to the results of those actions. The design guru Tim Brown, CEO of IDEO, writes in *Change by Design* "Don't ask *what?* ask *why?*" and continues: "asking 'why?' is an opportunity to reframe a problem, redefine the constraints, and open the field to a more innovative answer. [...] There is nothing more frustrating than coming up with the right answer to the wrong question" (2009: 236-237). Warren Berger reminds us of the power of inquiry, encouraging us to ask 'beautiful questions' using *why?* and *what if?* as a path to breakthrough innovation. The art of asking beautiful questions is about i) challenging assumptions, ii) inquiring about things normally taken for granted, and iii) wondering about new possibilities (Berger, 2014).

The practice of *living the questions together* starts by frequently asking yourself and others: are we asking the right questions? Which questions will help us make wiser decisions? What if we did things differently? What informs our current perspective? If we answer the question "why is the human species worth sustaining" in a neo-Darwinian way, along the lines of 'because we are the most intelligent and competitive species and therefore should continue to exploit nature for our benefit', we are unlikely to find timely responses to climate change and ecosystems degradation, and will be confronted with deepening ecological, social and economic crises. We will live into a very different future if we answer the question in a different way: we are co-creative participants in a 14-billion-year process of universe becoming conscious of itself. We are a keystone species capable of creating conditions conducive to all life. We can design for human, ecosystems and planetary health, and nurture resilience, adaptability, transformability and vitality. We care; we are compassionate beings able to love and to express this unifying emotion through poetry, music and art. Like all other species we are life's gift to life, creating meaning by being *in* and *through* relationship.

In a conversation I had with Professor David Orr in 2006, he suggested that we must ask *why* humanity is worth sustaining before considering *how* we might do so (see Introduction). He did so in response to a question I had asked him about the role of spirituality in the cultural transformation and transition ahead. David started his answer by saying:

> Humans are inevitably spiritual and the question is not whether we are, but whether we are authentically spiritual or not. It bubbles out of us. We are meaning-seeking creatures, and if the highest meaning in my life is soccer, I will make soccer my religion and it will orient my life. It will give my life meaning and gravity and direction. It just happens to be a bad religion. I could make environmentalism a religion. That happens to be a bad religion, too. We can't help but make something into a belief system, and you can argue why this is for us. This goes back to the early cave paintings. This is part of humanity. As soon as we identify the human species, we see a species trying to grapple with: what does this mean? Where are we? Who are we? How did we get here? You see these questions being asked. They pop up in early philosophy, early art. This is what it means to be human.
>
> David Orr, personal comment (2006)

He emphasized that to ask "why we should sustain humanity" is not an "idle debating question, and it takes you to the core of spirituality. What do we owe? How are we obliged? What do we owe to the far distant future? What do we owe to the distant past? What does it mean for us to be stewards or trustees?" Finding answers to all these questions can help us to re-contextualize our existence in a meaningful universe rooted in our interbeing. Beyond all religious dogmas or denominations of faith, beyond all our differences, we can find common ground in the communion of our interbeing with each other and all life. The future of our species depends on finding this higher ground *as* humanity, *as* nature, *as* life, *as* expressions of a living, transforming whole capable of self-reflection.

All the world's faith groups could express the meta-narrative of interbeing in diverse ways without opposing their foundational scriptures. At the heart of spirituality and the root of all religions lies a process of making sense of the relationship between the intimate and the ultimate. In *Lamps of Fire – the spirit of religion* Juan Mascaró offers a synthesis of the spiritual essence of religion through selected passages from Hinduism, Buddhism, Jainism, Taoism, Confucianism, Shintoism, Judaism, Christianity, Islam and Sikhism. Mascaró believed in the recuperation of a profound humanism to unite humanity beyond its differences (east and west, north and south) and offered his book in the hope that it would become "a light in deep darkness and a refuge in the storm" (1961: 9-11).

In the face of gut-wrenching attempts to justify inhuman barbarity with the misguided righteousness of religious fundamentalism inciting crimes against humanity, on the one hand, and ever more urgent warnings from the scientific community that we have dangerously over-shot planetary boundaries and are facing catastrophic climate change, on the other hand, humanity needs to find common ground for a coordinated, cooperative response. We also need to find a higher ground of shared meaning and significance so we all know *why* we are in this together and *why* it is worth transcending and including all our differences in pursuit of a shared vision of *thriving together*.

Spirituality, soul and solitude in nature

In December 2014 the 'Action and Research Centre' of the RSA (Royal Society for the encouragement of Arts, Manufacture and Commerce) published a report of a two-year conversation about why spirituality needed to play a greater role in the public realm. The report argues that "the spiritual injunction is principally an experiential one, namely to know oneself as fully as possible. For many, that means beginning to see beyond the ego and recognise being part of a totality, or at least something bigger than oneself" (Rowson, 2014). Referring to the epidemic of loneliness associated with big city living, the report muses: "We are all surrounded by strangers who could so easily be friends, but we appear to lack cultural permission not merely to 'connect' – the opium of cyberspace – but to deeply empathise and care" (p.7). Trying to heal causes instead of symptoms, the report calls for "the spiritual to play a greater role in the public realm, because it highlights the importance of personal and social and political transformation" (p.8). It asks the important question: "How can we best speak of the spiritual in a way that helps us understand how best to live?"

Reflecting on Martin Luther King's insight that "power without love is reckless and abusive, and love without power is sentimental and anaemic" and his observation that "it is precisely this collision of immoral power with powerless morality which constitutes the major crisis of our time" (see also Kahane, 2010), the report calls for the spiritual practice of tapping "into the deep source of our own power and love" and embarking "on a lifelong challenge to bring them together in practice" (Rowson, 2014: 59).

The RSA project reviewed how deeper questioning into the nature of love creates a sense of belonging. Inquiry into death helps us live a deeper life. Questioning the nature of our 'self' catalyses personal transformation; and exploring the nature of the soul gives our life meaning and informs our creative expression (p.78) The final report suggests a need to revitalize spirituality in order to more deeply address the challenges of the 21st century. Deep questioning into the nature of the soul will inevitably lead us to rediscover the soul of nature. Richard Tarnas writes in *Cosmos and Psyche*:

> Not only our personal lives but the very nature of the universe may demand of us now a new capacity for self-transcendence, both intellectual and moral, so that we may experience a new dimension of beauty and intelligence in the world – not a *projection* of our desire for beauty and intellectual mastery, but an *encounter* with the actual unpredictably unfolding beauty and intelligence of the whole [...] the open encounter with the potential reality of an *anima*

> *mundi* makes possible its actual discernment. In this view, only by opening ourselves to being changed and expanded by that which we seek to understand will we be able to understand at all.
>
> Richard Tarnas (2007: 487)

Questions that invite us to explore the relationships between the intimate and the ultimate also help us to understand who we are and to find our place in the wider community of life and within a living and transforming cosmos. By living these questions together, the process of collective meaning-making in the face of uncertainty can itself become our guide and inform our appropriate participation. Bill Plotkin describes soul as our 'ultimate place'. "David Whyte speaks of the soul as 'the largest conversation a person is capable of having with the world'. Here 'conversation' is the poet's way of saying *relationship*. [...] the largest relationship a person can have with the world is the same as his 'ultimate place'" (2008: 36-37). To find our ultimate place in the world, we have to enter into a deeper conversation with each other, with nature and with the cosmos. We have to explore: how do we belong? Where are we? Who are we? What are we here to do? In living into these questions more deeply we might live into the answer to the question: why we are worth sustaining?

Bill Plotkin offers his seminal book *Nature and the Human Soul* as a "contribution to the global effort to create a viable human-Earth partnership" and bases his exploration on three premises: i) "a more mature human society requires more mature human individuals", ii) "nature (including our own deeper nature, soul) has always provided and still provides the best template for human maturation", and iii) "every human being has a unique and mystical relationship to the wild world, and that the conscious discovery and cultivation of that relationship is at the core of true adulthood." He adds: "True adulthood is rooted in transpersonal experience – in a mystical affiliation with nature, experienced as a sacred calling – that is then *embodied* in soul-infused work and mature responsibilities." Plotkin lays out a model for individual human development that offers "a narrative of how we might grow whole, one life stage at a time, by embracing nature and soul as our wisest and most trustworthy guides" and "a strategy for cultural transformation, a way of progressing from our current *egocentric* societies (materialistic, anthropocentric, competition-based, class-stratified, violence-prone and unsustainable)."

Bill Plotkin explores why being truly human is only possible in relationship with the natural world and how our soul and the soul of nature as our larger being are not separate but co-arise. "All places and all things and all roles speak to us, if only we have the ears to listen. Likewise, your soul, your ultimate place, evokes something from you, wants something from you, speaks to you, sometimes in a quiet voice, sometimes in a roar" (2008: 39). He speaks of *"living the questions of soul"* in reference to Rilke's letter to a young poet, cited at the start of this book. In this letter, Rilke encourages the young poet to spend time in nature paying attention to the little things "that can so unexpectedly become big and beyond measuring"; and his advice for finding one's true work in the world is "to go into yourself and test the depths in which your life takes rise" (in Plotkin, 2008: 280). The encouragement to seek solitude and insight in nature and the advice to go within are mutually reinforcing. In John Muir's words: "I only went for a walk and finally concluded to stay out til sundown, for going out, I found was really going in" (in Knapp & Smith, 2005).

Ecology and spirituality are two sides of the same coin – understanding and making sense of our own interbeing with the world, and our interdependence. You can enter into an embodied experience of wholeness and meaning through the door of the natural world or through spiritual practice. In fact, the two are ultimately not separate but they are pathways to the same *oneness* of existence *in* and *through* relationships. A oneness we experience most of the time from the limited perspective created by the 'illusion of separation'. If we want to reconstitute this oneness – the whole whose conscious reflections we are – we need to do so through the way we create meaning together and through the narrative we tell about our interbeing. Making time for solitude in wild nature helps us to have the largest conversation we are capable of having with the world. Communion with wild nature helps us embody our ultimate place and act wisely in recognition of our kinship with all life.

Parker J. Palmer (2004) reminds us that "to understand true self – which knows who we are in our inwardness and who we are in the larger world – we need both the interior intimacy that comes with solitude and the otherness that comes from community" (p.54). Palmer calls the soul "that life giving core of the human self, with its hunger for truth and justice, love and forgiveness" and continues "when we catch sight of the soul, we can become healers in a wounded world – in the family, in the neighbourhood, in the workplace, and in political life" (p.2). Deep listening can help us catch sight of the soul: listening to our inner voice, listening to our community, listening to wild nature, *listening for wholeness*. Without listening for wholeness, truth and beauty we will not find the answer to why we are worth sustaining – the key to our regeneration.

> Up North, in the wilderness, I sense the wholeness "hidden in all things"
> [Thomas Merton]. It is in the taste of the wild berries, the scent of sun-baked
> pine, the sight of the Northern Lights, the sound of water lapping the shore,
> signs of bedrock integrity that is eternal and beyond doubt. And when I return
> to a human world that is transient and riddled with disbelief, I have new eyes
> for the wholeness hidden in me and my kind and a new heart for loving even
> our imperfections.
>
> Parker Palmer (2004: 5)

Sustainability as a learning journey: pilgrims and apprentices

Sustainability is not a fixed state that can be achieved and then maintained forever after. Sustainability is a dynamic process of co-evolution and a community-based process of continuous conversation and learning how to participate appropriately in the constantly transforming life-sustaining processes that we are part of and that our future depends upon. If we are not asking the right questions, it is very easy to get confused with the diversity of answers on offer. As practitioners in your own field you will have noticed that often there are a number of 'sustainable design solutions' competing to be applied to a specific problem. Even for the experts it is difficult – if not impossible – to decide with certainty which answer offers the better solution.

One example of competing 'sustainable solutions' is the issue of whether tomorrow's road transport system should be based on renewably generated hydrogen or a shift towards electric vehicles powered by renewably generated electricity. I have met many informed and passionate advocates for both of these solutions and – at points – have found myself swayed towards one or the other by the force of conviction and evidence provided for either of them.

There are also many examples of how the powerful lobbies of the global petro-chemical, agro-industrial and pharmaceutical industries have used 'scientific evidence' and well-funded misinformation campaigns to sell the consumer supposedly sustainable solutions that at best sustain the short-term economic growth imperative of these multinationals but do so at the expense of people and planet. One such example is the way giant agribusinesses have patented GM seeds and have lobbied national governments to make traditional seed-saving of heirloom varieties illegal, while spending millions on campaigns to promote themselves as working for global food security. Surely the diversity of local varieties of food plants adapted to different ecological and climatic conditions is a vital factor in food security? In a culture of corporate greed and insidious disinformation it is hard to know which expert to trust and which proposed solution is worth implementing.

Any technology-based solution that needs energy and materials can always be criticized on the grounds that these techno-fixes fall short of delivering lasting results, since we are (globally) running out of the materials and energy we need to implement these technologies and to maintain the associated infrastructures over the long term. We are approaching shortages of many of the key chemical elements that are the basis of our current high technologies. For example, indium is a rare earth element that is crucial for modern photovoltaic technologies and touch screen displays, yet it is on the growing list of 'endangered elements' published by the Royal Society of Chemistry (Davies, 2011). At current rates of consumption many of these 'endangered elements' might not be available within 10 to 50 years (Cohen, 2007).

In thinking about the implementation of sustainable solutions we have not only to consider the limited availability of certain key materials but also the energy required to develop and deploy these solutions. In the last few years the fossil fuel industry has tried to silence the debate about peak oil with reports on new discoveries. Ever more expensive, complicated, and dangerous technologies (e.g. the fracking of shale gas and the exploitation of tar sands) are opening up access to more fossil fuels stored in the Earth's crust. The message is: there are a lot of fossil fuel resources left!

This is certainly true. Yet, these reports fail to say that the 'energy return on energy invested' (EROEI) along with the environmental impacts of the extraction and use of these reserves will make it uneconomic and unfeasible ever to use these fuels. More importantly still, the International Panel on Climate Change makes it clear that if we were to burn the remaining fossil fuel reserves we would affect global climate patterns in ways that would trigger catastrophic climate change. It matters little how much of this "unburnable carbon" (Carbon Tracker, 2013) is left; we have to switch to renewable resources for our fuels and material culture long before we run out of fossil resources. As Bill McDonough has suggested: "the Stone Age did not end because humans ran out of stones"; nor will the fossil fuel age end because we are running out of oil, coal or gas. It is time for us to shift towards a regenerative use of renewable resources.

If we take the current speed of technological innovation into account, it may indeed be possible to achieve radical resource and energy efficiency improvements that will help us in the transition towards a more sustainable culture, but if we see this transition only as a technical problem we are unlikely to create a truly regenerative human culture. We might develop new graphene-based nanotechnologies that will help us to filter water, store energy and find even more effective ways to collect and distribute renewable energy. We might be able to develop a new material culture based on additive manufacturing if we can grow feedstock for 3D printing technologies based on renewable materials and a new bio-economy. Yet, if we don't ask deeper questions about our current consumer culture and its value systems and worldview, we are unlikely to use these technological innovations to humanity's and life's long-term advantage.

Technology is a double-edged sword. Even if new 'green' miracle technologies did come riding over the hill to save us, in the short term, we need more than technological innovation to steer our way into an uncertain and unpredictable future. We need to develop a new sensitivity to the way life as a whole sustains itself and flourishes on a finite planet. Such deeper sensitivity and the humility of acknowledging the limits of our knowing is essential if we hope to apply our technological capabilities with wisdom and foresight.

Since the 1950s our economic system has been driving ever-increasing consumption on the premise that more (growth and consumption) is better. We need to learn from the kind of growth found in natural systems, which shifts from quantitative growth to qualitative growth as the system matures (see Chapter 7). It's not that more is better; better is better! Technological change is now so fast that we will also have to address important ethical questions:

Q How do we best apply the Precautionary Principle with regard to new technologies that seem promising but might have far-reaching environmental and social consequences if employed at a global scale?

Q Is it wise to mass-deploy all technologies that are technically feasible, or should we choose more carefully how and for what we employ our technological capabilities?

Q How do we choose wisely between one technological 'solution' and another, if experience shows that most of today's solutions turn into tomorrow's problems?

Q   How do we stay humble and act with 'precaution' in the face of uncertainty and constant change?

We will never reach 'destination sustainability'. Instead, we had better prepare for the long – and at points surprising – learning journey that will allow us to chart our path into an uncertain future. To walk the path into an uncertain future we would do well to cultivate the *attitude of a pilgrim* – with respect for all of life, in gratitude for the abundance we can share along the way, and with reverence for the magnificence of participating in this beauty. We would also do well to cultivate the *attitude of an apprentice* – acknowledging that nature in all its forms – whether through our fellow human beings or through the multitude of fellow species on this planet – has so much to teach us. As pilgrims and apprentices we have to be willing to question and, at times, give up what we know and who we are for what we could become. Herein lies one of the secrets of transformative innovation for a regenerative culture.

The learning journey that will take us beyond sustainability towards a regenerative human presence on Earth will have to be travelled with a pilgrim's humility and reverence for life and an apprentice's questioning and open mind. If we stop reminding ourselves of the limits of our own knowing and stop seeing the intrinsic (not just the utilitarian) value of all life, we will lose our responsiveness to what nature/life has to teach us. If we cease to understand ourselves as apprentices and begin to believe we have permanent answers to offer, we leave the path of 'living the questions' and we run the risk of stifling creativity, adaptive capacity and transformative innovation.

Sustainability is not enough; we need regenerative cultures

Sustainability alone is not an adequate goal. The word sustainability itself is inadequate, as it does not tell us what we are actually trying to sustain. In 2005, after spending two years working on my doctoral thesis on design for sustainability, I began to realize that what we are actually trying to sustain is the underlying pattern of health, resilience and adaptability that maintain this planet in a condition where life as a whole can flourish. Design for sustainability is, ultimately, design for human and planetary health (Wahl, 2006b).

A regenerative human culture is healthy, resilient and adaptable; it cares for the planet and it cares for life in the awareness that this is the most effective way to create a thriving future for all of humanity. The concept of resilience is closely related to health, as it describes the ability to recover basic vital functions and bounce back from any kind of temporary breakdown or crisis. When we aim for sustainability from a systemic perspective, we are trying to sustain the pattern that connects and strengthens the whole system. Sustainability is first and foremost about systemic health and resilience at different scales, from local, to regional and global.

Complexity science can teach us that as participants in a complex dynamic eco-psycho-social system that is subject to certain biophysical limits, our goal has to be appropriate participation, not prediction and control (Goodwin, 1999a). The best way to learn how to participate appropriately is to pay more attention to systemic relationships and interactions, to aim to support the resilience and health of the whole system, to foster diversity and redundancies at multiple scales, and to facilitate positive emergence through paying attention to the quality of connections and information flows in the system. This book explores *how* this might be done.

Using the Precautionary Principle

One proposal for guiding wise action in the face of dynamic complexity and 'not knowing' is to apply the *Precautionary Principle* as a framework that aims to avoid, as far as possible, actions that will negatively impact on environmental and human health in the future. From the United Nation's 'World Charter for Nature' in 1982, to the Montreal Protocol on Health in 1987, to the Rio Declaration in 1992, the Kyoto Protocol, and Rio+20 in 2012, we have committed to applying the Precautionary Principle over and over again.

The Wingspread Consensus Statement on the Precautionary Principle states: "When an activity raises threats of harm to human health or the environment, precautionary measures should be taken even if some cause and effect relationships are not fully established scientifically" (Wingspread Statement, 1998). The principle puts the burden of proof that a certain action is not harmful on those proposing and taking the action, yet general practice continues to allow all actions that have not (yet!) been proven to have potentially harmful effects to go ahead unscrutinized. In a nutshell, the Precautionary Principle can be summarized as follows: practice precaution in the face of uncertainty. This is *not* what we are doing.

While high-level UN groups and many national governments have repeatedly considered the Precautionary Principle as a wise way to guide actions, day-to-day practice shows that it is very hard to implement, as there will always be some degree of uncertainty. The Precautionary Principle could also potentially stop sustainable innovation and block potentially highly beneficial new technologies on the basis that it cannot be proven with certainty that these technologies will not result in unexpected future side-effects that could be detrimental to human or environmental health.

> Q   Why not challenge designers, technologists, policy-makers, and planning professionals to evaluate their proposed actions on their positive, life-sustaining, restorative and regenerative potential?
>
> Q   Why not limit the scale of implementation of any innovation to local and regional levels until proof of its positive impact is unequivocally demonstrated?

Aiming to design for systemic health may not save us from unexpected side-effects and uncertainty, but it offers a trial and error path towards a regenerative culture. We urgently need a Hippocratic Oath for design, technology and planning: do no harm! To make this ethical imperative operational we need a salutogenic (health generating) intention behind all design, technology and planning: *We need to design for human, ecosystems and planetary health.* This way we can move more swiftly from the unsustainable 'business as usual' to restorative and regenerative innovations that will support the transition towards a regenerative culture. Let us ask ourselves:

> Q How do we create design, technology, planning and policy decisions that positively support human, community and environmental health?

We need to respond to the fact that human activity over the last centuries and millennia has done damage to healthy ecosystems functioning. Resource availability is declining globally, while demand is rising as the human population continues to expand and we continue to erode ecosystems functions through irresponsible design and lifestyles of unbridled consumption. If we meet the challenge of decreasing demand and consumption globally while replenishing resources through regenerative design and technology, we have a chance of making it through the eye of the needle and creating a regenerative human civilization. This shift will entail a transformation of the material resource basis of our civilization, away from fossil resources and towards renewably regenerated biological resources, along with a radical increase in resource productivity and recycling. Bill Reed has mapped out some of the essential shifts that will be needed to create a truly regenerative culture.

> Instead of doing *less damage* to the environment, it is necessary to learn how we can *participate with* the environment – using the health of ecological systems as a basis for design. […] The shift from a fragmented worldview to a whole systems mental model is the significant leap our culture must make – framing and understanding living system interrelationships in an integrated way. A place-based approach is one way to achieve this understanding. […] Our role, as designers and stakeholders is to shift our relationship to one that creates a whole system of mutually beneficial relationships.
>
> Bill Reed (2007: 674)

Reed named 'whole-systems thinking' and 'living-systems thinking' as the foundations of the shift in mental model that we need to create a regenerative culture. In Chapters 3, 4 and 5, we will explore these necessary shifts in perspective in some detail. They go hand-in-hand with a radical reframing of our understanding of sustainability. As Bill Reed puts it: "Sustainability is a progression towards a functional awareness that all things are connected; that the systems of commerce, building, society, geology, and nature are really one system of integrated relationships; that these systems are co-participants in the evolution of life" (2007). Once we make this shift in perspective we can understand life as "a whole process of continuous evolution towards richer, more diverse, and mutually beneficial relationships". Creating regenerative systems is not simply a technical, economic, ecological or social shift: it has to go hand-in-hand with an underlying shift in the way we think about ourselves, our relationships with each other and with life as a whole.[†]

[†] Wherever the obelisk appears, it indicates that more materials on the subject are available online at www.triarchypress.net/questions

1: Living the Questions

Figure 1 shows the different shifts in perspective as we move from 'business as usual' to creating a regenerative culture. The aim of creating regenerative cultures transcends and includes sustainability. *Restorative design* aims to restore healthy self-regulation to local ecosystems, and *reconciliatory design* takes the additional step of making explicit humanity's participatory involvement in life's processes and the unity of nature and culture. *Regenerative design* creates regenerative cultures capable of continuous learning and transformation in response to, and anticipation of, inevitable change. Regenerative cultures safeguard and grow biocultural abundance for future generations of humanity and for life as a whole.

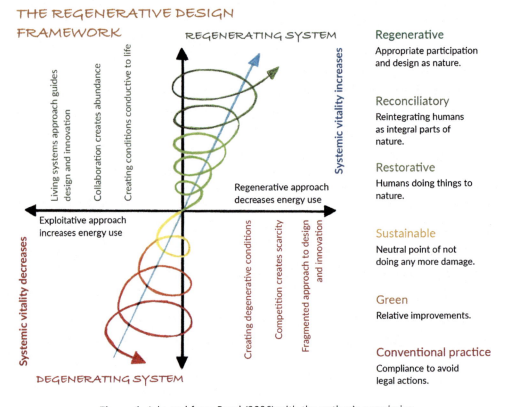

Figure 1: Adapted from Reed (2006) with the author's permission

The 'story of separation' is reaching the limits of its usefulness and the negative effects of the associated worldview and resulting behaviour are beginning to impact on life as a whole. By having become a threat to planetary health we are learning to rediscover our intimate relationship with all of life. Bill Reed's vision of regenerative design for systemic health is in line with the pioneering work of people like Patrick Geddes, Aldo Leopold, Lewis Mumford, Buckminster Fuller, Ian McHarg, E.F. Schumacher, John Todd, John Tillman Lyle, David Orr, Bill Mollison, David Holmgren, and many others who have explored design in the context of the health of the whole system. A new cultural narrative is emerging, capable of birthing and informing a truly regenerative human culture. We do not yet know all the details of how exactly this culture will manifest, nor do we know all the details of how we might get from the current 'world in crisis' situation to that thriving future of a regenerative culture. Yet aspects of this future are already with us.

In using the language of 'old story' and 'new story' we are in danger of thinking of this cultural transformation as a replacement of the old story by a new story. Such separation into dualistic opposites is in itself part of the 'separation narrative' of the 'old story'. The 'new story' is not a complete negation of the currently dominant worldview. It includes this perspective but stops regarding it as the only perspective, opening up to the validity and necessity of multiple ways of knowing. Embracing uncertainty and ambiguity makes us value multiple perspectives on our appropriate participation in complexity. These are perspectives that give value and validity not only to the 'old story' of separation, but also to the 'ancient story' of unity with the Earth and the cosmos. These are perspectives that may help us find a regenerative way of being human in deep intimacy, reciprocity and communion with life as a whole by becoming conscious co-creators of humanity's 'new story'.

Our impatience and urgency to jump to answers, solutions and conclusions too quickly is understandable in the face of increasing individual, collective, social, cultural and ecological suffering, but this tendency to favour answers rather than to deepen into the questions is in itself part of the old story of separation. The art of transformative cultural innovation is to a large extent about making our peace with 'not knowing' and living into the questions more deeply, making sure we are asking the right questions, paying attention to our relationships and how we all bring forth a world not just through what we are doing, but through the quality of our being. A regenerative culture will emerge out of finding *and living* new ways of relating to self, community and to life as a whole. At the core of creating regenerative cultures is an invitation to *live the questions together*.

CHAPTER 2

WHY CHOOSE TRANSFORMATIVE OVER SUSTAINING INNOVATION?

> For both the poor of the world living in largely degraded ecosystems and the so-called wealthy in the developed world, transformational change now seems to be required. Humanity cannot survive without functional ecosystems, and the actions of all people are needed to act together as a species on a planetary scale.
>
> John D. Liu (2011: 24)

Clayton Christensen (1997) identified two fundamentally different kinds of innovation. The most common kind simply aims to keep 'business as usual' going on for longer by improving upon already established ways of doing things and existing systems structures. It helps a company, organization or culture to keep doing what it is known for and used to without fundamentally changing services, products or the system's structure and identity. Christensen called this *'sustaining innovation'*, not because it is 'sustainable' but because it sustains 'business as usual' and helps established systems to function in the way they are used to.

The second type of innovation described by Christensen is *'disruptive innovation'*. He identified a wide range of cases where companies were caught out by competitors that had invented a completely new kind of service or product that made the offers of 'business as usual' companies in their industry sector obsolete. This kind of innovation is a game changer. Disruptive innovation can lead a company to compete with its own 'business as usual' offer in a disruptive way. The challenge becomes how to introduce the disruptive innovation in a sequenced way that allows the company to keep the lights on while preparing to phase out obsolete ways of working and technology and, at the same time, phase in the innovation that reinvents, redesigns and redefines the 'new business as usual'.

Taking a closer look, we can distinguish between two qualitatively different kinds of disruptive innovation. There is the kind that makes certain technologies and products obsolete by offering an improved and innovative way of obtaining better results than the old system. A simple example would be the change from magnetic tapes to compact discs as devices to store music. This fundamentally disrupted the business of those who were still trying to sell tapes, but the companies distributing the music were able to stay more or less the same. Another kind of disruptive innovation not only makes older technologies obsolete but initiates a process of transformation that leads to companies innovating a whole new way of doing business and providing service and value. The change from compact disc to digital media files downloadable from the Internet led to fundamental changes in the music industry. Established companies were forced to transform themselves in order to stay alive and companies like Apple and Spotify were able to capitalize on these fundamental changes by taking the first mover advantage.

In other words, one form of disruptive innovation leads to a change in technology without fundamentally transforming the industry in itself. The second type offers a bridge into a deeper cultural transformation that will lead the company, community, or society to transform and reinvent itself.

Building on Christensen's work, the International Futures Forum distinguishes a third type of innovation that describes the long-term innovation process of fundamental changes in culture and identity. In the context of sustainability and the transition towards a restorative culture, it is this kind of *'transformative innovation'* that is particularly of interest to us.

> Q How do we keep the lights on, avoid revolution and turmoil, keep children in school and people in work, yet still manage to fundamentally transform the human presence on planet Earth before 'business as usual' leads to run-away climate change, a drastically impoverished biosphere, and the early demise of our species?

Metaphorically speaking we are challenged to redesign the plane we are on in mid-flight. How do we keep the basic needs met while we are preparing and experimenting with the kind of transformational change that will make 'business as usual' obsolete and offer a qualitatively different alternative? Only by experimenting with and accepting change can we bring about transformation. Transformative change requires us individually and collectively to live differently, rather than to continue repeating unhealthy patterns of behaviour and ways of thinking that no longer serve us.

We have seen how we are living in between two narratives – separation and interbeing – and we will have to carefully evaluate what aspects of the old story can continue to serve us once we re-contextualize them from the more inclusive and integrative perspective of the 'new story' of interbeing.

We would be unwise to dismiss all our current systems and processes outright. In this time of cultural transition, we have to live the questions more deeply rather than jump into answers and solutions too quickly. Innovation for cultural transformation towards a regenerative culture is about finding the right balance between envisioning and designing our common future and letting it simply emerge while we pay close attention to how we relate to ourselves, our communities and the world. One of the questions we should keep asking is whether these relationships are nurturing, loving and healthy, or whether they are stifling, aggressive and pathological. Transformative innovation is as much about deep listening into what wants to emerge as it is about conscious and intentional interventions on the path from our current industrial growth society and culture of competitive individualism to a life-sustaining society and truly regenerative cultures.

We live in extraordinary times

We are living in extraordinary times and transformation is already happening and accelerating all around us. In almost every area of our lives old structures are breaking down as we witness the unfolding impacts of unprecedented technological innovation. All of this is happening within the context of an expanding human population, profound societal and economic transformation on all continents, and – most urgent of all – a dangerous destabilization of global and local climate patterns. There is a scientific consensus that we need to take immediate action if we are to avoid catastrophic climate effects on the future of humankind, the diversity of life and the entire planet. Already hundreds of thousands of people die every year due to climate change-related extreme weather events and millions lose their homes, go hungry or are forced to migrate. Ecosystems everywhere, and the biosphere as a whole, are reaching dangerous tipping points. The prolonged impact of an industrial growth society addicted to fossil fuels and the rapid extraction of non-renewable resources is pushing against planetary boundaries.

Our current economic system is structurally committed to ever-increasing economic growth and intertwined with a financial system based on debt, and currencies that are not backed up by real material value. Attempts to resuscitate this structurally dysfunctional system are getting more and more expensive, as the cycles of economic crisis and costly (temporary) recovery are getting shorter and shorter.

Continuing economic crisis, along with fear of war and terrorism have effectively kept climate and environmental issues at too low a level of political priority. Whether our structurally dysfunctional economic system can ever deliver sustainability is being questioned more and more. Not just anti-globalization activists but people in institutions such as the World Bank (Soubbotina, 2000), government think tanks (Jackson, 2009a), academia (e.g. Victor, 2010, Jackson 2009b) and the World Economic Forum (2012) are questioning the economic growth paradigm.

At the same time, the evidence that inequality has devastating social and health impacts is mounting (Wilkinson, 1996, 2005, Wilkinson & Pickett 2011, Stiglitz, 2013); yet the gap keeps widening globally. Demographic changes are challenging some countries, such as Germany and Japan, with the effects of over-ageing populations, while other countries in South America, Asia, Africa and the Middle East have a growing population of disenfranchised youth with poor economic prospects and inadequate education, facing a century of potential turmoil.

Rising fundamentalism and resource conflicts over oil, water and land have led to a series of wars which have caused humanitarian crises in the Middle East, Africa and Europe as rising numbers of refugees herald another era of mass migration. Environmentally, politically and economically induced migration are on the rise, driving potential conflicts between immigrant and resident populations, and adding to a resurgence of xenophobia just at the time when humanity has to pull together in order to successfully chart the turbulent waters ahead.

Food, water and energy supply issues are already leading to localized scarcities, famine and conflict in many parts of the world. Nevertheless, some predatory multinational corporations are still actively exacerbating these problems in the interests of a few, rather than helping to find solutions that protect the global commons and ensure basic access to essential needs for all of humanity. The root cause of this misguided behaviour is the narrative of separation that justifies aggressive competitive behaviour and generates artificial scarcity. This 'old story' still fundamentally informs our culture.

Education and health systems the world over are stretched to their limits as they are forced to reinvent and restructure themselves while at the same time maintaining and improving their services in a difficult economic climate. Even in the privileged and wealthy nations most education systems have not been able to come to grips yet with the profound reorganization of their mandate since information and knowledge is now more accessible than ever due to new information technology. Most university graduates are equipped with outdated knowledge and skills by the time they graduate, and are unable to grasp the big picture connections of the world they inhabit. Overspecialization has limited their capacity for integrative, lateral and holistic thinking.

It is true that many generations before us have thought of themselves as 'living in extraordinary times', yet never before in human history have there been so many of us on Earth, nor have we ever been in possession of such powerful technologies capable of affecting large scale catastrophic change based on only a very few ill-fated and misinformed decisions.

Transformation is inevitable and already under way

The transformations afoot today will reshape the human presence on Earth in less than a century, and if we want to have a 'snowball's chance in hell' we need to learn how to see all the diverse change processes and transformations as part of a systemic transition which we are unable to control but which we can navigate more wisely if we learn to ask the appropriate questions.

If we nurture the ability to see the interconnections between the different crises we are facing, if we learn to pay attention to the underlying systemic structures and narrative that drive our current deeply unsustainable behaviour, we may be able to equip communities everywhere with the ability to respond appropriately to the challenges ahead at their local and regional scale, while offering them a global context for collaboration in the transition towards regenerative human cultures. We live in a time of extraordinary opportunity. The Renaissance and the Enlightenment were relatively minor variations on an already existing theme in comparison to the transformation that is now under way. The birth of regenerative cultures and a regenerative human civilization is the most profound transformative innovation that our species has undergone since we started to turn from nomadic hunters and gatherers into settled agriculturalists some eight to five thousand years ago.

The ancient Greeks had two words for the concept of time: *chronos* – sequential, quantitative, chronological time – and *kairos* referring to extraordinary periods when culture transforms qualitatively and profoundly as individuals and collectives seize the transformative future potential of the present moment. The fall of the Berlin Wall and the Soviet Union, Nelson Mandela's transformation from prisoner to president, and the end of the British Raj through non-violent direct action led by Gandhi are all examples of *kairos* moments that affected the course of history. We are now in the midst of a *kairos* moment at the level of our entire species on a planetary scale. Transformation is inevitable and already under way.

The Three Horizons of innovation and culture change

In the autumn of 2009, I was invited to join the International Futures Forum (IFF) as one of a small group of 'next generation' members. The IFF is an international collaborative network of people committed to pooling their experience and insights to explore "the complex and confounding challenges that our world faces", to "support a transformative response to those challenges" and to "enhance our capacity for effective action".

One common perspective shared between the members of the IFF is that we need a more systemic approach to the complexity of the interconnected problems and opportunities that we face. Another shared belief is that, in order to appropriately respond to the changes around us, organizations, communities, businesses and governments must not only pay attention to possible short-term responses to symptoms of these crises, but must also address the underlying structural and systemic causes that drive these symptoms. In addition, working with complex systems requires us to befriend uncertainty, change and unpredictability. We aim to engage communities in the deeper cultural dialogue that asks the kind of questions and proposes the kind of provisional answers that drive cultural transformation and continued learning.

IFF members and other futures practitioners (see Hodgson & Sharpe, 2007; Curry & Hodgson, 2008; Sharpe 2013) developed the 'Three Horizons' framework collaboratively over the last 10 years. 'Three Horizons thinking' is an effective method for making sense of and facilitating cultural transformation and exploring innovation and wise action in the face of uncertainty and not-knowing. The framework has been applied in a variety of contexts, including the future of intelligent infrastructures in the UK, technological foresight in the IT industry, transformative innovation in the Scottish education system, the future of Alzheimer's research, rural community development, and executive leadership programmes. It is a versatile methodology for inviting people to explore the future potential of the present moment through a number of perspectives that all have to be considered if we are to steer our course wisely into an unpredictable future.

The 'Three Horizons' framework is a foresight tool that can help us to structure our thinking about the future in ways that spark innovation. It describes three patterns or ways of doing things and how their relative prevalence and interactions evolve over time. The change from the established pattern of the first horizon to the emergence of fundamentally new patters in the third occurs via the transition activity of the second horizon. The model not only makes us think in interactive patterns, but more importantly "it draws attention to the three horizons always existing in the present moment, and that we have evidence about the future in how people (including ourselves) are behaving *now*" (Sharpe, 2013: 2).

THREE HORIZONS FRAMEWORK APPLIED TO THE TRANSITION TOWARDS A REGENERATIVE CULTURE

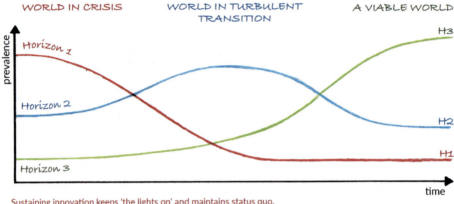

Sustaining innovation keeps 'the lights on' and maintains status quo.
Disruptive innovation identifies opportunities to change the scope of what is possible.
Transformative innovation facilitates the transition towards regenerative cultures.

Figure 2: Adapted from bit.ly/DRC229 with permission from IFF

The framework helps us to become more aware of how our individual and collective intentions and behaviours actively shape the future today. By mapping three ways of relating to the future from the perspectives of the three horizons we can bring the value of each of them to the conversation in a generative way that fosters understanding and future consciousness as the basis for collaborative action and transformative innovation.

I believe the three horizons offer an important framework for thinking about transformative innovation that can be used to facilitate the transition towards regenerative cultures. It can help us to structure our collective exploration as we start living the questions together as conscious participants in this transition. In this context, the first horizon (red) represents the currently prevalent systems that are beginning to show symptoms of decline and shortening cycles of crisis and temporary, but never fundamental, recovery.

In other words, Horizon 1 is 'business as usual', or 'the world in crisis' (H1). It is characterized by 'sustaining innovation' that keeps 'business as usual' going. Horizon 3 (green) is how we envision a 'viable world' (H3). We may not be able to define this future in every detail – as the future is always uncertain – yet we can intuit what fundamental transformations lie ahead, and we can pay attention to social, ecological, economic, cultural and technological experiments around us that may be pockets of this future in the present. Horizon 2 (blue) represents 'world in transition' (H2) – the entrepreneurial and culturally creative space of already technologically, economically and culturally feasible innovations that can disrupt and transform H1 to varying degrees and can have either regenerative, neutral or degenerative socio-ecological effects.

At the point where these H2 innovations become more effective than the existing practices, they begin to replace aspects of 'business as usual'. Yet some forms of 'disruptive innovation' ultimately get absorbed by H1 without leading to fundamental and transformative change, while other forms of 'disruptive innovation' can be thought of as a possible bridge from H1 to H3. Within the context of the transition towards regenerative cultures we introduce a value bias into our use of the Three Horizons methodology: solutions that create conditions conducive to life and establish regenerative patterns are valued more highly than those that don't. Throughout this book I refer to H3 as perspectives and patterns that intend to bring about a 'viable world' of regenerative cultures able to creatively transform in continuous exploration of the most appropriate responses to a rapidly changing socio-ecological context.

Cultivating future consciousness with Three Horizons perspectives

> The essence of Three Horizons practice is to develop both an individual and a shared awareness of all three horizons, seeing them as perspectives that must all come into the discussion, and to work flexibly with the contributions that each one makes to the continuing process of renewal on which we all depend. We step out of our individual mindset into a shared space of creative possibility.
>
> Bill Sharpe (2013: 29)

Horizon 1 is based on practices that have worked for a long time and have a proven track record based on past experience. H1 thinking – dominated by the narrative of separation – has shaped most of the practices that seem vital to our continued existence. Our education systems, our systems of production and consumption, our health system, communication infrastructure, transport and housing infrastructures, all of these systems and the vital services they provide will have to be transformed during the transition towards regenerative cultures.

From the perspective of the present moment, H3 describes regenerative cultures capable of constant learning and transformation in adaptation to and anticipation of change. Yet, as we approach H3, it recedes, or better, it transforms in response to wider systemic change. By the time we reach the cultural maturity that we today describe in terms of the third horizon, this H3 will have turned into the new H1 and we will face new and unpredictable challenges that will require us to take a new H3 perspective. The pilgrimage towards a sustainable and regenerative future has an endless string of false summits. As we reach the top of the green summit (H3) of our horizons map, we stand on the red ground of our new H1. Looking ahead with future consciousness we see the new second and third horizons stretched out in front of us.

Since the process of cultural evolution and transformation is continuous, there is no arriving at and maintaining an H3 scenario forever. Moving towards the third horizon always entails acknowledging our 'not knowing' and therefore staying with an apprentice mindset – ready to learn from experience; humble enough to regard no solution as final; and open to acknowledging the valuable perspectives of all three horizons.

While aspects of today's H1 are obsolete and among the root-causes of unsustainable practices, other aspects of H1 are also helping to provide vital services without which we would face almost immediate collapse. The transformation has to occur while these vital services continue to be provided. It is not possible for humanity to switch off the lights, leave the room, and start afresh in a different room that holds more promise. We only have one home planet. We have to find ways to transition from a status quo that is now deeply unsustainable to a new one. Sustainability and regenerative cultures are not endpoints to be reached but continuous processes of collective learning. As we move towards the third horizon we are likely to be surprised by the emergence of new challenges. To respond wisely to these challenges the perspectives offered by all three horizons should inform our actions.

> Three Horizon Thinking transforms the potential of the present moment by revealing each horizon as a different quality of the future in the present, reflecting how we act differently to maintain the familiar or pioneer the new.
>
> Bill Sharpe (2013: 10)

In order to avoid the common mistake of 'throwing out the baby with the bathwater', it is important to see all that is valuable about H1 and understand the importance of the contributions it makes to co-creating regenerative cultures. Bill Sharpe compares the H1 perspective to the role of the *manager* responsible for keeping the lights on and the business operational without massive disruption to its basic functioning. The H2 perspective is that of the *entrepreneur* who sees the potential advantage of doing things differently, challenging the status quo in operational ways but often without questioning the cultural narrative that maintains the H1 culture. The perspective of the H3 *visionary* calls for profound transformation towards a better (more just, fair, equitable, thriving and sustainable) world.

In the transition context, H3 thinking is informed by the new cultural narrative of interbeing and the scientific evidence for our interdependence with the rest of life. As such, it is defining a new way of being and relating based on a fundamental shift in worldview acknowledging the valuable contributions of H1 and H2 perspectives and putting them into the context of wider eco-social transformation.

In charting a path to regenerative cultures that aims to avoid massive disruption and suffering, we need to value the bridge that certain types of H2 innovation offer. Most H1 systems might be in need of profound transformation, but still have to be valued as a basis from which innovation and transformation become possible while we avoid the often regressive rather than evolutionary effects of revolution and systemic collapse.

The H3 perspective itself is populated by many different visions of the future. In the context of this book I concentrate on those that value viability and regeneration, yet it is important to stay open for the lessons we can learn from all three horizons and the diversity of perspectives on the future they represent. Maintaining an open mind and learning from multiple perspectives can help us to develop 'future consciousness' as we chart our path into a future that will always be characterized by the emergence of novel conditions - some predetermined and inevitable, others unpredictable.

Diverse H3 visions and experiments are needed to take our collective conversation about the future to a level that is inclusive and participatory. We need to question our own cultural conditioning and the myopia caused by H1 education and cultural discourse. H1 managers can often be locked into a specific way of doing things and a specific mindset (the narrative of separation) – a kind of self-fulfilling prophecy. H3 visionaries remind us to see future potential and possibilities beyond the rigid H1 mindset that resists change, in particular those kinds of change that invite cultural transformation.

The bridge between H1 and H3 is constructed by paying discerning attention to the space of innovation and the period of transition that is opened up by the second horizon. The H2 perspective sees opportunities in the shortcomings of H1 and aims to ground the visionary possibilities of the third horizon with some practical next steps. Many of them are likely to be 'stepping stones' or transitional innovations. Since H2 innovation takes place in an economic climate and within power structures dominated by H1, many of the proposed H2 innovations are ultimately captured to serve H1 goals. As the second horizon is about experimentation and entrepreneurship, many of its initiatives fail, offering opportunities for learning. Only a small percentage of innovations succeed in building an effective bridge between H1 and H3, enabling implementation of H3's high visions in tangible, convincing and 'positively infectious' ways.

Three Horizons thinking allows us to acknowledge what is valuable in each of the three horizons' distinct perspectives and ways of relating to the future. It helps us to see the opportunities and future potential of the present moment. It can help us to ask deeper questions as we engage in conversations informed by 'future consciousness' that turn rigid mindsets into valuable perspectives.

> Transformation happens as the emergent result of everything going on in the world – there is always an emerging third horizon at every scale of life from the individual to the planet and beyond. Some things will be the result of conscious intent, others will surprise us for good or ill. The way we live now was once the third horizon, partly imagined and intended, largely unknown. Future consciousness will not bring the future under control, but allows us to develop our capacity for transformational response to its possibilities.
>
> Bill Sharpe (2013: 15)

Three Horizons thinking offers a methodology and practice of seeing things from multiple perspectives and valuing the contribution that each perspective makes to the way we bring forth the world together. Simply holding a facilitated conversation using the Three Horizons framework in your local community group, business, organization or local council already has the potential for transformative cultural innovation within it.

Evaluating disruptive innovation in the age of transition

It is useful to classify H2 innovations into two categories. The first category is called H2 minus. H2- innovations change the technology employed and therefore disrupt 'business as usual' temporarily but without leading to a profound systemic transformation. The second category is H2 plus. H2+ innovations offer a bridge to H3, leading to a structural change and transformation of the system in question.

For example, providing power to the national grid via large-scale wind-farms is on the one hand part of the H2+ strategy of moving towards a 100% renewable energy based system, and on the other hand an H2- innovation locked into an H1 mindset as it is still structurally supporting a centralized energy system. An example of a genuine H2+ innovation in this area would be a blend of diverse and decentralized renewable energy technologies that combine stand-alone and grid-connected options in order to increase the flexibility, efficiency and resilience of our energy system overall. Figure 3 shows how we can evaluate potentially disruptive innovation within the context of the longer-term transition towards regenerative cultures, applying the Three Horizons' framework.

For practitioners aiming to facilitate the transition towards regenerative cultures, the art of *evolutionary* rather than *revolutionary* cultural transformation is to avoid systems collapse and subsequent rebuilding and to avoid dismissing the 'old story' categorically (throwing out the baby with the bathwater) but to build the 'new story' by transcending and including the 'old story'. To do so effectively we need to be able to distinguish between H2- and H2+ innovations, and support the latter as a way to drive the deeper transformation towards a regenerative H3 culture.

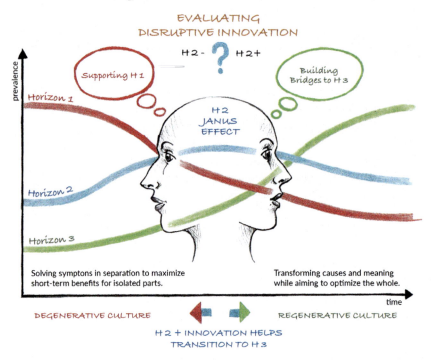

Figure 3: Adapted from Bill Sharpe (2013) and expanded, with permission from the author

H2+ type *disruptive innovation* tends to disrupt H1 ('business as usual') by offering improved solutions that buy us time to evolve the deeper H3 type transformative innovation. Widespread, culturally creative behavioural changes and worldview shifts only come about if we involve everybody – those who are invested in maintaining the status quo, those who see the entrepreneurial potential of doing things in a different way, and those who can envision fundamental worldview and value changes that would create a more regenerative culture. All three perspectives need to inform an ongoing conversation about our collective future.

Three Horizons thinking and practice is an invitation to move from rigidly held and defended 'mindsets' to being able to develop future consciousness by valuing the perspectives of all three horizons. As a sustainability educator and consultant with a particular interest in bridging between organizations in order to find common ground for co-creating a regenerative economy and culture, I have witnessed many entrenched arguments in rooms full of people who all wanted to do the right thing. Three Horizons thinking is a way to discover common ground and move forward together.

Paying attention to, and trying to support, both H2+ and H3 types of innovation is very important during the turbulent transition period we are in, but we also need to value the perspectives of H1 and H2- innovators trying to meet basic operational needs during the transition. If the lights go out, we risk taking a revolutionary – not an evolutionary – path, which could set us back into anachronistic, them-against-us thinking.

In a rigid mindset even H2+ innovators and H3 visionaries will tend to argue with each other rather than seeing that they are powerful allies. Far too often I have witnessed well-meaning visionary people wasting time over arguments that were trying to critique H2+ innovations as insufficiently transformative. Arguments between rigid mindsets tend to compare and contrast the slower, more complex transformative innovation (which often includes social innovation, value and behaviour change, and the redesign of economy, society and governance) with the more rapidly deployable technological changes in our energy, transport or production systems. In my opinion, we need technological innovators who are developing, say, new kite-based wind energy technologies that use less energy and materials than large turbine-towers, just as much as we need innovators who are designing complementary exchange and currency systems to enable a cooperative economy.

It is important to be aware that all three horizons are present at any point on the time axis. They do not fully replace one another, but simply change in their relative 'prevalence' (as scored on the y axis). This is a reminder to carefully assess what aspects of the 'old system' are worth saving. Humanity too often disregards the wisdom of the past in the name of 'progress'. In response to the dysfunctional aspects of 'business as usual' we often over-swing the pendulum and change from one extreme to another, rather than maintain what is good and useful of the old and blend it in a creative way with the new. The red line at the right end of the diagram represents just these useful aspects and structures of Horizon 1 that are worth maintaining and transforming.

Similarly, the green line of Horizon 3 on the left side of the diagram reminds us that "the future is already here, it's just not evenly distributed" as the science fiction writer William Gibson has put it. One way to accelerate the transition towards a regenerative culture is to identify these pockets of the future in the present and work to amplify and spread the transformative innovations generated by such visionary experiments.

Examples of experiments in transformative innovation are all around. Here are just a few areas where it is useful to evaluate disruptive innovations (H2-/+) for their role in the transition towards regenerative cultures: the fields of 'collaborative consumption', 'distributed manufacturing', bio-inspired innovation in industrial product and process design, 'open P2P innovation'; 'socio-cratic systems of governance' and 'restorative justice'; 'complementary exchange media' at the local, regional and global scale; work on 'the circular economy' and 'regenerative economics'; transition (town) initiatives and ecovillages, as well as work on eco-cities and bioregional development plans. The path of cultural transformation is made by walking it with an open mind and a willingness to learn from each other, from our mistakes, and from the community of life.

Transformative innovation is about deep questioning

> True innovation occurs when things are put together for the first time that had been separate.
>
> Arthur Koestler and John Smythies (1969)

The third horizon gives us a long-term guiding vision and invites us to expand the time horizons we are thinking in. In the search for a sustainable and desirable future we would do well to remember the wisdom of many traditional cultures that thought in much longer timeframes than our fast-paced modern culture. Many traditional cultures took important decisions with future generations in mind. Most of our current decision-making on the other hand seems to aim for short-term maximization of limited systems parameters, like for example the increase of GDP from one year to the next, or at the most, from one election cycle to another. The Native American Iroquois Nation famously had the practice of taking any important decision with special consideration for its possible effects on the seventh, yet unborn, generation in mind. This is the kind of cultural and civilizational guidance system that can create regenerative cultures.

We have to relearn what Peter Schwartz (1996) called the *Art of the Long View* and Three Horizons thinking is a good way to do so. Just as the builders of medieval cathedrals had a vision of the building they were constructing even if they would never see it finished, we need an inspiring vision of the regenerative culture we would like to co-create even if the journey of cultural transformation might take more than one lifetime or generation.

We'd better get used to constant transformative innovation and a rapid creation of new transitional structures that may soon dissolve to give way to the next creative adaptation to changing circumstances and another cycle of transformative innovation. In my own opinion, the 21st century will mark an unprecedented transformation of human culture as we will redesign our presence on Earth in adaptation to the ecological reality of our planetary life-support system. The emerging narrative of interbeing will come to express itself in a kaleidoscopic diversity of thriving regional cultures developing a new intimacy, reciprocity and care for their local ecosystems as contributors to human and planetary health.

Structural, cultural, technological, political, educational and economic transformations will occur not just once or twice but in a continuous sequence, at different scales, and in different regions at different times and in different ways. Both H2+ and H3 transformative innovation has the potential to drive the cultural evolution from our current industrial growth society of resource exploitation and social competition to a life-sustaining society of humanity *as nature* caring for systemic health and resilience out of enlightened self-interest and rooted in local, regional and global collaboration aimed at optimizing the system for all.

Our species, inquisitive *Homo sapiens sapiens*, is dancing with the real danger of triggering irreversible run-away effects within the biosphere that will influence life on Earth for many millennia. In the transformative journey towards regenerative human cultures, *how* we get there – what relationships we form within the human family and with the community of life, our path of continuous learning and transformation along the way – matters more than arriving. In fact, there is no arrival at the end of this journey, only continuous adaptation and transformation. We are participants in life's continuous exploration of novelty.

Guiding questions are a more useful way to chart such a continuous transformative path than fixed answers. This does not mean we do not have to propose answers and implement solutions; we simply have to be aware that they will only serve temporarily.

Q   What are the basic assumptions and beliefs that inform how we define the problem and offer solutions?

Q   What are the unmet real needs that are obscured by the perceived needs we are focusing on?

Q   How can we more effectively work with the people affected and involve them in finding solutions that work for them?

Q   How can we design flexibility and the capacity to transform and adapt into our proposed solutions?

Q   What can we learn from nature's patterns and processes in order to create solutions that strengthen rather than weaken local ecosystems and the planetary life support system?

Q   Why are we focused on this particular issue and how does it relate to its wider context (are we asking the right question)?

Q   Are there related problems that we could include in finding a more systemic way of dealing with multiple interconnected issues at once?

- **Q** How does what we are proposing to do affect ourselves, our community and the world?

- **Q** What implication might our 'solution' have for future generations?

- **Q** How do we stay flexible and keep learning from systemic feedback and unexpected side-effects?

Sensitivity to scale, uniqueness of place and local culture

One way to avoid – or at least minimize – the risk that new 'solutions' will result in catastrophic and widespread unintended consequences is to limit the scale of experimentation. At the local and regional scale, feedback is faster and ecological limits are more immediately identifiable. Furthermore, by focusing on the local and regional scale, we can adapt solutions better to the specific conditions of a particular place. Design that aims to meet basic human needs at the scale of the local community/region also creates systemic redundancies, so that unpredictable changes in one place are less likely to trigger domino effects in other places. In the dogma of neoclassical economics, redundancy is to be avoided as ever larger economics of scale are used to increase the profits of a few to the systemic detriment of many. However, if we aim to create circular economies based on local, renewable, biological resources, redundancy becomes a vital ingredient of vibrant local economies and regional resilience.

Good solutions and appropriate answers might be informed by global knowledge exchange but they are born out of the unique conditions of a specific place and its specific culture. Getting the questions right makes best practice transferable from region to region, turning 'best practice' examples into 'best process' methodologies. The right questions can help to guide the longer-term cultural transformation, enabling us to identify those past solutions that have turned into problems and invite more transformative innovation. Most solutions and answers are temporal, but good questions can guide us over the long term. The appropriate guiding questions can help us to assess when past solutions are beginning to turn into present problems as they do not adequately reflect or address the current circumstances any longer.

Creative problem-solving in a regenerative culture is not only about finding the answer to current needs but also about helping us to ask better questions. Ideally such questions help us to learn something about ourselves and about our relationships with the wider context. As we begin to understand the inadequacies of past solutions in the light of a more systemic awareness, we are developing a new social and ecological awareness. Transformative innovation promotes life-long learning for individuals and communities.

We need to co-create diverse models for systemic solutions at a local and regional scale. Some of them will inform through their successes and others through their failures. Repetitive failure and experimentation at a small scale can help us to learn faster. As Thomas Watson Sr., president of IBM for 42 years, said so aptly: "If you want to succeed, double your rate of failure". The response time and cycles of transformative innovation can be faster at the local scale. If you want to effectively adapt to and influence economic, social, cultural and environmental change, start with small-scale experiments that give you quick feedback as to what works and what doesn't. Deeper questioning into the underlying real or perceived needs that make us identify and frame the 'problem' in the first place might lead us to discover that we are treating symptoms rather than causes.

Sometimes the feedback from the system in question (for example, your local community) might be that a more effective and transformative solution can only be brought about at the next scale up – the regional scale. We need a new sensitivity regarding which problems to solve at which scale. Maybe we should ask ourselves:

Q How do we create functional experiments and case studies of the transition towards regenerative cultures at a scale where feedback is rapid enough so we can learn from mistakes before unwanted side-effects lead to catastrophe and systemic collapse?

Q How do we discern which issues and problems are best solved at which scale, building local and regional resilience through redundancies and self-reliance while nurturing regional and inter-regional collaboration on national and global issues?

The solutions we propose at the local, regional, national and global scales have to be interlinked in such a way that they become mutually reinforcing and supporting. Policy and governance needs to enable local and regional problem-solving rather than impede it by generalized regulations that do not adequately reflect the local conditions of a specific ecosystem and culture. Paying close attention to the uniqueness of place and regional culture reveals opportunities for transformative innovation and preservation of biocultural diversity.

All over the world our ancestors evolved unique cultural expressions, informed by a sense of place and a deep reciprocity with the unique ecological, geological and climatic conditions of that particular place. The local and regional scale is not only the scale at which we can act most effectively to preserve biological diversity, it is also the scale at which we can preserve cultural diversity and indigenous, local wisdom as expressions of living in long-term connection with the uniqueness of any given locality.

Much can be learned from such place-based knowledge. At the same time we have to be aware that most local cultures have already undergone a profound transformation and erosion of local tradition and language. We need to value traditional place-based knowledge and culture without falling into the traps of a resurgence of radical regionalism and narrow-minded parochialism. We need to value local and regional solutions supported by global collaboration and knowledge exchange. A regenerative human culture will be locally adapted and globally connected. The future will be glo-cal, enabled by collaborative, peer-to-peer networks and social innovation.

The transformative power of social innovation

> The results of social innovation are all around us. Self-help health groups and self-build housing; telephone help lines and telethon fundraising; neighbourhood nurseries and neighbourhood wardens; Wikipedia and the Open University; complementary medicine, holistic health and hospices; micro-credit and consumer cooperatives; charity shops and the fair trade movement; zero carbon housing schemes and community windfarms; restorative justice and community courts. All are examples of social innovation – new ideas that work to meet pressing unmet needs and improve people's lives.
>
> Geoff Mulgan (2007: 7)

One of the most promising areas of transformative innovation for a regenerative culture is the widespread emergence of social innovation in its diverse expressions all over the world. It is hard to offer just one definition of social innovation that works for all who are involved in this powerful impulse of cultural transformation. The examples of successful social innovations are as diverse as the different change agents who have created them. Social innovation is a cross-sector phenomenon, including 'collaborative consumption' business models, novel approaches to helping people help themselves through micro-loans pioneered by Muhammad Yunus, peer-to-peer lending or crowd-funding websites like Zopa or Kickstarter, and the co-production of social services in a collaboration between local government, service-providers and service-users. Such diverse applications drive transformative innovation in business, civil society and government, and even more excitingly in the fertile space between these sectors. *The Open Book of Social Innovation* (Murray *et al.*, 2010) offers an excellent introduction to the broad field of social innovation along with numerous examples that illustrate the different strategies and methodologies social innovators employ to create effective initiatives and businesses.

'Social enterprise' is a subset of 'social innovation'. Not all social innovation has to be business driven. In general, 'social innovation' can be understood as any initiative that employs innovative and experimental methods to tackle one or many of the problems we face (social, ecological, economic, cultural) to improve people's lives, community resilience and the health of ecosystems. 'Social enterprise' does the same but uses innovative business models, for example the provision of goods or services that help in linking unmet needs with spare capacity through win-win-win problem-solving.

A social enterprise or social business's primary objective is to have a positive social and/or environmental impact and to contribute to the wellbeing of society and local communities. Rather than aiming to generate profits for owners and shareholders beyond reasonable salaries for those running the business, surpluses in social enterprises are primarily reinvested in improving the business's ability to achieve its social impact effectively. Let me illustrate this distinction by two brief examples: Avaaz and Zopa.

Avaaz describes itself as a "global web movement to bring people-powered politics to decision-making everywhere". Launched in 2007, by early June 2015 Avaaz had already connected 41.5 million people in 194 countries around the world. Run by a small decentralized team spread over six continents and campaigning in 15 languages, Avaaz empowers a vast diversity of concerned global citizens to take action on pressing local, regional and global issues. It enables people to sign global petitions on a broad range of social, economic and environmental issues. These are then presented to the politicians responsible for taking related decisions or ratifying related policies. The crowd-sourced campaigns are supported through local volunteers who engage in direct action and demonstrations that highlight the global support of the campaign to local and global media.

From campaigning to stop deforestation, keep the Internet free of censorship, support the land-rights of indigenous communities and protect biodiversity initiatives, to advocating an end to violence against women, peace activism, and campaigns in response to climate change or the destructive practices of multinationals in the agro-industrial, pharmaceutical and petro-chemical industries, Avaaz has fought and won many campaigns of considerable impact at a global, regional and local scale. Avaaz is entirely member-funded via online donations. This helps to maintain its absolute independence from the lobbying interest of large corporations and government politics. Avaaz is an example of social innovation that is not a social enterprise, but finances its activities through a global network of supporters who value its work for the benefit of people and planet.

An example of a social innovation based on a for-benefit social enterprise business model is the UK peer-to-peer social lending service, Zopa. Since its launch in 2005, Zopa has enabled more than £900 million in peer-to-peer loans by connecting savers and borrowers directly through its website. Its lean business model means it can offer higher interest rates to savers and lower rate loans to borrowers. By June 2015, Zopa had connected over 59,000 lenders with over 110,000 borrowers and had been voted the 'most trusted personal loan provider' by the Moneywise Customer Awards for 6 years in a row.

Zopa by-passes the large banks with their huge overheads and service charges by connecting lenders and borrowers directly and creating a basis of trust through the 'Zopa Safeguard', which covers savers should a borrower be unable to pay. A low and transparent fee enables the social enterprise to offer the service, pay its 97 staff and invest in developing its services. Savers pay a 1% annual lender fee and borrowers pay a small borrowing fee once their loan is approved. Many of the loans are used by social innovators to set up as self-employed or start small businesses with a social, environmental or local community benefit.

The potential for social innovation and social entrepreneurship as drivers of transformative innovation and culture change is not to be underestimated. These pathways offer a participatory, locally responsive and globally collaborative way to address some of the most pressing issues. The field of social innovation is in constant flux. Its very nature as a type of transformative innovation is to break with established ways of doing things and to question established patterns and outdated assumptions in order to find new and more appropriate ways to solve social problems (Buckland & Murillo, 2013: 158). There are many foundations, academic institutes, and civil society organizations that have set up excellent programmes for people who want to learn more about social innovation and social entrepreneurship.[†]

Collaborative consumption and peer-to-peer collaboration

The field of collaborative consumption is one of the areas of social innovation that most excites me. Rachel Botsman and Roo Rogers (2011) offer an introduction to this rapidly evolving approach to participatory culture change in *What's Mine is Yours*. Fundamentally there are two different ways to engage with collaborative consumption, either as a 'peer-provider' offering assets to borrow, rent or share, or as a 'peer-user' renting, borrowing or sharing the assets offered by peer-providers (p.70).

> Swap trading, time banks, local exchange trading systems (LETS), bartering, social lending, peer-to-peer currencies, tool exchanges, land share, clothing swaps, toy sharing, shared workspaces, co-housing, co-working, CouchSurfing, car sharing, crowdfunding, bike sharing, ride sharing, food co-ops, walking school buses, shared microcrèches, peer-to-peer rental – the list goes on – are all examples of Collaborative Consumption. Some of these may be familiar already, some not, but all are experiencing a significant growth surge. Although these examples vary in scale, maturity and purpose, they can be organized into three systems – product service systems, redistribution markets and collaborative lifestyles.
>
> Botsman & Rogers (2011: 71)

One of the underlying shifts in worldview and thinking is that from needing to own to preferring simply to have access to shared goods and services. A *'product service system'* (PSS) allows people to receive the benefits of a product without having to actually own it themselves. Car sharing, co-working spaces or launderettes, for example, allow people to use products owned by service providers for a usage fee. Another kind of PSS enables people to share or rent privately owned items via a social P2P (peer-to-peer) market place, for example companies like Zilok or Erento. The global-local arts and crafts market place Etsy allows small scale artisan producers anywhere to have access to a global market; while *redistribution markets* like eBay and Around Again enable goods no longer needed by their original owner to be reused elsewhere. Many specialist online redistribution business have been set up, ranging from trading books (readitswapit) and baby clothes (tradingcradles), to fashion items (swapstyle). Sites like Gumtree and Craigslist offer a wide variety of items for sale or exchange, as well as listing diverse jobs, community services and more.[†]

The third type of collaborative consumption identified by Botsman and Rogers, *'collaborative lifestyles'*, extends the P2P exchange from physical goods to the sharing of time, skills, space and money. Both PSS and 'redistribution markets' are also enablers of 'collaborative lifestyles', which make use of hybrid systems of all three types of collaborative consumption. 'Collaborative lifestyles' generate the additional benefit of exchanges on a local or regional scale leading to human connections beyond the virtual platform by matching spare capacity with unmet needs. Examples range from co-working spaces, like the global networks of ImpactHubs, to the sharing of land for farming (e.g.

Landshare), horticulture (e.g. Edinburghgardenpartners) and garden produce (e.g. Neighbourhood Fruit), to sharing parking space (e.g. ParkatmyHouse).

One particularly inspiring example is the story of CharityFocus, now ServiceSpace, which started in 1999 with a group of successful Silicon Valley entrepreneurs who decided to offer their unique skill sets to help worthwhile causes and not-for-profit organizations. In only 15 years ServiceSpace has grown into a global network of more than 400,000 people who volunteer their skills and time to help initiatives for positive change. Among the projects that grew out of ServiceSpace are gift-economy restaurants called Karma Kitchens, a fundraising support site called PledgePage, and positive news platforms like DailyGood or Karmatube. Nipun Mehta, a co-founder of ServiceSpace, speaks about four behavioural shifts that are already beginning to transforming culture: from consumption to contribution, from transaction to trust, from isolation to community, and from scarcity to abundance (Mehta, 2012). Many more inspiring examples of peer-to-peer collaboration, open innovation and P2P technology development have been collected and explained by Michel Bauwens and his team at the p2p Foundation. The foundation's wiki-site is a treasure trove of inspiration on how peer-to-peer collaboration can catalyse the transition towards regenerative cultures.†

Facilitating systems innovation and culture change

> Social innovation doesn't have fixed boundaries […] we define social innovations as new ideas (products, services, and models) that simultaneously meet social needs and create new social relationships or collaborations. In other words, they are innovations that are both good for society *and* enhance society's capacity to act.
>
> Robin Murray et al. (2010: 5)

As individuals, communities and societies we are faced with rapid and profound changes, the breakdown of old structures, institutions and ways of working. We are already in the middle of profound systems innovation and cultural change. In the absence of effective political leadership and faced with the increasing inability of national governments to provide important public services, we are seeing a resurgence of self-help initiatives based on community-level citizen collaboration. Many of the examples reviewed in the last two chapters are part of this (r)evolution in social innovation. Increasingly, such initiatives will find the active support of local, regional and national government. In the UK the emerging 'co-production sector' is offering a culturally transformative alternative to providing public services.

> Co-production means delivering public services in an equal and reciprocal relationship between professionals, people using services, their families and their neighbours. Where activities are co-produced in this way, both services and neighbourhoods become far more effective agents of change.
>
> David Boyle and Michael Harris (2009: 11)

The 2009 Nobel prize winner for economics, Elinor Ostrom, pointed out the importance of co-production as early as the 1970s when she investigated why large-scale, top-down deliveries of public services without the human face of direct community involvement were frequently not as effective as more participatory approaches based on human-scale collaboration between service providers and the communities receiving these services.

When service users are only passive recipients and their skills, time and knowledge are not valued, community cohesion and collaboration atrophy and systems become stagnant. If you ask people for help in providing the services that are important to their communities and find ways to use their skills, systemic change occurs with renewed vibrancy. "The people who are currently defined as users, clients or patients provide the vital ingredients which allow public service professionals to be effective. They are the basic building blocks of our missing neighbourhood-level support system – families and communities – which underpin economic activity as well as social development" (Boyle & Harris, 2009: 11). Edgar Cahn, the inventor of time banking, summarizes 20 years of experimenting with this complementary exchange mechanism as a means of enabling co-production. Time banking can help to build neighbourhood-level mutual support networks that are not dependent on the rules of the market economy. It enables widespread and equitable participation, and creates community.

> It will take massive labour of all kinds by all to build the core economy of the future – an economy based on relationships and mutuality, on trust and engagement, on speaking and listening and caring – and above all on authentic respect. We will not get there simply by expanding an entitlement system which apportions public benefits based on negatives and deficiencies: what one lacks, what disability one has, what misfortune one has suffered. We have to begin creating a new species of entitlements: *earned entitlements* that vest by virtue of how one contributes to rebuilding the core economy. That is the new path we must blaze through co-production if co-production is going to transcend professionally defined domains of problems and rebuild an organic world of community that reunites the human family. Timebanking supplies a tool and a medium of exchange to help do that.
>
> Edgar Cahn (2008: 3-4)

Time banking is one way to unlock the flow of mutual support between people and organizations in a given region. Instead of using money as a medium of exchange, people and/or organizations are able to collaborate and organize themselves around a common purpose simply by keeping track of the amount of hours each person dedicates to the project at hand. "For every hour participants 'deposit' in a time bank, perhaps by giving practical help or support to others, they are able to 'withdraw' equivalent support in time when they themselves are in need" (Time Banking UK, 2015). This system enables the growth of social cohesion and social capital, by making it easier for people to get to know and help each other in ways that allow everyone to share what they are good at or what they are able to offer in support of others. Time Banking is one of many innovations in the design of complementary exchange systems of currencies; others include the

Metacurrency Project, Open Money and a wide range of regional and local currency projects (for examples, see Rogers, 2013).

If they don't take care of social capital, societies will fail. Social capital is rooted primarily in the social economy with its home-base in households, neighbourhoods, communities and civil society. Co-production aims to strengthen and re-grow this core-economy. "Co-production involves reclaiming territory for the core economy – territory lost to the commodification of life by all sectors of the monetary economy, public, private and non-profit." Edgar Cahn argues that "we will be unable to create the core economy of the future so long as we live in a bifurcated world where all social problems are relegated either to paid professionals or to volunteers whose role is typically restricted to functioning as free labour within the silos of the non-profit world" (2008: 3). For-benefit social enterprises and cooperatives based on social innovation, peer-to-peer collaboration and co-production are ways to overcome this blockage.

The rise of the so-called 'fourth sector' unites a wide diversity of such initiatives. In a nutshell, the fourth sector creates social, ecological and economic benefit by using some of the effective tools of the 'first sector' (private for-profit) to address some of the core challenges that the 'second sector' (government, public administration) is struggling with, and is informed by the social and environmental ethics and values of the 'third sector' (civil society organizations, non-profits, NGOs). Fourth sector networks are currently emerging in the USA, Denmark, the Basque Country, and on the island of Majorca. The Business Alliance for Local Living Economies (BALLE), co-initiated by Judy Wicks, is a similar type of network that is primarily focused on strengthening local economies through supporting locally-owned independent businesses, thereby creating an environment where fourth sector activities and co-production can flourish and help to build resilient communities.

"Co-production makes strengthening the core economy of neighbourhood and family the central task of all public services" (Boyle & Harris, 2009: 14). Inspired by the work of Nipun Mehta, Judy Wicks, David Boyle and Michael Harris, and Edgar Cahn, we can ask the following questions as we aim to strengthen our community exploration of what a regenerative culture might be like:

> Q Since people themselves are the real wealth of our communities and societies, how can we invite them to contribute their skills, knowledge and passion to meeting community needs?
>
> Q How can we value work differently so that we acknowledge the importance of what people do to raise families, look after others, maintain community health and cohesion, and to promote social justice and good governance?
>
> Q How can we promote reciprocity and generosity ('giftivism'), giving and receiving, as pathways to deeper trust and mutual respect between people?

Q   Since our physical and mental wellbeing depends on strong, enduring relationships, how can we build effective social networks and foster community?

Co-production, social innovation, social enterprises, fourth sector networks and initiatives like BALLE are just some of the diverse ways we can facilitate the kind of transformative systems innovation that will drive culture change.

Systems innovation is "an interconnected set of innovations, where each influences the other, with innovation both in the parts of the system and in the ways in which they interconnect" (Mulgan & Leadbeater, 2013: 7). This very general definition of systems innovation highlights the complexity – and, therefore, to some extent the unpredictability and uncontrollability – of systemic transformations. It is rare, if not impossible, for a single individual to design and execute a blueprint for widespread systemic change because such changes tend to emerge from the quality of interactions and relationships of diverse agents (participants or stakeholders) in the system.

In aiming to facilitate systems innovation we have to accept that designing and implementing systems-level interventions can contribute to systems change but cannot control it. There is a balance between emergence and design, which I will return to. Transformative systems innovation, in the face of complexity and uncertainty, means getting clear about 'why' we design something, our guiding values and visions for a better future. Once we have done that we can evaluate better 'what' we design, and how our interventions are likely to contribute to positive culture change.

Clearly there are many other aspects and examples of transformative innovation: the technologies we employ; how we behave as individuals and communities; changes in systems of governance, economic systems, or food, energy and transport systems; changes in worldview and value systems which will require changes in our education system; and ultimately changes in the predominant cultural narrative. I will offer some perspectives and questions on all of these in the following chapters. But first, here are some general questions we might want to explore in any attempt to drive systems and culture change. They can help to guide our actions as we aim to become positive and effective change agents in the transition towards regenerative cultures (based on Mulgan & Leadbeater, 2013: 18-20).

Q   What are the new ideas, concepts and perspectives (paradigms) that can inform and drive systemic transformation?

Q   Which policy changes, including new laws and regulatory changes, will support positive culture change?

Q   How can we create supportive networks of collaboration and coalitions united by common values and intentions?

Q   What are our new indicators of success, new ways of monitoring progress, and how can we shift what is valued by the market?

Q   Which relationships and power structures need to be transformed for systems change to occur and how will we go about this?

Q   What kind of technological innovation will assist the transition towards a regenerative culture and how will we deploy these technologies and choose not to use potentially harmful technologies?

Q   What kind of new skill sets and new professions are emerging in support of systemic transformation?

Q   How can we catalyse and support social innovation and behaviour change?

Q   What is the appropriate scale on which to focus, and how do we link local, regional and global transformation?

Q   How can we most effectively keep the big picture in mind and take small realizable steps that can offer feedback and learning locally?

Q   Who are the visionary individuals and/or organizations that act as change agents by going beyond the conventional to develop the new?

Q   How can we create projects that demonstrate viable and desirable alternatives to 'business as usual'?

Q   How can we invite as many people as possible to join the conversation about creating regenerative cultures of thriving communities in local-global collaboration?

CHAPTER 3

WHY *DO* WE NEED TO THINK AND ACT MORE SYSTEMICALLY?

> The power and majesty of nature in all its aspects is lost on one who contemplates it merely in the detail of its parts and not as a whole.
>
> Pliny the Elder

An increasing number of people are beginning to understand that the world we participate in is too complex, magnificent and changeable for any single perspective to do justice to its diversity and complexity. There is more to life than a 'theory of everything' that reduces the awe-inspiring diversity, creativity and beauty surrounding us to a series of abstract mathematical equations.

We live in networks of relationships defined by qualities that make life worth living. Most qualities escape quantification and mathematical abstraction. We need to acknowledge and value multiple perspectives and find ways to integrate their different contributions into a framework of thinking that can inform wise action.

In order to achieve a collaborative way of acknowledging, integrating and evaluating multiple perspectives, we need to move beyond dualistic either-or logic which suggests that, if two perspectives seem to contradict each other, one of them must categorically be wrong in order for the other perspective to be right. Yet, at a time when our cultural belief in the ability of science and technology to fix all our problems is beginning to wane, we also need ways to evaluate and compare different perspectives. Science might not offer us the 'objective' picture of reality we were taught in school, but it remains a powerful method of inter-subjective consensus-making and constitutes a fairly reliable basis upon which to act – more so, say, than the opinion, intuition or spontaneous insight of a single individual – in most but certainly not all cases. We should neither exclusively favour inter-subjective 'rational' reasoning nor only rely on individual insight and intuition, but let ourselves be informed by both, as and when appropriate.

Whole-systems thinking allows us to co-create rich pictures of the 'system in question' – pictures which can accommodate multiple points of view. Mapping the diversity of perspectives and insights that these pictures offer helps to make it possible for us to act more wisely in the face of uncertainty and in recognition of the limits of our knowing.

Whether the call is for joined-up thinking, 'multiple ways of knowing', systemic thinking, an integral approach or holistic thinking, all of them are inviting us into a deeper understanding of the interrelated crises/opportunities we are facing, and thereby to open up the potential of 'transformative innovation' as we begin to see the synergies and the potential for creating win-win-win pathways into the future. If the core of innovation is – as Arthur Koestler put it – to connect two or more previously unconnected things or issues, then we will innovate more appropriately once we learn from multiple perspectives in order to integrate ecological, social and economic concerns into solutions that are good for people, planet and shared prosperity.

Beyond promoting innovation and leading to more systemic and synergistic solutions, integrating multiple perspectives also serves to make us more aware of our own particular perspective and how that perspective influences our way of responding to a situation. What kind of action or response we might consider appropriate in a given situation critically depends on our worldview, our value system and the perspective we choose.

Whole-systems thinking can help us in complex situations where diverse stakeholders are trying to create a common basis for collaborative action that acknowledges diverse needs and points of view *and* still allows for a way to move forward together. It is important that we are not only integrating different material or exterior aspects of reality (the system in question), but also trying to pay attention to the immaterial or interior aspects of the situation at hand. Conflicts of opinion can be mediated once we are aware of how individually and collectively we assign meaning and significance to an issue. We need to become more aware of our own worldview and value system and how they inform our favoured perspective. This opens up a pathway towards both individual transformation (personal development) and cultural transformation through more inclusive decision-making.

Applying 'integral theory'

One way to map this complexity of experiences and perspectives available to us is the four-quadrant framework that forms the backbone of integral theory (Wilber, 2007). It maps our four dimensions of experience: the individual – interior (I), the individual – exterior (IT), the collective – interior (WE), and the collective – exterior (ITS). These four quadrants respectively address the intentional, the behavioural, the cultural and the social aspects of how we experience the world. Figure 4 shows a graphic representation of this framework, which has been applied to map a wide diversity of human affairs in the fields of philosophy, psychology, business, ecology, medicine and design (to mention just a few).

There is no room to examine integral theory in detail here, but I encourage you to explore this useful framework further. I do, however, need to address very briefly one common critique integral theorists have of systems thinking. Integral theory's four quadrants framework classifies all systems perspectives as belonging only to the exterior collective (ITS), which is to say the material world of physical systems. A common critique of the 'Gaian worldview' is that it reduces reality to the physical/material reality of the 'living planet' or the 'web of life'. While this might be true for some proponents, it certainly is not the approach explored here. As should have become clear already, this book aims to invite deeper questioning into the way consciousness and matter, the interior (subjective) dimensions and exterior (objective) dimensions of reality, interrelate. Exploring this relationship will inform the way we set about creating a regenerative culture. Yes, the language of 'systems' belongs to the exterior/collective quadrant (ITS) but a participatory whole-systems approach to our participation in living systems explores the relationship between all four quadrants.

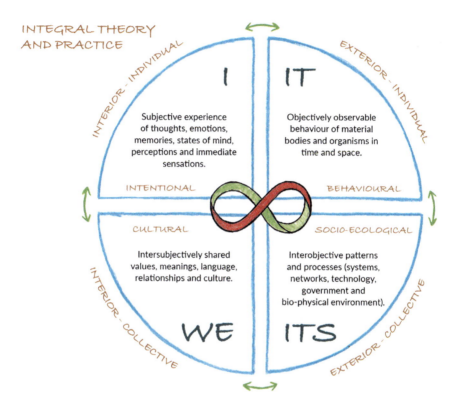

Figure 4: The Four Quadrant Framework of Integral Theory (adapted from Wilber, 2007)

The integral map can make our experiences of participation more intelligible in ways that can guide wise action. Our individual and collective relating to the world actually brings forth the world we experience. The whole-systems or living-systems perspective explored here transcends and includes the dualism of the 'out there' of objective description and the 'in here' of subjective experience. Our cultural narrative shapes our individual experience of how we perceive and explain what is out there. Becoming more aware of this process is the first step towards what Einstein referred to as the new way of thinking that might help us to resolve the 'problems' created by the narrative of separation (the way of thinking that created these problems in the first place). I believe that the narrative of interbeing and participatory whole systems thinking will help us to transform and/or resolve many of these problems.

Believing is seeing and seeing is believing

One of the crucial first steps in any process that lets us learn how to think differently is to begin with questioning our own assumptions and the mental models we employ.

- Q   What are we taking for granted?
- Q   What 'facts' we are interpreting to reach our conclusions and why?
- Q   How do the mental models and metaphors we use influence our understanding of the situation we are faced with?

Most people think that perception is the simple act of opening our eyes and seeing what is out there – a world made up of the clearly observable facts that constitute 'reality'. This is not actually the case. Neuroscientists and quantum physicists agree that every act of perception also contains an act of conception. The observer and his or her methods of observation affect what is observed. Reality shows up in diverse ways depending on the way of thinking and the way of seeing we employ, and the mental models we use to make sense of what we observe.

Imagine you are an anthropologist coming across a tribe hidden in a remote corner of the world, meeting people who so far had no contact with modernity. The members of the tribe would not see the equipment you are carrying, like your camera, your mobile phone, or the glasses you might be wearing, in the same way that you or I would perceive those objects. The glasses, for examples, would simply be 'something strange sitting on your nose'. They might be interpreted as an ornament that denotes your social position in your tribe.

The words, mental models and worldview we employ act as 'organizing ideas' that help us to structure what we see and pay attention to. These mental models shape how we see systems and processes. All too often we confuse the map with the territory. Even the systems view itself is only a map – a way of seeing relationships and interactions more clearly depending on how we define 'the system in question'. In the real world everything is connected and interacting with everything else, boundaries dissolve into places of encounter and exchange, uniting just as much as separating one aspect of the transforming whole from another.

Most of us will have been in situations where we found ourselves disagreeing with someone over how to assess a certain situation or interpret a certain reaction by someone else. If you take the time to pay attention to, and make explicit, the basic assumptions and mental models that people are applying in the process of interpreting a given situation, such conflicts can more easily be resolved. At the very least, it becomes possible to 'agree to disagree' and accept that there are different perspectives or interpretations depending on the core beliefs, worldview and value system we employ to interpret a given situation. The Three Horizons approach introduced in Chapter 2 offers a methodology for doing this.

Many processes of mediation and conflict-facilitation are based on slowing down the process through which we jump from observations to interpretations and conclusions, making us aware that even in the initial observations we were already selective with regard to what we chose to notice. This choice is influenced by our dominant worldview, the narrative in which we live our lives. Mediation techniques like Non Violent Communication invite the conflicting parties to return to what they observe, how it makes them feel, and what needs they might have with respect to the situation at hand. If we can get people to first agree about some level of 'consensus reality' regarding a given situation, it is much easier to make them aware of their core beliefs and assumptions and how these lead them to interpret or judge that situation in different ways. Being able to question our own assumptions and paying attention to how we think and interpret situations is a crucial skill for anybody in a leadership position, and anybody wanting to co-create a regenerative culture.

The *ladder of inference* is a model that makes us pay attention to how we think and create and reinforce assumptions and beliefs. First developed by Harvard Professor Chris Argyris, the model highlights our tendency to confuse our assessment of a given situation with the supposed 'facts' of the situation. The model illustrates how our assumptions shape the way we see the world and how we form conclusions about a certain situation based on our assumptions. Figure 5 illustrates how beliefs and assumptions have a critical effect on what we choose to pay attention to. It offers a series of questions we can ask ourselves to become more conscious of this process.

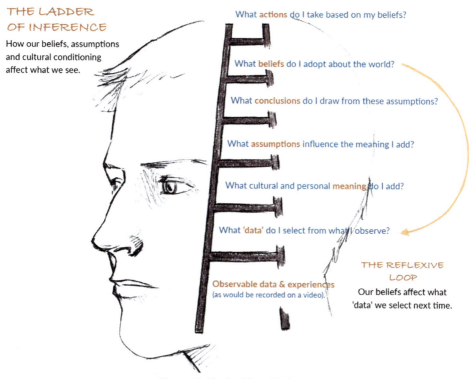

Figure 5: The Ladder of Inference

The *ladder of inference* explains in a simplified way that we select certain data out of the observable facts in front of us. We then add meaning to these experiences, which in turn influences the assumptions we make, and how we draw certain conclusions that shape our beliefs about the world. These beliefs guide how we respond to situations and act in the world. Most importantly, the ladder of inference highlights that there is an often ignored 'reflexive loop' through which the beliefs we formed based on past experiences and cultural conditioning actually influence what facts we choose to pay attention to in the first place. Our dominant belief system and worldview critically influence which alternative – possibly important – facts or interpretations we choose to ignore.

By becoming more aware of the different steps we are taking on the ladder, we can question our own assumptions, conclusions and beliefs and those of others. Here is a list of questions that can be used in taking individuals or groups through their own process of reasoning and reaching proposals for action. They invite us to apply the 'ladder of inference' to our own perspectives and those of others:

- Q Which observable facts and experiences am I basing my reasoning on, and are there other facts to consider?

- Q How and why did I choose certain data and regard other data as less relevant?

- Q What are the underlying assumptions I am employing and are they valid? (Based on what underlying assumptions am I judging their validity?)

- Q What beliefs underlie my perspective and how have these beliefs influenced what I observed and which data I chose?

- Q Why am I proposing to follow this course of action and what alternatives or complementary actions should/could we consider?

Going through such a process of conscious questioning of different perspectives in a group that faces disagreement might not fully resolve the conflict, but it will certainly help to better understand the different perspectives. This increased understanding of multiple perspectives can help us to form a more systemic understanding of the issue, which in turn might offer an opportunity to discover common ground (shared needs, values and beliefs) which can help us to move forward on the issues in a more inclusive and participatory way. It may help us to act more wisely in the face of not knowing and uncertainty.

In my own experience of facilitating and taking part in such processes of 'deeper questioning', simply the practice of asking such questions to get clear about the different perspectives and the assumptions that inform us can help to open up a gateway towards the resolution of what can initially be perceived as a irreconcilable conflict. It allows people to see their own 'issue' within the context of a broader, whole-systems perspective that includes multiple 'issues'. Simply being heard, valued and acknowledged can generate a willingness to compromise one's own needs in a collaborative attempt to acknowledge and address the needs of others and the health, wellbeing and resilience of the system as a whole. This is an important step in moving towards a regenerative culture.

The whole is more than the sum of its parts

The worldview we live in today began to take shape in that remarkable period in European history called the Renaissance which sparked the scientific revolution and enabled the first violent globalization in the form of colonialism and – later – the first industrial revolution. At the heart of these changes was a powerful new way of thinking and a change of attitude towards nature. Tens of thousands of women with knowledge of herbal medicine and natural remedies were burned as witches during a 300-year period which coincided with the development of the scientific method. Science began to replace religion as the 'ultimate authority' and arbiter in questions of right and wrong. Our perception of the natural world shifted from a nurturing view of 'mother nature' and the belief that all life was connected (*anima mundi*) to seeing nature as a resource to be exploited, controlled and conquered.

The powerful scientific method offered a conceptual separation between subject and object, mind and matter, and humanity and nature. It taught us how to understand things 'objectively' by taking them apart and out of their context. The detached observer, relying on dualistic logic and the power of reason, aims to explain the functioning of each part in order to get an understanding of the whole. This mechanistic approach took its guiding metaphors from how a clock-maker or mechanic takes apart a watch or a machine, in order to understand or 'fix' their workings. This is clearly a useful method for machines, but life is much more complex than a machine. Organisms and ecosystems cannot be adequately understood within a mechanistic explanatory framework.

The Renaissance and the scientific revolution have shaped our worldview and who we are today, and by no means should they be regarded as a mistake or negative development. The mechanistic, reductionist methodology of science, along with the specialization of human knowledge and activities, enabled a breath-taking explosion in knowledge, insight and technological development. The approach will continue to be useful to humanity, if we learn to put it in its place and recognize that it offers a simplified metaphor – an approach to making sense of the world – but it is not the only, and by no means the most important, way of seeing the world. Even more importantly, it is not the only valid way of making sense of our participation in the process of life. Like all other perspectives, it has serious limitations and perceptual blind-spots.

The flipside of reductionism and specialization is that we run the danger of not paying enough attention to the fundamental interconnectedness and interrelatedness of all the fields we have categorized into separate 'subjects' or disciplines. The often primarily qualitative emergent properties that give complex dynamic systems their unique identities are for the most part invisible to the myopia of single disciplines and reductionist, purely quantitative analysis. Just as the many surprising properties of water could never be explained or expected by only looking at oxygen and hydrogen on their own, important aspects of all living systems escape purely reductionist and mechanistic analysis. Failure to balance this approach with more holistic and systemic approaches can lead to many unintended and often negative consequences.

Whole-systems thinking

The whole-systems understanding of the world acknowledges that a whole is always more than the simple sum of its parts, paying attention to the diversity of elements, the quality of interactions and relationships, and the dynamic patterns of behaviour that often lead to unpredictable and surprising innovations and adaptations. Many of the interrelated problems we face, as change agents in the transition towards a more sustainable human presence on Earth, have their root cause in a way of thinking that has not paid enough attention to *whole systems* and their dynamic interconnectedness, dynamic relationships and context.

Whole-systems thinking has to be a transdisciplinary activity that maps and integrates relationships, flows and perspectives into a dynamic understanding of the structures and processes that drive how the system behaves. Experts and specialists are important contributors to most sustainability projects, but we also need integrators and generalists who can help to put the contribution of each discipline into systemic relationships and help to contextualize the contributions made by the specialists. Too often we employ limited progress indicators or inadequate measures of success based on the dominance of a particular discipline or perspective.

One way to define the word 'system' is as a set of interconnected elements that together form a coherent pattern we can refer to as a 'whole'. Such a system exhibits properties of the whole that emerge out of the interactions and relationships of the individual elements. This systems definition could be applied to a molecule, a cell, a human being, a community or the planet. In many ways a system is less a 'thing' than a pattern of relationships and interactions – a pattern of organization of constituting elements. The Greek root of the word system is 'synhistanai' and literally means 'to place together'.

Systems thinking and systemic intervention is a possible antidote to the unintended and dangerous side-effects of centuries of focusing only on reductionist and quantitative analysis informed by the narrative of separation. Yet, it is important to maintain the awareness that the systems view itself is also just another map that, as Gregory Bateson put it, should not be confused with the territory. We can reduce the world to a whole just as easily as we can reduce it to a collection of parts. Neither the whole nor parts are primary; they come into being through the dynamic processes that define their identity through relationships and networks of interactions.

One of the most important questions in any systemic approach is to ask 'what is the system in question'. In doing so we define boundaries that provide us with the necessary 'enabling constraints' to make sense of a situation. Yet, these boundaries are themselves a way of seeing that make a distinction between the system in question and its environment.

We should regard the boundaries that delineate one system from another as places of connection and exchange rather than barriers that separate or isolate.

In more general terms, whole-systems thinking invites us to see complex issues from multiple perspectives, to suspend our judgement by questioning our own assumptions, and to honour insights from different disciplines and different ways of knowing. Thinking in this way helps us to pay attention to the fertile ground of synergistic, whole-systems solutions. It can help us to more clearly see the opportunities in the multiple converging crises around us. Whole-systems thinking stops us from seeing ecological, economic and social constraints as irreconcilable challenges. It invites us not to view different stakeholder perspectives in a competitive, win-lose frame of mind, and encourages us to explore win-win-win solutions that improve the overall health and sustainability of the system as a whole. Whole-systems thinking is living systems thinking. I believe that a systemic understanding of processes by which life continuously regenerates conditions conducive to life offers a pathway to creating regenerative businesses and organizations within a regenerative economy as enabling factors of a regenerative culture. We will explore many examples in subsequent chapters. Here are some questions to contemplate when dealing with systems:

- Q What is the system in question and how are we defining what belongs to the system and what does not?

- Q What is the wider context that the system in question operates in?

- Q What are the key agents whose interactions and relationships define the system structure and drive the system's behaviour?

- Q How is our perspective of the system in question shaped by our worldview and value system?

- Q What are the key 'emergent properties' of the system that could not have been predicted by simply looking at the individual 'parts' of the system?

- Q How does our participation in the system and our way of describing it affect what we are observing?

From the 'crisis of perception' to the 'systems view of life'

After initially training as a zoologist and marine biologist at the University of Edinburgh and the University of California (Santa Cruz), I have spent the last 20 years of my life in search of answers to one extremely complex challenge: *How can we create a more sustainable human presence on Earth?* I still remember the day, in spring 1994, when I realized that the most effective way I could contribute to future generations being able to experience the bliss of swimming with a school of dolphins in their natural habitat was not by continuing on my path towards becoming a marine mammal biologist, but by working in whatever small way I could to help my own species change its perspective and way of relating to *life as a planetary process*. We are participants in that process and our future depends on it.

I dedicated the past two decades to investigating and learning how to apply 'sustainable solutions'. In the process I spent time as an academic, grassroots activist, business consultant and educator, and worked with public authorities at the local, national and international (United Nations) level. I investigated, advocated and helped to implement sustainable solutions in many areas of human activity like transport, housing, community development, food production, water treatment, sustainable production and consumption, and education.

Luckily everyday there are more sustainable solutions available to us, but applied at an inadequate scale or without paying attention to their systemic context, today's solutions can quickly turn into tomorrow's problems. Without the cultural ability to see our actions and the changes around us from a systemic perspective, combined with the wisdom to evaluate any proposed solutions in the context of their effects on the health and resilience of life as a whole, even well-meant attempts to create sustainability can have ill-fated results.

Einstein's widely quoted advice that "we cannot solve our problems with the same thinking we used when we created them" seems more appropriate than ever. We are dealing with the complexity of a profound societal change and the transition towards diverse regenerative cultures as manifestations of not only a different way of being in the world, but also a different way of seeing the world. In a letter to Jan Christiaan Smuts, Einstein congratulated him for publishing *Holism and Evolution* (1926) and suggested that two concepts would shape human thinking in the next millennium, his own concept of 'relativity' and Smuts's 'holism' defined as "the tendency in nature to form wholes that are greater than the sum of the parts through creative evolution" (Smuts, 1927). Holistic thinking is the new way of thinking needed to (dis)solve the problems created by reductionist thinking. But we should not over-swing the pendulum and favour holistic thinking in all circumstances over reductionist thinking. We should regard reductionism as a useful method to be applied if and when appropriate and within a whole-systems context that acknowledges the valuable contributions of diverse perspectives, as well as the limits to our knowing. We might prefer definitive answers and solutions, but what if they simply cannot be given?

Q   Are we chasing a mirage of certainty in a profoundly ambiguous and unpredictable world?

Q   Is the best we can ever do to live the questions more deeply?

Q   How will the questions we choose to guide us affect the world we will end up experiencing and co-creating in the process?

In spring 2002 I had the good fortune to meet the physicist Fritjof Capra at Schumacher College. Capra clearly articulated something that I had intuitively known and was trying to understand better. He suggested that the ecological, environmental, social and economic crises we are facing are not separate but interconnected expressions of one single crisis: *a crisis of perception*. He explained how our culturally dominant worldview is informed by outdated scientific theories and a tendency to lose ourselves in the details of the perspective of a single discipline, rather than to see the 'hidden connections' that maintain the long-term viability of life as a whole.

The neo-Darwinist story of individuals and species in fierce competition for limited resources is an inadequate and limited conception of life. Nature sustains life by creating and nurturing communities. In today's leading life sciences, evolution is no longer seen as a struggle for existence but as a collaborative dance and exploration of novelty. Capra pointed out that "sustainability is a dynamic process of co-evolution rather than a static state. Sustainability is a property of an entire web of relationships" (personal comment) rather than a characteristic of a single individual, company, country or species.

The understanding that the common root cause of the multiple crises we are facing is in fact a *crisis of perception* offers us hope that we will be able to respond before it is too late. It suggests that if we were to employ a different way of thinking to the one that got us into this mess in the first place, we might realize how many interconnected problems can be combined in ways that point us towards a series of interconnected opportunities and systemic win-win-win solutions by addressing root-causes rather than symptoms.

Taking a systems view of life is an important step towards addressing the crisis of perception. Realizing our intimate kinship and communion with the process of life as a whole will trigger a shift in consciousness that will enable us to radically improve the quality of our lives and the health of the ecosystems and planet we inhabit. It will change the ways we relate to each other and the rest of the natural world and allow for the emergence of health as a systemic property linking human and planetary health.

Individually and collectively we are beginning to learn how to ask better questions as we become aware of interconnections and relationships we have so far failed to pay attention to. The quality of the air we breathe, the quality of the water we drink, the quality of the food we eat, the quality of the clothes we wear, the quality of the houses we live in, the quality of the communities we participate in, the quality of our human relationships, the quality of the ecosystems we inhabit, the quality of the education we offer to our children – all these qualitative aspects of our lives depend not only on detailed, quantifiable specifics that can be understood within the confines of separate and narrowly defined disciplines. These important qualitative aspects of our lives depend on the complex relationships and networks that connect all these aspects into one dynamically transforming whole. These relationships and networks connect our individual and collective future to the health, resilience and wellbeing of *life as a whole*.

Advances in biology, ecology, neuroscience and complexity theory are now offering us a *systems view of life* (see Capra & Luisi, 2014b), defined in detail over the past decades. Society is beginning to catch up and most of the leading-edge initiatives to promote the transition towards regenerative cultures are informed by this systemic understanding of living systems and our intimate relationship with them. Peter Senge has been an important advocate of the importance of systems thinking for people in business leadership positions:

> The innovators creating tomorrow's regenerative economy have all, in their own ways, learned how to *see the larger system* in which they live and work. They look beyond events and superficial fixes to see deeper structures and forces at play, they don't allow boundaries (either organizational or culturally imposed) to limit their thinking, they make strategic choices that take into account natural and social limits, and they work to create self-reinforcing cycles of innovation – change strategies that mimic how growth occurs in the natural world. They have learned to see systems by cultivating an intelligence that we all possess. Human beings are natural systems thinkers, but like any innate capacity, this talent must be understood and cultivated.
>
> Peter Senge (2008: 167)

The systems view understands life as networks of relationships. We can find network patterns at the scale of individual cells, organs, organisms, communities, ecosystems or the biosphere as a whole. The qualitative emergent properties that make life worth living and sustain life as a whole are not located within one or many organisms, they are distributed across all of these scales as systemic properties of a living and transforming whole in which every participant counts and we *all* co-create the future.

If we aim to sustain humanity's common future, we need to learn how humanity can become a positive live-sustaining influence on ecosystems everywhere and the planet as a whole. This is the essence of creating a sustainable and regenerative human culture. By designing our technological, social and economic solutions around the principles of ecology and biology and informed by a systems view of life, we can transform culture so it becomes a restorative and regenerative force.

The continued emergence of self-reflective consciousness and our subjective and inter-subjective (cultural) experience of being living reflections of life's continuous explorations of novelty depend on maintaining the health and integrity of the biological and ecological basis for our continued evolution. The 'living systems view' of life is not an objectification of nature and biology as separate from the interior (individual and collective) experience of consciousness, but understands life and consciousness as fundamentally intertwined manifestations of one and the same process. In self-reflective consciousness we are becoming conscious of the role of how-we-experience and what-we-pay-attention-to in the experience itself – paying attention to how we are bringing forth a world together. We are only beginning to understand the co-dependent arising of life and consciousness as a fundamentally participatory process of entering into relationship and taking perspective:

> [...] consciousness is so much more than an evolutionary accident or epiphenomenal to biochemical processes in our heads – consciousness is, in fact, *fundamentally woven into the universe itself.* [...] What we *are* saying is

that some degree of subjectivity is indeed present all the way up and all the way down the evolutionary ladder, from the tiniest quarks to the biggest brains. This consciousness can be loosely described as a 'perspective-making, perspective-taking' system that creates, collects, and organizes deeper, wider, *more sophisticated* points-of-view as it develops.

Ken Wilber & Allan Combs (2010)

Interbeing

The practice of systems thinking is the practice of thinking about the world through the concept of a system (Checkland, 1981). It can help us to make complex dynamic interactions more intelligible and can inform wise initiatives and appropriate actions. The practice of looking at a set of participants and their relationships and defining them as a 'system' creates a framework within which we can ask deeper questions about the structures and behaviours that influence these relationships. By defining a system's boundary we are not isolating this 'system in question' from all others, but we are creating a frame to explore how it might be related to the wider systems that contain it. We may also realize that our 'system in question' might itself be made up of a series of other sub-systems.

Too often systems thinking is equated with a set of very specific methodologies, like the drawing of influence diagrams, feedback loops, and stock and flow systems models. These are all useful tools in the toolbox of systems thinking, but to equate them with whole-systems thinking itself would be analogous to equating a set of brushes, an easel and a canvas with the art of painting. More than a set of tools, systems thinking is an art form of creatively dancing with complexity that has the power to transform us and our world. It can make us see ourselves, and our world, with different eyes.

As the poet David Whyte observed: prose is about words describing an experience, whereas poetry elicits an experience itself. So let me offer you the poet Thich Nhat Hanh's take on whole-systems thinking:

> If you are a poet, you will see clearly that there is a cloud floating in this sheet of paper. Without a cloud, there will be no rain; without rain, the trees cannot grow; and without trees, we cannot make paper. The cloud is essential for the paper to exist. If the cloud is not here the sheet of paper cannot be here either. So we can say that the cloud and the paper inter-are. 'Interbeing' is a word that is not in the dictionary yet, but if we combine the prefix 'inter' with the verb 'to be,' we have a new verb, inter-be. Without a cloud we cannot have paper, so we can say that the cloud and the paper inter-are.
>
> If we look into this sheet of paper even more deeply, we can see the sunshine in it. If the sunshine is not there, the forest cannot grow. In fact, nothing can grow. Even we cannot grow without sunshine. And so, we know that the sunshine is also in this sheet of paper. The paper and the sunshine inter-are. And if we continue to look, we can see the logger who cut the tree and brought

it to the mill to be transformed into paper. And we see wheat. We know that the logger cannot exist without his daily bread, and therefore the wheat that became his bread is also in the sheet of paper. The logger's father and mother are in it too. When we look in this way, we see that without all these things, this sheet of paper cannot exist.

Looking even more deeply, we can see ourselves in this sheet of paper too. This is not difficult to see, because when we look at a sheet of paper, the sheet of paper is part of our perception. Your mind is in here and mine is also. So we can see that everything is in here with this sheet of paper. You cannot point out one thing that is not here – time, space, the earth, the rain, the minerals in the soil, the sunshine, the cloud, the river, the heat. Everything co-exists with this paper. That is why I think the word interbe should be in the dictionary. 'To be' is to interbe. You cannot just be by yourself alone. You have to inter-be with every other thing. This sheet of paper is, because everything else is.

Suppose we try to return one of the elements to its source. Suppose we return the sunshine to the sun. Do you think that this sheet of paper would be possible? No, without sunshine nothing can be. And if we return the logger to his mother, then we have no sheet of paper either. The fact is that this sheet of paper is made up only of 'non-paper' elements. And if we return these non-paper elements to their sources, then there can be no paper at all. Without non-paper elements, like mind, logger, sunshine, and so on, there will be no paper. As thin as this sheet of paper is, it contains everything in the universe in it.

Thich Nhat Hanh (1988: 3-5)

Reprinted from *The Heart of Understanding: Commentaries on the Prajñaparamita Sutra* with permission of Parallax Press, Berkeley, California, www.parallax.org

Thich Nhat Hanh offers a great example of seeing and understanding whole systems. Starting with a simple sheet of paper, he offers us a window onto the fundamental interconnectedness of our planetary system, which we are now also beginning to understand through physics, complexity science, ecology and earth systems science. We are participants in a dynamic whole within which we define ourselves and create our reality through our participation in relationships. To be *is* to interbe.

In many ways, the word 'interbeing' describes a shift in the perception of self and other that lies at the heart of co-creating regenerative human cultures and a sustainable human presence on Earth. Transformative innovation for regenerative cultures drives the shift from an industrial growth society, based on extraction and exploitation of natural resources and informed by the 'narrative of separation' to a life-sustaining society, based on regenerative agricultural and industrial processes and informed by the 'narrative of interbeing'. The word 'interbeing' describes the shift towards a new story about humanity's relationship with the wider community of life and its dependence on the planet's life support system. Here are some questions we could use to catalyse conversations about this shift in community groups, business boardrooms and government departments:

> Q To what extent is the way we are framing the problem and proposing solutions informed by the 'narrative of separation' and how could we reframe them from within the 'narrative of interbeing'?
>
> Q How do our real and perceived needs change as we shift from a perspective of separation to a perspective of interbeing?
>
> Q How do we propose solutions informed by interbeing and evaluate their effect on the wider community of life and the lives of future generations?

How can we participate appropriately in complex systems?

> In the early 1950s, the Dayak people in Borneo suffered from malaria. The World Health Organization had a solution: they sprayed large amounts of DDT to kill the mosquitoes that carried the malaria. The mosquitoes died, the malaria declined; so far, so good. But there were side-effects. Among the first was that the roofs of people's houses began to fall down on their heads. It seemed that the DDT was killing a parasitic wasp that had previously controlled thatch-eating caterpillars. Worse, the DDT- poisoned insects were eaten by geckoes, which were eaten by cats. The cats died, the rats flourished, and people were threatened by out-breaks of sylvatic plague and typhus. To cope with these problems, which it had itself created, the World Health Organization was obliged to parachute 14,000 live cats into Borneo.
>
> Hunter Lovins & Amory Lovins (1995)

The story serves to illustrate that, in complex dynamic systems, any attempt to solve isolated problems without adequate consideration of their systemic context can trigger multiple unintended side-effects and even new and often more severe problems.

The German systems scientist, Professor Frederick Vester (2004: 36-37), identified a number of common mistakes that occur as teams are asked to intervene in or 'manage' complex dynamic systems. Vester's insights drew on a series of experiments by the psychologist Dietrich Dörner who had challenged various transdisciplinary teams of 12 different specialists to improve the overall system and infrastructure design of a fictitious country in the developing world. A computer program modelled the impact of their strategies over a century of repeated cycles of interventions. The focus of the study was how teams of experts approach problem-solving, planning and systems interventions. Vester's analysis of Dörner's work provides the basis for a useful list of questions that we can ask ourselves to avoid the most common mistakes in dealing with complex systemic issues.

> **Q** Have we defined our goals correctly? – Are we trying to maximize isolated parameters or to optimize the whole system?

Instead of focusing on increasing the ability and probability of survival for the system as a whole, we tend to get lost in solving individual problems, one problem at a time. We tend to search out 'manageable problems' and inadequacies in the system, and we tend to define these problems from the perspective of a single discipline rather than a whole-systems perspective.

> **Q** Have we attempted a joined-up systems analysis by paying attention to dynamics rather than getting lost in static data?

We tend to be obsessed with the collection of huge amounts of measurable (quantitative) data. This results in very large data sets, but without paying attention to the qualitative aspects of the underlying interactions and relationships we often fail to generate a joined-up and coherent understanding of the whole system. By exploring the potential feedback loops, limits, dynamics and key relationships within the system we can move to a deeper questioning in search of organizing principles and policies that structure the system and drive its behaviour. Since complex systems are living entities that change over time, it is often more useful to focus on dynamics and qualitative relationships than to obsess over collecting quantitative data at a particular point in time.

> **Q** Are we avoiding the trap of creating irreversible emphasis?

There is a tendency to target issues that were initially identified as being the central parameters. If there are partial successes within a particular problem, it can become a favourite at the neglect of others. 'Blind spots' in our systems understanding can have severe consequences. We can be surprised by unexpected side-effects of particular actions, and fail to prevent dangerous run-away effects as our focus is elsewhere.

> **Q** Are we paying enough attention to the potential side-effects of our actions?

It can also be helpful to work with different scenarios. This allows us to explore and compare the potential outcomes of proposed actions and anticipate the possible results.

> **Q** Are we carefully avoiding over-steering or over-reacting?

Initial interventions aimed at problem-solving tend to be made hesitantly and usually start small. If, over the short term, there are no visible effects on the system, what follows tends to be a large-scale intervention. Once faced with the first unexpected feedback from the system – as the time-delayed effects of the initially small interventions have accumulated and are now amplifying the effects of the large-scale intervention – the most common reaction is to hit the brakes or try to reverse the interventions.

Q Are we avoiding acting in an authoritarian way?

Knowing or believing that we have the power and ability to change the system, along with the often mistaken belief that we have understood the system, often results in dictatorial behaviour. This is absolutely inadequate when dealing with complex dynamic systems. A more appropriate and effective way to affect such systems as a participant is to change them while going with rather than against their flow. Frequently personal aspirations to gain professional or political prestige are the main drivers behind large-scale changes that jeopardize systems dynamics. Individuals try to impress through the size of the project they are proposing rather than its functionality. The striving for power and respect tend to negatively influence the way we deal with complex systems. Appropriate participation in complex systems is about living these questions in humble awareness of the limits of our knowing. We have to keep asking ourselves:

Q How can we act with humility and future consciousness, applying foresight and transformative innovation in the face of the unpredictability and uncontrollability of complex dynamic systems?

The IFF World System Model

> The World System Model establishes a holistic structure for visioning the state of the world and, thereby, a platform for understanding our global predicament, assessing innovations and designing wise initiatives.
>
> Anthony Hodgson (2011: 43)

The IFF World Systems Model and the associated IFF World Game were developed to help people explore what a transformative response to our current 'crisis of perception' or 'conceptual emergency' might look like. They are effective tools for facilitating joined-up, systemic thinking about the converging and interconnected crises we are facing, and offer a way to connect currently proposed solutions into a more synergistic framework. The idea for this approach was inspired by Richard Buckminster Fuller, but the bulk of the development of these tools is the work of Anthony Hodgson (with the support of the International Futures Forum). In *Ready for Anything – Designing Resilience for a Transforming World*, Tony describes different uses and the rationale behind the IFF World System Model, offering a number of case studies of effective applications so far. The figure below shows the basic IFF World System Model.

The IFF World System Model (WSM) connects 12 key dimensions (or nodes) of a regenerative system. The 12 nodes have been carefully chosen to map out vital components or issues for creating a viable and thriving human system at any scale. As such, the model can be used to map – in a systemic and transdisciplinary way – the vital aspects of a community, a neighbourhood, a city, a bioregion, a nation or the planet (hence 'world' system model). The WSM acts as a question-generating engine or catalyst for joined-up thinking.

3: Why DO We Need to Think and Act More Systemically?

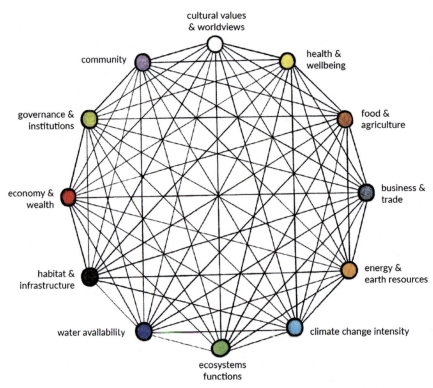

Figure 6: The IFF World System Model, reproduced from Hodgson (2011) with the author's permission

Each of the 12 nodes is joined in a map resembling a clock face with 66 interconnecting lines. Each of those lines creates a 'dyad' of two interconnected factors, inviting the question how these two factors might be related to each other. The question of 'interconnection' can be asked with regard to how failure or decreased viability in one node might affect other nodes. It also invites us to explore how a proposed solution in one node could simultaneously affect other nodes positively. The WSM can be used to generate joined-up design solutions aiming to create synergies between the different nodes by optimizing the whole system. For example, the model might invite us to investigate how a proposed improvement in the use of 'renewable energy and earth resources' could positively affect improvements in 'habitat and infrastructure' and vice versa; or it might ask us to explore the connection between 'health and wellbeing' and 'ecosystems functions' (the functions of healthy ecosystems providing clean air, fresh water, food and biological resources, as well as the regulation of climate and disease, erosion control, nutrient cycling and pollination).

Whether we are working on the specific case of a sustainable urban neighbourhood project, or on improving a country's sustainability performance at a national scale, the model can be applied to any scale from local to global, and by doing so can also invite questions about how work on one scale might affect the other, a practice referred to as 'scale-linking design' (van der Ryn & Cowan, 1996; and Wahl, 2007). The model can not only be used to invite questions about how to create more joined-up, sustainable design solutions and systemic improvements in overall viability; it also can be applied to auditing the 'status quo' of any system, by inviting us to map the strengths and weaknesses of a given system with regard to each one of the nodes.

In combination with the Three Horizons model, introduced in Chapter 2, the WSM can be used to map a system with regard to each horizon: the actual 'world in crisis' situation of H1, the potential for H2 transition innovations and systemic improvements, and H3 visions of a viable system. Ideally the 12 nodes mutually reinforce the viability of all the other nodes, thereby creating a healthy and thriving system overall. In order to create locally and globally appropriate synergistic whole-systems design solutions we must begin with a better understanding of the interconnected nature of the problems we face in each of the different nodes.

The international security analyst and consultant Thomas Homer-Dixon observed how failure in viability in one aspect of a system is frequently accompanied by simultaneous failures in other aspects of that system. He referred to this situation as *synchronous failure* (Homer-Dixon, 2006). The WSM can make us more aware of the way changes in viability in one node might cause domino effects throughout the system, resulting in changes in other nodes. A solution proposed from the isolated perspective of one particular node and focused only on improving the viability of that node can actually result in negative effects (decreased viability) in one or many other nodes. To avoid this we need to learn to think and act more systemically.

An obvious example of our systemic myopia is how many decision-makers focus only on 'rescuing the economy' by driving economic growth and, in doing so, their short-term 'solutions' actually decrease viability in most other nodes of the system. Many measures that are aimed at increasing economic growth end up having a negative impact on 'Community'. This is because they often increase inequality and decrease the viability of 'Ecosystems Services' while, at the same time, increasing 'Climate Change Intensity'.

So far, the WSM has been used to map out the potential impact of diverse *synchronous failure* or *synchronous success*, and domino-effect scenarios in a number of case-study applications ranging in scale from small communities to cities, regions, islands, and even entire countries (see Hodgson, 2011). By engaging diverse groups of stakeholders and experts in the process of questioning the possible connections between different nodes, we challenge them to connect issues that might previously have been viewed in isolation. This creates not only a 'fast and frugal' way to generate a range of possible future scenarios, it also invites lateral thinking and innovative ideas that might lead to pathways for transformative innovations. Once a series of scenarios have been generated, they can be explored within the context of the Three Horizons model. We can ask ourselves whether proposed innovations are indeed likely to catalyse the transition towards the viable world of Horizon 3 or are more likely to be captured by the first horizon to prolong 'business as usual'.[†]

The WSM and the associated *World Game* are particularly useful in raising awareness of connections and possible interactions at and across different scales (recursion and scale-linking). They are effective ways to generate rapid scenarios and promote systemic 'future thinking'. As a tool for 'advance facilitation' in strategy workshops and multi-stakeholder situations, the World Game liberates creativity through 'play' and gives decision-makers a direct experience of whole-systems thinking and its potential benefits for wise action. Creative gaming is a powerful way to liberate lateral and generative thinking (Hodgson, 2012).

The emergence of systemic health, wellbeing and regenerative cultures can be facilitated by integrative whole-systems design (see Chapter 4). Engaging in systems thinking and design is *not* an exact science but the art of appropriate participation. We are still at the beginning of our journey of putting Humpty Dumpty back together again – of undoing some of the side-effects of the story of separation. We have to accept that we don't have all the answers and we will have to frequently re-examine the questions we are asking. Whole-systems integration and synthesis is the task ahead of us all.

> We are drowning in information, while starving for wisdom. The world henceforth will be run by synthesizers, people able to put together the right information at the right time, think critically about it, and make important choices wisely.
>
> E.O. Wilson (1999: 294)

Learning to see nature everywhere

When on 4th November, 1869 the first edition of the scientific journal *Nature* went on sale it carried a foreword by the British biologist T.H. Huxley. In his introduction, Huxley quoted the German poet-scientist Johann Wolfgang von Goethe (1749-1832) at length and concluded with the following sentence: "it may be, that long after the theories of the philosophers whose achievements are recorded in these pages, are obsolete, the vision of the poet will remain as a truthful and efficient symbol of the wonder and the mystery of Nature." Here is an excerpt of Goethe's vision of nature:

> NATURE! We are surrounded and embraced by her: powerless to separate ourselves from her, and powerless to penetrate beyond her. […] We live in her midst and know her not. She is incessantly speaking to us, but betrays not her secret. We constantly act upon her, and yet have no power over her. […] She has always thought and always thinks; though not as a man, but as Nature. […] That which is most unnatural is still Nature; the stupidest philistinism has a touch of her genius. Who so cannot see her everywhere, sees her nowhere rightly. […] The spectacle of Nature is always new, for she is always renewing the spectators. Life is her most exquisite invention; and death is her expert contrivance to get plenty of life. […] We obey her laws even when we rebel against them; we work with her even when we desire to work against her. […] She has isolated all things in order that all may approach one another. She holds a couple of draughts from the cup of love to be fair payment for the pains of a lifetime. […] She is complete, but never finished.
>
> Johann Wolfgang von Goethe in T.H. Huxley (1869)

What would it mean to see nature everywhere? This is not a simple question of semantics. Our world would change, if we began to understand culture, society and technology as expressions of the same creative natural process that helped to create the atmosphere we breathe today and shaped the history of our planet for millions of years. It is quite a challenge to entertain this shift in perspective. If everything is nature, then nothing is un-natural, artificial or not part of natural process. Can we really call an atomic power plant, a nuclear bomb or genetically manipulated organisms 'natural'? Including everything in existence within the constantly transforming whole of nature becomes a necessity if we want to overcome the false dualism between nature and culture. Even dangerous technologies cannot be separate from the whole. The atoms they are made of are part of the universe and nature transforming. But even to put it this way can take us away from understanding the 'authentic wholeness' (Bortoft, 1971) of nature, since we *should not* think of nature's wholeness as an additive wholeness – the sum of its parts.

The whole comes forth *within* all of its parts and the parts find their significance and identity through the belonging to the whole. Henri Bortoft writes in his mind-bending and deeply insightful book about Goethe's way of science, *The Wholeness of Nature*:

> We cannot know the whole in the way in which we know things because we cannot recognize the whole as a thing. [...] The whole would be outside its parts in the same way that each part is outside all the other parts. But the whole comes into presence within its parts, and we cannot encounter the whole in the same way that we encounter the parts. We should not think of the whole as if it were a thing.
>
> Henri Bortoft (1996: 14)

Bortoft dedicated his life to the exploration, teaching and communication of what he called *a dynamic way of seeing* that allows us to experience "the coming-to-presence of the whole within the parts". He warns us of the epistemological pitfall of a purely analytical and objectifying approach to 'systems' (as objects out there) as it predisposes us to explore counterfeit rather than authentic wholeness (2012: 17).

If we see nature everywhere, even in our way of seeing, we can begin to pay attention to the 'coming into being' of the whole through mutual reciprocity (interbeing) with its parts. Neither the whole nor the parts are primary. They co-arise. Nothing is outside the wholeness of nature, as it is not a thing, but a process of 'coming into being' through relationship. From this perspective everything is 'natural' and 'nature' manifests through everything. I am not at all suggesting that because – from this perspective – nuclear bombs and GM crops are natural too, that they are expressions of appropriate participation in nature's life-sustaining and regenerative processes. They are better understood as dead-ends in nature's evolutionary exploration of novelty. It is up to us to recognize them as such and dismiss them as inappropriate before their effects on life and whole-systems health dismiss us.

This step towards fully embodying our own nature as 'nature at large' is crucial for cultural transformation towards a regenerative culture. To move on from the dominance of the 'narrative of separation' and into the 'narrative of interbeing' we have to heal the 'Cartesian split', embracing our experience of being separate individuals not as proof of separation but of being undividable from the wholeness of nature.

The narrative of separation brings forth a world where we separate mind and matter, self and world, humanity and nature into mutually exclusive categories, while the emerging cultural 'narrative of interbeing' brings forth a world in which we see ourselves and our technologies as expressions of life's natural process. From this inclusive and participatory perspective of nature we can re-evaluate all our social and technological achievements in the light of the crucial questions:

- Q How does this innovation affect nature's life support systems?
- Q Does this innovation increase systemic health and resilience?
- Q Is the proposed 'solution' likely to lead to an evolutionary dead-end or does it create conditions conducive to life?

We should neither condemn nor reify science and technology. *When, where* and *how* to use these tools in ways that create conditions conducive to life is a crucial public dialogue in regenerative cultures. Seeing nature everywhere and understanding the wholeness of nature as a living process in which we participate, will lead us to understand collaboration as the prevalent mode of maintaining the health of the whole. Competition is both self-perpetuating and ultimately self-defeating. Gregory Bateson warned us: "The creature that wins against its environment destroys itself" (1972: 501). Seeing nature everywhere can help us create technologies that contribute to the health of the whole rather than eroding it.

Being a process, and seeing in relationships

> I live on Earth at present, and I don't know what I am. I know that I am not a category. I am not a thing – a noun. I seem to be a verb, an evolutionary process – an integral function of the universe.
>
> R. Buckminster Fuller (1970)

Ask yourself: who am I? Am I just this body? Am I a thing, a noun, an object? Or am I a process of constantly transforming interactions and connections that define self and world as temporary expressions of my *being in relationship*?

Allan Watts referred to the separate self as the "skin-encapsulated ego". In biology classes we are taught to collapse the important question about the identity of our being into a conditioned answer that would read something like this: 'I am a biological being of the species *Homo sapiens sapiens*; a product of evolution based on random genetic mutation and the struggle for survival in the face of competition and scarcity, possibly with the predisposition to project meaning into a fundamentally meaningless universe.' Does this sound like a rational scientific hypothesis or an extremely limiting dogma to you?

The question 'who *or* what am I?' takes us to the core of culture and the way we understand the relationship between self and world, as well as culture and nature. Our answer affects not only our personal experience of life, but also how we are related to other human beings and the community of life. Culture transforms once we understand ourselves as 'processes' that define 'self-identity' through being in and (made) of relationships.

> Through thousands of years of anthropocentric conditioning […] we have inherited shallow, fictitious selves, and created a pervasive illusion of separation from nature. […] As long as the environment is 'out there,' we may leave it to some special interest group like environmentalists to protect while we look after our 'selves.' The matter changes when we deeply realize that the nature 'out there' and the nature 'in here' are one and the same, that the sense of separation no matter how pervasive is nonetheless totally illusory. I would call the need for such realisation the central psychological or spiritual challenge of our age.
>
> John Seed (2002)

Paradoxically we are 'self' *and* we are 'world'. The two emerge in our experience of *being* through the relationships we participate in. From a participatory understanding of the wholeness of nature, the *whole* of life is not a thing but a process that comes into being through all living beings and their relationships. We can describe life as the sum total of trillions of 'individuals' of a breathtaking diversity of species, *and* it is equally valid to understand life as the transformative process that weaves all of these temporary manifestations of *being alive through and in relationships* into an underlying unity. Focusing on separation reveals competition, while focusing on inter*being* reveals collaboration as the basis of all life. Gregory Bateson saw the "false reification of the self" – the idea of a separate self rather than one emerging out of and sustained by relationships – as a root-cause of our "planetary ecological crises". He argued:

> We have imagined that we are a unit of survival and we have to see to our own survival, and we imagine that the unit of survival is the separate individual or a separate species, whereas in reality, through the history of evolution it is the individual plus the environment, the species plus the environment, for they are essentially symbiotic.
>
> Gregory Bateson in Joanna Macy (1994)

Bateson's 'ecology of mind' was an attempt to invite people into a relational way of seeing. He understood that we live in a world entirely made of relationships and used to quip "there are days when I catch myself believing that there is such a thing as something, which is separate from something else". For Bateson, experiencing our own relational existence – the way we continuously bring forth the world and ourselves through relationships – could help us "unify and thereby sanctify the total natural world, of which we are" (Nora Bateson, 2010).

Bateson's unifying view of the natural world (life) is not collapsing life and our experience of it into the bottom right quadrant of the integral framework. He did not reduce 'what is' to the exterior collective of systems, of 'ITS', of material objects. His 'ecology of mind' referred to the "the ocean of mind" that we find ourselves in when we shift from seeing the world as a collection of objects to experiencing the coming into being of perspectives and identity through the act of relating itself. Conceiving of ourselves as verbs rather than nouns, as processes rather than isolated individuals, facilitates this shift in perspective that makes us see the world and ourselves as coming into being through relationships. Maturana and Varela later referred to it as structural coupling and autopoiesis, the self-making by which we are 'bringing forth a world'.

Bateson believed that "the major problems in the world are the result of the difference between how nature works and the way people think". He referred to the shift in thinking we are exploring here as the "difference that makes a difference". When Bateson asked his students "What pattern connects the crab to the lobster, and the orchid to the primrose and all four of them to me? And me to you?", he was not really looking for an answer. He was inviting people to notice the act of questioning itself and in doing so making them aware of the fact that everything changes if we change the way we think about 'self' and 'world' (2015). David Abram beautifully describes how our human identity is born out of our relationship to the rest of the community of life.

> Caught up in a mass of abstractions, our attention hypnotized by a host of human-made technologies that only reflect us back to ourselves, it is all too easy for us to forget our carnal inherence in a more-than-human matrix of sensations and sensibilities. Our bodies have formed themselves in delicate reciprocity with the manifold textures, sounds, and shapes of an animate earth – our eyes have evolved in subtle interaction with other eyes, as our ears are attuned by their very structure to the howling of the wolves and the honking of the geese. To shut ourselves off from these other voices, to continue by our lifestyles to condemn these other sensibilities to the oblivion of extinction, is to rob our own senses of their integrity, and to rob our minds of their coherence. We are human only in contact, and conviviality, with what is not human.
>
> David Abram (1996: 22)

I believe that at the core of the cultural shift that will lead to the emergence of regenerative cultures everywhere is the realization that *we are a process of relating* in 'delicate reciprocity' with a living planet, and that our individual and collective success depend on the health of the whole and the community of life.

CHAPTER 4

WHY NURTURE RESILIENCE AND WHOLE-SYSTEMS HEALTH?

> Oh, what a catastrophe for man when he cut himself off from the rhythm of the year, from his unison with the sun and the earth. Oh, what a catastrophe, what a maiming of love when it was made a personal, merely personal feeling, taken away from the rising and setting of the sun, and cut off from the magic connection of the solstice and equinox! That is what is the matter with us. We are bleeding at the roots […]
>
> D.H. Lawrence (1930)

The constitution of the World Health Organization (WHO) defines the concept of health as "a state of complete, physical, mental and social well-being and not merely the absence of disease or infirmity". In 1986, the WHO's 'Ottawa Charter' listed a series of conditions and prerequisites for health. These included: "peace, shelter, education, food, income, a stable ecosystem, sustainable resources, social justice and equity." The 1991 Sundsvall Statement emphasized that the "way forward lies in making the environment – the physical environment, the social and economic environment, and the political environment – supportive to health rather than damaging to it" (Waltner-Toews, 2004). The WHO's recommendations imply a salutogenic design approach that promotes individual, community, societal and ecosystems health as a scale-linking pattern. Design for human and planetary health aims to (re-)integrate humanity into the health-maintaining and life-supporting processes of the biosphere (see Wahl, 2006). The WHO Commission on Health and Environment emphasized:

> There is a powerful synergy between health, environmental protection, and sustainable resource use. Individuals and societies who share the responsibility for achieving a healthy environment and managing their resources sustainably become partners in ensuring that global cycles and systems remain unimpaired.
>
> World Health Organization (1992: xxx)

Complexity theory, a systemic understanding of health, transformative resilience, symbiosis, synergy and integrative salutogenic design are related scale-linking concepts and frameworks that can help us to structure an integrated strategy to maintain human and planetary health and create regenerative cultures. In this context, sustainability gets redefined from referring to the 'neutral' – do-no-more-harm – to a systemic understanding of the relationship between human, ecosystems and planetary health:

> Sustainability is a relationship between dynamic human economic systems and larger, dynamic, but normally slower-changing ecological systems, such that human life can continue indefinitely, human individuals can flourish, and human cultures can develop – but also a relationship in which the effects of human activities remain within bounds so as not to destroy the health and integrity of self-organizing systems that provide the environmental context for these activities.
>
> Brian G. Norton (1992)

Maintaining and restoring a healthy and resilient environment – at the community, ecosystem and the planetary scale – are inextricably linked. Ecological and societal health, as a system-wide emergent property, enables and supports healthy human development, and enables diverse cultural expressions of regional identity.

Systemic health as an emergent property of regenerative cultures emerges as locally and regionally adapted communities learn to thrive within the 'enabling constraints' and opportunities set by the ecological, social and cultural conditions of their local bioregion within a globally collaborative context. In a continuously changing, complex system, the promotion of health and sustainability requires constant learning in order to adapt appropriately to change. 'Living the Questions Together' and regionally focused design-based conversations about how to nurture systemic health can promote this constant learning.

Robert Costanza (1992: 239) reviewed a number of conceptual definitions of 'ecosystem health' based on health as: homeostasis, absence of disease, diversity or complexity, stability or resilience, vigour or scope of growth, and as balance between systems components. All of these perspectives on health are useful and also have their limitations. Costanza calls them "pieces of the puzzle". He proposes that ecosystem health should be understood "as a comprehensive, multi-scale, dynamic, hierarchical measure of system resilience, organization and vigor", and argues, "these concepts are embodied in the term 'sustainability', which implies the system's ability to maintain its structure (organization) and function (vigor) over time in the face of external stresses (resilience)". He emphasizes the important scale-linking aspect of health: "A healthy system must also be defined in the light of both its context (the larger system of which it is part) and its components (the smaller systems that make it up)" (p.240).

Similarly, David Brunckhorst (2002), the director of the UNESCO Institute for Bioregional Resource Management, emphasizes that "resilience, like sustainability, has multi-faceted elements affecting it through scales of space and time – it does not simply occur at a local or global scale." He explains: "To sustain and restore resilience in ecological and social systems for long term sustainability, we must begin to integrate our planning and operate our management across multiple scales […]" and we will best be able to do so by "nesting functional requirements of ecological systems and social systems for an enduring future" (p.16). This nested or scale-linking perspective is very important, as it invites us to ask questions about the synergistic integration of local, regional and global solutions, and reminds us to pay attention to how short-, mid- and long-term processes and cycles are interconnected.

Systemic health (as a scale-linking emergent property) enables regenerative systems to respond to disruption with resilience. Linking global, regional and local efforts to collaborate in designing resilience into the system at and across scales is an important aspect of creating a regenerative culture. We do have to pay attention, though, to what kind of resilience we nurture. Sometimes the ability to persist and bounce back to 'business as usual' is hindering rather than helping the transformation to a regenerative culture. Resilience is a multifaceted capacity closely linked to systemic health and vitality. In particular, a regenerative culture will depend on 'transformative resilience'. Let's take a closer look at the different aspects of resilience and why they are so important to our common future. At points the theoretical framework can seem a little dense, but resilience thinking is a profoundly practical way to face an unpredictable future by nurturing our ability to respond wisely and work with the disruptions that will challenge us.

Rolling back Earth Overshoot Day

Humanity first overshot the Earth's annual regenerative capacity in the early 1970s. That is to say our species reached a point where every year we started to consume more resources and produced more waste than the natural bioproductivity of the planet and ecosystems functions are able to regenerate and safely absorb in a year. In other words, we started to live off the capital that life built up over millions of years rather than taking the wiser path of making do with living off the annual interest on that capital. We are drawing down the natural capital account and in the process are diminishing the capacity of ecosystems functions to regenerate.

According to the Global Footprint Network which developed this measure together with the New Economics Foundation, the first Earth Overshoot Day fell on 23rd December, 1970. Rapidly rising population numbers and rates of material and energy consumption, along with the accelerating erosion of ecosystems everywhere have resulted in the decline of the planet's annual 'bioproductivity' and a reduction in ecosystems functions each year since. Thus, the day on which we overstep the limits of Earth's annual productivity is occurring earlier and earlier. By 1995 it was on 10th October, in 2005 we reached overshoot by 3rd September (Global Footprint Network, 2008), and in 2015 we reached it on 13th August (based on National Footprint Accounts, 2015 edition).

Figure 7 illustrates how humanity as a whole went into ecological overshoot (using more resources that one Earth can provide) in 1970 and how we will have to try to return to 'one-planet living' as soon as possible, ideally by 2050.

4: Why Nurture Resilience and Whole-Systems Health?

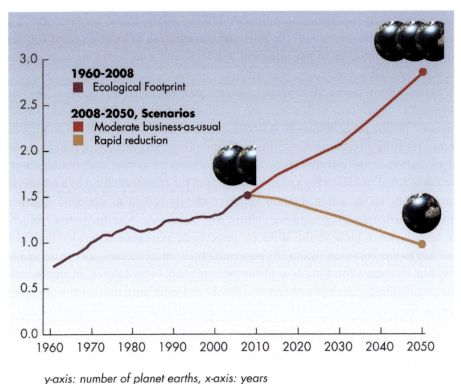

y-axis: number of planet earths, x-axis: years

Figure 7: Earth Overshoot, © 2015 Global Footprint Network. www.footprintnetwork.org

Moving towards a regenerative human culture depends on first stopping and then reversing this steady trend towards Overshoot Day occurring earlier and earlier each year. Until one day in the future we can celebrate the fact that Earth overshoot day exists no longer and we have collectively managed to meet human needs within the limits of the planet's capacity to regenerate and provide.

Sounds idealistic and utopian? Well, the science is simple: there is no other way to chart our path into a distant future on this planet. We need to first roll back Earth Overshoot Day and then begin to create a culture that aims to leave a richer, more vibrant and more ecologically productive planet to each subsequent generation. To achieve this transformation we will need the participation of all of humanity. We will need open and free education for all to raise everyone's ecological and social literacy. The narrative of separation has taught us how to see the world through the lens of difference, competition and scarcity – consequently we learned to compete. The narrative of interbeing reveals not only our interdependence but also the abundance that emerges from collaboration, sharing and caring for the whole community of life. We need to learn together how to collaborate effectively in nurturing the social and ecological capital of our communities.

I refuse to believe that 'human nature' is mainly competitive and individualistic; as a matter of fact, I am convinced that, by and large, the opposite is the case (see evidence for this in Chapter 7). We all have the capacity to understand that humanity's future depends on learning to live within the biophysical limits of the biosphere. War and fundamentalism are deeply anachronistic. It is time for humanity to come together and learn how to become a regenerative presence on Earth.

I am writing these lines while the news is full of the conflicts in Syria, Iraq, Israel/Palestine, Afghanistan, Libya and Ukraine. In asserting our fundamentally collaborative human nature I am not ignoring these horrors. Why are so many young people willing to join terrorist organizations fighting with blind hatred, barbarous brutality and complete disregard for the values of peaceful co-existence shared by all the world's religions? I believe many young people - particularly men - are disenfranchised and hurting from the lack of meaning propagated through the effects of the narrative of separation, desperately looking for a place to belong. The misguided ideologies that drive war, fundamentalism and conflict attract people who are looking for meaning and identity through creating an *other* to oppose.

Imagine humanity united in the meaningful work of creating a more thriving future for all of life. From within the narrative of separation this might seem like a naïve vision. From within the narrative of interbeing, and in full awareness of our dependence on the planetary life-support system and ecosystems functions, to do anything else and waste time in the fight between mal-adaptive ideologies is deluded. To care for the Earth and to care for others *is* to care for ourselves. Let's find meaning in co-creating a thriving world together, rather than in fighting each other blinded by outdated ideologies and divisive narratives. Let's roll back Earth Overshoot Day! Let's find that higher ground of interbeing that lies beyond all our differences. Let's value our divrersity as we come together in global unity.

Learning to live within planetary boundaries

In 2009, a landmark study by an international group of scientists led by the Stockholm Resilience Centre (Rockström, *et al.*, 2009) identified at least eight critical *planetary boundaries* that we will need to pay close attention to if we hope to create a more sustainable human presence on Earth. At least three of these boundaries have already been breached. We have already caused dangerous *climate change* and are getting close to triggering run-away feedback cycles in Earth's climate system that could have catastrophic effects for all of humanity and most life on Earth. We have a relatively small window of opportunity to avoid this, and the window is closing. *Biodiversity loss* has reached alarming rates that are on a par with the six other major extinction events in the history of life on Earth. Our unsustainable methods of agricultural production have interfered with biogeochemical flow boundaries like the *nitrogen cycle* and the *phosphorus cycle*.

Not enough research has been done yet to understand to what extent we may also have breached the planetary boundaries for *chemical pollution* and *atmospheric aerosol loading*. Evidence is mounting that endocrine system-disrupting chemicals (hormone mimics) in plastics and cosmetics are interfering with sexual differentiation and fertility in many species, including humans. *Ocean acidification, stratospheric ozone depletion, land system changes* and *global freshwater use* will have to be monitored closely as they are all rapidly approaching the point where safe planetary boundaries will be breached. A recent study has updated our understanding of planetary boundaries. It argues that "by identifying the safe operating space for humanity on Earth, the PB [Planetary Boundaries] framework can make a valuable contribution to decision-makers in charting desirable courses for societal development" (Steffen *et al.*, 2015).

Many of these boundaries are interrelated. Most of them cause a loss of biodiversity, resilience and ecosystem health at multiple scales, from local to global. With each species that is lost, we weaken the complex web of interdependencies and connections that support the health of the world's ecosystems. Each species that disappears into extinction might have held a treasure trove of biomimetic inspirations for us. It might have harboured a cure for cancer and will have played an important role in the ecosystems it inhabited. Every species plays a systemic role, the absence of which will transform the biosphere as a whole, affecting not just the future of humanity, but the future of all life. *Biodiversity loss* as a planetary boundary addresses both *genetic diversity*, as a repository for life's innovation, and *functional diversity*, as the diversity of interacting species that give a given ecosystem or the biosphere the capacity for healthy self-regulation. Both are key factors in the resilience of natural systems.

We have to go beyond valuing purely the utilitarian value of every species for human survival, the narrative of interbeing recognizes that each species is a unique expression of life with intrinsic value. As we lose biodiversity, we unravel the complex pattern of health based on diversity, symbiotic relationships, multiple redundancies, and complex interconnections, feedback loops and nested collaborative networks. The resilience of an ecosystem or a community critically depends on this scale-linking pattern of health that connects individual health with community health, ecosystem health and planetary health. A regenerative culture is a culture that has learned to thrive within planetary boundaries. Some questions that can guide our learning:

> Q How can we meet human needs within the limits set by planetary boundaries?

> Q What are the most effective ways to limit, ameliorate and reverse the effects we have already triggered by overstepping planetary boundaries like climate change, biodiversity loss, the limits of the nitrogen and phosphorus cycle, and land-system change?

One attempt to answer the question of how to return to living within planetary limits was made by Donella Meadows, Dennis Meadows and Jorgen Randers in their book *Beyond the Limits* (1992). They suggested a series of actions humanity will need to take. Amory and Hunter Lovins reviewed these actions, adding some of their own suggestions in *How Not to Parachute More Cats* (1996). Let's have a brief look at the questions they raised and some hopeful responses.

> Q How can we return to living within the limits?

The answers will include creating policies that enforce the pricing of resources in a way that includes the environmental and social effects of their extraction, use and recycling, along with the elimination of hidden subsidies to the fossil fuel, chemical, and nuclear industries and other major polluters. Creating regenerative agricultural practices is also critically important.

> Q   How do we best protect, restore and improve our resource base?

We will have to learn how to use the remaining fossil fuels, groundwater and mineral deposits with the utmost efficiency and only as long as we cannot substitute their use with recycled and renewable alternatives. It will require us to readdress how natural resources are managed and can be regenerated, including a more equitable ownership of them. We will have to make the protection of biodiversity, fisheries and watersheds, along with a shift towards organic regenerative agriculture, long-term reforestation programmes and agreements on the limitation of greenhouse gas emission an international and national priority.

> Q   How do we ensure more immediate feedback by tracking the right signals and improving our capacity to respond appropriately to change?

There is a clear need for more adequate indicators of progress (e.g. GPI instead of GDP). We will return to this in Chapter 7. The planetary boundaries framework can help us to better monitor how human activity affects wellbeing, local ecosystems and the biosphere. Our ability to respond appropriately to systemic changes depends on improved education that increases our capacity for systemic and critical thinking, and our ecological literacy.

> Q   How can we slow and eventually stop the growth of the human population?

This difficult question will not only require institutional and policy changes but, more importantly, a change in awareness driven by education and social innovation. We will need to define sustainable levels of population and industrial output, based on an understanding of the purpose of human existence that is decoupled from physical expansion and consumption. We have to value the idea of 'enough' rather than 'more' (Lovins & Lovins, 1996). There is a well-documented relationship between family size, poverty and women's access to education (Connor, 2008; Borgen Project, 2015). By creating a more equitable system of resource-sharing and improving global access to quality education we can create conditions leading to a reduction of family sizes in the mid-term and a gradual population decline in the long term.

Depending on the language used, reports on the biophysical boundaries of our planet and population pressures tend to reinforce cultural conditioning of the mindset of scarcity and competition. This does not have to be our response. Many of the innovations, technologies and culturally transformative questions explored in this book offer collaborative pathways for the transition from growth-obsessed cultures of consumption to regenerative cultures. The role of formal and informal education and life-long learning for all sectors of society and all of humanity is crucial. We need to educate about, and give voice to, a new cultural narrative that inspires humanity to co-create a new reality where we choose to see collaboration in nurturing whole-systems health and shared abundance as an expression of our interbeing with life. It is the most promising individual and collective survival strategy on a crowed planet.

In *The Open-Source Everything Manifesto*, Robert David Steele argues that to unleash the potential of collaborative abundance, human ingenuity and creativity, we need to give all humanity open access to information, education and 'liberation technology'.

> Liberation technology creates wealth, and open source technology creates wealth. In both instances the 'centre of gravity' for dramatic change towards resilience and sustainability is the human brain mass of five billion poor – the one billion rich have failed to 'scale'. The human brain is the one unlimited resource we have on Earth. The potential for innovation and entrepreneurship on the part of five billion poor is the most underdeveloped and underutilized resource.
>
> Robert David Steele (2012: 7)

Steele argues that taking the path of open-source everything will allow us to foster citizen participation and public intelligence as the basis for a truly participatory open democracy, informed and guided by our collective intelligence (p.141; see also Chapter 7). Together, we can learn to thrive within planetary boundaries. Rather than seeing 'planetary boundaries' as curtailing our freedom (and rebelling like teenagers against this imposition), we can choose to mature as a species and come to regard these boundaries as 'enabling constraints' that give us the context (safe operating space) within which we can apply our creativity to meeting everybody's needs, creating abundance for all without detriment to the wider community of life.

What exactly are resilience and transformative resilience?

In ecosystems science, resilience research started more than 40 years ago. In 1973, C.S. Holling published the first results of his studies of the complex dynamics of change within ecosystems. Holling saw that ecosystems could exist in a variety of dynamically stable (dynamic equilibrium) conditions, and that, after disturbance, ecosystems could either bounce back to their initial state before the disturbance or they could degenerate to less diverse and less vibrant new equilibrium conditions. Too much disturbance could lead to systemic degeneration, but at the same time periodic disturbance (within limits) could also contribute to an ecosystem's transformation to a more diverse and more vibrant dynamic equilibrium condition. For example, Allan Savory's work on the holistic management of degraded grasslands mimics the periodic disturbance caused by herds of migrating grazers as a key factor in maintaining and improving soil health, water retention capacity, biodiversity and the bioproductivity of the ecosystem as a whole (see Chapter 7). In ecosystem science the word resilience refers to the ability of ecosystems to respond to disturbance and environmental change with either persistence, or gradual adaptation and more fundamental transformation.

Scale-linking, interlocking change processes drive the dynamics of natural systems. These processes occur simultaneously at different temporal and spatial scales. Local changes are influenced by regional and global patterns of change, which are in turn affected by local changes. 'Dynamic equilibrium' conditions at a particular scale are regions of dynamic (relative) stability within a wider landscape of constant change and transformation. Resilience research started by investigating these dynamics in ecosystems and has since been expanded to the interlocking dynamics of change in eco-social systems, as it is impossible to study ecosystems without including the impact of human activity upon them.

The planet's self-regulating and climate-regulating processes have actively created and maintained relatively stable conditions conducive to the continued evolution of life. *Resilience* contributes to maintaining the relative stability of living systems over time, while transformative resilience describes a living system's capacity to transform itself in response to changing conditions and disruptions. We need both capacities to navigate our path towards a regenerative future. Our human capacity for foresight and anticipation adds an important component to an eco-social systems ability to respond to change with transformative resilience.

The systems view of life understands the presence of dynamic conditions of disequilibrium (continuous change and transformation) as a signature signal of living process. When James Lovelock worked at the Pasadena Jet Propulsion laboratories in the late 1960s, designing equipment for NASA's mission to Mars, a colleague's data set describing the atmospheric composition of the different planets in our solar system landed on Lovelock's desk. It struck him almost immediately that only Earth had an atmosphere in stark chemical disequilibrium while on the other planets the balance of different gases in the atmosphere were such that few chemical reactions were taking place. Our blue planet's dynamic disequilibrium sparked Lovelock's intuitive leap to ask some important questions. Maybe the presence of life is actively creating this disequilibrium? Could it be that life creates conditions conducive to life? Maybe life is a self-regulating and self-organizing process at the planetary scale? These questions were the basis for the Gaia Hypothesis and led to the development of Gaia Theory and a revolution in Earth Systems Science (e.g. Lovelock, 2000).

A scale-linking, whole-systems understanding of change processes invites us to embrace the paradoxical co-presence of relative stability over extended periods and turbulent disruption at and across scales. In nature we can observe individual subsystems in phases of relative dynamic equilibrium while other subsystems are in phases of disruption, collapse or transformation. One particular ecosystem might undergo a phase of relative stability and smaller fluctuating changes within a bounded region. Yet that same ecosystem is also part of a larger context (biome, biosphere), and simultaneously contains smaller subsystems (communities and individuals) that are engaged in different phases of life's change processes. While some systems are relatively stable and their resilience maintains basic systems functions, other systems experience disruptive and transformative change as previously stable patterns and relationships break down and release energy and resources. Whether we observe relative stability or change in a system also depends on the temporal and spatial scales we are paying attention to.

The *interbeing* of slow and fast cycles at different spatial scales within an interconnected planetary whole turns our living, transforming bio-culture-sphere into an archetypal example of a complex, dynamic non-linear system. Just as our own individual health is dependent on our capacity to bounce back from disruptions, resilience – as a vital capacity of healthy systems – is also an important factor of community, ecosystems and planetary health (Wahl, 2006a).

Resilience and transformative resilience are indicators of systemic health at and across different scales. There are, however, cases where too much persistence and resilience within systems in need of transformation can slow down necessary transformation and decrease future adaptive capacity. We need the right kind of balance between resilience (as persistence of the status quo) and the transformative resilience that enables us to avoid collapse through transformative innovation. Working with disruptions as invitations to transformative change creates the exciting opportunity to turn breakdown into breakthrough (Hutchins, 2012).

The Resilience Alliance, an international network of researchers and practitioners focused on understanding the complex dynamics of change in socio-ecological systems, defines *ecosystems resilience* as "the capacity of an ecosystem to tolerate disturbance without collapsing into a qualitatively different state that is controlled by a different set of processes" (Resilience Alliance, 2015a). As human beings and communities we have conscious awareness of the systems we participate in. By paying attention to the patterns of natural change processes and learning from them, we can potentially add the capacity of foresight to the whole system. We can anticipate and plan for the future, even if we cannot accurately predict the exact future behaviour of the complex dynamic systems in which we participate. To better understand and reduce our negative impact and to transform humanity into a regenerative influence on the whole system, we need to pay attention to the interaction of social and ecological systems and regard them as one *whole* socio-ecological system (SES).

> Resilience as applied to ecosystems, or to integrated systems of people and the natural environment, has three characteristics:
>
> - The amount of change the system can undergo and still retain the same […] function and structure
> - The degree to which the system is capable of self-organization
> - The ability to build and increase the capacity for learning and adaptation.
>
> Resilience Alliance (2015a)

As the resilience of a system declines, "the magnitude of a shock from which it cannot recover gets smaller and smaller". In general, "resilience shifts attention from purely growth and efficiency to needed recovery and flexibility. Growth and efficiency alone can often lead ecological systems, businesses and societies into fragile rigidities, exposing them to turbulent transformations. Learning, recovery, and flexibility open eyes to novelty and new worlds of opportunity" (Resilience Alliance, 2015b). In full awareness of the limits to prediction and control, informed by our conscious participation in socio-economic systems, we can humbly aim to redesign the human presence on Earth, creating locally adapted and globally collaborative regenerative cultures everywhere. The generations alive today have the unique opportunity to shape a viable future for humanity. To do so, we need the right balance between persistent/adaptive resilience and transformative resilience in our SESs. Knowing when to maintain existing systems and when to transform them in response to outdated patterns is part of the systemic awareness and foresight and anticipation that humans can add to SESs.

The adaptive cycle as a dynamic map for resilience thinking

The three aspects of resilience (persistence, adaptive capacity and transformability) describe important capacities of living systems: to resist collapse and maintain vital functions, to adapt to changing conditions (learn and self-organize) and (in the case of SESs) to apply foresight and anticipation to 'design for positive emergence' – to transform the system towards increased health and an improved capacity to respond wisely and creatively to disruptions and change.

The theory of complex dynamic systems describes the periodic, rhythmic dance between order and chaos, between stability and transformation as a fundamental pattern of self-organization in complex (living) systems. As any system begins to mature, there is an accompanying increase in fixed and ordered patterns of interactions and resource flows. The system becomes over-connected, or better, the existing qualities and quantities of connections are such that they inhibit the formation of new pathways needed for the system's overall adaptation to outside changes and its continued evolution. Eventually this leads to rigidity within the system, and it becomes brittle, less resilient, and more susceptible to disturbances from the outside. At this point, the effects of detrimental run-away feedback loops inside the system can further challenge viability. The often resulting gradual or sudden breakdown of the old order and structures moves the system closer to 'the edge of chaos' – the edge of its current stability (dynamic equilibrium) domain. The reorganization of resource flows and changes in the quality and quantity of interconnections within the system at this point create a crisis that can be turned into an opportunity for transformation and innovation.

At the edge of chaos, complex dynamic systems are at their most creative (Kauffman, 1995). Ervin László argues in *The Chaos Point* that the world and humanity is currently at a crossroads between breakdown and breakthrough. If we take appropriate actions, the chaos point could be an opportunity to "leap to a new civilization" (László, 2006: 109).

4: Why Nurture Resilience and Whole-Systems Health?

Understanding the overall dynamics of change we are in the midst of is important. We need to learn to *work with* rather than *fight against* these cyclical patterns of creative innovation, consolidation, ossification and eventual dissolution to make room for transformative innovation and renewed creativity.

The adaptive cycle is a model of natural patterns of change in ecosystems and eco-social systems. It consists of four distinct phases: 'growth or exploitation' (r); 'conservation' (K) of established patterns and resource distribution; 'collapse or release' (Ω); and reorganization (α). The adaptive cycle (see Figure 8) is often drawn like an infinity symbol or Möbius loop that joins these four phases.

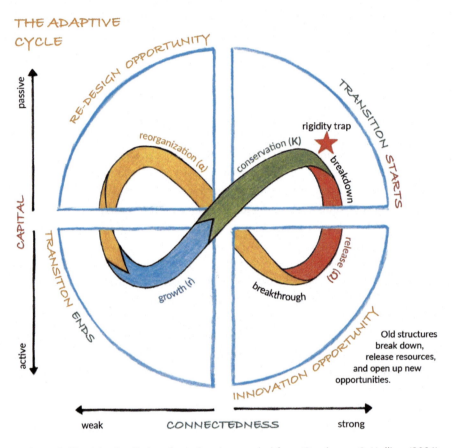

Figure 8: The Adaptive Cycle, adapted and expanded from Gunderson & Holling (2001)

The journey from exploitation (growth in the diagram above) to conservation is referred to as the 'fore-loop' (blue and green part of the loop). It describes the slow and often longer phase of growth and accumulation of resources in the system. Eventually, too much rigid structure, fixed connections and accumulation of resources in the system make it brittle and poised for release or collapse.

The transition from release to reorganization is referred to as the 'back-loop' of the adaptive cycle (red and orange part of the loop). This phase is often fast moving and relatively short. In this phase the opportunity for redesign, reorganization and renewal is high, due to the release of rigid structures, established patterns and the redistribution of resources throughout the system. In the adaptive cycle, the creative 'edge of chaos' is reached during the beginning of the 'release' phase and left at the end of the 'reorganization' phase.

During the α-phase the opportunities for and likelihood of creative change is highest. In the r-phase these opportunities for change are tested against each other and one or a few innovations begin to define the characteristics of the transformed system. This structure is conserved and then begins itself to rigidify during the K-phase, until the often rapid and sometimes catastrophic release (collapse) in the Ω-phase takes us back to the creative 'edge of chaos' conditions. This offers renewed opportunities for reorganization in a new α-phase and a new adaptive cycle.

The potential for regime shift or transformational change that moves the system into a new way of functioning (which may offer increased resilience and health) is highest during the α-phase. Transformative innovations introduced during this stage have the potential to lift the system into a new stability domain. Design interventions aiming to increase the resilience capacity of a system should use foresight and explore future scenarios to evaluate the potential effects of the intervention or redesign they propose.

In trying to navigate these natural change dynamics at different scales simultaneously, we have to remember that all three aspects of resilience are important. Finding a balance between persistence, adaptive capacity and transformative resilience will determine – to a certain extent – how turbulent, rapid and profound the transition will be. Since there is a scale-linking connection between systems at different spatial scale and the adaptive cycles of bigger systems tend to move more slowly while the adaptive cycles of smaller systems tend to move faster, we also have to pay attention to what aspect of resilience we are nurturing at what scale and how the different scales influence each other.

Panarchy: a scale-linking perspective of systemic transformation

Since nature is fundamentally scale-linking – connecting the molecular to the planetary and the local to the global – adaptive cycles of any particular system at any particular scale (e.g.: local community, bioregion, nation or planet) are linked to multiple adaptive cycles that are taking place simultaneously for smaller systems contained by that system and for the larger systems within which that particular system is embedded. This nested hierarchy of systems within systems – or holarchy (Koestler, 1989) of interconnected wholes within wholes – is also referred to as 'panarchy' (Gunderson & Holling, 2001). Gunderson and Holling explain that the word 'panarchy' describes nature's (w)holistic hierarchies and the complex dynamics that link different spatial scales and their fast- and slow-moving processes into an interconnected whole. The framework offers a deeper understanding of transformations in systems of humans and nature more deeply and this in turn might help us to navigate more wisely into an unpredictable future.

The panarchy model – interlinked adaptive cycles occurring at multiple temporal and spatial scales simultaneously – elucidates the interplay between change and persistence in scale-linked socio-ecological systems. The model can help us visualize the scale-linking complexity of natural processes. Facing this fractal complexity of interacting transformative processes – nested adaptive cycles spanning across temporal and spatial scales – reminds us to stay mindful of the limits of prediction and control that we face as participants in such complexity.

Generally speaking, the larger and longer the adaptive cycles, the less predictable and controllable they are. At a very limited spatial and temporal scale (and if we clearly define the boundaries of the system in question), prediction and control are possible, but since such reductions in complexity (e.g. controlled laboratory conditions) are artificially created by us and don't take into account the fundamental interconnectedness, interbeing and complexity of the scale-linking processes we participate in, such prediction and control is only of limited use. Figure 9 is a visual representation of panarchy depicted through dynamically interlinking adaptive cycles at different spatial and temporal scales.

Fast-moving cycles at smaller scales are more likely to innovate and test innovations. While slow-moving cycles at larger scales "stabilize and conserve accumulated memory of past successful, surviving experiments. The whole panarchy is both creative and conserving. The interactions between cycles in a panarchy combine learning with continuity" (Resilience Alliance, 2015c).

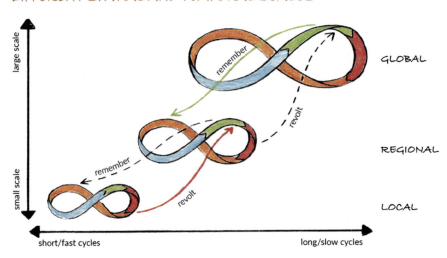

Figure 9: Panarchy of Adaptive Cycles, adapted and expanded from Gunderson & Holling (2001)

The larger slow-moving systems can stabilize the systems they contain by replenishing them and maintaining their established diversity and patterns of organization (remembering). The smaller fast-moving systems, in turn, can also affect the larger systems they participate in, either by a chain reaction of collapse – when loss of diversity, resilience, and viability at one scale is severe enough to affect the larger scale(s) – or through transformative (r)evolutionary changes that are innovated at the local scale and then spread to the regional and global scale (revolt). Figure 9 illustrates the interactions between fast- and slow-moving dynamic change processes at different spatial scales.

(R)evolutionary innovations are likely to occur in smaller systems that can respond to opportunity and change, while ecosystems and planetary health provide a stability that makes such innovation (and experimentation) at the smaller scale possible. Panarchy seems to suggest that innovation and the testing of viable alternatives in the transition to a regenerative culture are more likely to occur at the local and regional scale, and if successful, these innovations will spread globally (by adapting to local and regional conditions elsewhere).

In order for innovation to bubble up at a global scale we need to ensure open and transparent information flow, access to 'liberation technologies' (see Steele, 2012), and education that enables all of us to collaborate in local and regional adaptation and transformation supported by global collaboration. Transformative resilience has to be built from the bottom up and panarchy makes us understand that this requires both top-down and bottom-up collaboration and mutual support. Luckily this change is already under way.

Local and regional community resilience building is going global

In recent years the *resilience imperative* has made it onto the agenda of local and national governments, business leaders and international institutions like the European Union and the United Nations. In 2010, the UN Office for Disaster and Risk Reduction launched the five-year *Making Cities Resilient* campaign (UNISDR, 2015).

A 2012 report to the Secretary-General of the UN, prepared by the high-level panel on global sustainability and entitled *Resilient People, Resilient Planet – A Future Worth Choosing*, recommends three broad strategic actions: i) empowering people to make sustainable choices, ii) working towards a sustainable economy, and iii) strengthening institutional governance (UNGSP, 2012, p.79).

The 2013 World Bank report on *Building Resilience* recommends that the "international community should lead by example by further promoting approaches that progressively link climate and disaster resilience to broader development paths, and funding them appropriately" (World Bank, 2013: ix). In the UK there are now community resilience officers in local councils and the National Health Service.

The Rockefeller Foundation's *100 Resilient Cities Challenge* – funded with $100 million – says it "is dedicated to helping cities around the world become more resilient to the physical, social and economic challenges that are a growing part of the 21st century". The initiative will support 100 cities financially to enable them to employ 'chief resilience officers' (CROs). The city of San Francisco hired Patrick Otellini as the world's first CRO in early 2014 and by December 2014 another 64 cities had received funding to support this important whole-systems integration role in their city councils and town halls.

The Advisory Council on Global Change (WBGU) – the German government's foresight unit – published a 400-page report in 2011, entitled *World in Transition: A New*

Social Contract for Sustainability. It reviews historical examples of social change and suggests that individual actors and change agents are important drivers of cultural transformation, hence their role should be taken more seriously.

Socio-cultural innovators tend to stimulate change by questioning 'business as usual' practices and perspectives and introducing viable alternatives. The report highlights that such change agents appear "frequently from the margins of society where unorthodox thinkers and outsiders are at home" and then the change agents themselves and, more importantly, the issues they have raised begin to gain cultural interest and significance for the wider public and mainstream institutions (WBGU, 2011: 261-262). The way that the 'community resilience building' meme has reached the mainstream agenda seems to be an example of this.

At the Rio+20 conference I attended talks and participated in conversations in both the official UN summit programme and various venues of the parallel *Cúpula dos Povos Rio+20*. One of my highlights was an afternoon at the *Forum for Social Entrepreneurship in the New Economy* together with Ana Rhodes, then the chair of management at the Findhorn Foundation. We were both inspired by Michel Bauwens's lucidity about how we are already leveraging global social transformation through local actions powered by global collaboration. Ashoka's Dani Matierlo reported back from the event that the overarching credo was that: "we must build a win-win system" and "it must be a system that is a win to the environment as well". The resounding conclusion was: "[…] there is no better way to change the world than by having all sectors of society come together, to build a world guided by empathy – one in which everyone is a change maker" (Ashoka, 2012).

At the *Equator Price Awards*, local activists, scientists and change agents from around the world were recognized for "building resilient communities". UNDP's Helen Clark started her speech with: "Tonight's event is about honouring the great innovation and leadership which is coming from the world's local communities". Christina Figueres, Executive Secretary of the UN Framework Convention on Climate Change added: "I trust that we all know that we cannot address climate change globally unless communities claim their power to implement solutions – and creative solutions – on the ground." (EquatorInitiative, 2012). In a truly Brazilian finale, 1,700 attendants fell quiet whilst listening to Gilberto Gil closing with Stevie Wonder's mystical song about humanity's need to reconnect with nature and learn from The Secret Life of Plants.

Creating regenerative cultures and a regenerative human presence on Earth is first and foremost about re-connection with *life* as a whole, so that we can re-connect and collaborate with each other in new ways. In theory this should be easy since we were never truly separate, but the narrative of separation is strong and persistent. Profound cultural transformations take time. In a post-Rio+20 event organized by the UN Institute for Training and Research (UNITAR) and Instituto Ethos, the question was asked:

> Q Do we need a new Social Contract to address the sustainable development changes of the 21st century?

Referring back to Jean-Jacques Rousseau's *The Social Contract* (1762), UNITAR's executive director Carlos Lopez emphasized that Rousseau had been an 'agent provocateur' who questioned established ideas with his critique of inequality and call to reconnect with nature. Lopez suggested that the questions Rousseau asked have a new relevance and urgency today (UNITAR, 2012).

Rio+20 was a very mixed bag. I felt disappointed by the way the UN seems to have its hands bound by the big corporate lobbies and a few 'bully states'. The vibrancy at the people's summit was a welcome change from the posturing at the official summit, but I wished that 'the people', instead of running a parallel event, had created a broader conversation that involved everyone – heads of state and lobbyists included. The passion and enthusiasm at the Gaia Education/GEN/Transition Towns tent was infectious and nourishing. Overall, what most filled me with hope was that the conversations about local and regional resilience-building and the need for a deeper transformation are now global conversations, offering a common ground for collective action beyond multi-lateral dialogues.

We all need to become change agents who question inequalities and environmental destruction everywhere. We need to ask how we can co-create more equitable cultures that are deeply reconnected to nature and have a regenerative effect on their local and regional ecosystems functions and productivity. At those scales we can create true win-win-win solutions. Resilience thinking is beginning to unite global and local change agents working in civil society, business and governmental institutions in an effort to create a thriving future through global collaboration in support of local implementation.

Outside the circle of academics of the Resilience Alliance who started resilience research four decades ago, grassroots networks and civil society organizations were the first to understand the urgent need for local capacity-building and civic participation in the process of nurturing resilience at the community scale.

Among the early adopters and promoters of the resilience-building approach were the *Permaculture Design* movement (e.g. Holmgren, 2011; Whitman & Ferguson, 2014), the *Global Ecovillage Network* (GEN, 2015), the *Design for Sustainability* training programme of *Gaia Education*, and since 2006 the rapidly growing global *Transition Town* movement (Hopkins, 2011 & 2014). The enthusiastic response to the transition town approach by local community groups, first in the UK and then in Europe and globally, has helped to spread the meme of 'community resilience-building' to local and national governments around the world, in preparation for climate change and 'peak oil'.

> Q "What if the best responses to peak oil and climate change don't come from government, but from you and me and the people around us?"
> Rob Hopkins (2011)

Rob Hopkins, co-founder of the transition town movement, started his first experiments in community resilience-building in 2004 in the small Irish town of Kinsale, simply taking the opportunity of teaching a permaculture design course at a local community college to develop an 'energy descent plan' for the village together with his students. In 2006, he relocated to the Southern English town of Totnes and joined up with Naresh Giangrande and Sophy Banks to start the first transition town initiative. Within only three years the phenomenon had inspired more than a hundred communities in the UK and elsewhere to create local transition initiatives. By mid-2014 there were more than 1,500 communities around the globe registered with the Transition Network and many thousands of people had taken part in 'Transition Town Trainings' facilitated by a global network of transition town trainers. Rob Hopkins (2009) identifies three key design principles that resilience at a community scale depends upon:

> **Increased diversity**: a broader base of livelihoods, land use, enterprise and energy systems than at present.
>
> **Modularity** *(scale-linking design):* not advocating self-sufficiency, but rather an increased self-reliance; with surge protectors for the local economy such as local food production and decentralized energy.
>
> **Tightness of feedback** *(increased capacity to learn from local successes or failures):* bringing the results of our actions closer to home, so that we cannot ignore them.

Transition town groups around the world tend to be initiated by grassroots activists and educators. Many of them have successfully involved local business owners and gained the support of their local councils. Their success often depends on convincing the more 'mainstream' members of their communities to join in, for example through creating community enterprises that strengthen the local economy.

In 2013, the 'European Association for Information on Local Development' (AEIDL) published *Europe in Transition: Local Communities leading the way to a Low-Carbon Society*. The report reviews diverse local initiatives across Europe, including transition towns, ecovillage projects and low-carbon community groups. It shows that in the six years to 2012 the number of participatory, citizen-driven groups has grown from only a few to more than 2,000. This is an excellent example of cultural creative conversations already transforming communities. By collectively asking deeper questions about the future of their communities, and by experimenting with possible local solutions, these groups are contributing to the emergence of regenerative cultures.

> Meeting in living rooms, in local cafés, community centres and other public spaces, the focus is predominantly on practical initiatives that can be taken locally to reduce greenhouse gas (GHG) emissions and the dependence on fossil fuels, and strengthen the resilience and sustainability of local communities. Many of these initiatives involve the testing of new ideas, technologies and approaches in order to find the most sustainable and cost effective solutions. In this way, they act as important local laboratories, piloting and demonstrating how citizens and communities can live more sustainably.
> AEIDL (2013: 3)

How can we nurture transformative resilience?

The 2011 Nobel Laureate Symposium on *Global Sustainability* resulted in the publication of three scientific background papers that each named one important cultural transformation. The first called for *Reconnecting with the Biosphere* arguing "it is time for a new social contract for global sustainability rooted in a shift of perception – from people and nature seen as separate parts to interdependent social-ecological systems" (Folke *et al.*, 2011).

The second paper, *The Anthropocene,* encouraged humanity to adopt the planetary boundary framework to enable a complex systems perspective that is not myopically focused on climate change alone (Steffen *et al.*, 2011).

The final paper, *Tipping towards Sustainability,* said that while our human capacity for innovation was partially responsible for the crises we are now facing, "it is time to use this capacity and introduce innovations that are sensitive to the fundamental bonds between social and ecological systems" (Westley *et al.*, 2011).

Nurturing a healthy and mutually supportive relationship between social and ecological systems is primarily done at a local and regional scale. Global collaboration in the process of re-regionalization and re-localization based on biologically and ecologically inspired whole-systems design will enable the kind of transformative innovation that will create global sustainability based on locally adapted regenerative cultures and their circular regional 'biodiversity economies' (see Shiva, 2012: 143).

Transformative resilience at a global scale emerges from the scale-linking collaboration and interconnection of regional and local subsystems that have themselves high levels of transformative resilience. Efforts to nurture transformative resilience can learn from the scale-linking patterns of nature's life support systems – for example, by taking into account the dynamics described by the adaptive cycle and panarchy. Here are some *resilience lessons from natural systems* that can help us:

- Nature's pattern is modularity – interconnected, decentralized networks exhibiting redundancy at and across scales

- Diversity creates requisite variety and adaptive capacity

- Redundancy in the provision of vital resources and functions increases self-reliance and resilience in decentralized but globally connected collaborative networks

- The local, regional and global are scale-linked into symbiotic and mutually supportive relationships

- The primary source of energy is the sun (nature runs on current solar income)

- Resource and energy flows are predominantly local/regional and organized in circular and regenerative patterns

- Self-regulation and regeneration are based on information and resource exchanges within nested networks within networks

- Collaborative relationships that encourage diversity facilitate the sharing of abundance and maintain systemic health

Economic globalization has played a role in raising planetary awareness of the human family. Its effects confront us with our interdependence with each other and all of life as we face inevitable ecological limits. Caught up in the expansive movement of the globalization process – which started with colonialism and continued with economic globalization – we came to believe that bigger is always better, forever chasing efficiencies of scale.

I believe that regenerative human civilization will be structured as a globally collaborative network of diverse, regionally adapted, regenerative cultures drawing on different versions of a shared narrative of interbeing. Such a network will mimic nature's scale-linking pattern of diversity, health and resilience. The Stockholm Environment Centre, in collaboration with researchers from four continents, has proposed a series of 'policy-relevant principles' that could enhance the resilience of ecosystems functions (Biggs et al., 2012). Their recommendations invite these questions:

Q How can we maintain diversity and redundancy?

Q How can we enable connectivity?

Q How do we ensure that we pay attention to slow variables and feedbacks?

Q How do we foster a widespread cultural understanding of socio-ecological systems as complex adaptive systems?

Q How do we effectively encourage learning and experimentation?

Q How do we broaden participation?

Q How can we promote polycentric governance systems?

The salutogenic transformation of our global economy involves a re-patterning into a mosaic of vibrant regional and local economies with the means to meet basic needs in a decentralized way, trading predominately in those goods and services that cannot be provided locally. Peer-to-peer open knowledge-, skill- and information-exchange, along with the transfer of enabling technology, should be the focal point of global-local collaboration. Material and energy flows need to be predominantly at the local and regional scale.

This approach has multiple benefits, creating win-win-win solutions. Keeping material resource flows localized or regionalized, as far as possible, acts as a powerful 'enabling constraint' that i) reduces the energy and environmental cost of transporting resources, ii) stimulates innovation in regional circular bioeconomies adapted to local resource availability, iii) generates meaningful jobs in local living economies, iv) offers cultural opportunities to celebrate and express diversity in collaborative global unity, and v) nurtures a decentralized, networked pattern of organization that creates redundancy and resilience at and across scales. A single question, asked in the right moment and context, explored openly, can initiate a process of local and regional resilience building:

> **Q** How can we generate meaningful local/regional work by engaging in a gradual process of *import substitution*, nurturing our capacity to meet the needs of regional consumption as much as possible through regional production based on regionally regenerative resources?

In *The Resilience Imperative*, Michael Lewis and Pat Conaty (2012) show how energy sufficiency, local food systems, monetary reforms and low-cost financing, land reform and affordable housing, along with democratic ownership and nurturing sustainability, are all elements of the puzzle of creating a decentralized, cooperative, steady-state economy. As we will explore in Chapter 7, growth is not a problem in itself. It only becomes a problem if we don't learn to shift from the juvenile phase of quantitative growth to a more mature phase of qualitative growth, as occurs in the maturation process of ecosystems.

The steady-state economy approach is compatible with efforts to shift from quantitative growth (through accumulation and resource depletion) to qualitative growth (through qualitative transformation, regenerative resource use and leveraging the potential of synergies). Lewis and Conaty propose four mutually supportive strategic objectives that help to strengthen the resilience of communities: reclaiming the commons, reinventing democracy, creating a social solidarity economy, and "pricing as if people and planet mattered" (pp.21-32).

Their book is a valuable collection of tools for anybody who wants to begin building transformative resilience at the scale of their local community. It reviews many working examples showing how we can redesign our monetary and banking system, create affordable housing and energy sufficiency at the community scale, support the creation of local food systems, redirect the flow of finance to support vibrant local economies, strengthen cooperative business and cooperative ownership, and thereby accelerate the transition towards a resilient and regenerative culture.

In alignment with the narrative of interbeing, Lewis and Conaty refer to Desmond Tutu's suggestion that "We are not made for self-sufficiency, but for interdependence, and we break the law of our own being at our peril" (pp.336-337) and suggest that, "if interdependence is the essence, resilience and cooperation are the cornerstones" (p.337). The table below offers Lewis and Conaty's distilled advice on how to nurture resilience and cooperation.

Seven Resilience Principles	Seven Cooperative Principles
Promote and sustain social, economic, and biological diversity.	Member economic participation. Members contribute to and democratically control the capital of the cooperative but receive no or limited compensation.
Maintain modularity. Connect but avoid dependency, and ensure there are independent means to modify and adapt.	Each cooperative is autonomous and independent; external relations, financing, and federating are democratic decisions.
Tighten the community feedback loops to ensure awareness of what is happening and avoid crossing critical thresholds.	There is cooperation among cooperatives at local, regional, national and international levels.
Build social capital of strong networks, trust in relationships, and capable leadership that enables collective action.	Cooperatives have voluntary, open and inclusive membership.
Focus on learning, experimentation, building local rules, and change-oriented innovation.	Cooperatives provide education, training, and information to their members, elected representatives, and all staff. They also reach out to the public at large to educate about the nature and benefits of cooperation.
Design overlap and redundancy into governance systems and blend common and private property rights.	Democratic governance means a cooperative is accountable to its membership – one member, one vote.
Value and price all ecosystems functions.	Cooperatives work for community benefit. (The amendment of this principle to include respect for the environment is now formally under discussion)

Table 1: Principles of Resilience and Cooperation (Lewis & Conaty, 2012: 337)

Cooperation in community resilience-building improves systemic health as the basis for all regenerative cultures.

> This is the essence of the cultural shift we are struggling through in the early years of the 21st century, transitioning from cultural notions of independence and individualism to interdependence and mutualism, a reuniting of the 'I' and the 'We' as Martin Luther King prophesied. Perhaps a Declaration of Interdependence would concentrate our heads and hearts in ways that would crystallize the essence of the massive cultural shift we are in the midst of, and which we must organize and leverage in a big way if human kind is to survive with dignity.
>
> Michael Lewis & Pat Conaty (2012: 337)

The David Suzuki Foundation (1992) published such a declaration of interdependence for the 1992 Earth Summit in Rio de Janeiro. Its final sentence reads: "[…] at this turning point in our relationship with Earth, we work for an evolution: from dominance to partnership; from fragmentation to connection; from insecurity to interdependence". Cooperation for community resilience and systemic health is a natural consequence of understanding our interdependence, our *interbeing*.

From control and prediction to conscious participation, foresight and anticipation

One of the unique contributions that human beings offer to socio-ecological systems – and a possible response to the 'why-are-we-worth-sustaining?' question David Orr raised – is our capacity for foresight, or what Bill Sharpe calls 'future consciousness' (see Chapter 2). *Foresight is different from prediction!* Foresight scans and anticipates possible futures in recognition of the fundamentally unpredictable and uncontrollable nature of the complex dynamic systems we participate in. Through practising foresight and anticipation we develop 'future consciousness' and can more effectively work with the future potential of the present moment – aiming to participate wisely in full recognition of the limits of our knowing.

The need for prediction arises from a mindset of 'command and control' which is in itself a response to the isolation and alienation people begin to feel the more they experience life through the narrative of separation. The need for foresight to guide appropriate participation in the face of uncertainty arises from a deeper understanding of our fundamental interdependence. Life itself brings myriad perspectives into existence, bringing forth a world reflected in – maybe even to varying degrees pervaded by – consciousness.

The narrative of *interbeing* informs a sense of belonging that celebrates 'other' as a valued expression of a larger 'self' and unites us in the community of life. When we shift to experiencing the world from within this cultural narrative, we begin to heal the Cartesian split between mind and body. We reconnect with all our capacities to know the world as embodied subjects and participants. Rational thought is only one window onto the world. Apart from being able to think, we all have the ability to know and experience the world through thinking, sensing, feeling and intuition (Harding, 2009).

Good foresight is based on all four ways of knowing. It builds on our ability to anticipate a variety of future scenarios which are not only based on our understanding of current systemic dynamics and trends, but also on our sensing, feeling and intuiting into the future potential of the present moment. The practice of foresight and anticipation strengthens our awareness of system dynamics and potential future states – not as certainties but as possibilities. Identifying and collectively envisioning preferred future states are the first steps to exploring strategies for co-creating thriving, regenerative communities and cultures.

Rather than trying to manage the system through a 'command and control' approach as it were from the outside, foresight and future consciousness invites us into a new awareness and practice of 'living the questions' as embodied participants. Aware that ambiguity and uncertainty will never go away, we can give up our obsession with control; and aware of our participation and interbeing, we can take responsibility for our co-creative agency, aiming to participate appropriately through 'design for positive emergence' based on the underlying intention to benefit whole-system health by supporting regeneration and self-organization.

Regenerative cultures have to develop the resilience to know, sense, feel and intuit wise responses to disruptive change – sometimes with persistence and adaptive capacity and other times by choosing a transformative response. In order to meet this challenge, we need to deepen our understanding of the dynamics of natural change processes, informed by resilience thinking, living systems thinking and ecological literacy. All of them offer important insights into how to participate appropriately in the dynamics of complex socio-ecological systems (SESs).

In *The Pathology of Natural Resource Management*, Holling and Meffe (1996) explore several aspects of ecosystems pattern and dynamics at larger scales that provide insight into ecosystems resilience and stress the importance of retaining "critical types and ranges of natural variation in resource systems in order to maintain their resiliency" (p.328). We cannot force the complexity of nature's dynamic systems into our severely limited linear and mechanistic framework of prediction and control.

> The command-and-control approach implicitly assumes that the problem is well-bounded, clearly defined, relatively simple, and generally linear with respect to cause and effect. But when the same methods of control are applied to a complex, nonlinear, and poorly understood natural world, and when the same predictable outcomes are expected but rarely obtained, severe ecological, social and economic repercussions result.
>
> C.S. Holling and Gary Meffe (1996: 329)

Design for resilient and regenerative cultures is about facilitating positive emergence, co-creating collaborative networks of relationships that nurture the conditions in which we (life) can meet uncertainty with creativity, adaptive capacity and a readiness to transform in response to change and disruption.

From the genetic diversity of a population to the biological diversity of an ecosystem or the biosphere, diversity is life's strategy for keeping its options open in response to change. Nurturing diversity at and across different scales is best achieved by decentralized and networked distribution of vital systems functions. The resulting redundancy is not a superfluous repetition of functions at and across scales, it is a vital risk management strategy that ensures that diverse, locally adapted communities can meet their basic needs, and that the disruption of a vital function in one locality does not result in systemic failure across scales. Nurturing diversity generates requisite variety and redundancy at different spatial scales, and all three are characteristics of a resilient system. In the face of uncertainty, unpredictability and limited control, nurturing resilience in SESs is an appropriate anticipatory response to multiple risks.

Diversity is the bedrock of resilience and systemic health. In designing for resilience and systemic health we facilitate symbiotic relationships between diverse agents in the system and enable conditions for the restoration and regeneration of healthy ecosystems functioning.

Along with increased diversity and resilience, increases in bioproductivity, ecosystems functions, social cohesion, collaboration and wellbeing are all indicators of positive change in SESs and an increased capacity to respond to disruptions.

A resilient and regenerative culture aims to reverse the decline of bioproductivity through regenerative agriculture and ecosystems restoration, for example. One of the many synergistic effects of increased planetary bioproductivity, which is based on current solar income and CO_2 as a feedstock, is that carbon concentration in the atmosphere and the oceans would start to decline, as the carbon gets bio-sequestered into the corresponding increases in biomass everywhere.

There are many examples of how applying limited 'command and control thinking' to complex dynamic ecosystems has resulted in loss of diversity, decreased resilience and negative ecological and socio-economic effects. They include the disastrous effects large dams have on river ecosystems and native fish populations; the increased vulnerability to large fires resulting in severe systemic degradation that goes hand-in-hand with the suppression of frequent low intensity fires in 'managed' forest ecosystems; and the many ill-fated attempts at flood control by the canalization of rivers.

The detrimental systemic effects of energy-intensive, large-scale monoculture farming can be regarded as the "epitome of the reduction of variation and loss of resilience". Holling and Meffe conclude that the "suppression or removal of natural disturbances generally reduces system resilience" (p.331). We have to work with periodic disruptions rather than against them. They are part of the dynamics that increase systemic health and resilience. Here are some of the key lessons Holling and Meffe have learned from their comparative studies of ecosystems dynamics:

- Critical processes function at radically different rates and at spatial scales covering several orders of magnitude, and these rates and scales cluster around a few dominant frequencies.

- Scaling up from small scale to large cannot be a process of simple linear addition: non-linear processes organize the shift from one range of scales to another. Not only do the large and slow control the small and fast, the latter occasionally 'revolt' to affect the former.

- On the one hand, destabilizing forces are important in maintaining diversity, resilience, and opportunity. On the other hand, stabilizing forces are important in maintaining productivity and biogeochemical cycles, and, even when these features are perturbed, they recover rapidly if the stability domain is not exceeded.

- Ecosystems are moving targets, with multiple potential futures that are uncertain and unpredictable. Therefore management has to be flexible, adaptive, and experimental at scales compatible with the scales of critical ecosystems functioning.

C.S. Holling & Gary Meffe (1996)

I believe that these insights abstracted from the long-term study of dynamics in ecosystems can also inform appropriate participation in SESs. We need to be conscious of these lessons in our attempt to co-create communities, businesses and economies that are scale-sensitive, persistent, adaptable and transform appropriately in response to change.

Conscious participation in complex systems is about sensitivity to temporal and spatial scale-linking dynamics. *We need to learn to surf the 'edge of chaos' between structure, dissolution and transformative innovation.* Dynamic health embraces chaos and stability, each at the appropriate scale and time. Resilience thinking helps us to identify and then intentionally design pathways that support the emergence of systemic health as a basis for regeneration. Giles Hutchins draws some useful conclusions in *The Nature of Business – Redesigning for Resilience*.

> In becoming aware of the ever-present cycles of life within everything, inward and outward, we learn to recognise the breakdowns and breakthroughs as positive stages in our evolutions. Our organizations ought not to expend vital energy trying to control their environments, trying to resist any part of the adaptive cycle other than [excessive quantitative] growth. This is resisting evolution, and it is a futile waste of energy, while also slowing down effective transformation for the organization within its dynamic business environment. Of far greater use is the awareness and understanding of the dynamic environment one is operating in and the ability to adapt to it. Some parts of the organization may be in a rapid growth stage, while others may simultaneously be declining and heading for rebirth.
>
> Giles Hutchins (2012: 63)

CHAPTER 5

WHY TAKE A DESIGN-BASED APPROACH?

> If we don't change our direction, we're likely to end up where we're headed.
>
> Chinese Proverb

If we accept that questions rather than answers, and continuous experimentation rather than lock-in solutions are safer ways to guide us through these turbulent times and into the unpredictable future, then we also have to accept that there is a limit to the extent to which we can *design* our future in the face of complexity and uncertainty. Nevertheless, taking a design-based approach offers us a practical way to propose and implement solutions in order to continue to learn and improve our guiding questions.

On the one hand we have to accept that the future will remain unpredictable and uncontrollable; and on the other hand we can work creatively with the future potential of the present moment to envision and navigate towards the third horizon. Collective visioning focuses our attention on futures we want to co-create. It can help us agree on what we value and set the intentions that will inform our practice of regenerative design.

Culture change is first and foremost about a collective shift in perspective and consciousness, leading to a shift in values, intentions and behaviour. The technologies we employ and the designs we implement both support these changes and manifest our intentions materially and in the systems and structures we set up. Yet these relationships are circular, not linear. Our awareness and perspectives influence our behaviour, the technologies we employ and the way we 'design' solutions; while past designs and past solutions continue to shape our worldview and awareness.

We are all designers! We all co-create the world we live in through our relationships and our behaviour as citizens, community members and consumers. We all have real and perceived needs and we all *design* our own strategies to meet those needs. We all have intentions about what we would like to do and what kind of change we would like to see in the world; the ways we act (or fail to act) in accordance with those intentions are acts of design. Our intentions influence both our action and our inaction, they shape how we co-create the world.

Every time I spend a unit of currency on anything, I am directly participating in either maintaining past design decisions (possibly without questioning them) or encouraging a shift towards a regenerative culture by supporting ethical and sustainable business practices. The products and services we choose and offer in our work are important ways we all participate in the co-creation and design of the culture we live in. The stories we tell about ourselves, the education we offer our children, the way we share our wealth (of ideas, compassion, experience or money) all influence not just our lives but the culture we are co-creating.

> "Every act of knowing brings forth a world [...] All doing is knowing, and all knowing is doing [...] We have only the world we bring forth with others [...]"
>
> Maturana & Varela (1987: 25 & 249)

Design, in its broadest possible sense, can help us to integrate the remarkable wealth of specialized knowledge, skill and shared aspiration that rests within humanity. Design should not be considered a specialized field of human endeavour; rather, it can be understood as the integrative activity that connects human intentions to their material and cultural expression in the form of artefacts, institutions and processes. A design-based approach will not only help us to integrate many different perspectives and disciplines, it will also remind us that for the transition to be effective it will have to include not just a sound scientific basis informed by systemic thinking, but also ethical, aesthetic, social, cultural, economic and, of course, ecological considerations.

If we define design in its broadest sense, as *human intentionality expressed through interactions and relationships*, it becomes clear that any change that affects human intentions will redirect the entire design landscape downstream from that shift in intentionality. At first glance this design definition might sound a little broad, but if you think about it, whether we apply it to a product like a chair that expresses certain functional and aesthetic intentions of the designer, or to a monetary system that is also designed to perform a certain function based on a set of intentions, the definition holds. In the case of the chair the interactions and relationships are more focused on the different materials, production processes and spatial geometries involved, but also include the way the object, its designer, producer, distributor and user interact with the chair, and through it relate to each other. In the case of services and systems, for example a particular monetary system, design defines and shapes the interactions and relationships between the users of that particular medium of exchange. Design expresses *and* creates culture!

Design education enables cultural transformation

> Our eyes do not divide us from the world, but they unite us to it. Let this be known to be true. Let us abandon the simplicity of separation and give unity its due. Let us abandon the self-mutilation that has been our way [...]
>
> Ian L. McHarg (1969: 5)

> What we need is an education for collective living rather than for individual success. The collective to which we need to pay more attention includes all the other species of this planet.
>
> Brian Goodwin (2001)

In 2001, after an unsuccessful attempt to create a sustainability education centre and ecovillage in Southern Spain, I enrolled in the Masters in Holistic Science at Schumacher

College. At the time the word 'sustainability' had not yet entered the vocabulary of the vast majority of industrial designers and academic design educators. My own contact with 'designing' until then had been through the study and application of Bill Mollison's *Permaculture – A Designer's Manual* (1988) and a series of courses and internships at the Centre for Alternative Technology in Wales, where I had learned about the design of timber frame structures, basic ecological sewage treatment systems, compost toilets and off-the-grid photovoltaic, micro-wind and micro-hydro systems.

At Schumacher College I had the good fortune to attend a course with John Todd and Nancy Jack-Todd, two elders of the ecological design field and co-founders of the New Alchemy Institute in 1969, and David Orr, the USA's foremost environmental educator. After spending 3 weeks with them in the unique 'small is beautiful' environment of the enchanting Old Postern that houses the college, *the importance and transformative agency of design* suddenly struck me. I understood that the practice end of the emerging worldview we were exploring in holistic science (complexity theory, chaos theory, Goethean science, Gaia theory, deep ecology and eco-psychology) was in fact *design*. I realized that the overarching shift from, as Brian Goodwin put it, prediction and control of nature to *appropriate participation* in nature, would have to be implemented in our ways of living *by* and *through design*. As David Orr explains:

> The problem is simply how a species pleased to call itself *Homo sapiens* fits on a planet with a biosphere. This is a design problem and requires a design philosophy. The very idea that we need to build a sustainable civilization needs to be invented or rediscovered, then widely disseminated, and put into practice quickly.
>
> David W. Orr (2002: 50)

In my Master's thesis I argued that "ecological design is a participatory, interdisciplinary, community-based process that takes place, scale and appropriateness seriously and considers potential solutions within a holistic context" (Wahl, 2002: 58) and suggested that all design should aim to increase diversity and resilience as a means to increasing whole-systems health. During my time at Schumacher College I met Professor Seaton Baxter[†] who later supervised my PhD research. In 2008, he and I co-authored a paper in *Design Issues* in which we suggested that integral theory (Wilber, 2001), spiral dynamics (Beck & Cowan, 1996) and integral ecology (Esbjörn-Hargen, 2005; Zimmerman, 2005) offered designers a framework for facilitating multi-stakeholder dialogue and the integration of diverse perspectives in support of more sustainable and culturally transformative solutions:

> Designing for sustainability not only requires the redesign of our habits, lifestyles, and practices, but also of the way we think about design. Sustainability is a process of coevolution and co-design that involves diverse communities in making flexible and adaptable design decisions on local, regional, and global scales. The transition towards sustainability is about co-creating a human civilization that flourishes within the ecological limits of the planetary life support system […] Design plays a central role in shaping a

sustainable civilization. It does so in the material dimensions of product design, architecture, industrial design, and town and regional planning, as well as in the immaterial dimension of the metadesign of concepts and inclusive multiperspectives from which a holistic/integral worldview can emerge.

Daniel Wahl & Seaton Baxter (2008: 72-74)

The application of integral theory to design has since been taken up by a number of design practitioners and academics. In *Design Education for a Sustainable Future*, Rob Fleming (2013) applied Ken Wilber's integral framework (2001) and Mark DeKay's methodology for *Integral Sustainable Design* (2011) to reframing the role of design educators. Fleming argues that we need to reconsider design education "as an essential tool in the larger societal movement towards a sustainable future" (p.xxv) and asks the important question:

> Q How can design educators better reflect the zeitgeist of the new century by moving from well-intentioned but lightweight 'greening' to deeper and more impactful ideals of sustainability and resilience? (p.1)

Fleming stresses that "evolving the design professions to higher states of consciousness does not demand a paradigm shift so much as it does the transcendence to a new more integrated worldview, and the inclusion of all preceding worldviews"; and says that "the approach of 'both and' or 'transcend and include' recognizes the continuing value of all previous world views and plays an essential role in the establishment of new design consciousness not as a choice between the past and the present, but rather as an additional motivation to pursue sustainability" (p.4).

At a time when we are drowning in information and knowledge, while thirsting for meaning and wisdom, we need new pathways towards synthesis and integration. Fleming points to the fact that "design education, especially the studio, is one of the most powerfully effective vehicles for learning across the entire spectrum of higher education" (p.7). I agree with his conviction that "design educators hold the promise of a sustainable future in the hearts and minds of the students they teach". His book offers a wealth of useful frameworks and methodologies for students and educators alike. It will contribute further to the silent (r)evolution that is currently changing design education to serve the transition towards a regenerative human presence on Earth.

Gideon Kossoff (2011a) has recently articulated a framework for the emerging field of *transition design*. He explores the implications of a holistic participatory worldview for a design-led transition towards a more sustainable society through the reinvention of the domains of everyday life by design.

> The transition to a sustainable society will require the reconstitution and reinvention of households, villages, neighbourhoods, towns, cities and regions everywhere on the planet as interdependent, nested, self-organized, participatory and diversified wholes. [...] The result will be a decentralized and diversified structure of everyday life which is in contrast to the centralized and increasingly homogenized structures that we have become accustomed to. [...]

> Reconstituting the Domains is an inherently transdisciplinary and grassroots process that represents an opportunity to reintegrate and recontextualize knowledge, embedding it in both community and everyday life. It calls for the intentional, or designed, reintegration of all facets of everyday life in place, and suggests that a new kind of designer is needed, a *transition designer*.
>
> Gideon Kossoff (2011b: 22-23)

In collaboration with Terry Irwin and Cameron Tonkinwise, Gideon has help to establish a PhD programme in transition design and a professional doctorate (DDes) programme that includes transition design at Carnegie Mellon University's prestigious School of Design. They define *transition design* as "design-led, systems-level societal change towards a more sustainable future" and suggest "transition designers will use the tools and processes of design to re-conceive whole lifestyles and develop infrastructures, policies, systems (food, healthcare, education) and energy resources to support a more sustainable society" (Carnegie Mellon Design, 2015).

The approaches to transformative innovation and design for regenerative cultures explored in this book are *transition approaches*. They recognize that solutions are moving targets rather than fixed states. The community-based practice of living the questions is an invitation to take the design conversations about how to support the transition to a more sustainable future and regenerative culture beyond the academic environment and into the heart of communities, businesses and governance everywhere. Design education will be a critical enabler of the transition ahead. Well-facilitated design conversations can invite all of us to explore the transition within our communities, to collaborate with and learn from each other so we all become more effective in our role as transition designers. Design education can enable cooperative cultural transformation. We have to create a new kind of partnership between universities, civil society, the private sector, and governance by initiating integrative design conversations.

> Transition designers deploy a deep understanding of the interconnectedness of social and natural systems and conceive solutions that leverage the power of interdependency and symbiosis. We explore the role of design in negotiating between the transition our society is undergoing and the transition that it needs to make.
>
> Carnegie Mellon Design (2015)

Terry Irwin writes: "Until designers shift to a more holistic worldview, design will continue to be part of the problem, not the solution" (2012); and elsewhere: "One of the most fundamental changes for designers and design process will be a shift in focus from objects to relationship [...] An organic model of society and environment will replace the dominant, mechanistic one and this in turn will suggest a more respectful, iterative and inclusive process for designing solutions" (Irwin, 2011).

The number of design-focused programmes that share the *transition* perspective is growing steadily. Among them are Gaia University's programme in 'Integrative eco-social design', Gaia Education's 'Design for Sustainability', the Environmental Studies program at

Oberlin College and the postgraduate programme in 'Ecological Design Thinking' at Schumacher College. Other aligned programmes include Cornell University's programme in Sustainable and Regenerative Design; Regenerative Ecological Design at Prescott College, and the Sustainable Design programme at Philadelphia University.

Ezio Manzini's work at the Interdepartmental Centre for Research on Innovation for Sustainability at Milan Polytechnic has played a pivotal role in transforming the design community from within. He and François Jégou (2004) invite designers to ask important questions and to take an active role in envisioning and shaping a sustainable future:

- What might everyday life be like in a sustainable society?

- How will you take care of yourself and other people?

- How will you work, study and move around?

- How will you cultivate a network of personal and social relationships and create an undistorted relationship with the environment?

- What do the sustainable societies we are able to imagine today have in common?

- How wide a range of options do we have open to us on the basis of these common elements?

Manzini and Jégou have created the Sustainable Everyday Project as an open web platform to stimulate social conversation on possible sustainable futures. Manzini is also president of the 'Design for Social Innovation and Sustainability' (DESIS) Network, which works "with local, regional, and global partners to promote and support social change towards sustainability". The network's vision statement highlights that "social innovation is spreading and its potential, as a driver of sustainable change, is increasing. To facilitate this process, the design community, in general, and design schools, in particular, can play a pivotal role" (DESIS, 2015).

At Griffith University, Tony Fry, who created the EcoDesign Foundation in 1991, leads a Design Futures programme that aims to "better educate designers […] to become change agents, research based practitioners, critics, entrepreneurs, theorists, strategist and practical intellectuals" (Design Futures, 2015). Stuart Walker directs a research group in sustainable design at Imagination Lancaster. Bill Reed teaches integrative design at the Graduate School of Design at Harvard and the University of British Columbia. Alastair Fuad-Luke explores design as 'co-futuring' as Professor for Emerging Design Practices at Aalto University and Martin Charter directs the Centre for Sustainable Design at University College for the Creative Arts (UCCA).

By no means is this list exhaustive and there are many more design programmes worth mentioning, but the people and programmes mentioned here have all made an important contribution to taking the dialogue about the sustainability transition into design academia and professional design practice. They share an understanding of the central role of design and design education in cultural transformation towards sustainability. As such they are catalyst for the emergence of regenerative cultures.

Last but not least I would like to mention Gonzalo Salazar, at the Universidad Católica de Chile, who is working along similar lines. He also received his PhD at the Centre for the Study of Natural Design. I am indebted to Gonzalo for helping me appreciate more deeply how central *conversation* is to design. In a poetic language that carries the imprint of his native Chile, the land of Pablo Neruda, Humberto Maturana, Francisco Varela and Manfred Max-Neef, Gonzalo's doctorate concludes:

> Design is a human conversation about facilitating our existence in conversation […] design only becomes ecological when it is mainly guided by the emotion of loving through the ongoing process of creating and cultivating our (sense of) being at home in the world. […] attentive listening is the first and most important action of ecological design. […] ecological design is fundamentally cooperative. It is co-creation, co-facilitation; it is co-designing in love.
>
> Gonzalo Salazar-Preece (2011: 398-401)

Design is where theory and practice meet

All design is either consciously or unconsciously an expression of our theories about the world – our culturally dominant worldview. The shift from our current industrial growth society to a life-sustaining society of diverse regenerative cultures is fundamentally a shift in metadesign from the 'narrative of separation' to the 'narrative of interbeing'. Our worldview shapes our designs and our designs reinforce the worldview they were created in. That is one of the reasons why we cannot solve today's problems within the worldview that created these problems in the first place. Past design solutions in the form of the products, services and systems around us influence and reinforce culturally dominant perspectives, processes, structures and behaviours, mostly without questioning them.

We are faced with an urgent need for systemic transformation in so many aspects of our lives. Whether you live in London, New York or a 'slum' settlement on the outskirts of one of the world's rapidly growing mega-cities, people are calling for practical action and react with impatience if they perceive an approach to be 'too theoretical' rather than immediately practical and able to make a difference in the short term. I have experienced this bias against 'theory' and toward 'practical action' in my work with local, regional and national government officials, in consultancy work with individual businesses or business clusters of different industries, and in work with grassroots initiatives like ecovillage or transition town projects, even in many educational initiatives.

In my opinion, the separation of theory and practice is another false dualism that we have to learn to overcome. By classifying initiatives as either theoretical or practical we are not paying attention to the fact that our view of the world is already deeply informed by theories about the world. In saying "we don't have time to waste with theoretical considerations, let's get practical and start implementing solutions", what we are actually implying is that there is no need to question our perspective and explore alternative perspectives. We are jumping straight into action, offering answers to the questions and solutions to the problems at hand, without stepping back to make sure we are asking the right questions. We fail to explore whether the solutions we are aiming for are yet again solving one issue whilst causing harm and ugliness elsewhere.

Every practical act is deeply informed by a whole set of theories and perspectives. So the question is not whether we are practical or theoretical, but rather whether we are implementing practice in full awareness of the theoretical frameworks - the worldview and value systems - that inform our practice. Taking a design-based approach can help us to make our practice more theoretical and our theory more practical.

Design is at the nexus of theory and practice. Design is where art and science meet. In fact, it integrates information from almost all the disciplines into which we have separated human knowing and doing. Design is how we can acknowledge the influences of the past and give birth to visions of a different future. We all live our lives within buildings, cities, transport systems, economic systems, land use patterns and food systems that have been designed for a particular purpose at a particular point in time. Yet design goes on designing. In many of the world's cities, we move between buildings that were built decades and even centuries ago.

The transition towards diverse regenerative cultures, elegantly adapted to the uniqueness of the places they inhabit, will require us to re-examine how we have designed the world around us, our communities and institutions. We will have to combine the best of traditional, place-based wisdom, with the appropriate kind of modern technologies and innovation, and find creative ways to meet human needs, everywhere, within the limits of the natural cycles that sustain all life on Earth.

> As *Homo sapiens's* entry in any intergalactic design competition, industrial civilization would be tossed out at the qualifying round. It doesn't fit. It won't last. The scale is wrong. And even its apologists admit that it is not very pretty. The design failures of industrially / technologically driven societies are manifest in the loss of diversity of all kinds, destabilization of the earth's biogeochemical cycles, pollution, soil erosion, ugliness, poverty, injustice, social decay, and economic instability.
>
> David W. Orr (1994: 104)

Asking deeper questions and shifting the gravity of our approach away from quick answers and one-size-fits-all solutions is an invitation to become more conscious of how particular worldviews and value systems influence design and behaviour. If we change how we think of ourselves and the stories we tell about who we are and about our relationship with wider natural processes, we are making an up-stream change that will affect *why*, *how* and *what* we design.

Equally, just because complex and interconnected problems are hard to solve, it will not help to divide these issues into smaller and seemingly easier-to-solve problems. Such an approach, at best, leads us to temporarily alleviate symptoms, while the underlying problems might actually get worse.

Over and over again we commit the same mistake in politics, business, health care and other fields. We tend to treat symptoms rather than causes, while continuing with the worldview and the behaviour patterns that caused the problems in the first place.

Good whole-systems designs can make us more aware of *both* what we think and what we do. They can invite choices and behaviour change. Design-led system transformation in all aspects of our lives has a very practical influence on the world we live in and the cultures we co-create.

Design follows worldview and worldview follows design

How we see the world influences the real or perceived needs that inform our intentions. If I see the world as a place dominated by fierce competition for limited resources, I will fight others to get my own needs met. I will live a different life, interpret experiences in a different way, and design different products, services and systems, if I see the world as a place of abundance to be shared in solidarity and collaboration within the human family and with deep care for the ecosystems functions that are the basis for this abundance. These two different perspectives lead to fundamentally different approaches to defining our real and perceived needs and to meeting these needs by either competitive or collaborative means. *Design follows worldview.*

It is also true that, as Winston Churchill put it, "first we shape our buildings and then our buildings shape us". The design of buildings, products, services and systems is how we shape the world around us and these designs keep influencing our lives for decades and even centuries, as we maintain or replicate past design decisions in many cases without questioning them. Most of us grew up and were educated in a culture that primarily subscribed to the perspective of scarcity and competition – 'the narrative of separation'. The institutions, processes and incentives that shaped our experience of the world were informed by that point of view and thus reinforced experiences of competition and relative scarcity. The education system, the economic system and the way we relate with nature and with other human beings through the products and services we produce and exchange, all reinforce experiences of scarcity and competition. The design decisions we have taken in the past are continuing to influence how we experience and interpret the world. *Worldview follows design.*

So transformative innovation towards a regenerative culture is both about a shift in the worldview that informs our design solutions and a shift in design practice towards products, services and systems that engender experiences of collaboration and abundance that affect how we see the world. Since the relationship between worldview and design is mutually reinforcing, we can start by intervening in either. Transformative innovation and design for a regenerative culture is about enabling people to experience and live the 'narrative of interbeing' as a personal and social reality.

Design intentionally shapes interactions and relationships. It can do so in ways that favour the collaborative creation and sharing of abundance, or in ways that reinforce the narrative of separation. The recent upsurge of transformative social innovation –

enabled by online networks – is a good example of this. In particular, many innovations in the field of 'collaborative consumption' (see Chapter 2) enable people to gain economic benefit, human interaction and new friends and relationships by simply sharing access to a product or commodity that they would have previously owned and used 'only for themselves'. Collaborative consumption *by design* creates win-win-win situations. Its diverse applications give us a reinforcing experience of *shared abundance*, collaboration and trust. Transformative innovation for a regenerative culture will largely spread through this reciprocal relationship between design and worldview, turning the vicious circle driven by the mindset of scarcity and competition into a virtuous circle driven by the mindset of abundance, interconnection and collaboration.

Ethics and design for regenerative cultures

> Design is not so much about making things as about how to make things that fit gracefully over long periods of time in a particular ecological, social, and cultural context.
>
> David W. Orr (2002: 27)

Important lessons about environmental ethics can be learned from the world's traditional/indigenous cultures. Many of them managed to create regenerative systems that allowed them to live in a particular place for millennia. In Western culture, it was the conservation ecologist Aldo Leopold who provided the first modern formulation of an ecological and environmental ethic. He proposed that: "A thing is right when it tends to preserve the integrity, stability, and beauty of the biotic community; it is wrong when it does otherwise" (1949: 224). Leopold emphasized that ethics is not only a philosophical and social but also an ecological 'process'. Ethics ultimately concerns the relationship between the individual and the collective, aiming to define and guide appropriate participation in our immediate community, the human family and the community of life as a whole.

Moralizing masquerading as ethics can quickly be identified when we pay attention to the ecological component of ethics. Leopold argued that "the extension of ethics to include man's relationship to the environment" is an "evolutionary possibility" but an "ecological necessity". As such, "an ethic ecologically, is a limitation of freedom of action in the struggle for existence. An ethic, philosophically, is a differentiation of social from anti-social conduct." Leopold pointed out that "these are two definitions of one thing which has its origin in the tendency of interdependent individuals and groups to evolve modes of cooperation" (1949: 202).

Ethics in its wider context is not only about guiding human interactions within exclusively human communities. A solely philosophical ethic, considered only within the social and cultural dimension, is often criticized for moralizing from the position of a single cultural and societal context and set of values. The wider function of ethics – its *ecological imperative* – extends beyond anthropocentric concerns to biocentric concern for the continuing evolution of life.

The Australian eco-designer and design theorist, Tony Fry, calls for designers to stop absolving themselves from their ethical responsibilities by delegating these responsibilities to their clients. Beyond a basic code of professional conduct, the ethical implications of any design need to be discussed during the early stages of the design process. Fry argues: "an ethics of now crucially needs to confront our anthropocentric being as a structurally unethical condition" (2004).

The emergence of a biocentric ethic also found early expression in the work of Ian McHarg (1969) who insisted that humanity has to learn the "prime ecological lesson of interdependence" and understand that all humans are "linked as living organisms to all living and all preceding life". He was convinced that through understanding our interdependence "with the micro-organisms of the soil" and "the diatoms of the sea" humanity would learn that when it destroys nature it destroys itself and when it restores nature it restores itself (1963). This insight lies at the heart of the transition towards a restorative and regenerative culture, whether motivated by enlightened self-interest or *biophilia* – our innate love for all of life.

McHarg gave the opening address for the first Earth Day celebration in 1971 and his CBS television series 'The House We Live In' contributed significantly to the first wave of environmental awareness and ecological consciousness that swept the USA in the late 1960s and early '70s. McHarg foresaw the need to reintegrate human activity and the operating conditions of our planet's life support system. He was among the first to point out that when we design for sustainability and human survival and flourishing, what we are effectively trying to do is to support the systemic health of the whole system upon which we depend.

> Because this whole system is in fact one system, only divided by men's minds and by the myopia which is called education, there is another simple term which synthesizes the degree to which an invention is creative and accomplishes a creative fitting. And this is the presence of health.
>
> Ian L. McHarg (1970)

McHarg's definition of 'Design with nature' was a practice of design that increases interconnectedness, diversity, fitness and health throughout the system as a whole. To McHarg the system in question is nature *and* culture. He argues that culture change is the most rapidly adaptable way to re-establish a creative fit between humanity and nature. Biological adaptations to a changing environment take a lot longer to evolve than cultural adaptations. McHarg called for a shift from a culture that is intent on controlling and exploiting nature to a culture actively aiming for the restoration of the Earth and the health of nature (1996). He was one the earliest design professionals to promote transformative innovation for a regenerative culture, even if he did not use these terms.[†]

Before implementing any design solution we would do well to apply a series of checks to evaluate whether the proposed solutions are systemically integrated enough to contribute to the long-term health and resilience of people and planet. David Orr suggested that ecological design is about asking deeper questions. The list of questions below includes ones that he proposes we ask about any new design (adapted from Orr, 2002: 28). I could not resist adding two additional questions at the end.

5: Why Take a Design-Based Approach?

- Q Do we really need this new design?
- Q Is it ethical to produce, market and consume the new design in the intended way?
- Q What impact does the design have on the community that produces or employs it?
- Q Is it really safe to make and use the proposed design?
- Q Is it fair? (Does it contribute to greater social, economic and ecological equity without any form of exploitation?)
- Q Is it designed to be repairable and can it be reused over a long period?
- Q What is the full cost over its expected lifetime in terms of social, ecological and economic capital?
- Q Does this new design truly offer a better way to meet certain needs than already existing designs?
- Q How can we ensure that the proposed design does no harm *and* actively helps to restore damage already incurred – regenerating our capacity to meet an unpredictable future with community resilience?
- Q How does the design actively reinforce our lived experience of a regenerative culture and the 'narrative of interbeing'?

Aesthetics and design

In 2003 I attended a talk by William McDonough and Michael Braungart at a construction industry trade fair in Barcelona. They opened with this question:

- Q Can anything be truly beautiful if it causes ugliness, suffering or ill health anywhere else?

Most design academics and professionals suffer from a certain self-importance regarding their capacity to make aesthetic judgements while simultaneously holding a rather shallow and trend-serving notion of beauty. In sharp contrast, the indigenous people of the Navajo tribe describe their traditional way of living as the 'beauty way'. To them living in right relationship with the Earth is to 'walk in beauty' (*Hózhóogo Naasháa Doo*) and their advice is: 'if you walk into the future walk in beauty'. The way to walk in beauty is to 'witness the One-in-All and the All-in-One'. It is a path of appropriate relationship to self, to community and to the Earth. We have a lot to learn from this insight. It may guide us on our uncertain path towards a future where humanity has learned to be a regenerative rather than a destructive presence on Earth. It may also help us deepen into an ecological aesthetic of health and complexity.

The platitude 'beauty lies in the eye of the beholder' turns out to be a profound insight into the way we perceive beauty based on our culturally dominant worldview. The way we see the world determines our aesthetic experience. We already established in Chapter 3 that what we choose to pay attention to, and how we interpret the 'facts about reality' we are selecting, depends on already established beliefs we hold about the world. Likewise, our aesthetic perception is not a simple one-way process where we open our eyes and the world floods in and we see what is 'out there'. Rather, we employ organizing ideas, or beliefs about the world, to make sense of our perception and thereby structure what-is-seen in such a way that it makes sense to us. *Perception is a two-way process.* The act of seeing involves visual stimuli coming in and organizing ideas going out, or better 'making sense' of what is coming in. *Seeing is interpreting.*

Beauty thus depends to a large extent on what we have learned to see as beautiful. Beauty is primarily about relationships and our perception of relationships. Nicolas Bourriaud (1998), the director of the École Nationale Supérieure des Beaux-Arts in Paris, speaks of a "relational aesthetics" and Jale Erzen, a Turkish artist, architect, and member of the International Association of Aesthetics, equates the term relational aesthetics with ecological aesthetics, since ecology is fundamentally about interdependence and relationship. "Aesthetics and ecology can be said to be complementary and interdependent" (Erzen, 2004: 22). Aesthetics is a participatory exploration of the relationship between the one and the all. This understanding of aesthetics is getting closer to the traditional Navajo view.

The German artist Herman Prigann believes that the root of environmental problems lies in our "inability to understand the dialogue between nature and culture that defines their relationship through mutual dependence" (2004: 111). In Prigann's opinion the environmental problems we face demand "a new capacity for aesthetic judgement" (p.75). "It is not ecology that needs an aesthetic treatment, instead the aesthetic follows ecological insights. Nature does not need an aesthetic domestication" (p.180). Ecological aesthetics mediates an important shift in perception:

> An ecological aesthetic would be a perspective on our environment and society as well as the ensuing theory and practice. This perspective would annul current, standard contradictions such as nature – art // nature – technology // nature – civilization // nature – culture and proceed towards an insight of the principle of dialogue in and towards everything.
>
> Hermann Prigann (2004: 180)

Echoing Gregory Bateson's suggestion that we search for 'the pattern that connects', Prigann sees aesthetics as "the recognition of the pattern that connects everything". He believes that "through attentiveness to pattern, that connection in everything – the universal togetherness – evolves an aesthetic perspective of perception". In a regenerative culture, our perception of beauty and our aesthetic judgement would come to depend upon the effect that art, design and architecture, or indeed any creative activity, has on life as a whole. Once we begin to see things in their context – from a systemic perspective that is informed by ecological awareness of the impacts of production and consumption – what we perceive as beautiful changes. Aesthetic judgement informed by ecological literacy is not only influenced by how something looks but by a deeper questioning of how it was made, out of what materials, by whom and under what conditions.

Edwin Datschefski explores this expanded understanding of beauty in *The Total Beauty of Sustainable Products* (2001) and William McDonough and Michael Braungart (2002) build on Datschefski's concept of 'total beauty' in their ground-breaking book *Cradle to Cradle – Remaking the Way We Make Things*. Aesthetics, as a participatory and systemic understanding of our relationship with the rest of nature, is about perceiving beauty as an expression of our belonging and being in relationship. Beauty in a regenerative culture is about health, diversity, participation in complexity and about ethically appropriate relationships that create conditions conducive to life. A new aesthetic sensitivity of *interbeing* is emerging:

> Health is a term for the aesthetic understanding of complexity. There is a thread connecting biodiversity, cultural diversity and economic diversity. This is the metaphorical understanding of the health of a complex dynamic system. […] The perception of health is a relative term, it requires intimate knowledge over a period of time and a caring critical attention. In turn, a lack of health can be described in terms of emergent dominant systems that mitigate the constraint of diversity. […] Within the aesthetic perception of diversity lies systemic relationship, dynamism, complexity, symbiosis, contradiction to measurement and indefinite and procreative vitality.
>
> Timothy Collins (2004: 172)

In a regenerative culture any design, whether a product, a building, a community, or processes, services and systems, will be judged on its overall impact on health, resilience and sustainability. Any act of 'making' engenders the responsibility of material and energy use along with all other ways that the result affects the whole process in which it participates. The aesthetics of regenerative cultures will value how we can '*witness the One-in-All and the All-in-One*' in everything. Beauty draws us in and gives us a direct experience of our intimate communion with the world around us.

> *If it's not beautiful, it's not sustainable.* Aesthetic attraction is not a superficial concern – it's an environmental imperative. Beauty could save the world.
>
> Lance Hosey (2012: 7)

Emergence and design

> The beauty of living things stems from the fact that they are embodied solutions of individual-existence-in-connection.
>
> Andreas Weber (2013: 38)

I mentioned before that one of the key insights of complexity theory is the profound shift in perspective that results from acknowledging the fundamentally unpredictable and uncontrollable nature of complex dynamic systems.† The concept of *emergence*, which has become popular in management and design theory, describes how complex systems have characteristic emergent properties that cannot be predicted and therefore are impossible to control. They are novel characteristics of the system that emerge out of interactions and relationships which are governed by non-linear, iterative processes that drive the behaviour of complex systems.

Jeffrey Goldstein (1999: 49) defined emergence as referring to "the arising of novel and coherent structures, patterns and properties during the process of self-organization in complex systems". Emergence takes place at a higher explanatory level and the novel forms, behaviours and properties of the whole system "are neither predictable from, deducible from, nor reducible to the parts alone" (p.50). Brian Goodwin explains: "Emergent properties are unexpected types of order that arise from interactions between components whose separate behaviour is understood. Something new emerges from the collective – another source of unpredictability in nature." He continues: "The complex systems on which our lives depend – ecological systems, communities, economic systems, our bodies – all have emergent properties, a primary one being health and well-being" (Goodwin *et al.*, 2001: 27).

This insight has important implications for any exploration of how transformative innovation might facilitate the co-creation of a regenerative culture. It suggests that in working towards the health, wellbeing and resilience of our communities, economies and ecosystems we will always have to be prepared for the unexpected and new arising from the complex dynamics that characterize these systems.

> Q How do we facilitate the emergence of positive, salutogenic (health-supporting) systems properties and discourage the emergence of auto-destructive and pathological system properties?

Some properties like health, resilience and wellbeing might be regarded as desirable emergent properties, others might be regarded as undesirable: for example, fragility, sudden collapse of vital functions, and negative impacts on all or some system components.

> Q If the systems upon which our future depends are fundamentally unpredictable, how do we learn to participate in them appropriately?

> Q Can we actually design for human, community, ecosystem and planetary health, if these are in effect emergent properties of interdependent complex dynamic systems at different scales?

> Q Can we influence the emergence of positive systemic properties in our economies, societies and communities?

Since we cannot but participate in these systems and therefore cannot but affect them in one way or another, we simply have to try. If we do so with precaution, foresight and in constant awareness and anticipation of unpredictable change, I believe we can attempt to *design for positive emergence* by *designing for whole-systems health*. It is best to regard emergence and design as two sides of the same coin. As participants in these systems we are *all* co-responsible for what properties will emerge. Both the quality of our being and what we do or don't do affects the overall health and wellbeing of the complex dynamic systems we participate in.

Brian Goodwin taught me that the most important lesson of complexity science is a *shift of intention away from prediction and control to appropriate participation*. The mental, emotional and psychological state of an intervener affects the outcome of any systems intervention. If we stop wanting to control change and shift to a responsive dance with change, we will become more effective change agents capable of facilitating positive emergence. In doing so we become transition designers.

I believe that to design for appropriate participation is ultimately to design for human and planetary health. By paying attention to the underlying dynamics of the complex systems we participate in, we can learn how to increase their overall resilience, health and wellbeing. Resilience thinking and whole-systems thinking are crucial skills for transition design. So how do we design for positive emergence? One way is to support the ability of a complex dynamic system to keep adapting, learning and responding to internal and external changes. We can start by asking these questions:

- Q Are we weaving the appropriate synergies by valuing the degree and quality of interconnections between the different components or agents in the system?

- Q Are we paying enough attention to the diversity and quality of interacting systems components and their interdependence?

- Q Are we designing for the renewable use of vital resources (like energy and materials) on which these systems depend?

- Q Are we paying attention to the quality and speed of information that flows through these systems to enable the different components to learn from systemic feedback loops?

By paying attention to these questions we can effectively embrace the seeming paradox of unpredictable emergence and intentional design for systemic health and a regenerative culture.

Designing for positive emergence (a case study)

The last three sections on ethics, aesthetics and complexity might seem theoretical, but, as we saw earlier, to break through to a new way of thinking about our problems, we need to ask deeper questions about the theories that currently inform our practice.

Let me make the theory more palpable by relating it to aspects of the long-term project to promote transformative innovation and the transition towards a regenerative culture on the Mediterranean island of Majorca, where I live.

Clearly, even at the relatively small scale and within the defined boundaries of the island, I cannot predict – much less control – all the possible parameters that will affect whether the transition towards increased resilience, sustainability and a regenerative culture will be successful, nor can I force the speed of the transition. Yet I firmly believe that systemic interventions through processes that involve diverse stakeholders will contribute to this deeper culture change.

One useful entry point is the issue of local food production and the link between food and wellbeing, as well as food production and ecosystems health and societal resilience. I can't control to what extent the transition towards increased local organic food production will result from the systems interventions I engage in. Yet working with unpredictability and emergence rather than against it, I can facilitate the interconnections between certain parts of the system that were previously not talking to each other. The degree of interconnection and the quality of connections (what kind of relationships are established) do affect the behaviour of complex systems and the emergent properties they exhibit.

For example, facilitating meetings between the island's agricultural cooperatives and a large commercial kitchen that supplies hospitals, schools, business canteens and some hotels helped to initiate a dialogue about how this kitchen could include more local produce in its meal plans. This offered the kitchen and its clients an opportunity to support the local economy and will help to increase sales and eventually even the production of local foods. Since the kitchen has multiple customers, the project initiated a cascade of conversations that in many cases are the first step towards educating the people responsible for procurement about the systemic benefits of choosing regionally produced products.

A relatively small intervention can thereby affect the information flow in the wider system, via the newly facilitated connections and relationships and through the existing networks of the different stakeholders. What kind of information the system relies on crucially affects emergent behaviour. So, to stay with the example, educating farmers, hotel owners, local government, permanent residents and multipliers (like educators, academics, activists and journalists) about the potential impact of rapid increases in transport costs and food price – due to spiking oil proces, climate chaos, terrorist scenarios, food price speculation or economic crisis – will make the system as a whole more aware of its vulnerability to anything that affects cheap imports. Once these possible scenarios are – even only hypothetically – accepted, it will be easier to spread memes like the need for increased local food production and the advantages of an increased level of 'food sovereignty' as a risk management strategy.

Different actors in the system might pick this information up in different ways and for different reasons. Some might favour the idea of increased local self-reliance, while others might want to protect the profitability of their local tourism operations from being overly dependent on the availability of cheap imported food. Yet others might become motivated by the overall reduction in environmental impact that comes with increased local production of organic food, including the positive impact with regard to the protection of the beauty of the Majorcan countryside (which tourism also depends on). Local politicians and economists might see the multiple opportunities for generating more jobs through such a shift towards local production.

Entrepreneurial opportunities, protection of cultural heritage, local resilience building, and the link between local organic food, health and education are all additional reasons why the memes 'let's decrease dependence on cheap and low quality food imports' and 'let's increase the production of locally generated organic food' could spread through Majorcan society.

I cannot control exactly how people will respond to my systems interventions – or those of many others like me, but I can aim to work as a 'bridge builder' between different factions who previously thought that they had nothing to do and explore with each other. I can illustrate to them the potential for win-win-win solutions and systemic synergy. Once they understand this principle based on the easy 'entry issue' of food quality, food security and health, I can expand the learning and this 'whole-systems thinking approach' to other aspects of the island system.

For example, this can be done by exploring the benefits of decreased dependence on the importation of fossil and nuclear energy and the shift towards regionally produced, decentralized renewable energy. Apart from keeping the money spent on energy in the local economy and enabling Majorca to become an international example of a renewable energy and transport system, such a shift would help to diversify the local economy away from its almost exclusive dependence on tourism and generate new jobs, while protecting the beauty of the island and the integrity of its ecosystems.

In many ways, the most powerful act of transition design was simply to plant and distribute the seeds of a conversation by asking the following questions: What would a sustainable Majorca look like? How could Majorca become an internationally respected example for regional (island) transition towards a regenerative culture? Why is the current system deeply unsustainable, lacking resilience, and in danger of collapse? How can we co-create a better future for everyone living on Majorca and visiting the island?

By spreading these questions, I begin to work for positive emergence through connecting previously isolated parts of the system and affecting the quality of information in the system. Clearly, I am only one expression of an emerging culture. Some people before and many around me are also spreading their visions of a sustainable Majorca. As these people start to collaborate, we begin to live the questions together.

Education and communication are vital in any attempt to design for positive emergence. Outdated education systems and a media increasingly subservient to corporate interests propagate limited and biased perspectives of the complexity we participate in. The narrative of separation and specialization without integration engender narrow perspectives that can't do justice to the complexity we are faced with. These valid, yet severely limited, perspectives are influencing the solutions we implement and how our behaviour changes, thereby driving what systemic properties emerge. Regenerative design solutions are informed by a participatory systems view of life that is capable of integrating multiple perspectives. One of the design interventions with the highest leverage potential for the transition towards regenerative cultures is widespread education in eco-social and systems literacy.

Another important influence on the behaviour of complex systems is the way 'initial conditions' (like the dominant worldview, value systems or economic system) and 'iterations' (the unquestioned repetition of certain systemic patterns of organization and interactions) affect the system. It is important that as 'transition designers' or 'facilitators of positive emergences' we also take a closer look at the dominant patterns that impede positive systemic change and the emergence of systemic health.

Many of these patterns have to do with established power elites, insufficient education and the dominance of the 'narrative of separation'. Working with culture change in this way requires patience. One effect of the narrative of separation is to make individuals believe they do not have the power and influence to change the system, but the narrative of interbeing reminds us that every change at the individual level and every conversation does in fact change the system as we are not separate from it.

In my own work on Majorca, I have chosen a place to make a stand and do what I can do to contribute to positive emergence in a well-defined bioregion. Islands everywhere offer special case study opportunities for the regional transition towards a regenerative culture. Many share similar problems, for example their economies tend to be heavily dependent on tourism and their consumption tends to be largely based on imports. While there are limits to the possibilities of localizing production and consumption on an island, these limits can act as *enabling constraints* that challenge our imagination and drive transformative innovation. They also challenge us to think in a scale-linking, locally adapted and globally collaborative way.

Since local self-sufficiency in an interconnected world is a mirage not worth chasing, these island case studies can serve as experiments that show us how to find a balance between local production for local consumption promoting increased self-reliance and resilience, and local production of goods, services and know-how that forms an economic basis for trade, which in turn allows the import of goods that cannot be produced locally or regionally.

Before moving to the island, I spent four years living at the internationally acclaimed Findhorn Foundation ecovillage in Northern Scotland. I also worked with various transition town initiatives to understand how we can create increased sustainability and resilience as well as a deeper culture change at the community scale. In doing so, I realized that while local communities, whether rural or urban, are the scale at which the change towards a regenerative culture will be implemented most immediately, many of the systemic changes necessary require a larger (regional) scale and regional collaboration between communities.

I moved to Majorca to explore how to facilitate a scale-linked approach to transition design, by linking local communities within a regional context, and by connecting them with

Scale-linking, salutogenic design for resilience

> The etymology of the word 'health' reveals its connection to other words such as healing, wholeness and holy. Ecological design is an art by which we aim to restore and maintain the wholeness of the entire fabric of life increasingly fragmented by specialization, scientific reductionism and bureaucratic division. […] The standard for ecological design is neither efficiency, nor productivity, but health, beginning with that of the soil and extending upward through plants, animals, and people. […] It is impossible to impair health at any level without affecting it at other levels.
>
> David W. Orr (2002: 29)

Ecologically informed, health-generating (salutogenic), and scale-linking design for resilience and systemic health is not a recent innovation. This approach has emerged throughout the past century with the work of pioneers discussed elsewhere in this book. Most of them explicitly make the improvement of health a central aspect of their work. These pioneers have provided a solid foundation for the emerging theory and practice of transition design for resilient and regenerative cultures.

In socio-ecological systems (SESs) the effects of our actions can often only be observed and understood after long time-delays. In such complex dynamic systems, cause and effect is often non-linear with feedback loops leading to sudden escalations, unforeseen consequences and side-effects. What determines change in an SES over time are mainly the underlying, slowly changing variables such as climate, land use, nutrient stocks, human values and policies, as well as systems of governance and interdependencies between local, regional and global scales. SESs never exist in isolation; they are nested within a holarchical or scale-linking structure of other SESs (see Chapter 4).

How do we design for resilience at the scale of our communities and bioregions, as well as nationally and globally? By trying to create healthier systems capable of the appropriate transformative response in the face of sudden disruptions and crises, we need to pay particular attention to how proposed solutions are scale-linked spatially and temporally. *Spatial scale-linking* connects individuals, communities, ecosystems, bioregions and nations all the way to the planetary scale (and beyond). *Temporal scale-linking* can be understood as the way slow processes and fast processes interact. Many of the factors that will cause a loss of resilience at one particular scale, for example within a community and its local ecosystem, will also affect resilience at another scale, the national or planetary level. Localized actions, like the burning of fossil fuel, can accumulate to have global effects like climate change, which in turn can affect local conditions in multiple and unpredictable ways. This is the nature of the fundamentally interconnected nested system (holarchy) in which we live.

Among the factors that can degrade systemic health at multiple scales are: loss of biodiversity, toxic pollution, interference with the hydrological cycle, degradation of soils and erosion – but also, inflexible institutions, perverse subsidies acting as incentives for unsustainable patterns of consumption, and inappropriately chosen measures of total value that focus on short-term maximization of production and increased efficiencies at the loss of redundancy and diversity in the system as a whole.

The (re-)emerging *narrative of interbeing* helps us to see ourselves within the context of a fundamentally interconnected, constantly transforming complex whole. As human beings we both shape, and are shaped by, life's evolutionary process. Our actions and designs shape our world. The world we co-created, in turn, shapes current experience and our collective future. From the perspectives of many indigenous cultures, creating healing relationships is seen as a sacred act. Scale-linking and salutogenic design is also sacred design. It expresses our meaningful connection (interbeing) with this transforming whole through the way we participate in our human community and the community of life. This participatory perspective can also be found in the 'new sciences' as the notion of appropriate participation in complex systems.

> The new science keeps reminding us that in this participative universe, nothing lives alone. Everything comes into form because of relationship. We are constantly called into relationship – to information, people, events, ideas, and life. Even reality is created through our participation in relationships. We chose what we notice; we relate to certain things and ignore others. Through these chosen relationships we co-create our world. If we are interested in effecting change, it is crucial to remember that we are working within webs of relations, not with machines.
>
> Margaret J. Wheatley (1999: 145)

Ultimately, the shift towards a regenerative human civilization and increased human and planetary health will require a majority of global citizens to assume full responsibility for their co-creative involvement in shaping humanity's and the planet's future. To a greater or lesser extent, we are all designers of this future. We can *intentionally* choose to create healing relationships in the communities and ecosystems in which we participate. In 2006, my doctoral research concluded that if the basic intention behind all human design was salutogenesis, we would be able to facilitate a local and global shift towards sustainability (Wahl, 2006b).

Valerie Brown lists two criteria that should guide human behaviour if we hope to avoid serious damage to the natural processes that maintain systemic health. We need to i) "consume nature's flows while conserving the stocks (that is, live off the 'interest' while conserving natural capital" and ii) "increase society's stocks (human resources, civil institutions) and limit the flow of material and energy" (Brown *et al.*, 2005). Both are central aspects of a regenerative culture.

Salutogenic design aims to facilitate the emergence of health at *and* across all scales of the whole. It recognizes the inextricable link between human, ecosystem and planetary health. Rather than primarily focusing on the relief of symptoms of disease or ill-health, this approach tries to promote positive health and a flourishing of the whole. In other words, the aim of salutogenic design is to support healthy individuals in healthy communities acting responsibly in healthy societies to nurture and maintain healthy ecosystem functioning as the basis for healthy bioregions and ultimately a healthy biosphere. Scale-linking, salutogenic design aims to create resilient and regenerative systems at and across all scales.

The resurgence of a culture of makers: re-localizing production

One way to empower local communities and their regional economies to manifest their visions of a better future is to re-localize production and consumption and thereby strengthen regional economies. There is an important role for international trade and global exchange of goods and services, but not when it comes to meeting basic regional needs. Wherever feasible we should meet our needs as locally or regionally as possible and restrict the global exchange of goods to those that cannot be produced in a particular place. Open innovation and knowledge-sharing at a global scale will be an important part of the process of re-localizing production and some global companies are already beginning to explore how to reinvent themselves as facilitators of the shift towards 'distributed manufacturing' and 'the circular economy'.

Since 2013, together with Forum for the Future, I have been involved in conceiving and implementing a long-range innovation project for the Belgian manufacturer of ecological cleaning products and detergents Ecover. The project uses the unique island conditions of Majorca as a test field to explore how a global company like Ecover can help to facilitate a shift towards localized production for localized consumption based on local material and energy resources and in collaboration with local business partners. In the process we studied the potential of the Majorcan bioeconomy to deliver – in a regenerative way – enough biological raw materials (from waste streams) to produce cleaning products for the local market.

The island is particularly dependent on imports of consumer products and food, due to the increased demand caused by 16 million tourist visits each year. While the long-term sustainability of such mass tourism is more than questionable, these visitor numbers provide the economic engine that can finance the transition towards local production, food and energy infrastructures.

Ecover and 'Forum for the Future' collaborated with an on-island network of multi-sector stakeholders to create a showcase that, if successful, could serve as a transferable example and a model for a region-focused shift towards a renewable energy and materials-based circular economy (see Glocal, 2015). We learned some very important lessons. Simply embarking on the process of co-creating an inspirational experiment like this and involving diverse stakeholders in it contributed to the wider transformation towards a regenerative culture. The conversation about re-localizing production and consumption on Majorca has started.

The regional experiment aimed to take a step towards a circular economy based on re-regionalizing production and consumption. It was motivated less by the potential for short-term economic success and more by the power of experimentation as a way to make sure we are asking the right questions. It catalysed a local design conversation while Ecover explores how it could reinvent itself as a global knowledge and business partner with a wide network of regional collaborators enabling distributed manufacturing and promoting regional economic development.

The transformation of our systems of production and consumption is a creative design challenge that will require whole-systems thinking and transformative innovation at its very best. The resulting disruptive innovations will ultimately make the existing system obsolete. We were effectively trying to redesign production and consumption of chemical products, creating a local product by trying to operate more like an ecosystem. In an ecosystem, materials are sourced locally and assembled in non-toxic processes based on renewable energies.

The promise of this regionalized production system is a more diverse regional economy that generates jobs, encourages efficient use of regional waste streams as resources of production, helps local farmers get a good price for the food and biomaterials they grow, creates resilience by increasing self-reliance, reduces dependence on expensive imports, and contributes to the effort to quickly reduce greenhouse gas emissions by reducing transportation of feedstock and finished products.

The first steps towards achieving this are already being explored in many industrial ecology projects around the world (see Chapter 6). Even if some of these current projects are hybrid systems that still rely on fossil energy and non-renewable material resources, they are achieving increases in material and energy efficiency by connecting previously separate industrial processes in ways that turn one industry's waste (whether material streams or waste heat) into another industry's resource of production. They are second horizon (H2) stepping-stones to renewable energy-powered regenerative systems.

Unleashing the full potential of such ecosystems of production and consumption based on integrative industrial design requires regional collaboration across all sectors and all industries. The synergies that can be generated when previously separate industries are linked through ecological design thinking are substantial. The book *Blue Economy* summarizes a number of such ground-breaking design solutions that are being implemented or are in advanced stages of development (Pauli, 2010). It offers inspiration for green entrepreneurs to get involved in H2+ transformative innovation.

The overall shift is away from a fossil fuel-based industrial system with centralized production facilities that rely on bringing raw materials from all corners of the Earth only to then distribute the finished products globally again. This wasteful system is based on outdated industrial design solutions developed during the first industrial revolution where the economics of mass-manufacturing meant bigger was better, and cheap abundant fossil fuels and non-renewable materials were taken for granted.

Currently, the vast majority of our consumer products contain petroleum-based materials. During the first half of the 21st century we will witness the transformation of this global system of production. We will begin to co-create a material culture that relies on locally available materials, green (plant-based) chemistry and renewable energy sources for regional production and consumption.

Integrative design based on whole-systems thinking and the kind of nature-inspired design solutions explored in the next two chapters will help us create 'elegant solutions predicated by the uniqueness of place'. This is how my mentor Professor John Todd, a pioneer in his field, defines ecological design. Such solutions are an elegant blend of the best of modern technology and a rediscovered sensitivity to place, culture and traditional wisdom. New technologies are opening up a 21st-century, design-led re-localization enabled by global resource-sharing and cooperation.

Distributed manufacturing is becoming a reality as new 3D printing technologies enabling additive manufacturing at a small scale are developing rapidly alongside revolutionary approaches to open innovation based on peer-to-peer collaboration, the spread of 'Fab-labs' and a new maker culture, breakthroughs in material science, as well as diverse bio-economy projects. Much work is still needed in the area of developing locally grown and regenerated feedstock for 3D printing technologies.

The Open Source Ecology project started by Marcin Jakubowski demonstrates how inventors and technologists are already collaborating globally to recreate regional means of production that are increasingly independent of the centralized mass-production systems of multinationals. The project's aim is to create the 'Global Village Construction Set', an open-source design and engineering library of detailed blueprints that will enable people with basic engineering and technical skills to create the 50 most important machines needed to build a sustainable civilization. We are beginning to ask:

- Q How can we implement the global shift towards increased regional production for regional consumption?

- Q How can we create effective systems of open-source innovation that enable people globally to share know-how and design innovations?

- Q How can we ensure that re-regionalizing production and consumption will happen within the bioproductivity limits of each particular region, and strike a balance between growing food and growing industrial resources regionally?

- Q How can we make 3D printing technologies sustainable by ensuring that they use locally produced, renewable and up-cyclable feedstock in environmentally benign ways, powered by decentralized renewable energy?

- Q How can we use bio-refineries and advanced fermentation technologies to facilitate the shift from a fossil fuel-based organic chemistry to a solar-powered, plant-based and non-toxic chemistry in order to re-invent our material culture?

An early lesson we learnt in Majorca is that a successful bioeconomy requires widespread collaboration between sectors. Policy interventions are needed to regulate access to biological resources and their sustainable (regenerative) production and use. With limited bioproductive potential within a particular region, we must find ways to create ecosystems of collaboration that optimize the use of available resources.

Regenerative design solutions require whole-systems design conversations across all sectors of society. From these conversations a guiding vision will emerge. This vision can be made reality, one place at a time, by all of us. [At the time of writing, the Ecover Glocal project is not advancing, due to a lack of funding. It created a network of collaborators and planted a vision that is likely to be taken up again in the future.]

Collective visioning and design conversations change culture

> Vision without action is useless. But action without vision does not know where to go or why to go there. Vision is absolutely necessary to guide and motivate action. More than that, vision, when widely shared and firmly kept in sight, brings into being new systems.
>
> Donella Meadows *et al.* (1992: 224)

Any activity that involves a community, a business or an entire region in an open dialogue aiming to envision a more desirable future is the beginning of a design conversation that has the potential to become culturally transformative. Visioning invites us to not be restrained by the limitations we perceive in the status quo and to let go of linear predictions of what our 'unavoidable' future will be like on the basis of yesterday's and today's prevalent trends. Visioning opens up a space where we can have a multi-stakeholder conversation about the future we want, where we can design an ideal future and set clear intentions for what we would like to co-create.

Visions can serve as lighthouses that guide us towards a regenerative culture. Just as lighthouses are rarely the point of arrival, but only the beacons that direct us towards a goal that lies beyond them, so our current visions of regenerative cultures are unlikely to be accurate reflections of the regenerative culture we will co-create during the 21st century. Visioning together can serve as a catalyst for collective intelligence engaging all of us in a design-based conversation about a more meaningful and healthier future. Visioning processes educate and transform those involved in co-creating them.

The point is not to create a fixed vision. If we are truly 'living the questions' as we approach what we have envisioned, the vision will continue to evolve. Nevertheless, visions can help us to make sure we are going in roughly the right direction. It is important to understand that in the process of creating a vision of a sustainable community, society and civilization we should not be restricted by what may be perceived right now as insurmountable obstacles. The initial formulation of a vision has to be idealistic, creative, poetic, aesthetic, ethical, intuitive and imaginative. The process of creating it has to be inclusive, collaborative, non-dogmatic and participatory. The design conversations that are part of the visioning process invite us to listen to multiple perspectives, value the contribution of diverse points of view, and co-create the common ground from which we can move forward together, with mutual understanding and respect.

Reasoning from only one particular perspective should not restrict the integrative and participatory process of creating the initial vision. First, the best-case scenario, the win-win-win optimal future state has to be clearly *envisioned*. This creates a collective goal desirable to everyone and provides the basis for engaging the participation of diverse stakeholders in the long-term process of turning such a vision into reality through appropriate design.

While scenario planning and forecasting are ways to look at the trends we observe in the present and extrapolate them to the future, the visioning process first creates an ideal future state as clearly as it can be envisioned collectively. Only after the vision has been formulated in detail do we ask the question how we might get there, back-casting from that vision to establish a series of milestone achievements in the transition from today's 'business as usual' to the full manifestation of our vision. Here are some questions that can help guide an effective visioning process:

Q   Have we identified the appropriate representatives of each stakeholder group that needs to be present in order to create an inclusive vision?

Q   What are the different issues we need to include in our process of co-creating the vision in order to shape a comprehensive vision?

Q   How does the positive vision of the future we co-created differ from the status quo of today?

Q   Are we ensuring that our vision is not limited by our current, culturally dominant narrative and that it is based on the values we aspire to?

Q   What are our basic guiding values as we aim to achieve our vision, and what might the milestones along the way look like?

Q   What are the actionable steps that we can implement ourselves at the local level to manifest our vision step by step?

Q   Is our vision desirable environmentally, socially and economically; and is it meaningful to all stakeholders?

Whether in corporate boardrooms, government think tanks or community groups, the visioning and back-casting process is already being used effectively. The impact of this work will be even more culturally transformative when we apply these processes in teams that include members of each of these different sectors of society. The workshops of the transition town movement, for example, include future state visioning and back-casting along a timeline to help people envision the future of their community, town, or neighbourhood in transition. Unfortunately it is rare for representatives of all the different sectors to attend such workshops.

Likewise, the World Business Council for Sustainable Development has created a bold *Vision 2050 – The New Agenda For Business* (WBCSD, 2010) which details a series of 'must haves' (milestones) at certain points along the way which are necessary to achieve that vision. Bob Horn, a member of the International Futures Forum, summarized the content of this work as a timeline mural which can be downloaded on the WBCSD website along with a more detailed report. The initiative has many merits and highlights important issues that are helping to educate business leaders in a more systemic perspective of sustainability, yet the report has its own shortcomings as it has been created within a closed community of business leaders and lacked the participation of more diverse, cross-sector contributors in the initial visioning process. The report is an example of trying to solve our problems within the mindset that created them. It does not sufficiently question the underlying assumptions and the dominant worldview that informed the *Vision 2050*. Nevertheless, the 'must haves' invite business leaders to ask important questions:

Q How do we incorporate the costs of 'externalities', like carbon emissions, ecosystems functions and water, into the structure of the marketplace?

Q How do we double agricultural output without increasing the amount of land and water used for agricultural production?

Q How do we stop deforestation globally and increase the yields from planted forests?

Q How do we halve carbon emissions worldwide (based on 2005 levels) by 2050 through a shift to low-carbon energy systems?

Q How do we improve demand-side energy efficiency, and provide universal access to low-carbon mobility?

There are many visions of a more sustainable world. Maybe we can learn from all of them. They range from the Earth Charter's vision of globally shared human values, the UN's Sustainable Development Goals and the 'Future we really want' outlined by the Alliance for Sustainability and Prosperity, to Leister Brown's continuously up-dated 'Plan B', and visionary proposals for global systems changes made by Ross Jackson (2012), Albert Tullio Lieberg (2010), Roy Madron & John Jopling (2003) and others. These visions[†] and strategies for the transition to a sustainable civilization are excellent starting points for living the questions together and initiating design conversations in our communities and businesses and with our political representatives.

Collective visioning processes, structured through design conversations about the future we want to create together, need to take place in as many different contexts and locations as possible. The more diverse the participants in these processes, the richer the learning will be. Through collective visioning we can change the way we see the world around us. We can become hopeful again, inspired by the many opportunities for thriving together rather than struggling alone. Together we can co-design prototype expressions of this 'new story' which make us experience the benefits of regenerative cultures (H3 pockets of the future in the present).†

Social technologies that can be used to facilitate collective visioning and design conversations include the Bioneers' 'Dreaming New Mexico' methodology, the IFF's World Game and Three Horizons framework; future oriented versions of World Café (Brown *et al.*, 2005), John Crofts' 'Dragon Dreaming' process, Otto Scharmer's 'U process', the Elos Institute's 'Oasis Game', and Adam Kahane's 'transformative scenario planning' (2012). All of these processes can be engaging ways to learn from diversity and build communities of collaboration based on a shared understanding of the vast opportunities that lie in the transition towards regenerative cultures.

Culture evolves in conversations that help us question assumptions, evaluate our perspective, consider other points of view, inquire into meaning, and find shared values and intentions. These shared values and intentions form the basis for us to engage in co-designing our collective future. The mere act of engaging in transition design conversations with others is culturally creative. By learning from multiple perspectives, we learn to co-create a deeper systemic understanding. We begin to co-design our future together and thereby contribute to the emergence of regenerative cultures.

CHAPTER 6

How can we learn to better design *as* nature?

> If you do not rest upon the good foundations of nature, you will labour with little honour and less profit. Those who take for their standard any one but nature – the mistress of all masters – weary themselves in vain.
>
> Leonardo da Vinci (1452-1519)

Life has sustained its presence on Earth for about 3,800 million years. Life has done more than sustain itself; life has flourished, diversified and created the conditions for more complex life to evolve. During the vast time span of evolution, life has gone from strength to strength, overcome some catastrophic setbacks and continued to innovate, adapt to change and shape the conditions of the environment and the biosphere in ways that have allowed for more life to thrive. Life, as a process, is the grand mistress of transformative innovation.

Q What are life's operating principles that ensure long-term survival?

We would do well to ask this question and to pay attention to what we can learn from nature, as she expresses herself in a breathtaking diversity of species in interdependent communities of collaboration and symbiosis.

Here is where language lets me down again. When I say "learn from nature", I do not mean to create a distinction that sets us – humanity – apart from nature. *We are nature*, and as such we can design *as* nature. As a matter of fact, we can't do anything else. The main difference is that just as many of nature's 'design experiments' in the course of evolution have ended up in the dead-end street of extinction, so are we as a species along with our current version of industrial culture heading towards an early demise unless we pay more attention to the lessons we can learn from life's evolution. As Janine Benyus (2002) has put it so well, life has a 3.8-billion-year head start in research and development, so we might as well combine human ingenuity with the humility to become nature's apprentices.

Some of the most basic lessons we can learn from ecosystems everywhere are that almost all energy that drives ecological cycles flows from the sun. Even the kinetic energy of wind, waves and marine currents ultimately derives from the sun's energy reaching the Earth. Our industrial civilization, on the other hand, is driven by fossil fuel reserves in the form of coal, gas and oil, along with some other non-renewable sources like nuclear energy. Fossil fuels are nothing but *ancient sunlight* (Hartman, 1999) stored in the Earth's crust. These energy carriers are the compressed and transformed remains of plants and animals that populated Earth millions of years ago. The amount of fossil fuel humanity is currently using in a single year took approximately 1 million years to build up in the Earth's crust (Fischer, 2012: 36).

The word 'non-renewable' gives us an important hint: this pattern is far from sustainable! We have already seen that one of the first lessons we can learn from nature is that the biosphere's vast solar-chemical industry that drives bioproductivity and almost all energetic processes within the biosphere is based on *current solar income* rather than fossil reserves. Learning to better 'design as nature' means creating a solar powered, regenerative civilization based on current solar income and renewable energy and material resources.

Our industrial culture is not only addicted to the wrong kind of energy resources and therefore badly attuned to *appropriate scale*, it is also almost entirely based on the wrong kind of material resources. Life has evolved a diverse range of organic molecules and bio-chemical synthesis processes which are the building blocks and production processes of nature's design, tested over many millions of years.

For most of human history we used relatively few non-organic materials, apart from small amounts of minerals and ores, and stone for construction. With the industrial revolution we decided to take a perilous detour from life's tested metabolisms and began to create an energy system and a material culture that was based on fossil materials dug up from the Earth's crust and an ever increasing-variety of minerals and ores that we were able to mine because of cheap energy in the form of fossil fuels.

In the first half of the 19th century, the use of coal as a transportation fuel and energy source for heating and industrial production increased rapidly. In particular, the use of coal-based coke in steel production created a vast amount of waste in the form of coal tar. As this toxic, reeking paste started to build up we set about trying to find new industrial uses for it and, shortly afterwards, our fossil-fuel-based industrial chemistry was born.

It is not even 200 years since the German chemist Friedlieb Ferdinand Runge, in 1834, invented chemical paints and dyes from the aniline contained in coal tar (Fischer, 2012: 30). In 1889, the French chemist Hilaire de Chardonnet commercialized the first artificial fibre called rayon – an 'artificial silk'. In the early 1900s the Belgian chemist Leo Baekeland created 'bakelite', the first thermoset plastic. Polyethylene and polystyrene were not invented until the 1930s. In less than two centuries we have created a material culture almost entirely dependent on oil and coal as its key raw materials. Most of our textiles, plastics, paints, fragrances, cosmetics, detergents, fertilizers, technological gadgets, medicines and even food items contain chemicals derived from fossil fuels. The global chemical industry is now the most powerful industrial lobby on the planet and closely linked to the fossil fuel industry.

The 118 chemical elements can be combined into many millions of different chemical compounds and tens of thousands of new compounds are being created every year without stringent regulation on testing their effect on living organisms. All of us carry trace amounts of hundreds of human-made chemical compounds in our blood and fatty tissues; many of them are toxic and/or carcinogenic (Ewing Duncan, 2014).

The relatively new discipline of 'Green Chemistry' (Anastas & Warner, 1998) aims to create plant-based, non-toxic alternatives to many of our fossil fuel-based materials. It is of paramount importance to the redesign of our material culture. We should not make the mistake of seeing biomass simply as a possible energy source or as a way to make biofuel. If we humble ourselves enough to become apprentices of nature again, we can unlock the secrets of life's chemistry. Biomass, especially agricultural, forestry and organic household wastes, will become a precious resource for 21st-century chemists.

Understanding life's chemistry will help us in transforming our material culture – currently based almost exclusively on fossil, non-renewable material feedstock – into a material culture that will largely rely on plant-based chemistry, which is less toxic, requires relatively low energy inputs (from renewable sources), and does not create waste products which cannot be metabolized in other industrial processes. One of the biggest challenges for transformative innovation in the 21st century is to reinvent chemistry based on nature's metabolic processes.

From green chemistry, biomimetic product design, renewable energy systems and biomimetic architecture, to cities and industries that function like ecosystems, learning to better design *as* nature is one of the most exciting creative challenges in the transition towards regenerative cultures. In essence, by aspiring to design *as* nature in ways that create whole-system health we are aiming to learn how to participate appropriately in the life-sustaining cycles of the biosphere. This means meeting human needs within planetary boundaries while acting as a responsible keystone species that maintains and regenerates life's capacity to create conditions conducive to life. By aspiring to do this in local ecosystems everywhere, we will create resilience, health and the conditions for life to thrive across the globe.

If we truly live into the fact that *we are life*, that *we are nature*, and as such are bound by kinship and interdependence to the community of life that human and planetary health depend upon, we will come to regard the creation of a globally regenerative civilization expressed in exquisite locally adapted diversity as *the* creative challenge of our times. This is a challenge that not only unifies the human family behind a common vision of co-creative thriving rather than just survival, but also unites humanity with the ground of its own being – nature's genius unfolding through the diversity of life and the evolution of consciousness.

Once we understand that appropriate participation is the goal, we are at one and the same time *empowered* (as participants in nature we cannot but design *as* nature) and *humbled* (we still have so much to learn about how to creatively fit a vast global population of humans onto a planet with a fragile biosphere). Rather than forcing a natural world separate from us to fit our human needs, as the narrative of separation would have us do, we have to fit-*in* as a species that has a lot to learn from the rest of nature in trying to discern which design solutions better serve the whole system.

We need humility to use technology wisely. Living the questions together as a means to access collective intelligence will help us to distinguish which paths are conducive to life and which are maladaptive and will not only jeopardize the future of our children and our species, but the health and diversity of our wider family – life on Earth. Learning to design wisely *as* nature is a pilgrimage and an apprenticeship that will never end. How can we measure our success? We are doing well if we observe an increase in human thriving and planetary bioproductivity, a reduction in greenhouse gas concentration in the atmosphere, and the spread of elegant, regionally adapted communities of vibrant biocultural diversity in global solidarity and collaboration.

Ecoliteracy: Learning from living systems

> If we surrendered to earth's intelligence we could rise rooted, like trees.
> Rainer Maria Rilke, *The Book of Hours*

We need to reintegrate our economic activities, the way we meet our needs and how we produce and share value, with the basic rules of ecology. Our design and technology need to be aligned with the way that life and living systems are structured and how they maintain their vital functions in support of individuals and the whole system. The basic principles of ecoliteracy are a good starting point to explore some of the fundamental lessons we can learn from nature and how they might inform some guiding questions for the redesign of our economies, industries and society.

Ecoliteracy is the ability to understand the organization of natural systems and the processes that maintain the healthy functioning of living systems and sustain life on Earth. An ecologically literate person is able to apply this understanding to the design and organization of our human communities and the creation of a regenerative culture. Originally promoted by the environmental educator David W. Orr (1992) and the physicist Fritjof Capra (1995), nurturing ecological literacy in students of a wide range of ages has become the goal of sustainability education programmes worldwide.

The Center for Ecoliteracy in Berkeley, California has been instrumental in spreading its innovative secondary school ecoliteracy curriculum around California, Hawaii and now even some schools on the island of Majorca. School gardens become the living activity classroom where children learn maths, ecology and systems thinking while growing healthy food. Teachers and students, together, learn from nature, through nature and *as* nature. The centre defined a series of *ecological principles* (Center for Ecoliteracy, 2015) that can help us frame questions we might want to ask as we aim to design *as* nature:

Networks: All life in an ecosystem is interconnected through networks of relationship defining life-sustaining processes.

> Q   How can we increase the vitality and sustainability of our own communities by weaving mutually supportive relationships between our human community networks and the rest of nature's life-sustaining networks?

Networks are the patterns of organization expressing life's fundamental *interbeing*. They make mutual support, learning, exchange and nurturing relationships possible. One example of applying this lesson in human design is to avoid or decrease unnecessary disruption of life-sustaining networks within and between ecosystems. Nature-bridges over motorways in the Netherlands, Germany, France and in Canadian natural parks are doing just that. These artificially constructed, often hundred-metre-long over-paths across major motorways and railway lines are not for human use, but are designed to let migrating animals roam more freely without dividing up their habitat with insurmountable obstacles. In a more general sense the creation of 'wildlife corridors' from one wilderness reserve to another serves a similar function. By allowing for migratory patterns to continue and avoiding the fragmentation of a species habitat, we are maintaining biodiversity and the health and resilience of natural ecosystems.

Nested Systems: Nature is structured as nested systems within systems (or processes within processes). Each individual system is an integrated whole and is simultaneously comprised of smaller sub-systems as well as being integrated into larger systems. This scale-linking structure means that changes at one scale can affect all other scales.

> **Q** How can we scale-link our human systems in synergy within the nested eco-social systems that provide resilience and vitality?

Nested systems are part of nature's pattern of health and resilience as they create both interconnection and a degree of self-reliance at different scales. As we saw in Chapter 4, the resilience and vibrancy of systems at any scale depend on this interlinking 'panarchy' which maintains redundancy, diversity, adaptability and transformability. Re-localizing production and consumption will increase local/regional resilience and decrease the multiple negative impacts of unnecessary transport of goods and materials.

A sustainable community has a certain level of self-reliance with regard to meeting its needs for energy, food, water, shelter, transport, healthcare and education at the local community level. For these semi-self-reliant systems to work and be resilient they have to be designed as nested systems within a local, regional, national and global context, based on knowledge exchange, collaboration and the exchange of the materials, goods and services that cannot be easily provided at the smaller scale or by using only the naturally occurring regenerative resources of a particular locality.

Cycles: All ecological communities are defined and maintained through the cyclical exchange of resources between members. These continual cycles within an ecosystem also intersect with larger regional and global cycles in a scale-linking fashion. Fast- and slow-moving cycles are interlinked and interdependent.

> **Q** What can we learn from the patterns of nature's interlinking cycles at multiple scales in our attempt to create circular economies that link the local to the regional and the global in a life-sustaining way?

To create a truly regenerative culture, we must design processes in interconnected, closed-loop cycles. These include: cycles of primary production of biological resources and patterns of use that allow for equal or higher amounts to be harvested in a sustainable way in subsequent years; cycles of learning and adaptation in response to changes in the environment; cycles that maintain basic ecosystems functions like clean water, clean air, re-growing energy and material resources; and cycles that separate all our products into either an industrial metabolism for the recycling and reuse of technical resources or a biological metabolism of organic resources through composting and use as fertilizer to support more biological growth (see McDonough & Braungart, 2002 & 2013).

To create restorative and regenerative cultures we will have to re-learn how to work with natural cycles like the availability of daylight; the hydrological cycle and water-storage in the rainy season; the carbon cycle and restoring soil fertility; and the seasonal cycle of availability of local foods and materials. Our industries, buildings and food systems have to be carefully attuned to nature's local, regional and global cycles – not just to the annual seasonality, but also to '100-year floods, storms or droughts'. Planning for resilience pays attention to such cycles, which are local, regional and global in scale, as well as operating in the short-, mid- and long-term. Mimicking nature's closed-loop, no-waste, cyclical pattern of material flows based on renewable energy resources will help us to turn the vision of circular economies into reality.

Flows: Organisms depend on a continual flow of energy, water and nutrients to maintain their basic functions and stay alive. Solar energy sustains almost all life directly or indirectly and drives most ecological cycles.

> Q How can we redesign all our systems of energy generation and distribution to mimic nature's decentralized direct use of solar energy flows?

One of the most important flows to which a regenerative culture has to attune its patterns of energy consumption is the flow of energy from the sun. This energy initially hits the Earth in the form of sunlight and solar radiation, but then begins to drive other energy cycles like the flow of major wind systems, which in turn influence marine currents and waves. We have to link the energy flows of our human systems to these natural and renewable energy flows that ultimately come from the sun. We also have to redesign our chemical industries and material culture to depend pretty much entirely on material resource flows that are plant-based and therefore solar-based.

Development: Whether individual organisms, whole species or entire ecosystems, all life changes over time. Individuals develop and learn, while species adapt and evolve, and ecosystems transform through the co-evolution of the organisms within them.

> Q What can we learn from nature's patterns of development and evolution in order to create more adaptable and resilient ways of dealing with change through continuous learning and transformation?

In this ecological principle lies one of the keys to confronting the multiple converging crises that humanity has created due to centuries of design and technology that disregard natural patterns. The fastest way for humanity to respond to this unsustainable situation is through cultural transformation based on personal and collective development. Evolutionary adaptation by mutation and selection will take too long. Individuals change culture and culture changes individuals. We need individual, cultural and civilizational change to reinforce each other in order to respond in a timely manner to this opportunity to re-invent our human systems based on learning from other natural systems. Widespread education in ecological literacy will help this cultural transformation.

Dynamic Balance: Ecological communities are in constant flux and transformation, yet they also remain relatively stable over time. This dynamic balance is achieved through patterns of resource, energy and information exchange known as feedback loops.

> Q How can we design feedback loops at the appropriate scale into our human systems so we can stay adaptable and resilient in a changing environment?

The concept of 'dynamic balance' describes how, despite constant change and transformation, natural systems remain relatively stable over time. The key here is 'over time': what may seem like long periods of relative stability from the perspective of a human life-time are only the blink of an eye on the time scale of evolution. The interactions of short-term and long-term cycles create periods of dynamic balance and transformational change. At the core of dynamic balance are processes of self-regulation and self-organization based on feedback loops. Examples of dynamic balance and life's involvement in creating and maintaining conditions conducive to life are the regulation of salinity in the ocean, oxygen concentration in the atmosphere and the long-term regulation of global surface temperatures (see James Lovelock's work on Gaia Theory).

In the design of human systems we have to monitor our use of locally available renewable resources in real time to avoid depleting the regional capacity for regeneration. If we over-use a local resource, we have to reduce consumption and replace the resource with an alternative, or respond by ensuring that the annual sustainable harvest increases by raising the bioproductivity of this resource. By mimicking nature's patterns of self-organization based on feedback loops we can create dynamic balance in socio-ecological systems as a basis for long-term sustainability. The constant and long-term regeneration of the resources a culture needs to meet its basic needs is the defining characteristic of regenerative cultures.

Valuing traditional ecological knowledge and indigenous wisdom

> Let us put our minds together and see
> what kind of life we can make for our children.
>
> Tȟatȟáŋka Íyotake – 'Sitting Bull' (1831-1890)

6: How Can We Learn to Better Design AS Nature?

To overcome – once and for all – the false separation between nature and culture requires us to acknowledge that learning from human ingenuity and long-term adaptations to particular environments is also learning from nature. Among indigenous peoples there is a long tradition of solving human problems by learning from other species and from the wider natural processes in which we participate. Taking a long-term perspective, humanity has only managed to survive by doing exactly that. For most of our history we have carefully adapted to the sources of materials and energy that we could harvest in a renewable and non-depleting way from within the local and regional ecosystems we inhabited. One reason why we spent a good part of our history living nomadically is that our ancestors met their basic needs by following the migration routes of other animals and seasonally available food that could be gathered along the way.

For tens of thousands of years we have lived within the limits of our local bioregions, carefully learning – by trial and error – how best to meet the needs of our nomadic or resident population by drawing on local and regional energy and material flows. Culture is an epiphenomenon of nature and traditional place-based cultures are (or were) the result of the careful co-evolution of human settlements with the ecosystems they inhabit. Co-evolution means that the environment shaped human culture while humans shaped their environment.

I do not want to support an idyllic image that indigenous cultures have never overstepped ecological boundaries with negative effects on their local ecosystems. They certainly have (e.g. Easter Islands, Babylon). Yet, there are many more cases of indigenous practices helping to increase the productivity and vitality of the ecosystems they co-evolved with. Humans are capable of being a beneficial keystone species in an ecosystem, rather than an ecological disaster agent!

Indigenous cultures began to shape their environment as long as 50,000 years ago. By paying attention to our species' past we can learn lessons for ecosystems restoration. The oldest written document of humanity, the Epic of Gilgamesh, tells the story of Mesopotamia drying and salting up after the king killed the god of the forest, Humbaba, and cut down the cedar forests of Lebanon. Modern ecologists would call this 'down-wind desertification'. Most ecosystems today have been altered and degraded by human impact. *Used Planet: A global history* shows that many of the world's ecosystems underwent major ecological changes due to the interference of relatively small numbers of human inhabitants as long as 3,000 years ago. These changes have not always been negative, more often they increased bioproductivity (Erle *et al.*, 2012).

In recent years, research into *terra preta* – the human-facilitated black soil cultures enriched through the burial of charcoal, compost and beneficial fungal mycelia – is beginning to show that even the supposedly virgin rainforests of Amazonia, West Africa and Borneo are ecosystems affected by the forest-gardening practices of their human inhabitants. Similarly the great plains of North America, the 'wild' moorlands of England or the Highlands of Scotland are all examples of ecosystems that have been reshaped by human presence through repeated burning, deforestation and grazing (Pearce, 2013).

One way to rediscover the practices that helped *Homo sapiens* survive for over 200,000 years is to pay more attention to indigenous wisdom and traditional place-based knowledge (where it has not already been completely lost). Indigenous human cultures are an expression of generations of co-evolution of humans within the ecosystems they inhabited. Cultures that have managed to survive for millennia within their bioregions have a lot to teach us. Over the last few hundred years we have developed the unfortunate habit of dismissing such knowledge as antiquated and calling such cultures 'primitive'. Hypnotized by the apparent benefits of scientific and technological progress we made the mistake of dismissing traditional ecological knowledge that underpinned human survival for most of prehistory.

To re-evaluate the wisdom of traditional and indigenous cultures does not mean returning to some supposed 'golden age' when humanity lived in perfect harmony with the rest of nature. It simply means acknowledging that these cultures have managed to sustain themselves and evolve in intimate adaptation to the uniqueness of place for many more millennia. By comparison, the few centuries of modern industrialized civilization have brought us many great achievements but have also created some of the most pressing global problems we now face. We have to learn from both the successes and failures of modern technologies, and we have to pay more attention to the indigenous wisdom of local culture adapted to place.

Indigenous worldviews around the planet share a common perspective: *the world is alive and meaningful and our relationship with the rest of life is one of participation, communion and co-creation.* Creating regenerative cultures is also about finding creative responses to the questions:

Q   How can we combine the best of modern technology, science and cultural expression with the guiding wisdom of traditional, indigenous cultures?

Q   How can we innovate and transform our culture with one eye on the past (learning from traditional wisdom and practice), and the other on the future (social, ecological, economic and technological innovation)?

Individually and collectively we have lost our way. The poem 'Lost' by David Wagoner gives the kind of advice that a native elder would offer a young member of the tribe to find their way through the dark, tall forests of the Pacific North West. Stop and listen more deeply when you are lost. This is pertinent advice for humanity as a whole. Confronted with the sensory and information overload of modern life we have lost our ability to really listen to our own intuition, to consider the wisdom of others and to appreciate the insights we can gather by paying attention to life's 3.8 billion years of experience in not just surviving, but thriving, transforming and evolving. Humanity has lost its path!

Lost

Stand still.
The trees ahead and bushes beside you are not lost.
Wherever you are is called Here,
and you must treat it as a powerful stranger,
must ask permission to know it and be known.
The forest breathes. – Listen. – It answers,
I have made this place around you,
if you leave it you may come back again, saying Here.
No two trees are the same to Raven.
No two branches are the same to Wren.
If what a tree or a bush does is lost on you,
you are surely lost.
Stand still. – The forest knows where you are.
You must let it find you.

David Wagoner

I deeply believe that if we really want to create regenerative cultures of fairness and inclusion based on nurturing relationships with the community of life, one of the first things we have to learn to do is to listen more deeply. We have to learn to *listen* from our heart and our mind and *trust* our own inner wisdom, the wisdom of our community, the wisdom of indigenous cultures and the wisdom of the rest of nature. We should ask ourselves:

Q How can we learn to listen more deeply to our own inner wisdom and guidance that will speak to us if we quieten our mind or seek solitude in nature?

Q How can we learn to listen more deeply to the wisdom of the tribe, to the gifts that our community holds, and act wisely based on collective intelligence?

Q How can we listen more deeply and learn from the ingenuity of our animal and plant relations?

Another common characteristic of indigenous cultures everywhere is that they tend to have *modes of communication that involve respectful listening and sharing from the heart in a council circle*. In my own experience of working and communicating in this way, when we sit in council and offer the gift of attention and heart-full listening to each other, we are given the opportunity to directly live and experience the reality of *interbeing*. Together we enact the vast potential that unfolds by accessing collective intelligence and wisdom; we can experience the deeply healing effects of opening our hearts to the compassion we are able to feel for each other and the world because we never have been separated – only in our minds.

A third mental model or belief system that indigenous cultures the world over share is that *the rest of the natural world is in continuous communication with us if we only learn to listen*. We are capable of learning from plants, bacteria, fungi and animals with whom we share this experience of *being life on Earth*.

Deep listening lies at the heart of creating a regenerative culture. We have lost the path that nurtures all of life. We need to listen deeply in order to find it again: listen to each other and to the rest of the community of life. This is a wisdom we can recover by learning from indigenous cultures.

In 2010, while helping Marcello Palazzi and the Progressio Foundation to host the first European Bioneers conference in the Netherlands, I had the good fortune to meet Dennis Martinez, a native American elder who has been instrumental in establishing the 'Indigenous Peoples' Restoration Network' (IPRN). Dennis is widely recognized for creating a bridge between 'traditional ecological knowledge' (TEK) and Western science. His passion is 'eco-cultural restoration'. The preservation of ecosystems and biodiversity is critically linked with the preservation of the indigenous cultures that have co-evolved with these habitats. TEK can help us to tap into a long history of careful observation of the long-term cycles in a particular place that is held within the collective memory of the remaining indigenous cultures.

> While Western science is a powerful and successful methodology within its proper sphere – quantitative analysis – other valid epistemologies such as TEK offer complementary approaches to understanding the natural world and our relationship to that world with which we have co-evolved since time out of mind. TEK is a place based knowledge-belief-practice complex of ancient lineage. [...] The World Conservation Union estimates that tribal peoples occupy over 80% of the world's biological 'hotspots'. Locally adapted cultural diversity goes hand in hand with biological diversity. Together they constitute ecocultural diversity. [...] What we are really restoring is our relationship with the places we live in and depend on as we learn, once again, how to be native to these places: to be caregivers to the land; to participate with our elder brothers and sisters, the plants and animals, in the spiritual and physical renewal of the earth and of ourselves.
>
> Dennis Martinez (IPRN, 2015)

Creating regenerative cultures is a process of re-indigenization, of becoming deeply rooted in the unique condition of particular places again, of restoring and caring for a particular place over the long term. Now that humanity is globally interconnected and bound to a common fate, our challenge is to collaborate globally in the process of becoming carefully adapted to our localities again.

Gregory Cajete (1999), a native Pueblo science educator, emphasizes that traditional knowledge is a knowledge system that does not need external validation, just like Western science. The fact that TEK guided the sustainable and resilient co-existence of indigenous people with the wider community of life in their native ecosystem for many more centuries than Western science has existed is a proof of the validity and importance of this knowledge system. "Traditional knowledge is a fragile living library of oral knowledge passed down from generation to generation. It has always been adaptable and resilient. Because of its adaptive nature it cannot be preserved in libraries. Its survival depends on the survival of indigenous culture" (Martinez, 2010). If we lose the oral traditions of the world's indigenous cultures we are wiping humanity's collective long-term memory of what it means to live in a regenerative way *as* nature (see Nelson, 2008).

The preservation of indigenous languages is closely linked to the preservation of traditional knowledge. There are approximately 6,000 languages still spoken on Earth (most of them indigenous languages spoken by relatively small populations). "Each indigenous nation, tribe, band, community and clan will have different processes of 'coming to know' ourselves, each other, and the world. These metaphysical and epistemological processes of learning, knowing and being are not just abstract concepts but are embodied and animated in daily practices of survival and living" (Nelson, 2011). Preserving and learning from traditional knowledge, culture and language is humanity's common heritage and a vital contribution to a restorative culture. We can learn from traditional, place-based knowledge everywhere, also in Western culture. Transformative innovation for a regenerative culture is also about asking ourselves:

> Q   How do we re-indigenize and carefully adapt to place (home), while maintaining planetary awareness and global collaboration among all of humanity?

Even in the so-called 'developed world' much of the traditional knowledge of how to meet needs within the limits of biologically regenerative resources of the region was still predominant only 150 years ago. That is only a few generations! If we re-value what that knowledge and indigenous wisdom holds for us, we can recover much of it and blend indigenous wisdom in creative ways with the best of modern technology and science.

In *The Time of the Black Jaguar*, Arkan Lushwala (2012) offers a deeply insightful indigenous perspective on the great transformation under way: the healing of our cultural pathologies. The 'medicine of the Black Jaguar' (transformation) is a rite of passage bringing the death of what no longer serves and rebirth of a new and ancient communion with life.

> I see Pachamama becoming once again the fertile ground of growth of healthy human communities. […] All humans have the right to return home and become indigenous to this Earth, to become real human beings living their full potential as caretakers of life, to become people with big hearts living in cooperation with each other and with other forms of life. […] At these times of renewal of life on Earth, new designs, new life, and new tribes are being animated. […] It is the essence of life that is seeking to continue living and multiplying itself through us, the human race.
>
> Arkan Lushwala (2012: 171-173)

How does life create conditions conducive to life?

To pay attention, this is our endless and proper work.

Mary Oliver

Almost 20 years ago, the science writer and naturalist Janine Benyus gave biologically inspired design and innovation a new name: biomimicry. Since then her work has communicated this long tradition to a mainstream audience outside the circles of a few dedicated ecologically and biologically inspired designers, engineers, material scientists, chemists, biologists and ecologists. Her humorous and engaging story-telling style and her well-chosen examples of nature-inspired, sustainable innovation do not cease to ignite the hearts and minds of corporate leaders, clean-tech investors, researchers and technologists alike. There is something that just feels intuitively right about biomimicry-based design and technology. Janine Benyus has brought the central lesson of a regenerative culture to the point: "Life creates conditions conducive to life".

In '*Biomimicry – Innovations Inspired by Nature*' (Benyus, 2002), she brought together a wide range of inspiring examples and stories of inventors that herald a new era in the process by which humanity designs ways to meet its needs. This new era resonates with ancient traditions of learning from nature. The technologists and scientists mentioned in the book draw on a long legacy of pioneers in ecological design, bionic engineering and 'design with nature'. The publication of *Biomimicry* might well be regarded as another watershed moment in our species' re-awakening to the need for re-integration of human affairs with the life-sustaining cycles of nature, just as the publication of Rachel Carson's *Silent Spring* or the publication of *Limits to Growth* marked quantum leaps in understanding our ecological impact on Earth.

Janine Benyus and her team have brought nature-inspired design to schools and universities all over the world. They have inspired national innovation strategies, and worked with many successful corporate leaders, among them companies like HOK, Nike, Patagonia, Seventh Generation, Natura, General Electric and NASA. The biomimicry revolution is spreading around the planet. Universities, R&D labs and professional networks are taking up the call to create solutions to our most pressing human problems, by following life's basic principles. We are re-learning to see, as she puts it, *nature as a mentor, as a measure, and as model to emulate.*

The 'Biomimicry Guild' was set up in 1998 and followed by the non-profit 'Biomimicry Institute' in 2005. Now they are combined within Biomimicry 3.8. Over the last 10 years, a number of network-based consultancy groups with experience in biologically and ecologically inspired innovation have set up across Europe and internationally; among them: The Symbiosis Group, Biomimicry NL, Biomimicry Europa, Biomimicry Iberia, Biomimicry for Creative Innovation (BCI), Biomimicry Switzerland, and the European Biomimicry Alliance. There are also biomimicry networks in South Africa, Latin America and Asia. In addition, there are a number of parallel networks and businesses focused on biologically inspired, technological innovation (without explicitly aiming for increased sustainability). Rather than using the word biomimicry, they tend to refer to their practice as biomimetics, bionics and bio-inspired innovation.[†]

Here are some of the questions that collaborative R&D teams can ask themselves in their pursuit of creating biologically inspired innovations. This list of questions is based on the evolving list of 'Life's Principles' collected and developed by Janine Benyus and her colleagues at Biomimicry 3.8.

LIFE'S QUESTIONS

How can we evolve and transform our technologies and processes in ways that offer a long-term future to our species and life as a whole?

- Q Which longer-term survival strategies have worked so far and how can we replicate them?
- Q How can we make sure we stay open to the unexpected and to new insights?
- Q If we reshuffle the information and capabilities we have and look at it with new eyes, can we generate new insights?

How can we make sure to maintain and increase our ability to adapt to changing conditions and to transform what no longer serves?

- Q In what way are we incorporating and safeguarding diversity?
- Q What strategies help to maintain systemic integrity while simultaneously ensuring continuous self-renewal and transformative innovation?
- Q How can we optimize resilience by designing redundancy, variation and decentralized vital functions into the system?

How are we making sure that our solutions are locally attuned and responsive to change?

- Q Are we making the most of cyclical processes and leveraging the systemic benefits of regenerative resource cycles?
- Q Are we creating solutions that use readily available (local) material and energy sources in a renewable way?
- Q Which systemic feedback loops should we pay attention to and/or design into the solution?

> Q What are the cooperative and symbiotic relationships that we can cultivate and nurture to create a better solution?

How are we ensuring we use only life-friendly chemistry?

> Q Can all the products we use be broken down into benign components without requiring excessive time spans or a lot of energy in the process?
>
> Q What is the optimal small set of constituent elements we can combine to create the desired solution?
>
> Q Are we making sure we employ water-soluble, non-toxic chemistry?

How are we ensuring that we create high levels of material and energy efficiency, while using minimal amounts of predominantly local resources?

> Q What low energy processes can we employ to create the solutions?
>
> Q How can we design multi-functionality into the solution?
>
> Q Are all the materials employed in creating the solution recyclable (preferably at the local and regional scale)?
>
> Q In what way is the proposed solution fitting form to function?

How can we integrate development with [qualitative] growth and heed the limits of [quantitative] growth?

> Q Is there a way to design self-organization and feedback into the proposed solution?
>
> Q Are we making sure to build from the bottom up?
>
> Q Can the combination of modular and nested components improve production and offer flexibility and adaptive capacity?

(based on Life's Principles by Biomimicry 3.8)

These questions can inform 'biomimicry thinking' and in multi-disciplinary design teams they can unlock innovation inspired by biological and ecological form, process and systems. The list of inspiring examples of biomimetic innovations is growing every year. It ranges from improvements in the energy use and aero/fluid-dynamics of trains, planes, cars and boats based on the optimal shapes of birds and fish to methods for carbon dioxide sequestration inspired by coral reefs or photosynthesis; from the creation of powerful non-toxic glues inspired by mussels to paints and surfaces inspired by shark skin that keep hospitals sterile, or reduce the fuel consumption of cargo ships.

Biomimicry at the ecosystem level is teaching us how to weave different technological processes into industrial ecosystems that mimic the nutrient cascades in a natural ecosystem, thereby building on one of life's principles: that the waste from one process is the food of another. We will revisit this insight in the chapters on industrial ecology and the circular economy.

Biologically inspired innovation

In general, the biologically inspired innovation process is to identify a particular need or design problem, for example, 'how can we create an effective non-toxic adhesive?' and then to identify a biological analogy to learn from and be inspired by – to follow the example: a species that manages to stick itself to a surface in an effective way. The common or blue mussel (*Mytilus edulis*) manages to 'glue' itself to rocks in the intertidal zone where it is exposed to strong wave and current forces.

Once we have identified a promising biological model, we study it in detail and explore what patterns, principles or processes can be emulated and abstracted to inform possible ideas on how to apply what we have learnt to our design challenge. The biological model can inspire innovation at different levels: either at the level of chemistry, form and function, process and pattern, or systemic integrations and synergies. At each of these levels we can find a series of biologically inspired design solutions. These are then applied to our prototype designs, tested, evaluated, and (if necessary) redesigned and optimized, until we reach a design solution that we are satisfied with.

In our mussel example, Dr. Kaichang Li, from Oregon State University's College of Forestry, found that the blue mussel's 'byssal threads' are made of a special protein that acts as a very strong and at the same time flexible glue. Funded by Columbia Forest Products, Li applied biomimicry thinking and eventually managed to create a new kind of adhesive resin by modifying soy proteins to function in a similar way to the byssal threads of mussels. The biomimetic invention led to a way to create urea formaldehyde-free plywood panels, which in turn help to reduce the build-up of toxins in indoor environments where these products are used (Columbia Forest Products, 2014).

Globally, we are at the cusp of a biologically inspired transformation of how we do business and innovate. In *The Shark's Paintbrush – Biomimicry and how nature is inspiring innovation*, serial entrepreneur and inventor Jay Harman (2013) shows how bio-inspired design is already transforming industry. The book offers hope for anyone still doubting that we are capable of co-creating regenerative cultures. Jay, the founder of Pax Scientific, has built-up, worked with and studied a number of different biomimetic businesses. He suggests that some of their defining characteristics are that they are built on transdisciplinary collaboration involving biologists, engineers and designers as well as entrepreneurs. He stresses that this creates a certain need for translation between the languages and perspectives of these different disciplines.

"Bio-inspired solutions usually represent not just an incremental change to an existing technology but also a total rethink of how to solve a problem" (Harman, 2013: 219).

Culture change takes time. Ground-breaking new technologies usually take at least 15 years to break into markets and replace established ways of doing things, but the transition towards bio-inspired technologies is already gaining speed. The numbers of registered innovations, publications on biomimicry and the amount of investment in biomimetic technologies have been growing rapidly over the last ten years (p.22). "Bio-inspired products already have generated billions of dollars in sales" (p.20).

A 2010 study predicted that, by 2025, biomimicry-based technologies and businesses could turnover a trillion US dollars (San Diego Zoo, 2010: 33). Many ethical investors are keen to invest in this growing sector (Katherine Collins, 2014). This shift in investment flows away from degenerative and towards regenerative investments actively contributes to the transition towards the "solar age" (Henderson, 2014) and the spread of regenerative culture. Ethical Biomimicry Finance offers support to such investors.

Major foundations in the USA and elsewhere are moving their investments out of fossil fuel sectors and into renewable energy, resilience building and innovation in biomimicry and green chemistry. When the heirs of an oil tycoon like John D. Rockefeller move their $870 million fund out of oil and gas investments, the writing is on the wall. Tim Dickinson reported in a *Rolling Stone* article that "as climate-change activists pressure public institutions to dump their fossil-fuel investments, it's becoming increasingly clear that the right thing to do is also the smart thing to do" (Dickinson, 2015). We are learning! Biomimetic innovation stands to benefit from this.

Biomimetic innovators aiming to bring transformative innovations and designs to existing markets will often hit the wall of first horizon management. H1 management is concerned with keeping the existing business going and biomimetic innovation tends to be disruptive innovation. It is also important to recognize that not all biomimetic innovation is necessarily sustainable. There is a lot of bio-inspired design advancing weapons and military technology. This is a clear example of disruptive innovation being captured by Horizon 1. Yet, by and large, biomimetic innovations have the inherent potential to be H2+ innovations helping us build a bridge towards cultural transformation and systemic biomimicry, towards the third horizon of a regenerative culture.

"Biomimicry lays the groundwork for future profitability and by providing solutions that don't create new problems; it offers something that short-term, cost saving solutions can't" (Harman, 2013: 231). Jay Harman knows from his own experience that "bio-inspired business needs to be prepared for the long haul" (p.233), yet it has an important advantage. "Biomimicry offers the ultimate in performance – which industry is increasingly recognizing" (p.247).†

The team at Biomimicry 3.8 describes three levels of biomimicry: learning from nature's patterns; learning from nature's processes; and learning from nature at the level of ecosystems. Each of these different levels can be applied to different scales of biologically inspired design. As I already mentioned, one of the great transitions of the 21st century will be the shift towards a solar chemistry inspired by the way that life creates effective chemical compounds based on renewable energy and material resources. 'Green chemistry' and biologically inspired material science are important foundations of design for regenerative cultures. Other scales of design to which we can apply biomimicry thinking are: product design, architecture, community design, industrial ecology, urban planning, and bioregionally centred circular economies. Figure 10 illustrates the different scales of design and how different design approaches reach across these scales in an attempt to connect them in a scale-linking manner. Let's explore some examples at these different scales of design in more detail.

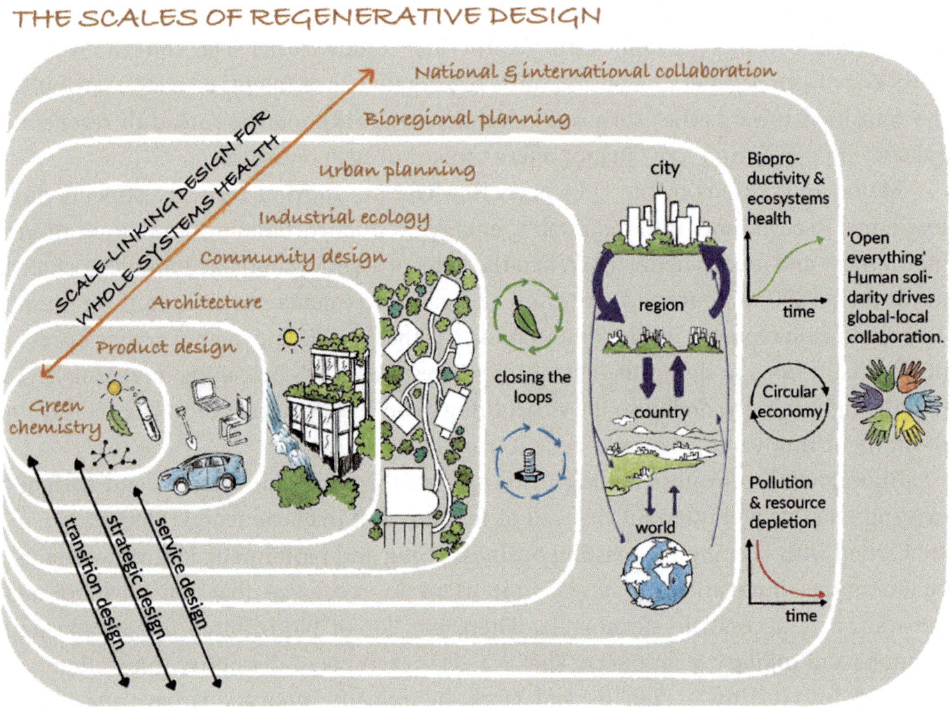

Figure 10: The Scales of Regenerative Design

Green chemistry and material science

> Studying and copying nature is one of the greatest tools in the green chemistry toolbox.
>
> Paul Anastas interviewed by Josh Wolfe (2012)

The chemists Paul Anastas and John Warner are the initiators of a global movement called 'green chemistry' aimed at designing chemical products and processes to eliminate, or drastically reduce, the generation of hazardous substances by the chemical industry. Anastas & Warner (1998) formulated twelve principles of green chemistry. Some of the questions these principles invite chemists to ask are:

Q How can we create chemical synthesis methods that maximize the incorporation of all materials used in the process into the final product?

Q How can we, as much as possible, rely on synthetic methodologies that use and generate substances with little or no toxicity to human health and the environment?

Q How can we (re-)design chemical products to preserve efficacy of function while reducing toxicity?

Q How can we minimize the energy requirements and associated environmental and economic impacts of chemical synthesis methods by conducting them at ambient temperature and pressure?

Q How can we favour raw material feedstock that is renewable rather than depleting (whenever technically and economically practical)?

Q How can we design chemical products that break down into innocuous products at the end of their function and do not persist in the environment?

In 2009, Paul Hawken, Janine Benyus, and John Warner (of the Warner Babcock Institute of Green Chemistry)[†] started an ambitious project to create a non-toxic, low-cost, solar energy technology, based on a series of non-toxic, photo-reactive dyes that are printed on a fully recyclable thin-film. Rather than following the conventional hallmarks of photovoltaic technology development by pursuing maximum durability of panels and maximum efficiency of conversion using silicon-based technologies, they decided to look at how nature creates its own solar panels.

Most leaves are renewed every year and are fully recyclable, and the efficiency of photosynthesis is low but based on renewable non-toxic materials that are assembled at ambient temperatures and ambient pressures. If their company, OneSun Inc., is successful in developing this biomimicry- and green chemistry-based 'dye-sensitized solar cell' technology, their invention will be a game-changer in the solar energy field and take us one step closer to creating more equitable regenerative cultures. There are other companies pursuing this goal, among them the Australian company Dyesol and the Irish company Solarprint.

The list of groundbreaking innovations based on green chemistry and biomimicry is rapidly growing. A number of research groups and clean-tech companies are trying to create a synthetic version of spider silk, which has a similar tensile strength to steel but is as flexible as rubber and produced without the need for high temperatures. The German company AMSilk announced in 2013 that it would start production of the "first scalable fibre with mechanical properties similar to natural spider silk".

Other leading businesses in the biotechnology and green chemistry field are working to support the shift towards regionally based circular bio-economies that use plant and waste materials as their main feedstock.[†]

Scott Allen, the co-founder of Novomer, a sustainable chemistry company based in the USA, was inspired by the fact that "nature uses billions of tons of carbon dioxide every year to make useful materials like cellulose" (Casey, 2011) and set out to create catalytic pathways in the production of plastics that use carbon dioxide and carbon monoxide as a feedstock. Currently, Novomer's plastics are still made from conventional petroleum feedstock, but the amount of feedstock needed is halved by also using carbon dioxide. The keys to Novomer's innovative approach are the catalysts that allow carbon dioxide and carbon monoxide to be transformed into a wide variety of industrial products (plastics, fuels, fertilizers, pharmaceuticals) in a cost-effective way. The development of these ground-breaking technologies has moved from initial laboratory tests to full-scale demonstration and is expected to reach commercial production soon.

> We are on the brink of a materials revolution that will be on a par with the Iron Age and the Industrial Revolution. We are leaping forward into a new age of materials. Within the next century I think biomimetics will significantly alter the way in which we live.
>
> Mehmet Sarikaya, Materials Scientist (in Janisch, 2015)

The Red Abalone (*Haliotis rufescens*) manages to produce an enormously tough, iridescent, coloured ceramic called 'mother of pearl' or nacre. It is twice as strong as any ceramic we currently produce using temperatures in excess of 2000°C. The abalone achieves this feat at ambient temperatures by laying down alternating layers of calcium carbonate (extracted from sea water) converted into its crystalline form (aragonite) and layers of a protein called Lustrin-A. At Sandia National Laboratories, a research team led by Dr. Jeffrey Brinker identified that the combination of very hard aragonite layers with flexible layers of protein gave nacre its ability to slide under compressive force. The resulting brick-wall architecture stops any cracks propagating. The team mimicked what they learned from the abalone in a self-assembly process, creating a layered structure of a mineral and a polymer. The resulting material is "optically clear but much tougher than glass. Unlike traditional 'heat, beat, and treat' technologies, Brinker's evaporation-induced, low temperature process allows liquid building blocks to self-assemble and harden into coatings that can toughen windshields, bodies of solar cars, airplanes or anything that needs to be lightweight but fracture-resistant" (Janisch, 2015). There are many other inspiring biomimetic innovations at the scale of green chemistry, molecular biology and material science:

> *Peter Steinberg* (Biosignal) has created an anti-bacterial compound that mimics the sea purse. These red algae keep bacteria from landing on surfaces by jamming their communication signals with an environmentally friendly compound called furanone. […] *Bruce Roser* (Cambridge Biostability) has developed a heat-stable vaccine storage that eliminates the need for costly refrigeration. The process is based on a natural process that enables the resurrection plant to remain in a desiccated state for years. […] *Daniel Morse* (UC Santa Barbara) has learned to mimic the silica-production process employed by diatoms. This could signal a low-energy, low-toxin route to computer components.
>
> Janine Benyus (in Biomimicry 3.8, 2014a)

The German entrepreneur, Hermann Fischer, who built up 'Auro', an international company producing plant- and mineral-based paints, coatings and glues with the highest environmental and performance standards, calls for a radical shift towards a "solar chemistry for the 21st century" by 2050 (Fischer, 2008). In his book *Stoffwechsel,* Fischer reviews the history of the petroleum-based chemical industry and explores in detail how the shift towards a non-toxic plant- and mineral-feedstock based chemistry is not only possible but an urgent necessity. As a successful entrepreneur in a sector dominated by the petrochemical industry Fischer spent more than 40 years demonstrating that this shift is possible and can be pursued in an economically viable way.

Biologically inspired product design

Starting at the scale of material science with new textiles, coatings and paints, the examples of biomimetic product design include improved medical tools, fans, propulsion mechanisms, vehicles, trains, boats, planes, renewable energy systems, smart meters, desalination technologies, carpets, windows and packaging systems; to name just a few of the breathtaking varieties of biologically inspired products on the market today. Let us explore a few of these innovations.

What can butterflies teach us about colours without pigments and dye? Butterflies in the genus *Morpho* can be recognized by their iridescent blue-toned colour which is not based on pigments but on how the surface structure of their wings diffracts and scatters light. The diverse species in this genus deploy colour to attract attention. Donna Sgro, an Australian fashion designer has created three dresses from a fabric called Morphotex, a pigment-free and dye-free textile developed by Tejin Fibres Limited in Japan. This iridescent blue material draws its colour from optical interference (Vanderbilt, 2012) based on the way fibres of different thickness and structure are inter-woven (Ask Nature, 2015a).

There are many examples of how nature has evolved functional surfaces based on their structure at the nano-scale. The micro-topography of the lotus leaf makes it extremely hydrophobic and therefore water repellent. This creates self-cleaning properties resulting in dirt-free surfaces. The leaf of the lotus (*Nelumbo nucifera*) forces water into droplets rather than letting it stick to it. These droplets then roll off, collecting dirt particles in the process (Ask Nature, 2015b). In 1982 Wilhelm Barthlott applied this biomimetic insight to the creation of a self-cleaning paint which is sold under the brand name Lotusan and is now used on hundreds of thousands of buildings.

What can we learn from sharkskin in the design of functional surfaces? Sharks are the fastest swimming marine organisms. This is due not only to their effective streamlined shapes, but also to their special skin that is covered in small teeth (*dermal denticles*) instead of scales. These denticles are aligned to produce vortices, spiral-shaped eddies that flow along the body of the shark, reducing friction (drag) as the animal glides through the water. Innovators at *Speedo Aqualab* applied this principle to the design of a revolutionary new swim suit which caused a stir at the 2000 Olympics when 80% of the medals were won by swimmers wearing this shark-skin inspired material. The Fastskin suits gave swimmers the advantage of a 3% increase in swimming speed (Waller, 2012). The suit has since been banned for competitions.

California-based Sharklet Technologies, has create a thin-film covered in microscopic diamond-shaped plates, which mimic the surface structure of shark-skin and effectively stop potentially dangerous microorganisms from establishing themselves on surfaces covered with this film. This method does not attack or kill the bacteria, but simply makes it so difficult to stay attached to these surfaces that they cannot form colonies and spread. As a result, this approach – unlike the use of antibiotics – will not create resistant microbes (Cooper, 2009). This is important as the spread of so called 'super-bugs' like MRSA and other potentially fatal strains of *Staphylococcus* and *Escherichia coli* is one of the growing concerns of the World Health Organization. Sharklet Technologies is collaborating with the US Navy to create an alternative to copper-based paints now in use as marine anti-fouling agents (Sharklet Technologies, 2015). Replacing such paints would not only drastically reduce a major source of marine pollution, but also keep ships' hulls free of attached barnacles and algae which reduce their fuel consumption by preventing drag.

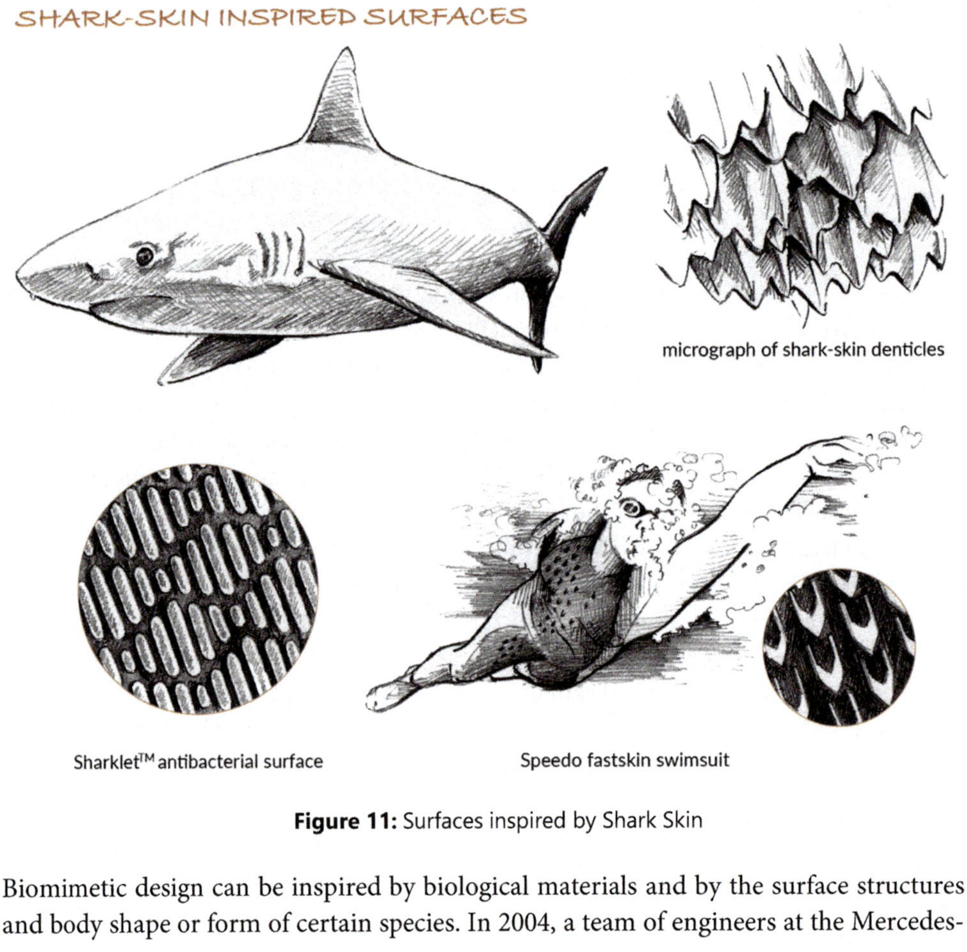

SHARK-SKIN INSPIRED SURFACES

micrograph of shark-skin denticles

Sharklet™ antibacterial surface

Speedo fastskin swimsuit

Figure 11: Surfaces inspired by Shark Skin

Biomimetic design can be inspired by biological materials and by the surface structures and body shape or form of certain species. In 2004, a team of engineers at the Mercedes-

Benz Technology Centre and at Daimler Chrysler Research decided to develop a bionic concept vehicle, looking for ways to optimize the mono-volume approach with aerodynamic performance and strength. The biological model from which they drew their design inspiration and lessons was the boxfish (*Ostracion cubicus*). Surprisingly the cube-shaped body of this tropical fish is extremely streamlined. Models of the fish tested in a wind-tunnel achieved wind drag coefficients of just 0.06, an aerodynamic ideal. The resulting full-scale concept car was among the most aerodynamic vehicles in this size category ever developed. According to Daimler, fuel consumption was reduced by 20%.

In addition to taking inspiration from the boxfish's aerodynamic shape, the team also studied the strength-to-weight ratio of the skeletal structure of the fish that gives it optimal strength with minimal material (weight) use. Again according to Daimler, transferring the optimized skeletal design of the boxfish to the concept car allowed the engineers to increase the rigidity of the external door panelling by 40% compared to conventional designs and led to a reduction of one third in the overall weight without diminishing strength or crash safety (Daimler Chrysler AG, 2004).

BOXFISH CAR

Figure 12: Boxfish Car

Can whales teach us to build more effective windmills? The inventor Frank Fish studied the humps on the front edge of the fins of humpback whales (*Megaptera novaeangliae*).

He discovered that these so-called tubercles compress the fluid flowing past the fins, giving the whales extra lift and propulsion to engage in their breathtaking 'breaching' when these animals (weighing up to 36 tonnes) propel themselves out of the water.

The Whalepower Corporation is now applying this insight to the design of new fans with improved efficiency and wind-generator blades that increase the power output at a given wind regime. The technology can also be retrofitted on existing turbine blades. The application of this tubercle technology to the aircraft industry might result in more efficient planes with more lift. Maybe humpback whales will inspire the next step in aircraft efficiency?

There are already many biomimetic designs in the airline industry. Swans inspired the Concorde's distinctive nose, for example, and the up-turned wing tips now common on most aeroplanes are turbulence-reducing measures inspired by birds of prey.

BIRD OF PREY AND PLANE WINGLETS

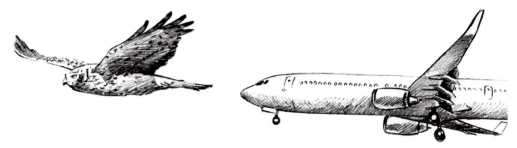

Figure 13: Wing tips

One of the most famous examples of biomimicry-based innovation is the Shinkansen 500-series bullet train that was made faster, more energy efficient, and quieter by using design principles copied from the beak of a Kingfisher (*Alcedo atthis*) (Ask Nature, 2015c). Many fast and efficient train designs have since been based on the aerodynamic shapes of other birds like the Spanish AVE 102 series with a locomotive that was shaped like a duck's bill.

KINGFISHER AND SHINKANSEN 500 BULLET TRAIN

Figure 14: Beaks

Learning from natural processes does not have to be limited to mimicking specific species, but can also be based on the general patterns and processes we can observe in nature. Jay Harman spent time as a designer of boats. His love for the ocean and obsession with the way water flows inspired him to study the 'streamlining principle' behind the formation of whirlpools.

Learning from the geometries formed by flowing and whirling water, Harman created PAX Scientific to bring the exceptional efficiencies of natural flow to fluid-handling technology like mixers, pumps, turbines, heat exchangers, ducts and propellers. One of the company's products, the Lilly Impeller, is a highly efficient water-mixing device based on these principles. Other examples include more efficient fans for cooling applications, ship propulsion systems and a new kind of desalination system.

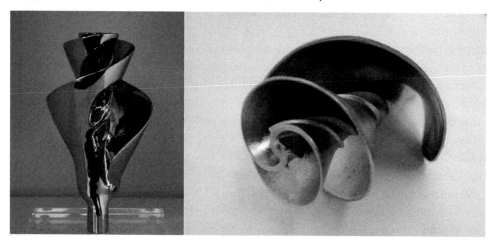

Figure 15: The Lilly Impeller (Images reproduced with permission of PAX Scientific Inc.)

The list of biologically inspired product design innovations is almost inexhaustible. These examples simply illustrate the diversity of applications of biomimicry at the product scale. There are many more.†

Biomimetic architecture

> Through its infinite complexity, nature is an instructive and inspirational influence that can expand the aesthetic horizons of the building arts and confirm the inalienable right of humanity to try to salvage a place on this planet before it's too late. The mission now in architecture, as in all human endeavour, is to recover those fragile threads of connectedness with nature that have been lost for most of this century. The key to a truly sustainable art of architecture for the new millennium will depend on the creation of bridges that unite conservation technology with an earth-centric philosophy and the capacity of designers to transform these integrated forces into a new visual language.
>
> James Wines (2000: 237)

There are countless examples of architects taking inspiration from biology. The Uluru-Kata Tjuta Cultural Centre in Australia, designed by Gregory Burgess Architects, mimics the interwoven bodies of two battling snakes. Foster & Partner's Swiss Re Headquarters in London, known as the 'Gherkin', is a 40-storey tower inspired by marine organisms called 'glass sponges'. These suck in water at the bottom and expel it at the top to filter nutrients; the building's ventilation system mimics this flow. Many other internationally recognized architects often rely on zoomorphic inspiration for the designs, processes and concepts that shape their buildings.[†] While many of them are inspired by natural and biological forms, Michael Pawlyn's approach to biomimicry in architecture is to focus on what he can learn from biological processes to make buildings more efficient by modelling nature's closed-loop, renewable energy, no-waste systems in the design of buildings (2011).

In helping to design the indoor environments for the Rainforest and Mediterranean biome exhibitions at the famous Eden Project, Pawlyn learned a lot about how water and energy cycle through natural ecosystems and how processes and functions in ecosystems are integrated and interlocking to create synergies. His design for the 'Sahara Forest Project' (Figure 16) makes use of such biomimicry thinking. The bold proposal aims not only to generate large amounts of renewable energy based on concentrated solar power and to desalinate large amounts of seawater. It integrates these functions through the use of seawater-cooled greenhouses for the horticultural cultivation of food and biomass, creating a long-term strategy to reverse desertification and regenerate productive ecosystems where the Sahara Desert borders the sea.

The project is on its way to implementation. A pilot test and demonstration centre has been built in Qatar in collaboration with two giant fertilizer companies, the Norwegian Yara ASA and its Qatari joint-venture partner Qafco. It would be good to keep in mind that in the long term the fertilizers used in such a facility will also have to be produced from renewable sources and with renewable energy. Nevertheless, this experiment at scale will give us many opportunities to learn. It will teach us how to ask the right questions in an attempt to re-green the world's deserts.

Figure 16: Reproduced with the permission of the Sahara Forest Project Foundation

Growing vegetables and biomass in the desert with external fertilizer inputs, but also using renewable energy and innovative desalination and horticulture approaches, can be considered a Horizon 2 stepping-stone technology, offering us important opportunities to innovate even more closed-loop systems that are based, as much as possible, on organic fertilizers and on-site nutrient cycling.

> Conventionally, human-made systems tend to be fossil-fuel dependent, linear and wasteful, mono-functional and engineered towards maximising one goal. Here the aim is to pursue a different paradigm – that is demonstrated by mature ecosystems which run on current solar income, operate as zero waste systems, are complex and interdependent, and have evolved toward an optimised overall system. The Pilot Project will demonstrate concentrated solar power, seawater-cooled greenhouses, evaporator hedges creating conditions for restorative agriculture, halophyte cultivation and algae production in an interdependent cluster that achieves significant increases in productivity for all elements of the system.
>
> Michael Pawlyn (2014)

Human beings, as expressions of *life-generating-conditions-conducive-to-life*, are capable of creating designs that are both restorative and regenerative. We can go beyond simply not doing any harm and start to regenerate health, resilience and thriving communities everywhere. This is the promise of biologically and ecologically inspired design and architecture.

The Eastgate Centre is a multi-storey office building in the Zimbabwean capital Harare. It uses a passive cooling system inspired by the way termites (*Macrotermes michaelseni*) cool their mounds. Mick Pearce and engineers at Arup designed the building to use only a tenth of the energy normally needed to cool a building of this size in the hot African climate (Biomimicry 3.8, 2014b). The Swedish architect Anders Nyquist of EcoCycleDesign applied a similar termite ventilation to the Laggarberg School in Timrå, Sweden.

The visionary architect and writer Jason McLennan, a Buckminster Fuller prize winner and Ashoka Fellow, created the Living Building Challenge in 2006 as a new kind of building certification system that goes beyond international or national standards like LEED or BREAM and sets a standard for regenerative architecture based on biologically inspired and ecologically informed design. There are currently 192 projects on four continents spanning a range of building types. The 'Living Building Challenge 3.0' challenges us to ask some fundamental questions about architecture and design:

Q What if every single act of design and construction made the world a better place?

Q What if every intervention resulted in greater biodiversity; increased soil health; additional outlets for beauty and personal expression; a deeper understanding of climate, culture and place; a realignment of our food and transportations systems; and a more profound sense of what it means to be a citizen of a planet where resources and opportunities are provided fairly and equitably?

International Living Future Institute (2014: 7)

McLennan's vision is to take what has already been learned through previous versions of the *Living Building Challenge* and incorporate these insights and new questions within the framework of the *Living Future Challenge*. McLennan regards the *Living Future Challenge* as "an opportunity to rethink and redesign all our systems and provide a vision for a truly regenerative society" (Living Future Institute Australia, 2014). He is a driving force in the transition towards a regenerative culture who has inspired architects around the world to take up his challenge to create buildings conducive to life.

Nature's whole system optimization informs community design

All our actions affect the sustainability, resilience and health of the communities in which we live, work and learn. The relationships we create and the collective vision of the future we create with our communities will shape whether they are sustainable and capable of regeneration. The community level is where we can all contribute to the emergence of a regenerative culture. The nested networks of interactions we co-create shape the present and future of our community and its participation in local ecosystems.

Sustainable community design is about becoming conscious of these nested networks of relationships and processes and then optimizing them in ways that support the health of the community and all its participants. The aim is to synergistically integrate the social, ecological, economic and cultural (worldview/narrative) dimension of community, creating a culture of collaboration and solidarity capable of being regenerative in the long term. Communities that succeed in this are thriving, healthy and inspiring places that offer an exceptional quality of life to their residents while having a positive impact on the local and regional environment.

Understanding ecological communities (ecosystems) better can help us fit in and optimize human communities in symbiosis with the rest of life. Rather than maximizing the numbers and short-term success of one individual species, ecosystems tend to optimize the whole system in ways that support diversity, health, resilience and the capacity for regeneration of the ecosystem as a whole. The most successful and long-term strategy for an individual or community is to emulate nature's fundamentally collaborative pattern of whole-system optimization and mimic its processes and relationships. Long-term success and vitality of all participants depends on the health of the whole system.

> Q How can we create human settlements based on learning from the patterns of organization and collaboration that we find in ecosystems?

Professors Declan Kennedy and Margrit Kennedy dedicated most of their professional and community lives to the exploration of sustainable community design and sustainable regional economic exchange mechanisms. Both worked in academia as professors for Urban Planning in Berlin and simultaneously experimented with sustainable community design within the 'Lebensgarten' ecovillage they helped to create in Steyerberg, near Hannover, Germany. In 1996, an EU-funded project initiated by them investigated many best practice and best process examples of community planning across Europe. The project resulted in their book *Designing Ecological Settlements* (Kennedy & Kennedy, 1997) in which they propose an ecologically informed standard for redesigning community. Here are some of the questions they invite us to ask:

Q How can we design ecological and sustainable settlements?

Q How are we celebrating and nurturing human and natural diversity in our community?

Q How can we focus our community around a human scale of personal interactions and collaboration between people so residents can form personal bonds with each other?

Q How can we create a settlement of short distances and integrate important community functions at a walkable scale?

Q How can we use as little space as possible for our human infrastructures and create high-density living spaces that integrate nature into the community fabric?

Q How can we encourage community participation and inspire all community members to co-create the collaborative advantage of responsible participation?

Q How can we use local and regional renewable energy resources, and energy-saving design, to create an energy-efficient settlement?

Q How can we create a climate-responsible, emissions-free community?

Q How can we create a quiet and beautiful settlement?

Q How can we use integrated design to value water and help to regenerate local watersheds?

Q How can we create effective patterns of circular resource use at a local and regional scale to make our settlements predominantly waste-free?

Q How can we design healthy buildings for healthy communities?

Q How can we integrate living space for native species and productive plants (horticulture, forest gardens, etc.) into the fabric of our settlement?

> Q How can we nurture ecological and social literacy in the community and establish effective processes of creative conflict mediation and resolution?
>
> Q How can we co-create a guiding community narrative of human values shared by all residents?

These questions challenge us to design our communities *as* nature. "What unites all these aspects [...] is that they strive for [...] *an optimisation of the whole*, rather than a maximisation of individual parts, and thus a new quality of housing and indeed life itself" (Kennedy & Kennedy, 1997, p.211). This optimization of the whole is a crucial lesson in how life creates conditions conducive to life. Sustainable community and human settlement design based on this systemic ecological insight will help to create communities capable of regeneration, adaptation and transformation. Optimization of the whole goes beyond the immediate concerns of present generations to create abundance for future generations.

Transformative innovation in existing communities means retrofitting design elements inspired by these questions into existing cultural patterns and infrastructures. It is almost impossible (and undesirable) to impose them from above. Policies must encourage and enable citizens to engage in the redesign of their community fabric. A *sense of place* and *sense of community* are nourished through participation in these collective visioning processes.

'Living the questions' is a community process. The questions above invite us to enter into dialogue and relationship with the people around us and the place we inhabit. They invite the first step of engaging participation and conscious co-creation at the community level. By exploring together how our community might become an example of a regenerative culture, we are giving each other an opportunity to learn together. This collective journey of learning in itself creates the path towards a community capable of wise decisions and regeneration. Community creates the conditions for the emergence of a regenerative culture. How do we design *as* nature and in community in elegant adaptation to this unique place and culture? Diverse regenerative cultures can evolve from this question.

Living the questions together creates community

My personal interest in sustainable community design as the primary scale of participation in the creation of regenerative cultures led me to spend a good part of the last 15 years investigating ecovillages as test fields for sustainable community design. My own apprenticeship and pilgrimage of living the questions together, of discovering in community with others what might be the appropriate questions to ask, has taken me to many ecovillages and community initiatives. To participate in intentional communities that are actively living the questions together is a powerful learning accelerator.

While I lived in the Findhorn Foundation ecovillage, I had the privilege to co-direct Findhorn College and set up the world's first 'MSc in Sustainable Community Design' in collaboration with Heriot Watt University. Community design cannot be left to professional architects, engineers and planning officials alone but, once trained in whole-systems design, these professionals can become powerful change agents. Regenerative and sustainable communities emerge from the active participation of all (or most) of their members. Therefore, widespread education in community design and processes that stimulate civic engagement and community participation are essential.

Ecovillages (Gilman, 1991; Dawson, 2006; Joubert & Dregger, 2015) and more recently transition towns and similar community groups are a source of experience and insight into how to co-create sustainable community. The Findhorn ecovillage demonstrates the results of 50 years of collective inquiry into how service to the whole, co-creation with nature, and values rooted in deep listening can create thriving human cultures in conscious and responsible co-creation. Since their learning has for the most part been born out of experimenting – living the questions together – these insights and social technologies are of particular relevance now that we urgently need to engage people in their communities everywhere in order to scale up the shift towards regeneration.

The very process of engaging in conversations about what we can do together, in the place we inhabit and with the people around us, is a catalyst for the collective learning and awareness-raising that will make 'regenerative culture' spread like a virus of infectious health. At the human scale of community, we can co-create regenerative cultures that become a lived experience and expression of the narrative of interbeing.

Two of the most successful programmes capable of stimulating this kind of participation and creating multipliers who can facilitate culturally transformative conversations in their home communities are the EDE (Ecovillage Design Education) and the 'Design for Sustainability' (GEDS) course developed by Gaia Education. These intensive programmes offer participants a whole-systems design understanding of sustainable communities. Their curriculum explores four dimensions (social, economic, ecological and worldview) each containing a series of modules (see Figure 17). It expands on the academic orthodoxy that sees sustainability as a 'three legged stool' (ecological, economic and social) by adding the critical fourth dimension of 'worldview and value system'. This approach has since been more widely adopted and is now often called the 'cultural dimension' by UN agencies and national governments.

Between its launch in 2005 and January 2016, these programme were taught a total of 200 times in 41 countries on six continents. Over 5,000 people have graduated from this UNESCO-endorsed training, which has been recognized as a significant contribution to the UN Decade of Education for Sustainable Development. Many EDE and GEDS graduates are now actively working with their home communities. The curriculum has been translated into eight languages and is available as a free download on the Gaia Education website, supported by four collections of short essays, one on each of the four dimensions of the curriculum: worldview (Harland & Keepin, 2012); ecological (Mare & Lindegger, 2011); economic (Dawson, Norberg-Hodge & Jackson, 2010); and social (Joubert & Alfred, 2007).

Teaching on these EDE programmes, I never cease to be surprised by the effectiveness of the participatory teaching methodologies and design-based exercises in quickly creating a strong community bond among participants as a basis for collective learning. The course has inspired, informed and enabled culturally creative projects in the favelas of Brazilian

6: How Can We Learn to Better Design AS Nature?

mega-cities and in traditional villages in Asia, Latin America and Africa. It has helped to revitalize abandoned villages in Southern Europe and to create working models for local economic development in Northern Europe, North America and Japan. Urban ecovillage projects are transforming neighbourhoods around the world. People who trained with Gaia Education are now supporting many of the most successful transition town projects.

Figure 17: Gaia Education's Community Design Curriculum Mandala (www.gaiaeducation.org)

Graduates have created a multitude of educational initiatives that are spreading the culture of living the questions together with sensitivity to the uniqueness of place. Gaia Education and its partner-organization the Global Ecovillage Network (founded in 1995) have successfully taken their expertise in participatory sustainable community design to grassroots activists, local community groups, academia, local and national governments, and have actively consulted the United Nations as an ECOSOC NGO since 2000.

Ecovillages and transition towns are important examples of communities actively living the questions together. The experience of these initiatives is now informing conversations in communities everywhere. In the USA the <u>Alliance for Regeneration</u> unites professionals who help communities to "reclaim their identities and destinies"

(2015). Pioneers of the ecovillage movement have recently set up VillageLab, bringing decades of expertise and experience together to provide the sustainable communities movement with what they describe as "a systematic, centrally coordinated, yet grassroots-distributed research & development program for the demonstration of leading practices in all aspects of sustainable and regenerative human systems design". The London-based charity Clear Village helps communities build a better future through creative regeneration particularly of inner-city neighbourhoods.

These enterprises and many others are helping to revitalize communities at the human scale where regenerative cultures can emerge. They all share two important insights: we can design *as* nature by deeply listening to and learning from the places we inhabit; and the first step towards creating regenerative cultures is to engage people in conversations to re-envision the future of the communities they live in. To do this we also have to re-envision our systems of production and consumption.

Industrial ecology and symbiosis are closing the loops

> […] if we aim to change the energetic metabolism of modern industrial societies, for example, we should be aware of the scope of the project. It will not just be a technological task: it will in the end imply profound socio-economic, historical change […] you cannot profoundly alter a system's output (i.e. its waste and emissions) without changing also its inputs and the ways it works internally […] to be able to deal with industrial metabolism, social and natural sciences must co-operate intimately.
>
> Fischer-Kowalski (2003: 44-45)

Industrial ecology (Graedel & Allenby, 1995), industrial symbiosis, the 'Cradle to Cradle' approach (McDonough & Braungart, 2002), and 'The Natural Step' (Robert, 2008) are all exploring effective pathways to apply ecological insights to our systems of production and consumption. These approaches all aim to transform our industrial production processes from linear (open-loop) systems – based on investing capital to acquire resources that move through the production system to end up eventually as waste – into industrial processes based on circular (closed-loop) systems in which waste is ideally eliminated completely and all energy and material waste streams become inputs for other processes.

McDonough and Braungart contributed a useful distinction between industrial and biological metabolism. All material flows should remain within one of these cycles. That is the basis for creating circular economies (see Chapter 7). Figure 18 illustrates the approach.

To achieve this shift towards integrated, cyclical whole-systems design we need to transform products, and how we design and produce them, in ways that allow disused products at the end of their useful life to be disassembled into fully recyclable or up-cyclable industrial feedstock or organic feedstock. This fundamental transformation of our industrial system is under way. It requires a whole new level of multi-stakeholder engagement in the shared understanding that our regenerative future lies with the collaborative advantage of all rather than the competitive advantage of some.

6: How Can We Learn to Better Design AS Nature?

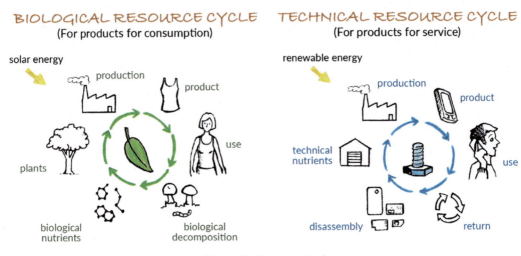

Figure 18: Resource Cycles

McDonough and Braungart ask the question: "How can humans – the people of this generation – upcycle for future generations? [...] How can people love all of the children, of all species, for all time?" (2013: 49). These are culturally creative questions that invite transformative innovation towards a regenerative culture. The graphic below illustrates the 'Cradle to Cradle Continuous Improvement Strategy' they propose in order to implement a transformation of our industrial systems. Rather than stopping at 'sustainable' (0% bad) the Cradle to Cradle approach is also regenerative, aiming for 100% good.

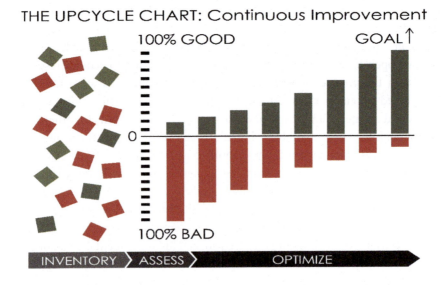

Figure 19: The Upcycle Chart – Reproduced with permission from MBDC LLC.

Simply to recycle is not enough, if it only leads to materials finding another use in less valuable and less complex products before ultimately ending in a landfill or as waste. Upcycling is about maintaining biological and industrial nutrients (resources) cycling through the biological and industrial metabolisms of our industrial processes so that they can be converted into higher quality or equal quality products at the end of a product's useful life. Being able to do this successfully is a major step towards creating regenerative cultures.

> Using the Cradle to Cradle framework, we can upcycle to talk about designing not just for health but for abundance, proliferation, delight. We can upcycle to talk about not how human industry can be just 'less bad,' but how it can be more good, an extraordinary positive in the world.
> William McDonough & Michael Braungart (2013: 11)

The Cradle to Cradle upcycling approach is applying biologically inspired design in order to have a regenerative impact. It mimics how production and consumption are organized in ecosystems. The approach builds on the wider field of industrial ecology and industrial symbiosis. Graedle and Allenby (1995: 297) defined a number of goals and principles to help us phase-in the industrial ecology and symbiosis approach in an effort to redesign our industries. These goals prompt us to ask the following fundamental questions:

Q How can we ensure that every molecule that enters a manufacturing process leaves that process as part of a saleable product?

Q How can we ensure that all the energy used actually produces the desired material transformation and waste energy streams are recovered and used elsewhere?

Q How can we create an industrial system that minimizes the use of energy and materials in products, processes and services?

Q How can we move towards using abundant (renewable), non-toxic materials when designing products?

Q How can we create industries that rely on recycling streams (theirs or those of others) as the predominant (ideally exclusive) source of material and avoid raw material extraction whenever possible?

Q How can we ensure that every product and process preserves the embedded utility of the materials used (e.g. by design for disassembly and modular design)?

Q How can we facilitate a transformation that reviews all industrial landholdings or facilities developed, constructed or modified with careful attention to improving local habitats and species diversity while minimizing impacts on local, regional and global resources?

> **Q** How can we design products so that they can serve to produce other useful products at the end of their product-life?
>
> **Q** How can we ensure this approach transcends and includes all industries, involving material suppliers, manufacturers and producers, and consumers, to weave a cooperative network that minimizes packaging and enables the recycling and reuse of materials?

At a local scale, eco-industrial parks are providing practical examples of ways to find innovative answers to these questions. By locating different production processes in the same place and applying a whole-systems design approach to connecting their resource and energy flows, we can create many win-win-win solutions. Among the economic wins are the reduction of overall raw material and energy costs, reduced waste management costs, better compliance, lower costs associated with environmental legislation, reduced costs from transportation, and economic benefits resulting from creating responsible brands for a responsible market.

The ecological benefits result from the reduced use of (virgin) raw materials and energy input through replacing imported raw materials with locally available waste streams. This in turn leads to a reduction in the waste and emissions generated by industries collaborating in the cluster. In addition, the re-localization of production and consumption, the use of local and renewable material, and the business opportunities that are created by interconnecting different industries, all generate local employment opportunities (Saikku, 2006) and diversify and strengthen local economies. Increased participation and cooperation along the entire product life-cycle strengthens community as a further social benefit.

The design of eco-industrial parks is, for example, being promoted by the Indian Government in collaboration with the German 'Gesellschaft für Internationale Zusammenarbeit' (GIZ). A recent report on eco-industrial development in India said: "It should be noted that not only new industrial parks can capitalize on the principles of *Eco Industrial Parks*. Experiences in India show that even old parks with serious environmental problems can be transformed with often simple and inexpensive measures" (GIZ, 2012: 73). The report highlighted the need for appropriate information systems and training programmes to help people apply ecological design thinking. To meet this need, the Asian Development Bank Institute has created a training manual to spread information and methodologies for the development of eco-industrial clusters (Anbumozhi *et al.*, 2013).

Among the particularly noteworthy examples of applying biomimicry at the ecosystems level are eco-industrial parks like Kalundborg in Denmark, industrial symbiosis at Östergötland in Sweden, the 'National Industrial Symbiosis Programme (NISP)' in the UK, and the 'Green Industrial Park' in Nandigama, India (still under development). Marian Chertow from Yale University has reviewed and compared a number of important examples of 'industrial symbiosis' worldwide and concluded that "environmentally and economically desirable symbiotic exchanges are all around us and now we must shift our gaze to find and foster them" (Chertow, 2007).[†]

The whole-systems design approach of industrial ecology is a powerful way to make re-localizing food production systems more effective and less wasteful, by applying ecosystems thinking through the synergistic integration of multiple food-producing processes. We will return to this powerful strategy for transformative innovation based on closing the loops and cross-sector collaboration in the next chapter, in the section on creating circular economies.

Ecologically informed urban and regional planning

> Everything that is white in the winter should be green in the summer.
> Everything that gets rained on, everything under the sun, belongs to the
> vegetable kingdom. Forests will grow in the valleys and on the roofs. In the city
> we should be able to breathe the pure air of the countryside.
> Friedrich Hundertwasser (in Senosiain, 2003: 157)

The global design, architecture and engineering firm HOK partnered with Biomimicry 3.8 to create a new process for innovation called 'Fully Integrated Thinking' which is now used in their projects around the world. The FIT framework enables design teams to tap into the wisdom behind the natural, social and ecological systems of a place to inform design and decision-making. It offers answers to today's design challenges by emulating nature's genius (HOK, 2015a).

Every FIT project aims to integrate multiple lenses (water, atmosphere, materials, energy, food, community, culture, health, education, governance, transport, shelter, commerce, ecostructure and value) to create a whole-systems design that works with and as the ecology of a given place. All FIT projects are rooted in place through an in-depth understanding of local ecologies. They are informed by 'Life's Principles' and the kind of questions we reviewed earlier. The framework helps to set goals, benchmarks and performance indicators that ensure all FIT projects are fully accountable with regard to their ecological, social and economic impacts (HOK, 2015a).

The collaboration between Biomimicry 3.8 and HOK also led to an exploration of what we might learn from nature's genius as expressed within the temperate broadleaf forest biome. This biome stretches around the planet and is home to the vast majority of the human population. Dayna Baumeister, Taryn Mead and the team from Biomimicry 3.8 helped HOK to ask the important question: *How can we create cities that function like ecosystems?* The project explored how to design cities based on 'ecological performance standards' by benchmarking the urban design project against the original ecosystem of the given locale and establishing the metrics of how the natural environment should perform: "How many millimetres of soil, how many tons of carbon, how much water stored, how much air purified?" Janine Benyus argues: "It is not enough to have green roofs and walls, we will need to ask how a building will store carbon. We need cities to perform like ecosystems, not just look like them" (Oppenheimer, 2010). The two pilot sites the project focused on were a new residential district around Meixi Lake in the city of Lang Fang in

6: How Can We Learn to Better Design AS Nature?

China, and a greenfield city development in Lavasa, a new hill town spread across 12,500 acres southeast of Mumbai (HOK, 2015c). These projects are still in development.[†]

Apart from these biomimicry inspired approaches, there are many other ecological design-based approaches to sustainable communities and urban planning. The global 'Eco-City Movement' and the work of eco-city pioneer Richard Register, who founded 'Ecocity Builders' in 1992, have helped to develop the 'International Ecocity Framework and Standards (IEFS)'. Ecocity Builders are now collaborating with UNISDR (The UN Office for Disaster Risk Reduction') to support the 'Making Cities Resilient' campaign which has already 1840 cities signed up (UNISDR, 2015.). Ecocity Builders supported UN-Habitat's 'City Resilience Profiling Programme' and also created the 'Ecocitizen World Map Project' which crowdsources and communicates tools, data and replicable methodologies from around the world to support urban sustainability.

Figure 20: Michael Sorkin's vision for a 'New York Steady State', Venice Biennale in 2010
(Reproduced with the permission of Terreform Inc.)

Designing Regenerative Cultures

These visions and tools for urban planning, many of them biologically or ecologically inspired, are supporting the growing networks of cities worldwide, like the 'World Urban Campaign' and the 'C40 Cities Climate Leadership Group', in the important task of redesigning our urban environment in ways that support the shift towards regenerative cultures.

> The best human innovations mimic and learn from natural systems. Cities need to reflect this approach to innovation in their planning, design, production, consumption, and governance.
>
> Peter Newman and Isabella Jennings (2008: 238)

Town planning pioneer, Sir Patrick Geddes, stressed in *Cities in Evolution* (1915) that effective urban planning must be based on a detailed survey of, and integration with, the surrounding region. He also demonstrated with his work on slum redevelopment that participatory processes and an educated and active citizenry were needed.

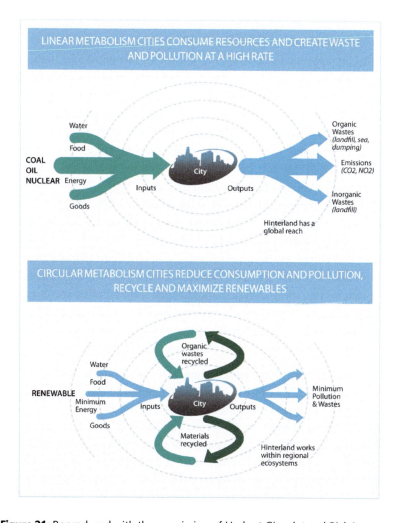

Figure 21: Reproduced with the permission of Herbert Girardet and Rick Lawrence

Almost 100 years later, Herbert Girardet wrote in *Regenerative Cities*: "Planners seeking to design resilient urban systems should start by studying the ecology of natural systems. On a predominantly urban planet, cities will need to adopt circular metabolic systems to assure their own long-term viability as well as that of the rural environments on which they depend." He suggests: "Policy makers, the commercial sector and the general public need to jointly develop a much clearer understanding of how cities can develop a restorative relationship to the natural environment on which they ultimately depend" (Girardet, 2010). Figure 21 shows how we can create regenerative cities by reducing their ecological footprint and redesigning the material and energy flows they depend upon primarily at the scale of their region.

His recent book *Creating Regenerative Cities* describes the evolution of cities from 'agropolis' to today's 'petropolis'. To create 'ecopolis, the regenerative city' we need to learn from ecosystems to help us reduce the ecological footprint of cities by optimizing the urban metabolism by designing for circular resource and energy flows and reliance on renewable energy and resources (Girardet, 2015).

The Smart City approach of optimizing the use of resources and the functioning of cities through widespread use of sensors and networks that give real-time (big-data) feedback on how the city is performing will certainly be part of the transition towards more sustainable cities, but we should be careful not to design in dependence on these high-tech systems. We need to design for resilience through including analogue alternatives and redundancy should these intelligent digital systems fail or be corrupted. A recent study by ARUP for the UK government estimated that the global market for smart city technologies will reach $408 billion by 2020 (ARUP, 2013).

Urban agriculture (Phillips, 2013) and vertical farming (Marks, 2014) will be equally important elements in tomorrow's regenerative cities as effective transport systems, urban industrial ecologies, ecological water treatment systems, building integrated renewable energy systems, and combined heat, power and cooling systems that are connected at the scale of city blocks or urban districts. Systems integration, win-win-win solutions and decentralized systems that meet local demand through local supplies, are all aspects of such urban and regional biomimicry at the ecosystems level. The movement of 'bioregionalism' (Brunckhorst, 2002) which started in the 1970s is worth revisiting in this context. The founders of the Bioregional Development Group suggest:

> […] the prices of many of the products and services we buy do not take into account the damage they cause to the environment, to people and communities. If we were to take these external costs into account, we would see the balance shifting towards smaller scale, more diverse local and regional development, or bioregional development. We can then reap the benefits of bioregional advantage. It will not take much to tip the balance and make bioregional development a much bigger part of the mainstream economy.
>
> Pooran Desai and Sue Riddlestone (2002: 82)

CHAPTER 7

WHY ARE REGENERATIVE CULTURES ROOTED IN COOPERATION?

We are beginning to learn from the way resource, information and energy flows are organized in ecosystems. We are learning to apply ecological insights to creating whole-systems design solutions that pay close attention to systemic interconnections and the potential for systemic synergies (or win-win-win solutions). Biomimicry at the ecosystem level, in the form of integrated whole-systems design based on ecological understanding, is the most complex and most promising way of applying nature's insights to creating regenerative cultures.

In mature ecosystems the health of the whole system is optimized by creating symbiotic relationships between the diversity of species in the system. Cascades and cycles of nutrients, information and energy create a diversity of interconnections throughout the system, in such a way that one organism's waste products become another organism's food, and feedback loops regulate temporary stability within a constantly transforming and evolving context. The community of organisms in an ecosystem – with its diverse roles, multiple redundancies and quick feedback loops – is interwoven into networks within networks to optimize the health, resilience and adaptability of the system as a whole. We have a lot to learn from this pattern of organization. It is the pattern that defines regenerative systems capable of self-organization.

The transition towards a regenerative culture requires the redesign of our communities, businesses, systems of governance, and how we meet everybody's basic needs in ways that learn from these patterns of organization of ecosystems. In doing so, we have to be careful to scrutinize the ways in which we apply our biological and ecological knowledge. While we urgently need to apply biologically inspired design and innovation, we must first examine the extent to which the 'story of separation' (scarcity and competition) has also coloured our perspective on life, biology and ecology.

The neo-Darwinian perspective, which still dominates the popular understanding of biology, isolates individual organisms or genes from the context of the living matrix that sustains them. Scarcity, competition and individual success are seen as the main drivers of evolution. This is an outdated perspective, based on outdated metaphors like Richard Dawkins's 'Selfish Gene' (1976).

The reductionist focus on genes and isolated individuals does not sufficiently reflect our current scientific understanding of how ecosystems and the biosphere maintain health and resilience. A more systemic and long-term understanding of how life creates conditions conducive to life has led scientists to recognize the vital importance of symbiosis, collaboration and systemic optimization in living systems. The maximization of efficiency of limited aspects of the system or the (temporary) success of certain individuals or species, on which so much of our biological (and economic) story-telling has focused, are of secondary importance for long-term survival. Collaboration and systemic optimization are more effective survival strategies.

Ecosystems are resilient because they have requisite variety (diversity) and multiple redundancies at different scales. The complex networks of relationships that create healthy ecosystems cannot be explained effectively by focusing only on the success or failure of individuals within them. The interconnections and symbiotic exchanges that create health and resilience as emergent properties of complex dynamic systems support the vitality of all participants and contribute to the survival of the system as a whole. Such health and vitality are emergent properties of the continuously transforming networks of information and resource flow across whole systems.

Think of the health and resilience of your own body (as a complex system). Our individual health is to a large part maintained by an ecosystem of bacteria and fungi inhabiting our intestines, our mouth and our skin. We are walking ecosystems! We carry ten times more non-human cells within us (and on us) than we have human cells in our bodies (Wenner, 2007). The diversity of life permeates us. Modern biology confirms that to be is to *interbe*!

> The emerging, more holistic paradigm of biological regulation and identity now holds that the identity of biological subjects is often not that of one species alone: the majority of organisms must be viewed as 'metabiomes' consisting of thousands of symbiotic, mostly bacterial species, according to recent research.
> Andreas Weber (2013: 29)

The American biologist, Craig Holdrege, offers a process-oriented understanding of biological organisms in his insightful article 'Where do organisms end?'. He suggests a shift "from a traditional notion of separate biological organism to the conception of ecological organisms, of which the biological organisms are part". In this perspective "the organism *is* interaction with other organisms within the context of a habitat. The single organism (or species) that is supposed to compete with others *does not exist* [original italics]. It is far more appropriate to view organisms as members of a differentiable whole that has never dissolved into discrete entities" (Holdrege, 2000: 16).

Whether we see isolated individuals in competition or interconnected communities in collaboration depends on our perspective. Both perspectives are useful and valid ways of approaching the individual-whole paradox of existing – subjectively and individually – in relationship and indivisible from the whole. In allowing both perspectives to inform our scientific investigations and our view of natural process, we overcome the perceptual blind-spot created by the dominant focus on competitive individual interactions.

Once we do this, we will find that the regenerative whole-system dynamics that create conditions conducive to life are predominantly collaborative in nature. Long-term survival (sustainability and regeneration) depends on these collaborative interactions, while the competitive interactions we have mainly focused on play a subordinate role of fine-tuning system dynamics in the short term.

The biologist and philosopher Andreas Weber argues that the leading edge of our scientific understanding of life is asking us to reintegrate the subjective experience of being alive as co-creative participants of evolution into our cultural narrative. He calls for an "enlivenment", a second enlightenment, which recognizes that our human meaning-making is in itself an expression of living process. If we are to co-create regenerative cultures everywhere, we have to come alive to the fact that we are *as life* capable of participating appropriately in living process. Our actions *and* how we create meaning are capable of creating conditions conducive to life.

The new biology, just like the new physics over one hundred years ago, is beginning to understand that we – and life as a whole – are far more interconnected and interdependent than our narrow focus on individual competition and scarcity has allowed us to see. The emerging understanding of life reflects the paradox of existing simultaneously as individual participants in – *and* as subjective reflections of – the whole.

We are – as individuals – indivisible from the ecosystem and the biosphere we co-create with all of life. Paradoxically, both collaboration and competition contribute to how life creates conditions conducive to life. "The biosphere is not cooperative in a simple, straight-forward way, but *paradoxically* cooperative. Symbiotic relationships emerge out of antagonistic, incompatible processes" (Weber, 2013: 32). We have to keep these new biological insights and the paradoxical relationship of individual/whole and competition/collaboration in mind when we aim to create regenerative human systems that emulate the dynamics and patterns of ecosystems. Andreas Weber points out:

> [Darwinian] evolutionary biology is a more accurate reflection of pre-Victorian social practices than of natural reality. In the wake of this metaphorical takeover, such concepts as 'struggle for existence', 'competition', and 'fitness' – which were central justifications of the political status quo in (pre) Victorian England – tacitly became centrepieces of our own self-understanding as embodied and social beings. And they still are. […] Biological, technological, and social progress, so the argument goes, is brought forth by the sum of individual egos striving to out-compete each other. In perennial rivalry, fit species (powerful corporations) exploit niches (markets) and multiply their survival rate (profit margins), whereas weaker (less efficient) ones go extinct (bankrupt). This metaphysics of economics and nature, however, is far more revealing about our society's opinion about itself than it is an objective account of the biological world.
>
> Andreas Weber (2013: 24)

Before we can explore how to redesign our industries, agriculture, the economy and the way we do business based on the regenerative dynamics that create ecosystems and planetary health, we have to raise awareness of how our understanding of biology and economics has for a long time been based on a series of blinkered assumptions and limiting metaphors. Many of the key concepts that helped Charles Darwin to construct the central argument of his theory of evolution by natural selection were influenced by the economic theories of his time, for example the work of Adam Smith and the political economist Robert Malthus's obsession with "the idea of scarcity as a driving force of social change" (Weber, 2013: 24).

The limited narrative of separation, with its exclusively competition- and scarcity-focused understanding of life, is supported by outdated biological and economic theories. Weber calls this an "economic ideology of nature" and suggests that an ideologically biased perspective "reigns supreme over our understanding of human culture and world. It defines our embodied dimension (*Homo sapiens* as a gene-governed survival machine) as well as our social identity (*Homo economicus* as an egoistic maximizer of utility). The idea of universal competition unifies the two realms, the natural and the socio-economic. It validates the notion of rivalry and predatory self-interest as inexorable facts of life" (pp.25-26).

If we understand life and evolution as a whole system in transformation, we begin to pay attention to relationships and networks of participants in that system, and suddenly we see collaboration, symbiosis and co-evolution as the prevalent patterns maintaining systemic health. Seeing competitive interactions between individual participants of the whole as the main characteristic defining and governing biological and socio-economic processes is a little bit like looking at the waves (competition) on the surface of an ocean but not seeing the immense body of water (cooperation) below. Life thrives through collaboration.

The optimization of resource-sharing and processing in order to share and generate abundance and systemic health equitably, rather than competition for scarce resources, is the basis of life's way of doing economics. In attempting to create a life-friendly economy, we need to understand the profound implications that the emerging 'systems view of life' has for our undertaking. Building on the notion of *a science of qualities* introduced by the biologist and mathematician Brian Goodwin, the physicist and systems thinker Prof. Fritjof Capra and Prof. Pier Luigi Luisi, a chemist working in the biology department of Roma Tre University, argue:

> As the twenty-first century unfolds, a new scientific conception is emerging. It is a unified view that integrates, for the first time, life's biological, cognitive, social, and economic dimensions. At the forefront of contemporary science, the universe is no longer seen as a machine composed of elementary building blocks. We have discovered that the material world, ultimately, is a network of inseparable patterns of relationships; that the planet as a whole is a living, self-regulating system. […] Evolution is no longer seen as a competitive struggle for existence, but rather a cooperative dance in which creativity and constant emergence of novelty are the driving forces. And with the new emphasis on complexity, networks, and patterns of organization, a new science of qualities is slowly emerging.
>
> Fritjof Capra and Pier Luigi Luisi (2014b)

What is being called into question here is not the overall process of biological evolution, but whether competition for scarce resources rather than symbiotic networks in which life creates conditions conducive to life are the main drivers of speciation and evolution of life as an interconnected process. New insights in biology, neuroscience and evolutionary theory are offering a perspective that helps us to retell the story about who we are as biophysical beings.

Truly understanding ourselves individually and collectively as 'being *in* and *through* relationships' is the conceptual/perceptual meta-design shift that underlies the cultural transformation that is under way. We are transforming a globalized but fragmented humanity based on the *narrative of separation* and competition into globally cooperative networks of locally adapted cultures sharing a unifying *narrative of interbeing*.

> Q How can we create a regenerative material culture and industrial system based on collaboration?
>
> Q How can we co-create a regenerative approach to agriculture that supports food and water security, climate change mitigation, local living economies, healthy local ecosystems and product diversity based on biomaterials?
>
> Q What would a regenerative economy with predominantly collaborative relationships look like?
>
> Q Understanding that long-term, collaborative advantage trumps short-term, competitive advantage as the success strategy in healthy systems, how would we redesign the way we do business?
>
> Q How will we redesign our economic systems to reflect the insight that collaborative participation in life-sustaining relationships is life's fundamental principle of evolution?

From a scale-linking, systemic and long-term perspective of natural processes we begin to realize that those isolated, competitive interactions we do observe from a short-term perspective are actually embedded in a context of systemic, long-term collaboration. All regenerative systems are fundamentally collaborative. Optimization of the whole based on symbiotic relationships over the long term is the hallmark of regenerative systems.

The *systems view of life* (Capra & Luisi, 2014a), as a fundamentally collaborative interconnected process, is inviting us to redesign the human presence on Earth based on our new understanding of the way life unlocks abundance through collaboration. The emerging practices of industrial ecology, integrated ecological design and regenerative agriculture, as well as the move towards circular regenerative economies based on locally regenerated biological resources, are part of a fundamental redesign that will lead to the emergence of regenerative cultures. Regenerative systems are primarily collaborative and regenerative cultures are cultures of collaboration.

Redesigning agriculture for food sovereignty and subsidiarity

> The world needs a paradigm shift in agricultural development: from a 'green revolution' to an 'ecological intensification' approach. This implies a rapid and significant shift from conventional, monoculture-based and high external-input-dependent industrial production towards mosaics of sustainable, regenerative production systems that also considerably improve the productivity of small scale farmers. We need to see a move from linear to a holistic management, which recognizes that a farmer is not only a producer of agricultural goods but also a manager of an agro-ecological system that provides quite a number of public goods and services (e.g. water, soil, landscape, energy, biodiversity, and recreation).
>
> *Wake up before it is too late*, UNCTAD Report (2013: 2)

To explore the transformation towards a regenerative culture without taking a closer look at how such deep societal change is dependent upon and reflected in the way we feed ourselves would be negligent. The primary sector – agriculture – is the basis of a thriving regenerative culture. There are many committed people promoting the shift towards more regenerative, restorative and sustainable farming practices.

Organic farming, bio-dynamic farming, sustainable agriculture, agroforestry, agro-ecology, permaculture and regenerative agriculture are just some of the names describing related and often complementary methodologies. They offer viable alternatives. Our current industrial farming practices are not only deeply un-economical (if energy and fertilizer inputs are fully costed), they are also destroying the quality and decreasing the quantity of the world's top-soil, on which we and so much of life depend.

Despite a vast amount of disinformation – in large part based on research funded by chemical agribusiness – the misconception that local organic agriculture cannot feed the world is finally being eradicated (Halweil, 2006; FAO, 2015). From the invention of agriculture until very recently, humanity has fed itself via local, small-scale farms that employ organic techniques to maintain and improve soil health and agricultural yields. Even with the global population in rapid expansion during the last century, the majority of the food that feeds the world still comes from small-scale local farms *and* is grown by women (FAO, 2011).

A 2013 review by the UN Conference on Trade and Development (UNCTAD) concluded that the adequate response to climate change and the challenge of feeding a prospective human population of 9 billion includes transformative changes in our agricultural, food and trade systems. We need to increase diversity on farms, reduce the use of fertilizers and other external inputs, and support local farmers to create vibrant and resilient local food systems (UNCTAD, 2013). Among the key challenges or questions highlighted in the report are:

> Q   How can we increase soil carbon content and achieve a better integration between crop and livestock production, *and* integrate agroforestry and wild vegetation into farming practices?

Q   How can we drastically reduce greenhouse gas (GHG) emissions associated with livestock production?

Q   How can we reduce GHG emissions through sustainable peatland, forest and grassland management?

Q   How can we optimize the use of organic and inorganic fertilizers, including through closed-loop nutrient cycles?

Q   How can we reduce waste throughout the food chain?

Q   How can we influence a change in dietary patterns towards climate-friendly food consumption?

Q   How can we transform the international trade regime for food and agriculture?

'La Via Campesina' is an international movement of farmers, indigenous people, women farmers, agricultural migrants, and farm workers representing more than 200 million small- and medium-sized primary producers in 164 local and national organizations in 73 countries. The main aim of this massive global movement is "to realize food sovereignty" and create organized resistance against an economic globalization that favours predatory multinationals.

In its own words, the movement aims to ensure that "small farmers, including peasant fisher-folk, pastoralists and indigenous people, who make up almost half of the world's people, are capable of producing food for their communities and feeding the world in a sustainable and healthy way" (Via Campesina, 2011).

Without food sovereignty, communities and regions lose their socio-economic resilience and vibrancy. Food sovereignty describes the rights of peoples "to healthy and appropriate food produced through sustainable methods" and the entitlement to "define their own food and agriculture system". Strengthening regional food sovereignty is a powerful win-win-win strategy in the response to the current food, inequity (poverty) and climate crises. Implementing food sovereignty leads to more decentralized and more highly diversified farming systems that are networked into regional food economies. This builds redundancies at different scales, and increases adaptability and resilience.

> Food sovereignty prioritizes local food production and consumption. It gives a country the right to protect its local producers from cheap imports and to control production. It ensures that the rights to use and manage land, territories, water, seeds, livestock and biodiversity are in the hands of those who produce food and not of the corporate sector. Therefore the implementation of a genuine agrarian reform is one of the top priorities of the farmers' movement.
>
> La Via Campesina (2011)

Without food, water and energy sovereignty at the regional level, subsidiarity will remain a political ideal. Subsidiarity describes the principles that any central (political) authority should have a subsidiary function of coordination, performing only those tasks that cannot be executed at a local level, and that decisions are to be taken as closely as possible to, and with the involvement of, the citizens affected by them. Without subsidiarity we will not be able to unleash the levels of locally grounded transformative innovation and widespread citizen participation necessary to co-create the transition to regenerative cultures in ways that foster health, diversity and local adaptation. Current global trade treaties and agricultural policies disregard subsidiarity and people's fundamental right to food sovereignty.

The global *Slow Food* movement, founded by the Italian Carlo Petrini, aims to promote the production of "good, clean and fair" food and to nurture the healthy connections between local food and culture, politics, agriculture and the environment. One of the roles of Slow Food was to catalyse the creation of Terra Madre, a network of networks comprising organizations, producer cooperatives and food communities in 160 countries. Slow Food published an important document on *The Central Role of Food*, inviting us to reflect upon the following questions (Petrini *et al.*, 2012):

- Q How can we strengthen and recreate food systems that build soil fertility?

- Q What is the connection between healthy food, healthy water and healthy air?

- Q How can promoting good, clean and fair food also act in defence of biodiversity?

- Q What role does food and agriculture play in maintaining local landscapes?

- Q How can we use the importance of good, clean and fair food to people's health as a way to engage participation in sustainable food production and consumption?

- Q What role does food and local food production play in the maintenance of biocultural diversity, knowledge and memory?

- Q What is food's cultural role in promoting pleasure, social relations, conviviality and sharing?

There are few better ways to engage a widespread section of society and local communities in a dialogue about creating a regenerative culture than by starting with the issue of food and how it relates to the health and wellbeing of individuals, communities and ecosystems. Local farmers and food producers, and the relationships local communities build with them, are critically important in creating regenerative cultures.

Slow Food actively helps people to stay in the countryside, encouraging young people to return to farming, fostering urban gardening and farming projects at the same time as creating co-producer networks that link urban consumers directly with rural producers. The organization is also actively working to reduce food waste – a direct result of a structural systems failure in the global industrial farming system that turns food into a commodity subject to speculation.

Local food sovereignty and the creation of a local living economy is a prerequisite for participatory democracy and vibrant socio-economic community life. Widespread citizen participation in the strengthening of local food economies requires open information sharing, continuous education and life-long learning. Slow Food therefore engages in education as a means of culture change promoting and supporting "mutuality, conviviality, the small scale and the protection of the common good" (ibid: 22).

Many inspiring organizations have been promoting the regenerative redesign of agriculture, the protection of heirloom variety seeds against corporate monocultures, and the creation of local food economies based on food, water and seed sovereignty, among them: the International Society for Ecology and Culture, founded by Helena Norberg-Hodge and the Navdanya network founded by the Indian physicist Vandana Shiva. Vibrant local food economies favour local production for local consumption where possible, yet do not oppose trade categorically.

Regenerative agriculture: effective responses to climate change

The Synthesis Report of the UN 'Millennium Ecosystem Assessment' (2005) called agriculture "the largest threat to biodiversity and ecosystem function of any single human activity". Everything we do is dependent on agriculture and many current agricultural practices are deeply unsustainable. In redesigning the way we 'do' agriculture, we can create the basis for the emergence of regenerative cultures everywhere.

The so called 'green revolution' of large scale industrial agriculture with its addiction to fossil resources and its systematic degradation of local farming communities and biocultural diversity in favour of predatory multinational corporations has been a failure with disastrous effects. Alternatives do exist. The Soil Association in the UK was started in 1946 and the Rodale Institute in the USA in 1947; both institutions promote and develop organic farming approaches. In 1972, the International Federation of Organic Agriculture Movements (IFOAM) was founded. It now has member organizations in 120 countries.

In April 2014, the Rodale Institute published a white paper that outlines how agricultural techniques available today could sequester sufficient amounts of atmospheric carbon to slow down climate change and reduce greenhouse gas concentrations in the long term by fixing carbon in agricultural soil. Regenerative agricultural practices can help to build fertile soils, to maintain and often increase agricultural yields, and to support ecological abundance by nurturing healthy ecosystem functioning:

> Simply put, recent data from farming systems and pasture trials around the globe show that we could sequester *more than 100% of current annual CO_2 emissions* with a switch to widely available and inexpensive organic management practices, which we term 'regenerative organic agriculture'. These practices work to maximize carbon fixation while minimizing the loss of carbon once returned to the soil, reversing the greenhouse effect. [original italics]
>
> Rodale Institute (2014)

Robert Rodale coined the term 'regenerative organic agriculture' to indicate that these practices are more than simply 'sustainable', taking advantage of the natural tendencies of ecosystems to regenerate when disturbed. Regenerative organic agriculture is "a holistic systems approach to agriculture that encourages continual on-farm innovation for environmental, social, economic and spiritual wellbeing". In general, "regenerative organic agriculture is marked by tendencies towards closed nutrient loops, greater diversity in the biological community, fewer annuals and more perennials, and greater reliance on internal rather than external resources" (Rodale Institute, 2014).

The techniques and methodologies used include the reduction or elimination of tillage in combination with planting cover crops on fallows in crop rotation cycles and maintaining the residue of these crops on the land (green mulch). Composting – the controlled aerobic decomposition of organic materials – and adding this nutrient and carbon-rich compost to the soil as fertilizer is a central practice of organic farming. It helps to accumulate carbon in the soil while increasing fertility and yields. The use of perennial plants, increased crop diversity including tree crops and maintaining a rich soil structure through plants with deep, bushy root systems, all support a healthy network of mycorrhizal fungi and encourage the long-term fixing of carbon in soils.

The World Bank has released a detailed report which reviews the different 'abatement rates' of different land management practices and how effective they are in different regions of the world. The report highlights that "in addition to storing soil carbon, sustainable land management technologies can be beneficial to farmers because they can increase yields and reduce production cost" (World Bank, 2012: xvi). One of the techniques that scores highest for its greenhouse gas abatement rate is the application of biochar (ibid: xxiii).

Biochar can be obtained on farms from the carbonization of biomass through pyrolysis or gasification. The International Biochar Initiative maintains that – applied correctly – "the carbon in biochar resists degradation and can hold carbon in soils for hundreds to thousands of years". It needs to be applied in combination with organic nutrients (e.g. liquid compost) to have a positive effect on yields. "Biochar and bio-energy co-production can help combat global climate change by displacing fossil fuel used and by sequestering carbon in stable carbon pools" (Biochar International, 2015).

Regenerative agriculture and the wide range of land management methodologies associated with it have the potential to create multiple win-win-win solutions. In addition to offering a timely response to the spectre of run-away climate change, these techniques help to restore soils, revitalize rural communities, build food, water and energy sovereignty, and support the process of re-localizing production and consumption – thereby building systemic resilience as the basis of thriving regenerative cultures.

Starting in the 1960s, the wildlife biologist Allan Savory developed one particularly promising methodology of regenerative agriculture that could be a game-changer for climate change mitigation. Holistic management and its associated technique of 'holistic planned grazing' are based on a systems thinking approach that mimics nature. Savory's 'Holistic Management' is "a Whole Farm/Ranch Planning System that helps farmers, ranchers, and land stewards better manage agricultural resources in order to reap sustainable environmental, economic and social benefits".

The four cornerstones of this practice are *Holistic Financial Planning* to "make a healthy profit"; *Holistic Grazing Planning* to manage the effects of resting the land combined with periodic disruption by grazers to improve "land health and animal health"; *Holistic Land Planning* to help "design the ideal property plan"; and *Holistic Biological Monitoring* using simple techniques for feedback on land health and productivity (Holistic Management International, 2015).

> Holistic Management teaches people about the relationship between large herds of wild herbivores and the grasslands and then helps people to develop strategies for managing herds of domestic livestock to mimic those wild herds to heal the land. […] Holistic Management embraces and honours the complexity of nature, and uses nature's model to bring practical approaches to land management and restoration.
>
> The Savory Institute (2015)

In the last 40 years more than 10,000 people have received training in 'Holistic Management' and globally there are now over 40 million acres managed using this system (Savory Institute, 2014). With long-term field trials on four continents, some of them running since the 1970s, the effectiveness of holistic management is well established.

In a 2013 white paper the institute suggested that holistic planned grazing could be applied to approximately 5 billion hectares of the world's degraded grassland soils in order to restore them to optimal health and thereby sequester more than 10 gigatons of atmospheric carbon annually into the soil's organic matter, "thereby lowering greenhouse gas concentrations to pre-industrial levels in a matter of decades. It also offers a path towards restoring agricultural productivity, providing jobs for thousands of people in rural communities, supplying high quality protein for millions, and enhancing wildlife habitat and water resources" (2013: 3). There is still some scientific debate about these claims and they are now being evaluated through research and field trials.

I regard holistic management as an excellent example of biomimicry at the ecosystems level. Its practice is adapted to the uniqueness of place and based on both scientific principles and local knowledge. Practitioners intervene in the dynamics of degraded grassland ecosystems by substituting absent natural grazers (whose absence is often attributable to past farming practices) with domesticated grazers like cattle, sheep, goats or bison, rotating them over the landscape in patterns that mimic the natural disturbance and fertilization caused by roaming herds of herbivores.

7: Why Are Regenerative Cultures Rooted in Cooperation?

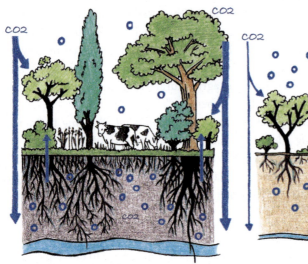
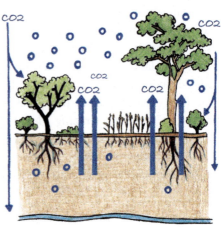

HOLISTIC LAND MANAGEMENT & OTHER TECHNIQUES OF REGENERATIVE AGRICULTURE

CONVENTIONAL LAND MANAGEMENT & INDUSTRIAL AGRICULTURE

Healthy soil as carbon sink
- More ground cover
- More roots
- More carbon stored in soil
- More water retention in top soil
- Recovering groundwater levels
- Less erosion
- More bioproductivity
- More diversity
- Less carbon in the atmosphere

Depleted soil as carbon source
- Less ground cover
- Fewer roots
- Less carbon stored in soil
- Less water retention in top soil
- Depleting groundwater
- More erosion
- Less bioproductivity
- Less diversity
- More carbon in the atmosphere

Figure 22: Holistic and conventional land management compared

Holistic Management influences natural ecosystem processes to support the conversion of solar energy by plants (efficient energy flow), improve the interception and retention of precipitation by the soil (effective water cycle), optimize the nutrient cycles (effective mineral cycle), and promote "ecosystem biodiversity with more complex mixtures and combinations of desirable plant species, otherwise known as community dynamics" (2013: 9). We are starting to (re)learn how to act as a responsible keystone species and participate appropriately in the emergence of increased health, bioproductivity and vibrant diversity in the ecosystems we inhabit. Figure 22 illustrates some of the multiple synergistic benefits of holistic land management and holistic planned grazing.

Regeneration means promoting diversity and resilience above and below ground, restoring watersheds and replenishing aquifers. Regenerative agriculture nurtures symbiotic inter- and intra-species relationships to support systemic health. It is an example of salutogenic (health-generating) design. The dynamics of healthy ecosystems are the measure, model and mentor of regenerative agriculture, which promises to feed humanity while restoring ecosystems, regulating climate and growing the resource base of regional bio-economies.

Learning from and mimicking healthy ecosystems

> Because ecosystems components are interdependent, by degrading or improving one aspect of ecosystem health, the entire system can likewise be degraded or improved. Rebuilding soil organic matter pumps carbon dioxide into the soil in the form of soil carbon and creates an upward spiral of ecosystem health. Making soil health a central goal of agricultural policies worldwide will be *essential* for achieving global food and water security and mitigating climate change.
>
> Center for Food Safety (2014: 19)

Since the very beginnings of large-scale industrial agriculture there have been wise voices of warning and dissent, along with innovators and pioneers seeking healthy alternatives. The petrochemical industry aggressively promoted the use of pesticides and large-scale monocultures farmed with heavy machinery after the Second World War. During the so-called 'green revolution' in the 1950s and '60s a handful of multinational corporations effectively took over the majority of global grain production. Soil became nothing but a substrate for growing and the rapid degradation of the world's farm and grasslands resulted. There are hundreds of millions of farmers worldwide, many of them keen apprentices of the ecosystems and unique places they inhabit. Let's have a look at some of the pioneering innovators who have developed *and* applied techniques that will support the transition to a regenerative agricultural system.

The plant biologist and farmer Wes Jackson co-founded The Land Institute in 1976 to work on the "problem of agriculture" and help to "develop an agricultural system with the ecological stability of the prairie and grain yields comparable to that from annual crops". Wes Jackson has taken a biomimetic approach since the very beginning. The Land Institute's mission statement reads: "When people, land, and community are as one, all three members prosper; when they relate not as members but as competing interests, all three are exploited. By consulting Nature as the source and measure of that membership, The Land Institute seeks to develop an agriculture that will save soil from being lost or poisoned, while promoting a community life at once prosperous and enduring" (Land Institute, 2015a).

Over the last 39 years the Land Institute has developed a proposal for 'Natural Systems Agriculture' and has demonstrated its scientific feasibility. The institute's extensive plant breeding programme has the long-term vision of creating "a domestic grain producing prairie with the four functional groups represented (warm season and cool-season grasses, legumes, sunflower family)" (Jackson, 2002: 7). Their efforts focus on both domesticating wild species and on turning domesticated annuals into perennials.

The development of perennial varieties based on traditional plant breeding takes generations. Wes Jackson loves to point out: "If your life's work can be accomplished in your lifetime, you're not thinking big enough" (Land Institute, 2015b). A regenerative culture needs such long-term thinking! The Land Institute has already had its first successes; for example, creating a new perennial grain they named 'Kernza'. Their long-term aim is to "design an agriculture that relies on proven ecological patterns and processes to achieve sustainability, changing agriculture from being extractive and damaging to restorative and nurturing" (Land Institute, 2014). Developing an agricultural system predominantly based on perennial grains is a 'Horizon 3' type long-range transformative innovation and we can learn a lot along the way.

> At The Land Institute, ecologists are exploring ways to grow grains, oilseeds and legumes together so cropland can once again benefit from the advantages of diverse perennial vegetation. These new crop arrangements will be less dependent on nitrogen-based fertilizers and better-equipped to anchor soil, virtually eliminating erosion and chemical runoff, and promise a much smaller energy cost. They interact in complementary ways to manage pathogens and pests naturally, all while providing food for years without replanting. In many situations, the deep roots of perennial grains will better withstand the drought or deluge likely to accompany climate change. They sequester carbon, which helps reduce greenhouse gases, and they host microorganisms and invertebrates that contribute to soil health.
>
> Land Institute (2014)

Regenerative agriculture pays close attention to improving soil quality. The diversity of microorganisms and fungal mycelia in the soil is the basis for a regenerative farming system. Plants need the microorganisms and fungi in the soil in order to take up nutrients effectively. So-called nitrogen fixing plants, used as green manure, are not fixing the nitrogen themselves but do so in symbiosis with bacteria (e.g. *Rhizobium*) living on their roots. Modern industrial farming tends to reduce the diversity of nutrients that support healthy and resilient plants to only three main fertilizers (phosphorus, potassium and nitrogen). They can support fast growth and high yields (for a while), but used without a wide variety of complementary nutrients they leave the plants more vulnerable to disease and parasites.

Another common agricultural practice that is brought into question by regenerative agriculture is the ploughing and turning of the soil through the use of heavy (and therefore soil compacting) machinery. Leaving the soil bare and turning it leads to a massive die-off of beneficial microorganisms in the soil and can lead to top-soil loss either through wind (in dry conditions) or water. Compacting the soil destroys the soil's water retention capacity and makes crops vulnerable to droughts.

The technique of key-line ploughing, developed by Percival Yeomans in the 1950s, is now applied with the plough developed by his son Allan. It involves ploughing just off the topographic contour lines with a very gradual slope (approximately 1 metre in 400 metres) in order to create a surface profile that slows water run-off and gives water time to sink into the soil. Most regenerative farming approaches do not turn the soil and only cut the soil using his innovative plough (Yeomansplow, 2015). The plough simply opens up the soil for water to sink in. The thin grooves can be cut to different depths and used to inoculate the soil with beneficial microorganisms and mycelia to help with the soil-building process. Biochar inoculated with liquid organic compost can be fed into the thin grooves for active carbon burial and soil building.

Maintaining a healthy bacterial and fungal flora and fauna in the soil increases the soil's carbon content. The win-win-win solutions of restoring the world's top-soils, actively sequestering atmospheric carbon and creating a more resilient and productive local agricultural system are practically begging us to engage local farmers everywhere in this process. Increasing the organic carbon content of our top-soil also has the important role of increasing the soil's water retention capacity (Rawls *et al.*, 2003) and the crops grown on them are therefore more resilient to unstable weather patterns and droughts. Regenerative agriculture aims to optimize the local water cycle, including recharging underground aquifers and restoring healthy watersheds. "Spread it! Slow it! Sink it!" is the mantra of the director of the Water Institute, Brock Dolman, who is a passionate advocate and practitioner of regenerative watershed stewardship.

The practice of Holistic Management mentioned in the last chapter also helps to increase water retention in the soil and is an effective means of regenerating degraded dry lands and even deserts. Applied at the farm scale it is also an excellent strategy for creating resilient, regenerative and lucrative farm businesses. Joel Salatin at Polyface Farm is a North American farmer who has built up a model farm attracting international attention. He created a highly productive and healthy agro-ecosystem by planting trees, digging ponds, building huge compost piles and raising grass-fed cows that he moves across the land with the help of portable electric fencing. Mimicking the grazing patterns of ecosystems with diverse grazers, the cows are followed by chickens and pigs using innovative mobile animal shelters. Each species takes a specific role in fertilizing and enriching the diversity of the perennial prairie polyculture it feeds upon (Polyface, 2015a). The 500-acre farm employs 10 people and generates over US$1 million in sales through direct marketing to local families, restaurants and retail outlets. Joel Salatin describes his farming method as a "symbiotic, multi-speciated synergistic relationship-dense production model that yields far more per acre than industrial models" (Polyface, 2015b).

The Australian farmers Colin and Nicholas Seis have turned their 2,000-acre farm, Winona, in New South Wales into an internationally acclaimed example of a technique called 'pasture cropping'. Cereal crops are sown directly into native perennial pastures, combining grazing and cropping into a single land-use method with synergistic economic and environmental benefits. Colin Seis started to develop this technique in 1992 running a herd of 4,000 merino sheep and cropping oats, wheat and cereal rye on the same land. In recent years it has become increasingly popular, with more than 1,500 farmers in Australia converting to the method and farmers in the Northern hemisphere adopting the approach (Pasture Cropping, 2008).

Another important set of techniques needed for successful regenerative agriculture is the production of farm-made BioFertilizers, in order to avoid the economically and environmentally disastrous effects of energy-intensive and expensive artificial fertilizers. Among the techniques used are the composting of on-farm organic waste in combination with beneficial microorganisms, fungal mycelia and rock dust for re-mineralization. Many new techniques for organic fertilizer production and soil fertility testing were developed by Latin-American scientists, among them are the Mexican Eugenio Gras, the Columbian Jairo Rivera and the Brazilian Sebastião Pinheiro. In recent years organizations like RegenAG, Agricultura Regenerativa Iberica, Regenerative Agriculture UK and MasHumus have started to promote and teach the diverse tools of regenerative agriculture internationally.

There are many complementary approaches to helping agriculture enable the transition towards regenerative cultures. Many people now promoting regenerative agriculture are experienced permaculture design practitioners and teachers. Bill Mollison and David Holmgren developed permaculture in the 1970s. This systematic, design-based method was originally aimed at creating a 'permanent agriculture' and has since been expanded into a multi-faceted approach to creating a 'permanent culture' (or regenerative culture), with applications in social dynamics, decision-making, community planning and economics.

Worldwide there are tens of thousands of people trained in permaculture and thousands of established permaculture farms. Bill Mollison's *Permaculture Design Principles and Ethics* (2011) offers a useful set of guidelines for the creation of locally adapted cultures capable of regeneration. The Essence of Permaculture can be downloaded on Holmgren's website in nine different languages (Holmgren, 2002).

'Forest gardening' is a prehistoric method of food production in many tropical areas. Robert Hart pioneered it in temperate climates and his work has been developed further by Patrick Whitefield and Martin Crawford, who runs the Agroforestry Research Trust. The related approach of 'Analog Forestry' uses "natural forests as guides to create ecologically stable and socio-economically productive landscapes". This whole-systems approach to silviculture "minimizes external inputs, such as agrochemicals and fossil fuels, instead fostering ecological function for resilience and productivity". Ranil Senanayake developed the 'analog forestry' approach in Sri Lanka in the early 1980s. It has since grown into a global practitioner network with a standard for certified 'Forest Garden Products' (IAFN, 2015).

Agroecology, as promoted by Miguel Altieri (1995) is also very much aligned with the shift towards a regenerative agriculture. Altieri has done important work on the preservation of indigenous agricultural knowledge and techniques while working for the UN's Food and Agriculture Organization (Koohafkan & Altieri, 2010). His work has supported an "agroecological revolution in Latin America" to help heal natural ecosystems, create food sovereignty and support peasants (Altieri & Toledo, 2011).

An important and still somewhat underdeveloped aspect of restoration and regenerative agriculture is the creation of mutually supportive plant-mushroom-soil relationships based on mycorrhizal symbiosis (see Smith & Read, 2008). Maintaining healthy soil ecosystems, in particular supporting the role of fungal mycelium in soil-root-plant nutrient exchanges, decomposition of organic matter, and soil remediation from pollutants is a central aspect of regenerative agriculture and ecosystems restoration.

Paul Stamets's *Mycelium Running – How Mushrooms Can Help Save the World* (2005) is an invaluable resource for regenerative culture designers. From high quality tasty protein sources, broad spectrum medicinal use and water filtration, to applications in agriculture, forestry, soil remediation and ecosystems restoration. Stamets explores *mycomimicry* and how we can apply *mycorestoration* to benefit ecosystems and people. I had the pleasure of taking various walks through the wooded corners of the Scottish Highlands with Paul. He believes that we have ignored or feared our fungal cousins for too long. Mushrooms *are* the molecular disassemblers of nature. Most cyclical and regenerative processes that take care of decomposition, nutrient cycles, soil fertility, soil water retention and soil health involve fungal mycelia.

Mushrooms have also learnt to defend themselves against bacterial infections and have been shown to not just have antibiotic but also anti-viral and anti-cancer properties. They practically 'created the first internet', networking entire forest ecosystems into a web of distributed collective intelligence and symbiosis. Paul likes to point out that "after every major extinction event it was mushrooms who inherited the Earth" and helped life to reboot.

Stamets has built his company, Fungi Perfecti, into a successful green business and has filed a long list of patents (to protect his innovations against what he calls "the vulture capitalists"). His work and collection of fungal mycelia will be a critical resource as ecosystems regeneration becomes a central activity for humanity in the 21st century.[†]

> On land, all life springs from soil. Soil is ecological currency. If we overspend it or deplete it, the environment goes bankrupt. In either preventing or rebuilding after environmental catastrophe, mycologists can become environmental artists by designing landscapes for both human and natural benefit.
>
> Paul Stamets (2005: 55)

There are so many committed practitioners of regenerative agricultural practices and ecosystems restoration worldwide. We can be very hopeful that co-creating regenerative human cultures is indeed a possibility of our choosing. Hopeful examples range from the reforestation of the Highlands based on the 500-year business plan of the Scottish Charity's Trees for Life to bring back the Caledonian Forest, to Treepeople in Los Angeles working on urban watershed and urban community forest restoration, The Wild Foundation, and almost 30 years of the Society for Ecological Restoration. People from all these organizations and many others like them have given us the know-how and experience to restore the world's ecosystems and watersheds. In 2002, I took part in the *Restore the Earth Conference*, when over 200 people from forty countries and six continents officially declared the 21st century the *Century of Earth Restoration*. Let's continue to work for this vision for the sake of future generations and our own.

The award-winning Chinese-American film-maker and senior research fellow at the International Union for the Conservation of Nature (IUCN) John D. Liu has documented a number of highly successful, large-scale regeneration projects in China (Loess Plateau), Ethiopia, Uganda and Latin America. Liu concludes: "From what I have seen, the determining factors for survival and sustainability on the Earth are biodiversity, biomass and accumulation of organic matter, the more the better". He suggests that "the lessons of the Loess Plateau show that it is possible to restore large scale damaged ecosystems and that this mitigates climate impacts, makes land more resilient and increases productivity" (Liu, 2011, p.24). Following these simple insights from ecosystems restoration we can create the basis for regeneration.

Restoring the world's ecosystems and increasing bioproductivity is a path towards a regenerative future. John Liu's photographs of the large scale environmental restoration project on the Loess Plateau in China (below) demonstrate that as human beings we are not condemned to having a negative impact on the community of life. We can be a regenerative and restorative influence in ecosystems. We can design *as* nature and generate shared abundance.

Figure 23: Restoration project on the Loess Plateau, China – © The Environmental Media Project

Regenerative agriculture is a growing practice of ecological intensification based on integrated food production systems that mimic natural ecosystems and maintain diversity and resilience by weaving the raising of animals, the growing of grains, horticulture, orchards turned into forest gardens, aquaculture ponds, and mushroom cultivation into highly productive agro-ecosystems that not only feed humanity, but maintain the health and diversity of the biotic community of Earth. In urban environments we are seeing the evolution of edible parks and sidewalks, green walls, vertical farming (Despommier, 2011), urban forestry (Clark *et al.*, 1997) and urban community gardens among many other urban agriculture initiatives. Wild lands, cities and farmed ecosystems can be both repositories and sanctuaries for the world's diversity of wild and domesticated flora and fauna.

Redesigning agriculture along the lines explored and demonstrated by the pioneers of regenerative organic agriculture offers us a timely way to avoid run-away climate change and work towards reducing carbon dioxide concentrations in atmosphere and oceans. Regenerative agriculture will also help to ensure food, water and energy sovereignty in a globally and locally equitable way. In the challenge to redesign our entire material culture and wean ourselves off our current dependencies on fossil fuels and resources from the Earth's crust, regenerative agriculture will provide regenerative resource streams that will be the basis of vibrant circular bio-economies locally, regionally and globally.

By carefully mimicking nature we can create agro-ecosystems that provide food, water, energy and the feedstock for our new material culture based on distributed manufacturing within regional, circular and inter-connected economies at different scales. In a regenerative culture we will do this not simply to meet human needs equitably. By regenerating ecosystems functions at a local and a planetary scale we are aiming to co-evolve with life as our larger community – recognizing both the utilitarian and intrinsic value of all life. Humanity is coming of age and becoming a conscious and responsible member of the community of life. *As life, we can create conditions conducive to life!*

Redesigning economics based on ecology

> To make the world work for 100% of humanity in the shortest possible time through spontaneous cooperation without ecological offense or the disadvantage of anyone.
>
> R. Buckminster Fuller

Much of our day-to-day behaviour and cultural activity is structurally determined by our monetary and economic systems. Their redesign is a crucial enabler of the transition towards a regenerative culture. To transform our economic system(s) at every scale is an audacious salutogenic design intervention, yet it is the only way we can effect changes deeply enough to avoid the collapse of civilization and further damage to ecosystems and the biosphere.

> Q Is it possible to create a regenerative economic system based on cooperation rather than competition?
>
> Q How can lessons from ecology – like symbiosis, circular no-waste systems and whole-systems optimization – inform the redesign of our economic and monetary systems?

In line with Buckminster Fuller's central design intention, we have to ask ourselves: does our current economic and monetary system work for 100% of humanity without ecological offence and disadvantage to anyone? Clearly it does not! We need new economic rules and fundamental structural changes that incentivize regenerative and collaborative relationships. The redesigned system will need to discourage the kind of pathological behaviour patterns our current culturally dominant narrative of separation, supported by neo-Darwinian biology and neo-classical economics, justifies and rewards.

As human beings, we are in our very nature compassionate and collaborative, but our current monetary and economic systems are based on the narrative of separation that creates and encourages competition. For too long, we have told a story about nature 'red in tooth and claw' and excused the worst of human behaviour as natural. Scarcity is primarily a mindset and lack of collaboration not a biophysical reality! Competition creates scarcity, which in turn is used to justify competitive behaviour (a vicious circle). The natural limits of bioproductivity and healthy ecosystems functions don't create scarcity as such. Collaboration can turn these natural planetary limits into enabling constraints to create abundance for all within healthy ecosystems and a healthy biosphere. Collaboration creates shared abundance, which in turn invites more collaboration (a virtuous circle). We choose which world we want to bring forth together!

Our economic systems have to be redesigned to enable rather than inhibit vital changes towards improved whole-systems health. The healthier the whole system is, the more abundance is generated by healthy ecosystems functions. Our current monetary system generates money out of nowhere based on debt (every time anyone takes out a loan). Differential interest for lending and borrowing, along with compound interest, further drive a system that is not only set up as a win-lose game, but also requires continuous economic growth to keep going. Furthermore, this system depends on continuous extraction of natural resources, turning them into (privatized) economic assets while externalizing the ecological and social costs. This is a structurally unsustainable system.

Rather than creating a medium of exchange and a store of value that incentivizes appropriate participation in the life-sustaining processes of the biosphere, we have created a monetary and economic system that drives the systematic exploitation and destruction of healthy ecosystem functioning. In addition, this badly designed system makes us compete rather than collaborate with one another. Our profoundly unsustainable monetary and economic systems lie at the root of many of the converging crises around us. They reinforce a self-fulfilling prophecy of competition and scarcity. A regenerative culture will only emerge if we address these necessary and fundamental structural changes.

On his website Peak Prosperity, Chris Martenson, a former Fortune 300 executive, provides an excellent crash course using a series of short video presentations exploring the interconnected forces of our structurally dysfunctional economic system. The economic growth phase of the global economy is nearing its systemic (structural) end. I recommend this resource to everyone willing to invest four hours in gaining a better understanding of why economic and cultural transformation is inevitable and urgently needed. Like an ecosystem reaching maturity, our economic systems need to shift from quantitative towards qualitative growth by revitalizing local and regional economies through the prosperity that comes from collaboration and community resilience.

The word 'regenerative' in 'regenerative culture' refers – in part – to a culture's ability to regenerate and transform *itself* in response to change. Most importantly it refers to a culture's ability to maintain and regenerate healthy ecosystems functions as the basis of true wealth and wellbeing. If we finally understand that our current monetary and economic systems are not fit for purpose, we can initiate structural changes that will create conditions for life as a whole, including *all of* humanity, to thrive.

The founder of the World Economic Forum, Klaus Schwab, said in the run-up to the 2012 forum that "capitalism, in its current form, no longer fits the world around us [...] a global transformation is urgently needed" (*Economic Times*, 2012). In Chapter 5 we explored how design keeps on designing, how there is a self-reinforcing feedback between our worldview and designs that reinforces the way we see the world. We need to break out of this vicious circle of bad economic design decisions – they reinforce a perspective of scarcity, separation and competition that drives ecological and social degradation. Human beings designed this system and human beings can redesign it to serve people and planet.

Nothing about our current economic system is inevitable or unchangeable. Remember, economics is at best a 'management system' and at its worst a dangerous ideology. Unlike biology and ecology, economics is *not* a science. We created our current economic system and we can redesign it, based on ecological insights, to better serve our common purpose: promoting the health and wellbeing of humanity and the community of life. To redesign economics from the ground up challenges us to design new monetary systems, trade policies and financial institutions, as well as scale-linked local living economies and regionally based circular bio-economies supported by global collaboration and resource- and information-sharing.

The structural failure of the current system is no longer a provocative hypothesis of a few thought-leaders. The World Bank, the United Nations, the world's financial institutions, many political leaders and most importantly a groundswell of increasingly informed global citizens, have all recognized the dysfunctionality of the current economic and monetary system. We are challenged to redesign the plane we are on in mid-flight. The necessity of 'Horizon 1' – to keep the lights on and people fed and in jobs – is driving many people in leadership roles to react to short-term electoral and economic cycles with little room to manoeuvre, rather than to initiate transformative change with the long-term benefit of humanity and life in mind. This structural lock-in drives 'business as usual'. Here are just some of the key faults in the current monetary and economic system:

- 'money as debt created out of nowhere' drives extreme inequality and sets 'competition' as the rule

- compound interest on loans and deposits creates an economic time-bomb that drives the perverse necessity for exponential growth and unbridled consumption, structurally establishing a win-lose rather than a win-win-win 'playing field'

- inappropriate and misguided measures of economic success like GDP divert our attention from creating systemic health and wellbeing (caring about qualities) to economic throughput (caring about quantities)

- anachronistic subsidies and international trade policies established under the economic stranglehold of big lobbies favour the wrong kind of industries and energy sources

- current trade rules favour financial gains for the shareholders of multinational corporations yet sabotage local and regional production and consumption (to the detriment of most of humanity's 5 billion poor and of ecosystems functions)

- tax systems that are set up to tax work rather than resource-use structurally increase inequity and drive environmental and social degradation

- value creation is based on an exploitative system of extraction, production and consumption that externalizes the social and ecological costs of (and damage caused by) degrading our resource base and causing dangerous climate change

- the flow of investments and subsidies is not supporting salutogenic and regenerative activities and technologies, as would be the case if value creation was based on healthy ecosystems functions and regeneration

Economic and monetary systems as they stand are structurally dysfunctional and at best serve a few (for a while). Under no circumstances will they deliver a healthy, meaningful and happy life for all. On a crowded planet with failing ecosystems we have to learn that out-competing others while destroying the planetary life-support systems is not an evolutionary success strategy. Win-lose games in the long run turn into lose-lose games.

Starting with the systemic leverage points mentioned above, we can transform our global economy and strengthen resilient regional and local economies as the foundations of thriving, diverse, regenerative cultures. If we want to create healthy economies that protect rather than destroy local ecosystems, we will need to rewrite international trade rules in ways that include the social and ecological costs of production and consumption, as well as trade. We need to protect local economies from 'cheap' imports made possible by hidden subsidies, externalizing true costs, and outsourcing production (exploiting international inequality). Re-localizing and re-regionalizing economics – while maintaining international collaboration and fair trade – creates jobs and community resilience. It supports an economics of positive social and ecological impact.

Neo-classical economic dogma would call this 'protectionism' and oppose it because 'we need deregulation instead of regulation to ensure the free-market'. What a pervasive myth this so-called free-market is proving to be! In a conditioned knee-jerk response, many intelligent people will defend an ideal (the free market) that simply does not exist. Kenny Ausubel, co-founder of Bioneers, hit the nail on the head:

> The world is suffering from the perverse incentives of 'unnatural capitalism'. When people say 'free market', I ask if *free* is a verb. We don't have a free market, but a highly managed and often monopolized market. […] we have banks and companies that are 'too big to fail,' but in truth are too big not to fail. The resulting extremes of concentration of wealth and political power are very bad for business and the economy (not to mention the environment, human rights, and democracy). One result is that small companies can't advance too far against the big players with their legions of lawyers and Capitol Hill lobbyists, when in truth it's small and medium-sized companies that provide the majority of jobs as well as innovation.
>
> Kenny Ausubel in Harman (2013: 77)

The transformation of our economic system is already under way. Social, cultural, ecological and economic innovators around the world are already offering and exploring a plethora of alternatives. Our socio-economic systems are being reinvented from the ground up. In *Money and Sustainability – The Missing Link*, Bernard Lietaer and his colleagues (2012) explore a variety of ways in which complementary regional currencies can be designed to address the problems created by our current monetary system. We have already started to ask different questions about the purpose and objectives of economics and money:

Q How can we reinvent our economic system to cure its current structural dysfunctionality and create an economy that is in service of all people and the planet?

Q What kind of monetary systems would serve us at what scale?

Q Can we design a full-reserve currency based on bioproductive capacity, biodiversity and the healthy functioning of ecosystems?

Q What would circular bio-economies look like and how do we effectively create them, and at what scale?

Q What kind of economic system would help us to optimize resource sharing and (biologically regenerative) resource creation locally, regionally and globally?

Q What would an 'economy for the common good', an 'economics of happiness' and a 'sacred economics' look like in our community and how do we co-create them?

Q How can new rules in economics facilitate a fair sharing of, and a common responsibility for, the global commons?

Q How do we create monetary and economic systems where value is ultimately based on healthy ecosystem functioning and where ecological and social regeneration are structurally incentivized?

Q How can ecological literacy and learning from the rest of nature help us to redesign a more fitting economic system for a regenerative culture?

I cannot do these important questions justice here. But I will highlight some of the excellent work of people who – to my mind – hold a piece of the puzzle. All these approaches are based on the important ecological insight that regenerative systems in nature are collaborative. Effective resource-sharing in natural systems is based on collaboration in circular patterns of resource use and regeneration. Creating a healthy economic system requires us to meet humanity's needs within the limits of the planet's annual bioproductivity and to do so while attempting to regenerate the bioproductive capacity of damaged ecosystems everywhere. Willem Ferwerda, Executive Fellow at the

Rotterdam School of Management and special advisor to the IUCN, explains why the restoration of damaged ecosystems is an economic imperative:

> Ecosystems form the basis of all wealth creation. Ecosystem services flow from natural capital and are an investor's primary asset. […] Ecosystems provide societies with soil fertility, food, water, shelter, goods and services, medicines, stability, pleasure, knowledge and leisure. […] Today 60 per cent of the services provided by ecosystems are threatened. Economic activities aimed at achieving short-term wealth are destroying ecosystems worldwide and thus economies' primary asset. Restoring damaged ecosystems is essential if we are to secure the livelihoods of future generations.
>
> Willem Ferwerda (2012: 13)

Creating circular economies

> The circular economy refers to an industrial economy that is restorative by intention; aims to rely on renewable energy; minimises, tracks and eliminates the use of toxic chemicals; and eradicates waste through careful design. The term goes beyond the mechanics of production and consumption of goods and services […] (examples include rebuilding capital including social and natural, and the shift from consumer to user). The concept of the circular economy is grounded in the study of non-linear, particular living systems. A major outcome of taking insights from living systems is the notion of optimising systems rather than components.
>
> Ellen MacArthur Foundation (2013a)

Questions about how to create a circular and regenerative economy based on the resource and energy flow patterns we can observe in ecosystems have inspired thought-leaders and innovators in ecological design and ecological economics for a number of decades; now these questions are being asked by global financial institutions, the European Commission, leading companies, and mainstream consultancies like McKinsey. I choose to take this as a positive sign that the culturally creative conversations started by ecologically literate pioneers decades ago are beginning to reach critical mass for a transformational cultural response to the converging crises.[†]

In recent years, the work of the Ellen MacArthur foundation and its CE100 initiative has taken the conversation about how to facilitate the transition towards a circular economy into corporate boardrooms around the world. The CE100 unites businesses and local authorities in different regions around the globe with innovators in ecological design to enable rapid information exchange and collective intelligence. It aims to facilitate the swift implementation of industrial process improvements that have been estimated to be worth more than US$1 trillion to the global economy. The CE100 offers a best practice and best process database so businesses can learn from each other's experiences. It also offers an online executive education programme to help get industry leaders and their management teams on board and informed.

The kind of transformation needed to implement the circular economy approach locally, regionally and globally can only occur if it is driven by widespread cross-sector collaboration. Business leaders are waking up to the multiple benefits of focusing on *collaborative advantage* rather than *competitive advantage*. Regenerative systems are defined by collaboration and win-win-win solutions, rather than competition and zero-sum games creating winners and losers.

Walter Stahel (2014) highlights characteristics of a circular economy that distinguish it from a linear economy based on extraction, production, consumption and disposal (waste):

1. "The smaller the loop (activity-wise and geographically) the more profitable and resource efficient it is." The aim is not to create one globalized circular economy, rather, the most effective strategy is to appropriately scale-link multiple circular economies at local, regional and global scales.
2. "Loops have no beginning and no end", so they require continuous collaboration along the entire value chain.
3. "The speed of the circular flows is crucial: the efficiency of managing stock in the circular economy increases with a decreasing flow speed"; and therefore companies will have to rethink strategies based on 'planned obsolescence' and create high-quality, durable products.
4. "Continued ownership is cost efficient: reuse, repair and remanufacture without change of ownership save double transaction costs." This creates an incentive for companies to sell (lease) the use or service provided by their products, rather than the products themselves.
5. "A circular economy needs functioning markets".

The current market system, far from being a free market, is regulated in ways that privatize profits and externalize the costs of the social and environmental damage done in the manufacture, distribution and disposal of the product as collateral damage rather than including them in the true cost accounting of a given product. To create functioning markets we need legislation insisting that social and environmental costs are included in product pricing, and a shift from taxing work to taxing resource and energy use.

The shift from a linear to a circular economy has multiple economic, social and environmental benefits. In 2014, McKinsey staff suggested that the circular economy is already "starting to help companies create more value while reducing their dependence on scarce resources". They concluded that "the era of largely ignoring resource costs is over" and that business leaders are starting to ask the important question: "Could an industrial system that is regenerative by design – a circular economy, which restores material, energy, and labour inputs be good for both society and business?" (Nguyen et al., 2014).

Renault has already created a remanufacturing plant where many mechanical components for their cars are remanufactured. Design for disassembly, closed-loop material recycling and working systemically along the entire supply chain have brought increased profitability along with a wide diversity of environmental benefits. Renault is applying Horizon 2 innovation by taking already profitable steps towards a circular economy. The team at McKinsey highlighted that there is:

> a growing body of evidence suggesting that the business opportunities in a circular economy are real – and large […] In fact, our research suggests that the savings in material alone could exceed $1 trillion a year by 2025 and that, under the right conditions, a circular economy could become a tangible driver of global industrial innovation, job creation, and growth for the 21st century.
>
> Hanh Nguyen et al. (2014)

The CEO of Philips, Frans van Houten, believes we are "on the cusp of a new economic revolution" and will need a fundamental rethink of how we define 'value' and 'ownership'. In line with Stahel's insights about the optimal functioning of circular economies, he suggests: "Perhaps instead of selling products, businesses such as Philips should retain ownership and sell their use as a service, allowing us to optimize the use of resources" (van Houten, 2014). In an interview about work within Philips he said: "It's rewarding to see how enthusiastic people can be when they learn what they can do from a circular thinking point of view" (Fleming & Zils, 2014). Enthusiasm is kindled by meaning rather than money alone. Given the chance, most people would prefer that their daily work contribute to the creation of a regenerative culture rather than simply to paying their bills on the Titanic.

To what extend this upsurge in interest in the 'circular economy' will lead to true Horizon 2+ innovation that builds a bridge towards the wider cultural transformation (H3), rather than being captured by 'business as usual' (H1) and turning out to be H2- innovation, will depend how deeply this approach transforms the businesses and institutions that engage with it. If large multinational companies retain ownership over their products and only sell access to them, this could further drive inequality and create unfair dependencies for the product users.

In order to achieve H2+ and H3 type transformation, the multiple social, economic and environmental benefits of the circular economy approach have to be communicated to, and understood by, the entire workforce not just top management. The technical changes in product design, production processes and product life-cycles need to be contextualized within the wider cultural change towards thriving local and regional communities and a regenerative culture. Transformative change in production and consumption will not just be a change in the *how*, but also a change in *why* and as such it will transform the very nature of large corporations. I believe their future lies in the role of global knowledge partners that support distributed manufacturing by facilitating global-local collaboration.

The schematic diagram in Figure 24 was created by the Ellen MacArthur Foundation and maps out the various elements of a circular economy.

I have had the opportunity to experience first-hand how the vision of co-creating a regionally based circular economy project can inspire people and create widespread collaboration among previously isolated stakeholders. While the 'Glocal-project' on Majorca for Ecover and in collaboration with Forum for the Future, mentioned in Chapter 5, was put on hold after the initial pilot, it has already created a shift in attitude among many of the island-based participants. Our work has seeded a new way of thinking that is more systemic, explores the potential of closing the loops, and the collaborations necessary to do so effectively. Other companies are beginning to show an interest in this long-range innovation experiment in how to create island-scale circular bio-economies.

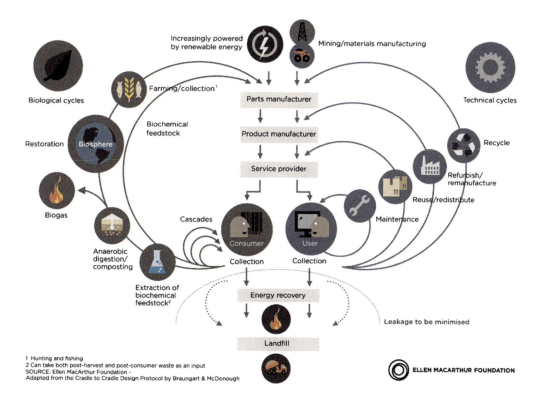

Figure 24: Circular Economy – Reproduced with permission of the Ellen MacArthur Foundation

Another Forum for the Future project with the aluminium recycling specialist Novelis Inc. supported the creation of the world's largest aluminium recycling facility in Germany. The facility is expected to process 400,000 metric tonnes of aluminium scrap every year in an optimized process that reduces carbon emissions and makes this valuable metal available for reuse in the can and automotive industry. The shift is from traditional 'supply chain thinking' to 'value network thinking'. The approach creates and incentivizes new ways to collaborate in the creation of win-win-win solutions. John Gardner (2014), vice-president and chief sustainability officer at Novelis, calls this "disruptive innovation through collaboration". Once the circular economy approach is more effectively linked with a re-regionalization of production and consumption this disruptive innovation will turn into transformative innovation for regenerative cultures. Regionally, circular bio-economies will create jobs and vibrant regional economies.

Towards a regenerative economy

> Ultimately, we need to transform finance and shift the flow of investment capital to perpetuate a Regenerative Economy that serves humanity and is a steward of Earth's ecosystems. [...] The transition to a Regenerative Economy is about seeing the world in a different way – a shift to an ecological world view in which nature is the model. The regenerative process that defines thriving, living systems must define the economic system itself.
>
> John Fullerton & Hunter Lovins (2013)

Redesigning our industrial system of production and consumption around the circular patterns of resource and energy use that we observe in mature ecosystems is only one part of redesigning our economy using the insights of ecology. To create a truly regenerative economy challenges us to ask deeper questions and initiate more far-reaching transformative change. The stock-market crash of September 2008 shocked many mainstream economists into realizing that the current system is fundamentally dysfunctional. Some of them have since become effective change agents of the transition towards a regenerative culture. Rather than condemning these highly intelligent, well-connected, well-resourced, and extremely capable people for their roles in creating some of the mess of Horizon 1 (which we all had a part in), we should celebrate the new-found support of people who have access to, and the respect of, important decision-makers.

John Fullerton, a managing director at J.P. Morgan until 2002 and now a member of the Club of Rome and president of the Capital Institute, is one of the most active facilitators of the dialogue about how we might create a regenerative economy. He has published a list of principles that could be used to characterize a regenerative economy (Fullerton, 2015). If we turn the list of proposed qualities of a regenerative economy into guiding questions, they might sound like this:

- Q How do we create an economy with its operations based on cooperative relationships (between each other and within the ecosphere)?

- Q How would a regenerative economy nurture the entrepreneurial spirit?

- Q How would a regenerative economy enable empowered participation?

- Q How can we ensure that the economy promotes robust circular flows?

- Q How would we design balancing mechanisms (feedback loops) into the economy?

- Q How can we enrich the interactions in our economy by mimicking "the edge effect" (the point where two ecosystems and their diversity meet)?

Q   How can we nurture regenerative economic activities that honour place by expressing the culture and ecology of place in their relationships?

Q   What would an economy that views wealth holistically look like?

Questions like these can serve as activators of important conversations in your local community, a boardroom, or in the newly enlivened political dialogue about redesigning economics.

A regenerative economy would have "critical value adding exchanges" occurring within networks of reciprocal relationships "in contrast with commoditized transactions" (ibid). An important aspect of the transition to such a system is to encourage people to "discover their essence, innovate, and create anew across all sectors and activities of society, not just the business sector". To stimulate participation, people need to feel empowered to contribute to a healthy human economy "negotiating in their own enlightened self-interest as they naturally promote the health of the whole" (ibid). If we learn to understand wealth holistically rather than just in monetary terms, we will understand that by regenerating the health and wealth of our communities and ecosystems we are creating wealth for all.

The material flows of a regenerative economy will mimic "the metabolic process found in resilient living systems" with wastes being fully recycled or upcycled in an "ongoing, productive, circulatory and value enhancing flow" (see circular economy). The flow of information and money would follow similar patterns. Self-regulating processes and feedback loops maintain the dynamic balance in ecosystems; by analogy, "a regenerative economic and financial system seeks a balance between efficiency and resilience, global and local, big and little, diversity and uniformity, innovation and conservation, flexibility and constraint" (ibid).

Creative use of the 'edge-effect' nurtures the qualitative growth of all sub-systems rather than pushing the unbridled quantitative growth of one isolated sub-system. Designing to increase the 'edge effect' is biomimicry applied to economics. The regenerative economy at and between different scales will aim to create 'edge effect' conditions with rich interaction and high diversity, that can manifest in "intense collaboration across diverse sectors (public sector, private sector, NGO sector), cultures and demographics, increasing the possibility of value-adding wealth creation through these human exchanges that occur 'in relationship'" (ibid).

Appropriately linking the local, regional and global scales of nested regenerative systems through collaboration will be a central achievement of a regenerative economy. Such a scale-linking design would nurture "healthy stable communities, locally, regionally and globally, both real and virtual, in a connected, place-centred mosaic" (ibid). Scale-linking collaboration between the different 'local living economies' (BALLE, 2012) and regional economies within a global context will be an important aspect of creating and maintaining greater equity locally and globally.

Wealth understood holistically is primarily expressed in the health of the whole system. Many aspects of healthy socio-ecological systems and a regenerative culture are not reducible to monetary values and numbers. They evade quantification since they are qualities rooted in being nurtured by and nurturing collaborative relationships.

A regenerative economy will redefine wealth in terms of multiple kinds of capital rather than just financial capital. Ethan Roland and Gregory Landua proposed a whole-systems map of economics which conceives of wealth as relying on eight forms of capital: living, cultural, experiential, intellectual, spiritual, social, material and financial capital (2011). We will revisit this model in more detail when we explore the role of regenerative enterprise.

The redirection of the flow of financial capital from the speculative to the real economy, and from exploitative and destructive to regenerative and for-benefit enterprises is also a crucial step towards creating a regenerative economy. Ethical Markets Media, a social enterprise set up by Hazel Henderson, has been reporting success stories of the transition towards a green economy for over ten years. The organization's 'Green Transition Scoreboard' monitors the amount of private green investment globally and has shown a steady increase over the last ten years to $US5.7 trillion by September 2014, predicting that the $10 trillion mark will be reached by 2020. Together with Biomimicry 3.8, Ethical Markets developed a set of "Principles of Ethical Biomimicry Finance" (Ethical Markets, 2012).

Henderson also offered a major step towards more qualitative and holistic ways of measuring economic success with a practical alternative to the dysfunctional success indicator GDP. Supported by the socially responsible investment firm Calvert, Henderson led the development of a new set of indicators, now called the Ethical Markets Quality of Life Indicators. This economic performance measure is based on education, employment, energy, environment, health, human rights, income, infrastructure, national security, public safety, recreation and shelter.

A regenerative economy will furthermore require us to redesign the role of the banking system. The Global Alliance for Banking on Values is an independent network of banks using finance to deliver sustainable development for "unserved people, communities and the environment". The alliance includes pioneering, innovative banks on six continents which are all committed to i) "delivering social finance products", ii) "financing community based development initiatives and social entrepreneurs", iii) "fostering sustainable and environmentally sound enterprises and fulfilling human development potential including poverty alleviation", while iv) "generating a triple bottom line for people, planet, and profit" (GABV, 2014). We are not starting the transition towards a regenerative economy from scratch. Many important tools, processes and innovations are already at our disposal and the transition is already occurring.

All over the world, individuals, organizations and businesses are asking how we might transform our dysfunctional economic system. In the USA, the New Economy Coalition (NEC) unites many of these pathfinders aiming to co-create "an economy that is restorative to people, place and planet, and that operates according to principles of democracy, justice and appropriate scale" (New Economy Coalition, 2015). In the UK, the New Economics Foundation is equally determined "to transform the economy so that it works for people and planet" (New Economics Foundation, 2015). We might not have worked out all the answers and solutions yet, but we are asking the questions that will allow us to take important steps towards a regenerative economy.

Thriving communities and the solidarity economy

> A green economy is not an end in itself. Rather, […] it is a means towards a shared and lasting prosperity. But what exactly does prosperity mean? We propose a definition of prosperity in terms of the capabilities that people have to flourish on a finite planet. It is clear that a part of our prosperity depends on material goods and services. Living well clearly means achieving basic levels of material security. But prosperity also has important social and psychological components. Our ability to participate in the life of society is vital. Meaningful employment, satisfying leisure, and a healthy environment also matter. […] Thriving communities are the basis of shared prosperity.
>
> Tim Jackson and Peter A. Victor (2013: 6)

In 2009, Professor Tim Jackson catalysed a step-change in the conversation about the 'growth imperative' that is structurally built into our economic system. In a report for the UK Sustainable Development Commission, Jackson dared to name the elephant in the room by asking whether "prosperity without growth" was a possibility, stating clearly why 'business as usual' was no longer an option (Jackson, 2009a).

The report showed that while the global economy has more than doubled in size in the last 25 years, it has severely degraded more than 60% of the world's ecosystems without delivering a more equitable sharing of wealth. To the contrary, inequality has grown both within and between nations. We live in a world with 5 billion poor and the bottom fifth of the world's population have to make do with just 2% of global income. According to a Credit Suisse report, the richest 1% of people now own more than half of the world's financial wealth (Treanor, 2014). This extreme inequality drives a series of devastating chain reactions, affecting health, community cohesion, national and international security, and the environment.

Yet prosperity and wellbeing are not simply a function of the (financial) wealth a person has. We need more than money to feel well. Participation in thriving communities makes individuals prosper and through collaboration in community we can create prosperity for all. The report by Tim Jackson and Peter Victor on *Green Economy at the Community Scale* (2013) concluded that communities can take independent positive action to create a green local economy and improve prosperity for all.

"At its best, green economy offers a positive blueprint for a new economics – one firmly anchored in principles of ecological constraint, social justice, and lasting prosperity" (p.6). Taking a systemic perspective on true prosperity means going beyond simply meeting material needs and giving equal importance to the establishment of social and psychological conditions in which individuals and communities can thrive. "Material bounds do not in themselves constrain prosperity; […] with appropriate attention to material limits, it may be possible to improve quality of life for everyone even as we reduce our combined impact on the environment" (pp.17-18).

At the scale of local communities, abundance and human thriving are not exclusively based on the availability of material resources and energy but on human creativity and relationships. Community and individual prosperity depend on how we collaborate to create win-win-win solutions for all. Jackson and Victor identified four enablers of thriving communities: "the role of enterprise, the quality of work, the structure of investment, and the nature of the money economy" (p.6). Entrepreneurial and business activities in a community need to offer people the opportunity to flourish. Beyond providing the basic needs of food, clothing and shelter, "prosperity depends on 'human services' that improve the quality of our lives: health, social care, education, leisure, recreation, and the maintenance, renovation, and protection of physical and natural assets" (p.7).

Almost all of us spend much of our lives working. In doing so we participate in important relationships that shape our culture. These relationships form part of the 'glue' of our society. "Good work offers respect, motivation, fulfilment, involvement in community and, in the best case a sense of meaning and purpose in life" (p.7). In the face of the multiple convergent crises that are challenging humanity, to participate in co-creating thriving local communities as expressions of a regenerative human culture can offer this sense of meaning and purpose in life. As previously mentioned, the restructuring of investment and the redesign of our monetary systems are two important enablers of such community-scale collaboration.

Many inspiring and informative examples from around the world show how communities and regions can start to create economic structures that facilitate the emergence of regenerative cultures. The website Global Transition to a New Economy maps many of these initiatives. They all have a common thread: *The path towards prosperity for all is co-created through collaboration.* Regenerative systems are collaborative! The 'solidarity economy' approach illustrates this. SolidarityNYC, for example, tries to give visibility to, and create synergies between, existing initiatives that are part of community collaboration within New York City's solidarity economy.

> The solidarity economy includes a wide array of economic practices and initiatives but they all share common values that stand in stark contrast to the values of the dominant economy. Instead of enforcing a culture of cut-throat competition, they build cultures and communities of cooperation. Rather than isolating us from one another, they foster relationships of mutual support and solidarity. In place of centralized structures of control, they move us towards shared responsibility and democratic decision-making. Instead of imposing a single global monoculture, they strengthen the diversity of local cultures and environments. Instead of prioritizing profit over all else, they encourage a commitment to shared humanity best expressed in social, economic, and environmental justice.
>
> SolidarityNYC (2015)

The US Solidarity Economy Network supports this transformative impulse in the USA. Internationally, The Alliance for Responsible Plural and Solidarity Economy has stimulated dialogue on how we can co-create a collaborative economic model that builds rather than divides community in Asia and Brazil, and www.socioeco.org offers an excellent resource in this area. A UN Research Institute for Social Development report concluded: "Policy makers and the international development community at large need to pay far more attention to ways and means of enabling SEE [Social Solidarity Economy]. This is particularly apparent in the current context of heightened risk and vulnerability associated with economic and food crises and climate change" (UNRISD, 2014: v). Ethan Miller (2010) has attempted to map the diverse economic strategies, organizational forms and tools that can contribute to the creation of a solidarity economy (Figure 25).

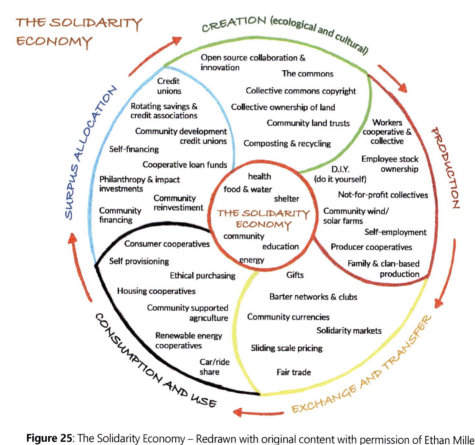

Figure 25: The Solidarity Economy – Redrawn with original content with permission of Ethan Miller

Once again, the important message is that we are not trying to reinvent economics with ecology and community in mind from scratch. There are many time-tested strategies and tools already available to us today. They have been developed on the innovation-rich fringes of the mainstream. Some of them may well be H3 'islands of the future in the present', waiting to be spread not necessarily by scaling-up but by employing and adapting them everywhere at the scale of local communities and regional economies. Even if the transformation of the wider macro-economic context will test our patience for a little longer, we are already beginning to meet the descending top-down globalized economic system with ascending H2+ bottom-up innovation. Applying scale-linking, health-generating design to economics means creating diversity and resilience by strengthening the solidarity economy at the local and regional scale.

Shifting from quantitative to qualitative growth

> Too much and for too long, we seemed to have surrendered personal excellence and community values in the mere accumulation of material things. Our gross national product, […] if we judge the United States of America by that – counts air pollution and cigarette advertising, and ambulances to clear our highways of carnage. It counts special locks for our doors and the jails for the people who break them. It counts the destruction of the redwood and the loss of our natural wonder in chaotic sprawl. It counts napalm and counts nuclear warheads and armored cars for the police to fight the riots in our cities and the television programs which glorify violence in order to sell toys to our children. Yet the gross national product does not allow for the health of our children, the quality of their education or the joy of their play. It does not include the beauty of our poetry or the strength of our marriages, the intelligence of our public debate or the integrity of our public officials. It measures neither our wit nor our courage, neither our wisdom nor our learning, neither our compassion nor our devotion to our country, it measures everything in short, except that which makes life worthwhile.
>
> Senator Robert Kennedy, 1968 in Capra & Henderson (2013:2).

We have known for a long time that judging an economy's progress and success in quantitative (financial) terms leads to dangerous distortions and misplaced priorities. In 1972, *Limits to Growth* warned of the potentially devastating environmental effects of unbridled growth and resource depletion on a finite planet. While some of the predictions made were delayed by the extraordinary resilience of the planetary system, recent research suggests that we are now very close to witnessing the collapse scenario of 'business as usual' that the authors warned of. In their 30 years up-date to *Limits to Growth* the authors emphasized:

> Sustainability does not mean zero growth. Rather, a sustainable society would be interested in qualitative development, not physical expansion. It would use material growth as a considered tool, not a perpetual mandate. […] it would begin to discriminate among kinds of growth and purposes for growth. It would ask what the growth is for, and who would benefit, and what it would cost, and how long it would last, and whether the growth could be accommodated by the sources and sinks of the earth.
>
> Meadows, Randers & Meadows (2005: 22)

The calls for 'de-growth' (Assadourian, 2012), post-growth economics (Post Growth Institute, 2015), prosperity without growth (Jackson, 2011), and a 'steady state economy' (Daly, 2009) have become louder and have found a much wider audience in recent years. All these more or less anti-growth perspectives make important contributions to our rethinking of economics with people and planet in mind, but they might be over-swinging the pendulum. As a biologist who is aware of how growth in living systems tends to have qualitative and quantitative aspects, I feel uncomfortable with demonizing 'growth' altogether. What we need is a more nuanced understanding of how as living systems mature they shift from an early (juvenile) stage that favours quantitative growth to a later (mature) stage of growing (transforming) qualitatively rather than quantitatively.

> It seems that our key challenge is how to shift from an economic system based on the notion of unlimited growth to one that is both ecologically sustainable and socially just. 'No growth' is not the answer. Growth is a central characteristic of all life; a society, or economy, that does not grow will die sooner or later. Growth in nature, however, is not linear and unlimited. While certain parts of organisms, or ecosystems, grow, others decline, releasing and recycling their components which become resources for new growth.
>
> Fritjof Capra and Hazel Henderson (2013: 4)

Capra and Henderson argue that "we cannot understand the nature of complex systems such as organisms, ecosystems, societies, and economies if we describe them in purely quantitative terms". Since "qualities arise from processes and patterns of relationships" they need to be mapped rather than measured (p.7). There are close parallels between the difference in how economists and ecologists understand the concepts of growth and development. While economists tend to take a purely quantitative approach, ecologists and biologists know how to differentiate between the qualitative and quantitative aspects of both growth and development.

> It appears that the linear view of economic development, as used by most mainstream and corporate economists and politicians, corresponds to the narrow quantitative concept of economic growth, while the biological and ecological sense of development corresponds to the notion of qualitative growth. In fact, the biological concept of development includes both quantitative and qualitative growth.
>
> (ibid: 9)

Life's growth patterns follow the logistic curve rather than the exponential curve. One example of aberrant quantitative growth in living systems is that of cancer cells which ultimately kill their host. Unlimited quantitative growth is fatal for living systems and economies. Qualitative growth in living organisms, ecosystems and economies, "by contrast, can be sustainable if it involves a dynamic balance between growth, decline, and recycling, and if it also includes development in terms of learning and maturing" (p.9). Capra and Henderson argue:

> Instead of assessing the state of the economy in terms of the crude quantitative measure of GDP, we need to distinguish between 'good' growth and 'bad' growth and then increase the former at the expense of the latter, so that the natural and human resources tied up in wasteful and unsound production processes can be freed and recycled as resources for efficient and sustainable processes.
>
> (ibid: 10)

The distinction between good growth and bad growth can be informed by a deeper socio-ecological understanding of their impact. While bad growth externalizes the social and ecological costs of the degradation of the Earth's eco-social systems, good growth "is growth of more efficient production processes and services which fully internalise costs that involve renewable energies, zero emissions, continual recycling of natural resources, and restoration of the Earth's ecosystems" (p.10). Capra and Henderson conclude: "the shift from quantitative to qualitative growth […] can steer countries from environmental destruction to ecological sustainability and from unemployment, poverty, and waste to the creation of meaningful and dignified work" (p.13). Nurturing qualitative growth through the integration of diversity into interconnected collaborative networks at and across local, regional and global scales facilitates the emergence of regenerative cultures.

Valuing the commons by cooperatively sharing the gifts of life

> Growing numbers of people are taking steps that move us, gradually, in the direction of a commons-based society – a world in which the fundamental focus on competition that characterizes life today would be balanced with new attitudes and social structures that foster cooperation.
>
> Jay Walljasper (2011)

The practice of 'commoning' – to collaboratively hold a natural or cultural resource as a 'commons' – is a way to collaborate in safeguarding the gifts of nature and culture that people share in a particular place and that humanity shares collectively. A regenerative culture will value and responsibly steward the biocultural commons we all depend upon: clean air, clean water, healthy ecosystems functions, abundant bioproductivity, on the one hand, and the fruits of diverse cultures (as epiphenomena of nature) on the other hand. This cultural heritage includes music, art, science, dance, literature, languages, liberator technologies like the open Internet, and the stories and questions of wisdom that have guided humanity on its journey so far.

In most indigenous cultures the natural resources generated in a particular place along with cultural traditions and knowledge are not anyone's 'private property' but are regarded as a 'commons' held in trust and stewardship by all, for the benefit of all. What is held in a 'commons' is not to be owned but to be cared for and regenerated so it can be passed on to the next generation in as good or better condition than the current generation received it.

As such, the commons of a particular locality or culture are a birthright of that community. The commons are about relationships and belonging, about interbeing rather than separation. Holding things in 'common' invites people to collaborate and share the abundance provided by a particular place and culture, while private (or corporate) ownership creates artificial scarcity and separation, driving us to compete.

Gareth Hardin's 1968 article 'The Tragedy of the Commons' offered a convenient justification for rapid privatization (enclosure) of the gifts of life during the period of rapid economic growth that saw the rise of large multinational corporations. Hardin argued that, with the population increasing, people would inevitably over-exploit and destroy the commons, and suggested that regulating population growth was the most important way to end the tragedy of the commons. He stressed that "every new enclosure of the commons involves the infringement of somebody's personal liberty" (1968: 1248), yet his work has since been used to justify more enclosure of the commons through privatization and strict government regulation. This process continues today.

Elinor Ostrom, the first woman to receive the Nobel Prize in economics, spent her life working on an economics of collaboration rather than competition. She demonstrated that "communities of individuals have relied on institutions resembling neither the state nor the market to govern some resource systems with reasonable degrees of success over long periods of time" (1990: 1). She reviewed a number of successful and unsuccessful cases of communities governing a common resource; and identified a set of 'design principles' leading to successful collective management of the commons:

1. define the community of people sharing the commons
2. adapt rules of use to the type of commons and its users
3. commoners themselves have to set the rules
4. the state of the commons has to be monitored in an accountable way
5. abuse by individuals needs to be curbed in a gradual way

Elinor Ostrom (1990: 185-186)

These principles basically encourage collaboration and discourage competition by creating a common interest community.

In recent years there has been an upsurge of interest in exploring what a commons-based collaborative economy would look like. Online resources include <u>On the Commons</u>, David Bollier's <u>News and Perspectives on the Commons</u> and the <u>P2P Foundation</u>. David Bollier explains that effectively "a commons arises whenever a given community decides to manage a resource in a collective manner, with special regard to equitable access, use and sustainability". Importantly, the commons is not simply a resource but "a resource *plus* a defined community *and* the protocols, values and norms devised by the community to manage its resource" (Bollier, 2011). Creating regenerative cultures will critically depend on our ability to collaborate in managing local, regional and global resources collectively. We need to learn *the art of commoning*.

Traditional commons systems have been small scale and usually focused on the collective stewardship of natural resources. About two billion people around the world still depend for their livelihood on commonly managed forests, fisheries, water and other natural resources. In spreading the practice of managing common resources collectively at the local and regional scale, we also need to connect local and regional 'commoners' into networks of national and global collaborations.

Enclosure is theft! Through this process, individuals or institutions claim the gifts of life as private property. A massive wave of enclosure took place with the institutionalization of nation states and colonization. During the last 50 years, aggressive economic globalization and the spread of corporate exploitative capitalism have gone hand in hand with a further wave of enclosure of the commons. The world over, we have witnessed "the expropriation and commercialization of shared resources, usually for private market gain". Examples of this practice are "the patenting of genes and lifeforms, the use of copyrights to lock up creativity and culture, the privatization of water and land, and attempts to transform the open Internet into a closed, proprietary marketplace" (Bollier, 2011).

As we are aiming to create regenerative cultures locally, regionally, nationally and globally we have to safeguard the remaining commons and re-establish commons-based resource management at various scales. We have to collectively 'live into' the important question:

> Q How can the practice of 'commoning' offer a scale-linking way to manage the gifts of nature and culture collectively?

David Bollier suggests: "to actualize the commons and deter market enclosures, we need innovations in law, public policy, commons-based governance, social practice and culture. All of these will manifest a very different worldview than now prevails in established governance systems, particularly those of the State and Market" (ibid). Creating a collaborative economy requires a shift in worldview and cultural narrative from separation to interbeing. Human beings are capable of empathy and collaboration just as much as they can be self-interested and competitive. Would we not create a healthier culture if our economic system was structurally designed in such a way that it incentivised collaborative behaviour and created conditions that made competition unnecessary?

Vasilis Kostakis and Michel Bauwens (2014) have explored what mature, commons-based peer production within a collaborative economic model might look like. They distinguish two scenarios that would *both* contribute: the global commons (GC) scenario in which the commoners create infrastructures for global sharing; and the resilient communities (RC) scenario in which the commoners design for increased local self-reliance through sharing and governing resources locally. Kostakis and Bauwens do not pretend to have definitive answers, rather they explore a number of questions and pathways that might help us build a collaborative economy.

The spirit of 'living the questions' so that we may one day 'live into the answers' which this book promotes can also be found in the work of the P2P Foundation and in the radical experimentation and disruptive innovation of the 'Cooperativa Integral Catalana' (CIC) set up in 2010. The CIC understands itself as a "transitional initiative for social transformation from below, through self-management, self-organization and networking" (CIC, 2015). Recently the CIC launched 'Fair Coop' as "the Earth cooperative for a fair economy" and introduced a new cryptocurrency called 'Faircoin' –"hacking the money markets to introduce the virus of cooperation" (Fair Coop, 2014). Such culturally creative H2+ and H3 experiments are examples of (salutogenic) design for infectious health, enabling us to share the gifts of nature and culture collaboratively.

Earth Law: the enabling constraints of collective living

> A thing is right when it tends to preserve the integrity, stability, and beauty of the biotic community; it is wrong when it does otherwise.
>
> Aldo Leopold (1949)

In order to share the gifts of life cooperatively we also need transformative innovation in national and international law. Laws provide enabling constraint and attribute rights and responsibilities. Ideally, they need to incentivize cooperation as appropriate behaviour and limit competitive behaviour that jeopardizes systemic health. What kind of laws and policies would facilitate the transition to regenerative cultures?

> What if there were another system and jurisprudence, based upon the concept that the planet and all of its species have rights – and they have those rights by virtue of their existence as component members of a single Earth community?
>
> Thomas Berry (2001)

By asking this important question and inviting others to explore it with him, Thomas Berry catalysed a global-local conversation that is reaching more and more people and institutions. Berry understood that for the "universe story" (Swimme & Berry, 1992) to continue in ways that would allow our young and immature species to grow into mature membership of the community of life, we have to accept the responsibility that comes with the gift of self-reflexive consciousness and safeguard the rights of all the participants of that community. In order to enable the creation of regenerative cultures everywhere "there is a need for a jurisprudence that recognizes that the well-being of the integral world community is primary and that human well-being is derivative" (Berry, 2001).

The 'original participation' expressed by the worldview of indigenous cultures means their members are born into that integral world community. They have been encouraged to speak on behalf of the four-legged-ones, the winged-ones, the finned-ones, the forest, the mountain, the river or the Earth. We label this practice as 'primitive culture' at our peril. It is in fact a sign of an evolved ecological consciousness that will be as vital to our future as it has been in our past, before the narrative of separation clouded our judgement.

The Great Work (Berry, 1999) of co-creating humanity's transition into the *Ecozoic Era* (Swimme & Berry, 1992) requires us to create a legal basis for speaking on behalf of and defending the community of life. Our current laws are based on the narrative of separation and still enable corporations and governments to criminalize opposition to crimes against nature. Berry's vision of an Earth Jurisprudence has inspired many others that are working in the same direction.†

From Cormac Cullinan's *Manifesto for Earth Justice* (2011), to work by Vandana Shiva (2005) and Polly Higgins (2010), and thanks to organizations like the Gaia Foundation, the Pachamama Alliance, Navdanya, and EnAct, the conversation about Earth Law has deepened and broadened. The Global Alliance for the Rights of Nature is now working for "a universal adoption and implementation of legal systems that recognize, respect and enforce *Rights of Nature*" (GARN, 2010).

Just as most people today would regard not awarding rights to someone on the basis of their sex, sexuality, ethnicity or the colour of their skin as an act of apartheid that is fundamentally unlawful and unjust, the regenerative cultures of the not-so-distant future will question how it was possible to believe that nature had no rights.

In *Making Peace with the Earth*, Vandana Shiva explores how the narrative of separation is a kind of "eco-apartheid" that causes human beings to be at war with the Earth and each other. She reviews the root causes of this war against nature and shows that a "destructive Anthropocene" is not the only possible future ahead, if we address the structural systemic conditions that are driving water wars, climate wars forest wars, and other resource wars.

Exploring the situation in India and globally, Dr. Shiva argues that we have designed hunger into the system via international trade agreements formulated under the control of multinational corporations. Shiva warns of the many pitfalls associated with the use of GMOs and certain types of synthetic biology. We have to ask important questions to ensure that our approaches to creating a 'bio-economy' are not simply an "industrialization of life" but maintain and create real "biodiversity economies" (Shiva, 2012: 143). The proliferation of industrial, petrochemical agriculture and GMO monocultures is a "biodiversity war" and the suppression of small farmers and eradication of local variety is a "seed war" (p.148).

To create regenerative 'living cultures', lasting peace within the human family and peace with the Earth, we need laws and policies based on careful deliberation of the following questions (based on Shiva, 2012):

Q How will we move from a system based on privatizing the Earth to respecting the integrity of the Earth's ecosystems and ecological processes?

Q How will we discourage and reverse the 'enclosure of the commons' and support the recovery of the commons?

Q How can we ensure that ecological costs are internalized and prohibit the externalization of environmental destruction?

Q How can we dismantle 'corporate economies of death and destruction' and create 'living economies'?

> Q   How can we reverse the erosion of democracy and create 'living democracies'?
>
> Q   How can we halt the destruction of cultural diversity and create 'living cultures'?

Earth Law, well formulated and locally and globally enforced, will be part of living into the answers on these questions, giving communities the legal means to defend the healthy functioning of the ecosystems that their wellbeing depends upon.

Life's collaborative lessons transform business

> Organizations have three options:
>
> 1. Hit the wall
>
> 2. Optimize and delay hitting the wall
>
> 3. Redesign for resilience – simultaneously optimizing existing networks whilst embracing disruptive innovation and working collaboratively with partners.
>
> Dawn Vance, Global Supply Chain Director at Nike, in Hutchins (2011)

Living the questions that initiate the transition to a commons-based collaborative economy describes transformative innovation from within the third horizon. It is an example of how H3 is already present today but unevenly distributed. A fundamental transformation of our economic and monetary systems is becoming a necessity, if not inevitability. So, how can today's businesses act in today's conditions while at the same time engaging in their own transformation and the transformation of the economic environment they are operating in? Transformatively innovative (H2+) businesses have to be viable in the current economy *and* simultaneously transform the business ecosystems they participate in.

A plethora of disruptive green technological solutions are on offer. How do we avoid H2- pathways and innovations that will eventually be captured by the first horizon to maintain 'business as usual'? There are immediate and diverse economic opportunities for regenerative businesses even under current economic conditions. How do we choose innovations that are truly transformative and lead us towards the third horizon and regenerative cultures? The goal is to create businesses that support win-win-win solutions, systemic health and collaborative networks that serve people and planet.

A fundamental pattern that defines regenerative living systems is the emergence of overall system health based on predominantly collaborative relationships among all the diverse participants of the system. Competition in such a system is about serving the whole system more effectively, rather than about who makes short-term gains at the expense of the collective and therefore to the long-term detriment of all.

In *Holonomics: Business where People and Planet Matter,* the authors argue that "we often have a mistaken view of competition, associating the word and its meaning with rivalry, the survival of one over the other". They continue: "Indeed, a competitive process may result in the failure of one of the participants, but, when seen from the perspective of the system, it is part of the whole evolutionary process" (Robinson & Moares Robinson, 2014: 214).

Not all competitive interactions have a detrimental effect on whole-systems health, just as not all collaboration leads to regenerative systems. Reflecting on our own lives, how often has failure to achieve a certain goal caused disappointment in the short term and a deeper understanding of our true gifts and their more effective application in the long term? Healthy competition teaches individual participants about appropriate participation and how best to apply their unique skills and knowledge to optimizing the whole system. Some forms of competition within predominantly collaborative systems can be beneficial for all participants.

In general terms, within a regenerative socio-ecological system, businesses and individuals meet their objectives most effectively by nurturing the collaborative advantage that emerges from connecting previously separate or competing participants in synergistic ways – connecting unmet needs with spare or new capacities, so that everyone wins. Life evolves towards increasing complexity through favouring non-zero sum (win-win-win) relationships over zero-sum (win-lose) relationships (see Wright, 2001). Collaboration is life's primary evolutionary strategy for the integration of diversity.

Strengthening collaborative (win-win-win) networks optimizes the system and builds social, ecological and economic capital. It prepares the system for disruptive events. As the 'perfect storm' of economic, political, cultural and ecological change is intensifying, strong networks of collaboration are better placed to weather the change ahead than isolated individuals or businesses.

Weathering the turbulent times ahead is about being embedded in wide networks of open information exchange with established means to keep competition 'healthy' – in support of optimizing the system as a whole. Such networks are based on collaborative relationships that value synergy and symbiosis, ensuring that information and mutual support flow rapidly, enabling us to respond with resilience, adapt appropriately and transform together when necessary.

The health and future of the planetary life support system and with it the future of humanity is at stake. Competitive strategies based on 'them against us' thinking will only delay our collective response and prove detrimental to all. At this stage of the game, either life as a whole wins and we stabilize and reverse global average temperature rise and halt rapid biodiversity loss, or nobody wins. All competitive wins will be short-lived. Business today has to serve all of humanity and life as a whole otherwise it will not effectively serve itself (in the mid- or the long term). Transformative enterprises are based on the ecological insight that optimization of the whole provides long-term benefits while maximization of isolated parts only leads to short-lived and questionable 'success'.

Collaborative businesses and regenerative business ecosystems will become the new mainstream of the third horizon. Ecologically inspired, collaborative businesses are capable of transforming the entire business ecosystem and the economic systems they operate in. How do we create such businesses? What can life teach us about business that creates conditions conducive to life? Giles Hutchins, a co-founder of 'Biomimicry for Creative Innovation' (BCI), explains:

> [Nature's Business Principles] are aimed at creating business conditions conducive to collaboration, adaptability, creativity, local attunement, multifunctionality and responsiveness; hence enhancing the evolution of organizations from rigid, tightly managed hierarchies to dynamic living organizations that thrive and flourish within ever-changing business, socio-economic and environmental conditions. Organizations that understand how to embed these principles from nature into their products, processes, policies and practices create greater abundance for themselves and their business ecosystems in times of rapid change, flourishing rather than perishing in volatile business conditions. Organizations inspired by nature are resilient, optimizing, adaptive, systems-based, values-led and life-supporting.
>
> Giles Hutchins (2012: 80-83)

The collaborators in the BCI network have used the list of 'Life's Principles' developed by the Biomimicry Institute (see Chapter 6) and have turned them into "a set of business principles for the firm of the future" aiming to "provide a framework to guide successful transformation towards […] business inspired by nature" (ibid: 81). Here are just some of the questions that Nature of Business (2013) and Hutchins invite us to explore, as we aim to transform business to support the emergence of a regenerative culture with a regenerative economic system:

Q   How can our business learn to use change and disturbance as opportunities rather than regarding them as threats?

Q   How can we restructure to decentralize, distribute and diversify knowledge, resources, decision-making and action throughout the business?

Q   How can we create a business culture that fosters diversity in people, relationships, ideas and approaches?

Q   How can we optimize what we do by fitting form to function, embedding multiplicity in functions and responses, and building complex and diverse products and services from simple components and patterns?

Q   How could we build a more adaptive business through appropriate information feedback loops, integrated cyclical processes and flexible responses to changes in resource availability?

Q   How can we support the resilience of our business and its socio-ecological context by fostering synergies within communities, within energy, information and communication networks, enabling effective cyclical resource use?

Q How can our business contribute to the wider socio-ecological system by using values as the core driver towards positive outcomes, respecting and measuring what is valued rather than valuing what is measured?

Q How can our business become truly restorative by supporting life-building activity through leveraging information and innovation rather than energy and materials, creating mutually supportive health-generating relationships between individuals and ecosystems, and making environmentally benign and socially beneficial products?

I first had the privilege to be in an environment where these kind of questions were being formulated and explored during my 18 months at Schumacher College. Since 2001, I have seen the culturally transformative meme of ecologically inspired design and innovation spread from the fringe into the heart of business, government, academia and, most importantly, communities everywhere. Biological, ecological and systemic insights can inform the design and creation of sustainable and regenerative businesses. This is not a new insight, but one we are finally beginning to act on. For more than two decades, business leaders in need of inspiration have been able to resort to insightful books[†] exploring the *what* and *how* questions of sustainable business. Most offer Horizon 2 perspectives and intimate a diversity of visions for Horizon 3. Nevertheless, we are in the early phase of our learning journey into how to create regenerative businesses that create conditions conducive to life.

Business can be a powerful catalyst in the transition towards a regenerative culture, and we need both disruptive innovation of the H2+ type and transformative H3 innovation. Business leaders are recognizing that in a resource-constrained world, creating waste is a luxury that we can no longer afford. As more people are becoming aware of the collateral damage associated with 'business as usual', customers everywhere are choosing businesses that are phasing out the pure 'shareholder profit maximization' model and, instead, are creating new 'for social and ecological benefit' business models.

In a rapidly changing world, nobody has definitive answers, but at least business leaders are now beginning to 'live the questions' – creating stepping stones towards a regenerative future. Second horizon signs of hopeful change in the 'mainstream' include: a new generation of sustainability metrics that report 'natural capital dependency' not just carbon footprints, pioneered by market-leader Trucost; management tools like PUMA's 'Environmental Profit and Loss Account' (co-developed with Trucost); the Circular Economy 100 Network; McKinsey's call for a *Resource Revolution* (Heck & Rogers, 2014); many of the solutions show-cased by *The Blue Economy* (Pauli, 2010), AskNature and EthicalMarkets; for-benefit business models (Plan C, 2014 & Bocken *et al.*, 2014), the WBCSD's *Vision 2050* (WBCSD, 2010), the work of CDP with Fortune 500 companies and investors (CDP, 2015), and the 'B-team' initiated by Richard Branson (B-Team, 2015).

By January 2016, B-Corporation had certified 1,577 businesses from 42 countries and 130 industries to be a committed force for good in the world (B-Corporation, 2015). To find out how to convert your business into a B-Corp and learn from many good examples have a look at Ryan Honeyman's recent book (2014).

The business world is changing rapidly in response to the accelerated environmental, technological, social and economic changes that are occurring all around us. Change is not only responsive to external forces; a key psychological driver is a deeper transformation fuelling people's desire for meaningful work and for making a difference in the world. Fulfilling work means earning satisfaction from the meaningful impact of one's work and not just earning more money. Together, we can find meaning in asking:

Q   What would a truly regenerative business look like?

Q   How can we create a business that restores ecosystems functions, regenerates bioproductivity, improves social solidarity and collaboration, and increases the health and wellbeing of our communities and ecosystems?

<u>The Firm of the Future</u> explores the major transformations that businesses and organizations will undergo in order to adapt to a changing world and in order to act more in tune with natural patterns. Figure 26 (below) illustrates the nature of this shift from linear hierarchies of control towards more flexible networks of collaboration.

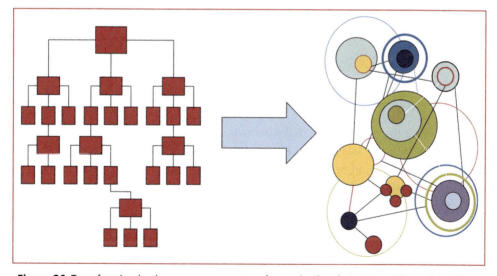

Figure 26: Transforming business management and organizational structures (Reproduced from DeLuca et al., 2010)

The table on the next page from the same report compares and contrasts the firm of the past (a classical Horizon 1 business) with the firm of the future (a H2+ or even H3 business integrated in adaptive and regenerative business ecologies).

Firm of the Past	Firm of the Future
Independent	Synergistic
Competitive	Collaborative
Controlled	Conducive
Closed-source	Open-source
Stable	Dynamic
Maximizes/Minimizes	Optimizes
Resists Change	Leverages diversity
Linear	Networked
Short-term	Long-term
Function fits form	Form fits function
Proactive, planned	Responsive, emergent
Self-focused	System-focused
Exploitation	Mutualism
Avoids disturbance	Leverages disturbance
Manages risks	Fosters resilience
Protects	Adapts
Forces	Fits

Table 2: Characteristics of the Firm of the Past and Firm of the Future (DeLuca *et al.*, 2010: 12)

The H1 firms of the past were created from within the mindset dominated by the narrative of separation, whereas the H3 firms of the future will be expressions of the narrative of interbeing, recognizing the need for collaboration and regeneration as effective strategies to chart their paths into an unknowable future within a complex and turbulent world.

Co-creating regenerative enterprises

> If the goal is to regenerate the health and vitality of living systems, then an enterprise will be most effective if it is designed: 1. To mimic living systems, following clearly defined ecosystem principles, 2. To be an integral part of living systems, building living capital through all their processes, and 3. Collaboratively with other enterprises, to form conscious enterprise ecologies.
>
> Ethan Roland & Gregory Landua (2013: 35)

Roland and Landua's book, *Regenerative Enterprise* (2013), provides a lucid and practical exploration of the question "What would a regenerative business do?" Ethan is a multiple entrepreneur and investor with a background in permaculture and sustainable agriculture. His work combines education, the restoration of degraded farmland and international development. Gregory also works in education and international development and helped to establish a direct trade chocolate business that supports reforestation in tropical Latin America. They define 'regenerative enterprise' as "a venture that pro-actively grows and cultivates the foundational pools of social, cultural, spiritual, and living capital by providing goods and services in a way that creates net positive gains for the system as a whole" (ibid: 22).

Such a business "does not harvest the roots of the tree of production, only its fruit". Working with and supporting healthy eco-cultural systems, such businesses are able to "gather the unique, surplus, place-based goods and services" emerging from healthy regenerative systems and enterprise ecologies. A "regenerative enterprise helps to grow the roots deeper and wider, healing the damage that has been done and eventually creating the possibility of new and larger fruits" (ibid: 24-25).

In general, regenerative systems create conditions conducive to life, nurturing diversity and complexity characterized by mutually supportive relationships that build resilience, adaptive capacity and transformability throughout the system as a whole. In the creation of a regenerative enterprise we should ask (p.17):

> How can our connection with the system we are harvesting from grow the integrity, resilience and long-term viability of these people and this place?

They explain their theory of how a regenerative enterprise should be designed and function in the context of a holistic model of the economy based on eight forms of capital:

> *Social capital*: the influence, relationships and networks an individual, business or community can draw upon
>
> *Material capital*: the physical resources, infrastructures and technologies
>
> *Financial capital*: money, currencies, securities and similar financial instruments currently facilitating the exchange of goods and services
>
> *Living capital*: soil, water, biodiversity, human health, the health of other organisms and healthy ecosystems functions
>
> *Intellectual capital*: ideas, concepts, and knowledge
>
> *Experiential capital*: actual embodied know-how, built from personal experience
>
> *Spiritual capital*: an entity's internal connection and awareness of a greater whole
>
> *Cultural capital*: emerging from the "shared internal and external experience of a group of people: Cultural capital is an emergent property of the complex inter-capital exchanges in a community, village, city, bioregion, or nation […]".
>
> Ethan Roland & Gregory Landua (2013: 12)

In this systemic model, "pools of capital can be held and developed by multiple entities, and various flows can occur within and between each form of capital". The economy is understood as "the sum total of global inter- and intra-capital exchanges". Roland and Landua argue that the current "international trend is to deplete the pools of most forms of capital while exponentially increasing the amount of financial capital". They warn "this mono-capital trajectory has significant impacts on the sustainability of current and future generations" (p.13).

By valuing financial capital above all others for too long, they say, we have severely degraded and destabilized the healthy dynamics of the whole economy (*oikos*). We have compromised the planetary life support system by degrading ecosystems everywhere along with human cultural diversity and community resilience. [Our current] "trajectory fundamentally limits the long-term viability of humans and other species on the planet – instead of life flourishing, it is degenerating" (p.15). Therefore, we need a regenerative systems design approach.

An extractive economy depletes diverse forms of capital in the system and damages the long-term viability, vitality and health of the whole system. A regenerative economy, on the other hand, does more than simply sustain the status quo by refraining from further depletion. It optimizes the whole system rather than maximizing privileged parts. Roland and Landua suggest that growth has to be reframed from our current obsession with increase in size to increase in surface area and connections. "Regeneratively cultivating capital means increasing the amount and complexity of edge, not just growing the size of the system" (p.19). By connecting diverse collaborative networks within and across localities into symbiotic relationships the economy grows qualitatively (optimizing all eight forms of capital) rather than quantitatively (maximizing financial capital in the hands of a few).

As a general rule, living capital should only be traded between localities if it is surplus (in terms of annual bioproductivity in that locality) and does not deplete "the living core of each locality, preventing regeneration and continued health of the system". They emphasize that "foundational pools of capital must be kept intact – enterprises must never extract more value than can be regenerated within the capacity of the living system itself"; and propose that "by cultivating capital instead of extracting it, growing the edges of a system, and increasing its internal and external connectivity, enterprises can proactively develop greater surpluses for harvest and exchange" (p.21).

Regenerative development at any scale will require us to reverse the current systemic trend of increasing financial capital while severely degrading and depleting ecological, social and cultural systems. Investors play an important role in redirecting financial capital into regeneration and the building-up of "the four nurture capitals" (social, living, spiritual and cultural capital). Impact investment can strengthen the virtuous circle of regeneration by "optimizing for multi-capital abundance".

Roland and Landua pay attention to the inner as well as the outer, the personal as well as the collective dimensions of regeneration. Success in regenerative enterprises, communities or cultures does critically depend on the level of personal development of the people that co-create these collectives. Our collective thriving depends on our individual "ability to articulate and achieve goals", the "capacity for clear communication", "integrity in making and keeping commitments", "intellectual and emotional flexibility", as well as self-acceptance and a deeper understanding of and compassion for different people and situations. Roland and Landua suggest that "clear-thinking, spiritually confident, emotionally resilient people are more effective at repairing the world's living and cultural capital" (p.32). Creating a regenerative culture asks all of us to revisit our personal strengths and weaknesses, our emotional scars and unhelpful patterns, and to transform them for the benefit of our community and our self.

Regenerative economic systems emerge out of following three closely linked and self-reinforcing "global imperatives" (p.48): i) the *personal imperative* that change starts with our individual intentions and actions; ii) the *trade imperative* inviting us to "stop buying, selling, and trading in degenerative goods and services"; and iii) the *capital imperative* requiring humanity globally to "reverse the dominant flow of capital, stopping financial capital's destructive processes, so that living capital can repair, grow and thrive" (pp.45-46). Figure 27 describes a regenerative enterprise as a nested system of personal, business and cultural transformation:

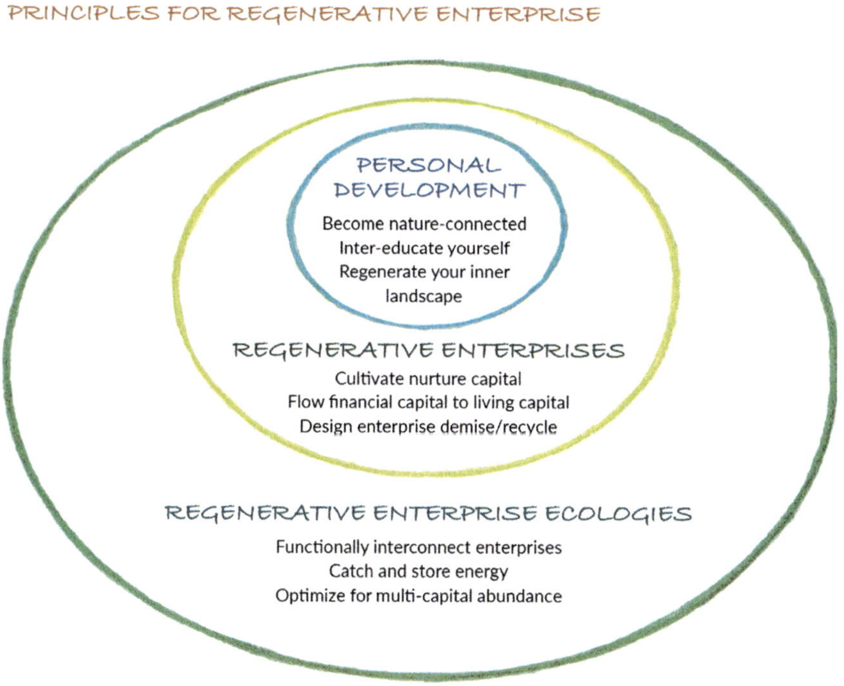

PRINCIPLES FOR REGENERATIVE ENTERPRISE

PERSONAL DEVELOPMENT
Become nature-connected
Inter-educate yourself
Regenerate your inner landscape

REGENERATIVE ENTERPRISES
Cultivate nurture capital
Flow financial capital to living capital
Design enterprise demise/recycle

REGENERATIVE ENTERPRISE ECOLOGIES
Functionally interconnect enterprises
Catch and store energy
Optimize for multi-capital abundance

Figure 27: Principles for Regenerative Enterprise (redrawn & reproduced with permission)

In summary, a regenerative enterprise aims to reverse the degenerative trends of our current (financial growth obsessed) economy by supporting a healthy pool of *nurture capitals* (social, cultural, spiritual and living capital) at local and regional scale. It does so by effectively transforming financial capital into living capital as the basis for supporting all other forms of capital. In supporting the personal development of all the people involved in a regenerative enterprise, a business increases its effectiveness and chances of success. Overall success critically depends on the way businesses optimize for multiple forms of capital by collaborating within the regenerative enterprise ecology they participate in. Such business ecosystems are culturally transformative as they offer "new routes for the flow of financial capital into regenerative venture" (p.57).

Many pioneering businesses and entrepreneurs are already exploring the vast potential for enterprise creation in service of regeneration through <u>regenerative design</u>[†] and are already living the question of how we can co-create enterprises that regenerate the health and productivity of our communities and ecosystems. By caring for and working towards the health and wellbeing of our communities and ecosystems, enterprises can collaborate to become catalysts of a culture of regeneration.

Collaboration and empathy as evolutionary success stories

> This world, in which we are born and take our being, is alive. It is not our supply house and sewer; it is our larger body. The intelligence that evolved us from stardust and interconnects us with all beings is sufficient for the healing of our Earth community, if we but align with that purpose. Our true nature is far more ancient and encompassing than the separate self defined by habit and society. We are as intrinsic to our living world as the rivers and trees, woven of the same intricate flows of matter/energy and mind. Having evolved us into self-reflexive consciousness, the world can now know itself through us, behold its own majesty, tell its own stories – and also respond to its own suffering.
>
> Joanna Macy and Chris Johnstone (2012)

We are life. We are nature. We are the universe. Self-reflexive consciousness allows us different perspectives on this ever-transforming and evolving whole we participate in – this *all* that we are reflections of. We bring forth a world together, as embodied manifestations of the universe co-creating the world through *how* we participate and *what* we pay attention to and care about. Spreading the story of *why* we care about life and the health of the whole and sharing the narrative of interbeing is culturally creative meta-design. By sharing the new and ancient story of interbeing we facilitate the emergence of diverse regenerative cultures scale-linked by empathy and cooperation.

As life, as nature, as the universe we can access the collective intelligence inherent in the whole. Collectively, we have the choice to cooperate with each other and with the community of life to nurture regenerative systems locally, regionally and globally. Living the questions together is about how we apply collective intelligence to cultural transformation, co-creating a new story of *why* humanity is worth sustaining and a powerfully infectious vision of a thriving future for all of life. The 'why' will guide the 'what' and the 'how'.

In a recent article in the journal *BioSystems*, John Stewart (2014) reviews evidence that throughout the evolution of life on Earth we can observe a general trend towards increasing complexity. He highlights two other general trends closely linked to this increase in complexity. Life seems to have a general tendency to diversify as it adapts to changing conditions and the uniqueness of place. Life's way of accommodating this diversity in ways that optimize the whole system is a general tendency towards increasing integration, forming scale-linking networks of life-supporting relationships. In general, life cooperates in creating conditions conducive to life through the creation of regenerative processes that benefit diverse locally adapted networks of life and thereby increase the health and resilience of the whole. "Integration has proceeded through a stepwise process in which living entities at one level are integrated into cooperative groups that become larger-scale entities at the next level, and so on, producing cooperative organizations of increasing scale" (ibid).

Cooperative advantage has driven major inventions throughout evolution: endosymbiosis – the evolutionary step towards nucleated cells (eukaryotic cells); multi-cellular organisms cooperatively integrate many such cells; and "cooperative groups of these organisms produce animal societies". The trend towards increasing complexity of living networks through diversification and integration is a core pattern in the evolution of life, from the scale of molecules to cells, organs, organisms, communities and ecosystems, to biomes and the biosphere.

John Stewart argues that this "trend towards increasing integration has continued during human evolution with the progressive increase in the scale of human groups and societies". He postulates that increasing diversification and integration "are likely to culminate in the emergence of a global entity. […] This entity would emerge from the integration of the living processes, matter, energy and technology of the planet into a global cooperative organization" (ibid). The word "entity" might be misleading here, as it invites us to think of a material superstructure or super-organism. I believe that Stewart is actually referring to a globally cooperative pattern of organization which integrates all of humanity's diversity through predominantly collaborative relationships that steward and regenerate the global commons. From a pack of wolves or a pod of dolphins, to a human family, a local community, a city, region, nation or the United Nations, these 'entities' are better understood as processes defined by patterns of collaboration.

The multi-lateral negotiations and agreements facilitated by the UN – with all its shortcomings *and* successes – are expressions of humanity living the questions together with a commitment to global solidarity and cooperation. The recently ratified Sustainable Development Goals with their emphasis on 'means of implementation' are a clear sign that despite all our conflicts and disagreements humanity is evolving its capacity for global collaboration. This emerging pattern of conscious collaboration can also be observed in a huge variety of civil society organizations and networks of cultural change agents involved in the transition to a more sustainable human presence on Earth. The only way to safeguard the privilege of abundance is to share it collaboratively with all of humanity and all of life. Evolutionary success for life as a whole has followed life's diversifying and integrative tendencies. This process is now finding expression in the integration of human diversity into global awareness and solidarity. Our individual and collective success depends on this integration through collaboration and empathy.

Stewart observes that "whatever the evolutionary challenges, living processes can respond to them more effectively if they are cooperative organizations and if their actions are coordinated". Life as a scale-linking planetary process thrives through the integration of diversity into circular flows of energy, matter and information which facilitate the emergence of collaborative and regenerative processes at local, regional and global scale. This creates shared abundance at multiple scales as the basis for individual and collective evolutionary success. Integration through collaboration offers a number of advantages:

- the opportunity to distribute key tasks in decentralized ecologies of collaboration

- the opportunity to create abundance within planetary boundaries through the sharing of common resource pools

- an increased capacity for collective intelligence to inform our collective resilience, adaptive capacity and transformability

- increased resource effectiveness as less energy and fewer resources are wasted on competitive interactions that damage systemic health

- the opportunity to create networks of mutual support characterized by non-zero sum or win-win-win relationships

The biologist Peter Corning, former president of the International Society for Systems Science and director of the Institute for the Study of Complex Systems, suggests that in the evolution of our own species, cooperation has played a particularly important role. Corning's 'synergism hypothesis' argues "that it was the bioeconomic payoffs (the synergies) associated with various forms of social cooperation that produced – in combination – the ultimate directional trend over a period of several million years, from the earliest bipedal hominids to modern *Homo sapiens*. […] we invented ourselves (in effect) in response to various ecological pressures and opportunities" (Corning, 2005: 40). Corning explains: "one implication of this more complex view of evolution is that both competition and cooperation may coexist at different levels of organization, or in relation to different aspects of the survival enterprise. There may be a delicately balanced interplay between these supposedly polar relationships." p.38). Evolving language and with it the ability to shape culture through narrative has allowed humans to develop complex patterns of collaboration.

Corning emphasizes: "If a society is viewed merely as an aggregate of individuals who have no common interests, and no stake in the social order, then why should they care? But if society is viewed […] as an interdependent 'collective survival enterprise,' then each of us has a vital, life-and-death stake in its viability and effective functioning, whether we recognize it or not" (p.392). Rather than getting lost in the disagreements and competitive episodes that are part of negotiating the integration of our human diversity, we are called to remember that "mutually beneficial cooperation is the fundamental organizing principle underlying all human societies" (p.393). Humanity's future depends on mutually beneficial cooperation at a planetary scale.

The evolutionary biologist and futurist Elisabet Sathouris describes how in the evolution of complex communities of diverse organisms a 'maturation point' is reached when the system realizes that "it is cheaper to feed your 'enemies' than to kill them" (personal comment). Having successfully populated six continents and diversified into the mosaic of value systems, worldviews, identities (national, cultural, ethnic, professional, political, etc.) and ways of living that make up humanity, we are now challenged to integrate this precious diversity into a globally and locally collaborative civilization acting wisely to create conditions conducive to life.

> We have now reached a new tipping point where enmities are more expensive in all respects than friendly collaboration; where planetary limits of exploiting nature have been reached. It is high time for us to cross this new tipping point into our global communal maturity – an integration of the economy and ecology we have put into conflict with each other, to evolve an *ecosophy*.
>
> Elisabet Sathouris (2014)

If *Homo sapiens sapiens* wants to continue its fascinating yet so far relatively short evolutionary success story we have to evolve wise societies characterized by empathy, solidarity and collaboration. Wise cultures, societies and a wise civilization will 'manage the household' with wisdom (*oikos* + *sophia*) and a love for all life (*biophilia*). Humanity's challenge in a constantly changing, complex world is to establish a set of guiding questions that focus our collective intelligence on responding wisely to often unpredictable and surprising change.

Such questions would guide our cultural activity to create regenerative and thriving communities and circular economies elegantly attuned to the unique conditions of local and regional eco-social systems. We need to respond to global challenges with effective local and regional actions enabled by global collaboration and exchange. To do this effectively we need more than policy change and participatory democracy; we need a shift in our way of thinking, from rigid mindsets to valuing multiple perspectives and recognizing our interdependence and common humanity.

The meta-narrative of *interbeing* informs a participatory whole-systems understanding of life and consciousness. It allows us to value a wide diversity of perspectives while unifying us with our larger identity as humanity and life. Transformative innovation and regenerative design are supporting the creation of thriving communities, shared natural abundance and systemic health by collaboratively nurturing regeneration everywhere. They are creative ways of giving form to the narrative of interbeing – ways that reinforce our experience of kinship and oneness with each other and with the ecosystems we inhabit. This collaboration is made possible by a new understanding of who and what we are.

> No longer need we be fragmented and boxed in; we have the option of seeing ourselves within a cosmic Oneness that eliminates all fragmentation; that joins our inner experience to our outer experience as it joins us to one another, to our planet and our Cosmos. Whatever the New Story is, however many versions of it we write and tell, it will reflect this new view of ourselves.
>
> Elisabet Sathouris (2014)

Jeremy Rifkin (2009) suggests that human nature is fundamentally empathic and cooperative rather than selfish and competitive. He reviews recent evidence from brain science and child development studies that shows how selfishness, competition and aggression are not innate aspects of human behaviour but learned and culturally conditioned responses. Our very nature is far more caring, loving and empathic than we have been educated to believe. While being empathic may have initially extended primarily to our family and tribe, our ability to empathize has continued to expand to include the whole of humanity, other species and life as a whole. Rifkin suggests that we are witnessing the evolutionary emergence of *Homo empathicus*:

> We are at the cusp, I believe, of an epic shift into a climax global economy and a fundamental repositioning of human life on the planet. The 'Age of Reason' is being eclipsed by the 'Age of Empathy'. The most important question facing humanity is this: Can we reach global empathy in time to avoid the collapse of civilization and save the Earth?.
>
> Jeremy Rifkin (2009: 3)

The narrative of *interbeing* informs and promotes global empathy as it makes us aware of our interdependence as relational beings with life's thriving on Earth and with the evolution of consciousness within the constantly transforming universe. The healthy evolution of consciousness is not a replacement of reason with empathy, but rather an integration of our capacity for reason with multiple ways of knowing and an increased capacity for empathy – what Albert Einstein referred to as "widening our circles of compassion".

Evolutionary maps of consciousness like the Wilber-Combs lattice of levels and states of consciousness (Combs, 2009), Clare Graves's 'bio-psycho-social systems' (Graves, 2004 & 2005) or Don Beck's and Christopher Cowan's 'spiral dynamic' map of worldviews and value systems (1996) all suggest that healthy development proceeds by a process of transcending *and including* (rather than opposing and dismissing) previous perspectives.

The evolutionary trend of *increasing integration of diversity* is not a path towards increasing homogeneity and one dominant monoculture but a path towards appropriate participation in complexity. Avoiding 'monocultures of the mind', valuing and nurturing diversity and cooperatively integrating this diversity by living the questions together will enable humanity to act wisely – informed by collective intelligence and multiple perspectives – in the face of unpredictable change.

Being fixed on finding silver-bullet solutions and universal or permanent answers predisposes us to frame progress as a replacement of one perspective or 'paradigm' with another. We tend to over-swing the pendulum from one extreme to another. We habitually move from thesis to anti-thesis, rather than searching for the fertile ground of synthesis that transcends and includes various perspectives in an attempt to inform wise action.

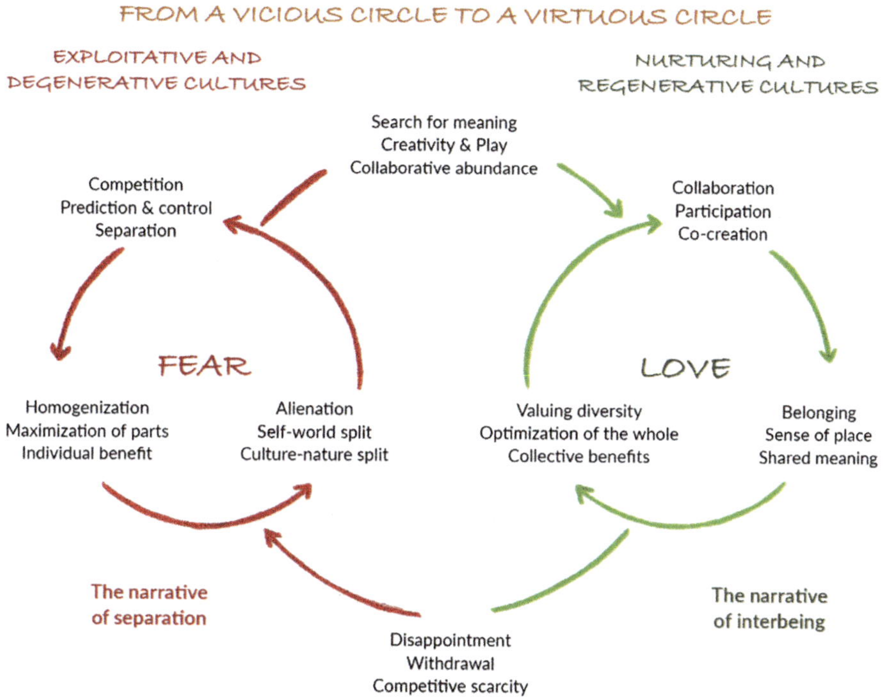

FROM A VICIOUS CIRCLE TO A VIRTUOUS CIRCLE

EXPLOITATIVE AND DEGENERATIVE CULTURES

- Competition
- Prediction & control
- Separation

Search for meaning
Creativity & Play
Collaborative abundance

FEAR

- Homogenization
- Maximization of parts
- Individual benefit

Alienation
Self-world split
Culture-nature split

The narrative of separation

Disappointment
Withdrawal
Competitive scarcity

NURTURING AND REGENERATIVE CULTURES

- Collaboration
- Participation
- Co-creation

LOVE

Valuing diversity
Optimization of the whole
Collective benefits

Belonging
Sense of place
Shared meaning

The narrative of interbeing

Figure 28: The Love and Fear Cycles

Cooperatively and empathically living the questions together – in humble recognition of the limits of our individual and collective knowledge and capacity – is a cultural guidance system capable of informing wise action in the face of change and unpredictability. Living the questions together creates regenerative cultures by nurturing resilience, adaptive capacity and transformability. By collectively exploring and valuing the perspectives that each of the three horizons has of the future potential of the present moment we facilitate the emergence of future consciousness that can help us to act with foresight in the face of unpredictable change.

On 12th September, 2001, the day after the traumatic events at the World Trade Centre in New York, the Catalan philosopher Jordi Pigem led a small group of students on the Masters in Holistic Science at Schumacher College in a collective exploration of the significance of this tragic yet catalytic blow to humanity's collective consciousness. Jordi started the session by lighting a candle and reading two poems by the Vietnamese monk Thich Nhat Hanh: *Interbeing* and *Call me by my true name*. During the subsequent dialogue we co-created an early version of the diagram in Figure 28, mapping the fundamental choice we have, both individually and collectively, to bring forth a world enabled by love or driven by fear.

Activism revisited: conscious participation and collective intelligence

> If success or failure of this planet and of human beings depended on how I am and what I do [...] HOW WOULD I BE? WHAT WOULD I DO?
>
> R. Buckminster Fuller

> We cannot individually comprehend the range, depth and detail of the consequences we are collectively generating for ourselves.
>
> Tom Atlee (2002)

During my time living and working at the Findhorn Foundation ecovillage, I had the opportunity to collaborate with May East on a wide range of projects. May is Brazilian and has been an activist since the late '80s. She is a co-founder of the Global Ecovillage Network and Gaia Education, and directs the United Nations training centre CIFAL Scotland. She has been repeatedly listed as one of the top 100 global sustainability leaders (ABC Carbon, 2012). More than most people I know, May embodies the role of a global change agent and bridge-builder between the often-separate worlds of civil society, business and governance.

Her work stretches from teaching capacity-building courses in sustainable community design and transition town trainings to activists all around the world, to working with local and national governments on a wide range of sustainability issues, and to international development work and sustainability training with UNITAR and UNESCO. May has actively contributed to the development of the new UN Sustainable Development Goals. May and I share a passion for helping diverse constituencies and stakeholders explore whole-systems design solutions that draw on collective intelligence, integrating diverse perspectives and needs. We thrive on building bridges of collaboration between activists and corporate leaders, between academia and civil society organizations, and between local and regional governments and the UN system.

There is a widespread tendency among activists to 'fight against' something, rather than extending our hands and opening our hearts to those whose unsustainable practices and attitudes we are hoping to transform. We are all part of the problem and we will all have to be part of the solution. May once shared her definition of activism with me: "The first thing I do after my morning meditation is to consciously choose where I will put my attention that day, what conversations and projects I will *activate* through the power of my attention".

We are all activists, activating one story or another through the power of our attention and the way we participate in our communities. We can choose to activate and embody the story of separation or the story of interbeing. We can choose what kind of world we want to bring forth together with the people we are in contact with. We can ask ourselves: What am I choosing to activate through the power of my attention? How does my participation contribute to the world I would want to live in?

We are all designers! We are all activists! Regenerative cultures are co-created by people who have become conscious of the way their participation activates certain possibilities, people who share a vision for a better world, collaborating to co-create a thriving future for all Life. Mindful practitioners and conscious activists live a simple question every day: *How can I be the change I want to see in the world?* They are aware of the 'future potential of the present moment' and aim to act wisely to facilitate positive emergence in an unpredictable world.

The first step is to be *aware* of what we are activating in the world by the power of our attention and the story we propagate through our thoughts, words and actions. When we reach out to our communities (families, neighbourhoods, colleagues and friends) and invite them to live the questions together, we are inviting multiple perspectives and diverse ways of knowing to inform our cooperation in the co-creation of regenerative cultures.

This kind of open exchange and inquiry can facilitate the emergence of collective intelligence and future consciousness to inform wise actions in the face of increasing complexity and in humble recognition of the limits of our own knowing. You too can become a conscious activist, change agent and bridge builder by starting such an inquiry in your community. The fact that you have read this far means that you probably already are. By exploring the questions in this book with others and refining them, or adding to them, we can continue our pilgrimage and apprenticeship in the transition to the third horizon of a regenerative human presence on Earth.

In *Reflections on Evolutionary Activism*, Tom Atlee highlights three evolutionary dynamics: i) integration of diversity, ii) constant alignment with reality, and iii) self-interest rooted in the wellbeing of the whole. These are key characteristics of regenerative cultures aligned with the evolution of life. They are also guidelines to help us, as individuals, keep on learning and contributing to the creation of regenerative businesses, communities and cultures.

Atlee begins his book by reminding us of the long evolutionary journey from the beginnings of the universe to our times. Our bodies literally contain atoms forged in the death of giant stars. As participants in this ever-transforming and evolving whole, we are expressions of what Atlee calls the Creative Power of the Universe. He extends an invitation to all of us:

> As evolutionary activists we can step out of [separation] and into the awareness that we are part of the ongoing creation of the universe, that our power is the Creative Power of the Universe working through us, and that we have a creative job to do, a really important undertaking to be part of. We are the eyes and ears and hands and feet and heart and mind of the Creative Power of the Universe at work in our world at this time forming the first sustainable self-evolving, wise civilization ever seen on this planet. Every decision we make – including how to spend this precious moment and where to put our precious energy and which precious people to work with and how we are going to be with them – all these decisions are the Big CPU feeling its way about what to do next here, what is possible now. [...] You and I are that Power, in that Power, of that Power. Welcome home. We're all in this job together, backed up by the greatest creative force on Earth – and beyond. Let's go to work, as consciously, in tune, and together as we can manage.
>
> Tom Atlee (2009: 33-34)

7: Why Are Regenerative Cultures Rooted in Cooperation?

Tom Atlee's work offers profound inspiration and practical support for people willing to live the questions together in order to redesign the human presence on Earth. He describes how a series of questions has guided his own journey as a life-long activist (pp.43-47):

- Q How can I help make a better world?
- Q What is the meaning of self-organized collective intelligence?
- Q How can activist groups become more collaboratively effective?
- Q How can communities and countries be more collaboratively effective?
- Q How can humanity wisely and creatively work with the crises of our time?
- Q How can we help our social systems and cultures consciously evolve?
- Q How can we grow into being evolution – and take responsibility for our own role *as* the increasingly conscious co-intelligence of the universe?
- Q How do we activists humbly become the world consciously evolving in directions that deeply support all forms of aliveness?

The last two questions invite us deep into a participatory and evolutionary perspective, which we are participants *in* and expressions *of*, aiming to become more fully conscious of how our *being and doing* creates conditions conducive to life.

The practice of Living the Questions Together and co-designing the transition towards regenerative cultures *is* a practice of evolutionary activism. The approach I have explored in this book is fully aligned with Atlee's principles for evolutionary activism:

i. promoting healthy self-organization and the conscious evolvability of whole systems

ii. using strategic questions and strategic conversations as primary transformational tools

iii. engaging diversity and dissonance creatively in service of greater life

iv. highlighting, using, and promoting the energy of positive possibility

v. consciously seeking and using guidance from evolutionary dynamics

vi. considering co-creativity the sacred essence and power of our work

vii. seeing evolutionary activism as part of the great story of evolution becoming conscious of itself, and inviting others into that story

(Atlee, 2009: 54-63)

In *Thoughts on Wisdom and Collective Intelligence*, Atlee says "if individuals cooperate they can generate collective intelligence". The world has become so complex, new technologies are developing so rapidly, information and knowledge are expanding at such a pace, and we are facing so many converging crises on multiple scales that we need the power of many minds to inform wise action. For collective intelligence to emerge we need to pay attention to "the presence of 'the whole' in the life and functioning of 'the parts'".

Atlee lists a number of conditions that facilitate the successful emergence of collective intelligence: a shared vision, an understanding of collective purpose, believing in shared work, dealing with diverse perspectives creatively, integrating multiple stakeholder perspectives into a "more complex big-picture reality", a shared ability to "encounter more of the whole" and a sense that the whole is working *through* all of us and *as* all of us. He offers an insight into wise participation by proposing that "wisdom characterizes any factor that facilitates greater engagement with more of the whole". In this context, "factors" can be as diverse as a worldview; a piece of insight, information, knowledge or understanding; a way of thinking, feeling or behaving; a narrative or a design. "Any of these can shape our engagement with the world in holistic ways and thus be wise." Atlee explains: "engagement here can be active or passive. It includes perceiving, reflecting on and understanding, as well as being with, responding to, influencing and changing reality, as well as being influenced or changed by it. Engagement here implies interbeing and interactivity. […] The 'whole' here refers to the deeper, fuller, more comprehensive reality of something – a person, a group or community, a situation, an idea, the world, or anything else" (2004).

The narrative of interbeing and a participatory living-systems view of life are important enabling factors in the emergence of collective intelligence through cooperation. At the level of the individual and the collective we have to consciously explore appropriate participation. To do so we need to make use of all our diverse ways of knowing: thinking, feeling, intuiting, and sensing. Wise action can only be guided by synthesis and cooperation. Leadership is increasingly recognized as a role that all of us can take and no longer personified by individuals who exert 'power over' through secret intelligence and proprietary knowledge and technology. Wise leadership in the 21st century has to be rooted in 'power with', public collective intelligence, and open sharing of knowledge and technology. Tom Atlee writes:

> Power-with is fast becoming as strategic and skilled a science as power-over. Even military and business schools are teaching the power of cooperation. Power-with is also becoming a source of power in sustainability practices working with bugs and bacteria to compost garbage and recycle wastes or working with wind and water to generate energy. All fields and practices that stress collaboration are exercising power-with.
>
> Tom Atlee (2012)

Atlee emphasizes that "just because our current systems of politics and governance – and economics and so many others – are designed to get us to compete, doesn't mean we have to always go there. We can create new systems that help us work together more powerfully." If we practise collaboration and live the questions together we can access the "power and wisdom that arises from *within* and *among* the group's members. This power and wisdom does not come from the individuals themselves so much as from their interactions, from a kind of group energy or intelligence that shows up because these people are together" (2012). Once you have experienced directly what Atlee talks about here, collective intelligence and wisdom cease to be abstract notions and become an attainable, lived reality and embodied experience. Sitting in council circles has given me this transformative experience.

In the autumn of 2014 I attended a remarkable gathering of activists and cultural creatives from 52 countries and 6 continents. Two years earlier, I had helped to conceive and plan the New Story Summit at the Findhorn Foundation. Among the many inspiring people I met was a former CIA spy turned whistle-blower and activist, who in 1988 – after years of covert operations – had come to understand his "life as a spy specializing in secrets was not only unproductive, it was in sharp opposition to what we actually need: full access to true information, to the complete diversity of views on any given issue, and consequently, the ability to create Open-Source-Intelligence (OSINT)." Robert Steele is a pioneer of this OSINT approach and he makes a convincing argument that it is in fact a necessary foundation for "direct democracy: participatory intelligence (decision support), open-source policy-making, and participatory budgeting" (Steele, 2012: xiii). Figure 29 shows the 'larger ecology' of the Open Source Everything approach:

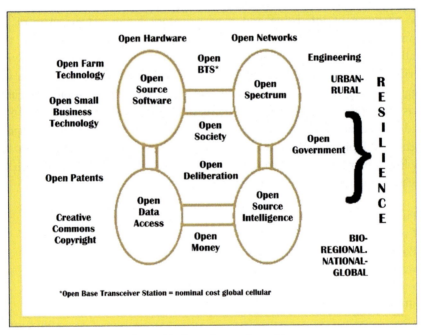

Figure 29: Open Source Everything

I highly recommend the *Open Source Everything Manifesto* Steele published in 2012. At the New Story Summit, he was invited to submit a research paper to the UN's high-level panel on the post-2015 development agenda. The paper is now online (Steele, 2014a).

Apart from offering the UN "a 21st century alternative approach for development" the paper argues that the 17 Sustainable Development Goals could effectively be achieved by 2050 at an estimated cost of $230 billion a year, a fraction of the $1.3 trillion the world's governments spend annually on their military. In a recent article, Steele wrote:

> [Collective Intelligence] in the 21st century – a human endeavor – must focus on the true meaning of intelligence as evidence-based decision-support, rooted in holistic analytics, true cost economics, and open source everything enabling open source engineering. […] My hope is that we can reinvent intelligence to re-engineer and re-open the human academy, economy, governance, and society such that the five billion poorest are empowered to create infinite sustainable wealth at the same time that we stop, in a non-violent manner, the pathologies of Western capitalism, colonialism, and militarism.
>
> Robert David Steele (2014b)

Applied collective intelligence – based on multi-national, multi-agency, multi-domain and multi-disciplinary collaboration in information-sharing and sense-making – can help us to co-create a world that works for all. In line with what we have explored in this book, Steele calls for a redesign of academia, economics, governance and our societies "to embed intelligence in what we build, how we build it, and how we use it". We need to go beyond the kind of embedded intelligence approach promoted by, for example, IBM's 'Smart Cities' and the current fad of 'smart everything'. Rather than doing the 'wrong thing righter' we need to redesign with appropriate decision support (ibid).

Collective intelligence and wisdom is an emergent property of complex dynamic eco-social-systems with predominantly cooperative rather than competitive relationships. If we cooperate effectively in the sharing of knowledge, information and technology and learn to distinguish education from indoctrination we can almost certainly find appropriate responses to the converging crises humanity is facing. If we learn to share the biocultural commons more equitably at a local, regional and global scale and create life-long-learning opportunities for all of humanity we can unleash the enormous abundance and ingenuity that lies in the creative and innovative capacity of billions of underprivileged people in the world.

We cannot create regenerative cultures without creating more equitable cultures. For this transition to be successful, we need the widespread participation of informed citizens collaborating in the creation of regenerative communities at every scale, empowered and enabled by global collaboration. When all your creative ability is absorbed by desperately meeting the immediate survival needs of yourself and your family and without basic education and access to higher education, it is hard to collaborate in long-term community projects and a globally collaborative effort to create a regenerative human civilization.

We need to enable all humanity to take an active role in the great transition to a regenerative human presence on Earth. As David Orr says: "It's all-hands-on-deck time! Hope is a verb with its sleeves rolled up" (personal comment). We need to share all our resources openly. There is, to some extent, also a leap of faith in moving from the competitive, depleting win-lose economy into the collaborative, regenerative win-win economy. We need to trust that by effectively sharing what we have (money, knowledge, skills, technology, productive ecosystems, a life-sustaining biosphere and other resources) we can co-create genuine abundance and a more meaningful and joyful life for everyone, including ourselves, our families and our communities.

Sharing and cooperation can spread through the system like infectious health. The more people meet with cooperative, empathic and sharing attitudes, the more they will step into the joy of cooperating, caring for and sharing with others. In these transition times, we all have to ask ourselves: What kind of world am I activating through the power of my attention? *Co-creating regenerative cultures is evolutionary activism*, and every day is a new opportunity to step into our role as evolutionary activists in this transition.

We are coming back to life and this changes everything

Evolutionary activism is socio-ecological innovation that drives transformative culture change. In *kairos*, this time of transformation that Joanna Macy calls the "Great Turning", the personal, the collective and the planetary are intertwined more than ever. She speaks of our dual role, of needing to be both hospice workers of the old "Industrial Growth Society" (with its habits, structures and stories that no longer serve) and midwives of the new, the emerging "life-sustaining society".

Macy identifies three dimensions of involvement with this process of cultural transformation. The world over, *we*, the people are engaging in: i) "actions to slow the damage to Earth and its beings", ii) "analysis of structural causes and creation of structural alternatives", and iii) "a fundamental shift in worldview and values" (Macy & Young Brown, 1998: 17).

> Many of us are engaged in all three, each of which is necessary to the creation of a life-sustaining society. People working quietly behind the scenes in any of these three dimensions may not consider themselves activists, but we do. We consider anyone acting for a purpose larger than personal gain or advantage to be an activist.
>
> Joanna Macy & Molly Young Brown (2014: 6)

In *This Changes Everything* Naomi Klein (2014) explores why the current system and, in particular, our current economic model is causing us to wage war against life on Earth. United in our love for life, we do *all* have the power, if not the obligation, to become active in changing this. The video trailer announcing her book ends with the words: "change, or be changed, but make no mistake: This changes everything!"

Everywhere, people are organizing in holding actions, opposing further crimes and violence against nature and calling for an immediate and transformational response to climate change and a structurally unsustainable economy of exploitation, waste and inequity. Violently silenced, ridiculed and disenfranchised for centuries, indigenous people are joining forces with a globally networked movement of change makers.

> As Indigenous people have taken on leadership roles within this movement, [their] long-protected ways of seeing are spreading in a way that has not occurred for centuries. What is emerging, in fact, is a new kind of reproductive rights movement, one fighting not only for the reproductive rights of women, but for the reproductive rights of the planet as a whole – for the decapitated mountains, the drowned valleys, the clear-cut forests, the fracked water tables, the strip-mined hillsides, the poisoned rivers, the "cancer villages." All of life has the right to renew, regenerate, and heal itself.
>
> Naomi Klein (2014)

There are many signs that we are in midst of a massive step change in our capacity and motivation for acting to protect a living planet and to co-create a thriving future for all. Non-violent direct action campaigns are gaining strength, proliferating and joining up. More than once I have cried tears of joy celebrating the widespread responses to global-local actions called by 350.org and Avaaz uniting human beings from all over the world in defence of our living 'Home' and social justice. Times *are* changing! People *do* care!

Ever larger sums of money are being 'divested' away from planet-destroying industries like the petrochemical, fossil fuel and agro-industrial giants. Institutions and philanthropic foundations are washing their hands of investment in Horizon 1 or Horizon 2- and putting their money behind systemic transformation – Horizon 2+ and Horizon 3 investments in restorative, renewable and regenerative alternatives. Naomi Klein has come to a conclusion that I and many others – every day more – agree with:

> Only mass social movements can save us now. This means laying out a vision of the world that competes directly with today's vision, one that resonates with the majority of people on the planet because it is true: that we are not apart from nature but of it. That acting collectively for a greater good is not suspect, and that such common projects of mutual aid are responsible for our species' greatest accomplishments. That greed must be disciplined and tempered by both rule and example. That poverty amidst plenty is unconscionable.
>
> Naomi Klein (2014)

We need to build on the emerging global-local movement of concerned Earthlings, *aligned with life* rather than with dangerous ideologies (like destructive economic dogmatism and religious fundamentalism). To do this we need a new story, "a story that serves". Or better, many stories giving voice to an underlying cosmology and narrative inspiring enough to galvanize humanity into action, awake to the promises and opportunities of *thriving together*.

This narrative needs to combine intellectual breadth with spiritual depth of meaning and significance that transcend and include all religions and paradigms. It needs to draw its transformative power from infectious idealism and grounded pragmatism, technological innovation and age-old wisdom, helping humanity to act wisely with power and love. It must encompass the immanence of our experience as embodied biological beings intimate with all life, and the transcendence of pure consciousness beyond mind-body, energy-matter dualisms; the immanence of being *on* and *of* the Earth and the transcendence of being self-reflexive consciousness.

John D. Liu observes a growing call for a new collective consciousness among activists and climate scientists:

> By valuing life higher than material things we are coming much closer to the spiritual teachings of all the world's great religions. This understanding is the next level of evolution for human consciousness. But it is not simply a profound philosophical understanding, it is a practical way forward to rebalance the climate, to create meaningful employment, to fairly distribute affluence and create an abundant and sustainable civilization.
>
> John D. Liu (2014)

The publication of Pope Francis's *Laudato Si* in 2015 marks a historic move not just for Catholics around the world, but even more importantly towards an alliance of all religious leaders in support of creating a globally regenerative civilization in which all humanity can thrive within planetary limits. The Pope calls for "a new dialogue about how we are shaping the future of our planet" and stresses that "we need a conversation which includes everyone, since the environmental challenges we are undergoing, and its human roots, concern and affect us all" (Vatican, 2015).

As discussed in Chapter 1, we need to recognize that ecology and spirituality are both ways to connect to and better understand wholeness and our participation in it. Once religious leaders facilitate a dialogue between their congregations that highlights their shared spiritual wisdom and values beyond the differences between religions, they can become catalysts of the transition towards a regenerative human presence on Earth.

The stories we tell as expressions of the meta-narrative of interbeing need to educate our systemic understanding of the converging crises and their root causes, thereby opening up perspectives on how to do things differently. Even more importantly they need to nurture our collective capacity for design conversations that create visions and practical examples of a regenerative and thriving human presence on Earth. These visions and 'pockets of the future in the present' will invigorate individual and collective creativity, inspire our aesthetic and moral imagination and offer everyone an opportunity for finding meaningful work inspired by active participation in the project of the century: creating regenerative cultures everywhere.

As we lend our voices, our hearts, our minds and our creativity to living the narrative of interbeing we change humanity's design-conversation to the guiding intentions of salutogenesis, the healing of the whole system and to co-creating win-win-win solutions in a world that works for all. As we join others in the process and learn together how to come home, how to design *as* nature, and how to cooperate in elegant adaptation to the uniqueness of place, the narrative of interbeing will unfold in its full fractal diversity. No longer one story, but a tapestry of stories in many languages, carrying the wisdom of cultural diversity woven together by the threads of life's fundamental interbeing, of diversity in unity, the pattern that connects.

Living the questions together is activism. It changes everything. As we become conscious practitioners of the art of living from our love for others, for humanity and for life – and others around us begin to do the same – we encourage each other to live in *active hope* and to bring forth a better world together.

> Active Hope is not wishful thinking.
> Active Hope is not waiting to be rescued
> by the Lone Ranger or by some saviour.
> Active Hope is waking up to the beauty of life
> on whose behalf we can act.
> We belong to this world.
> The web of life is calling us forth at this time.
> We've come a long way and are here to play our part.
> With Active Hope we realize that there are adventures in store,
> strengths to discover,
> and comrades to link arms with.
> Active Hope is a readiness to engage.
> Active Hope is a readiness to discover the strengths
> In ourselves and in others;
> A readiness to discover the reasons for hope
> and the occasions for love.
> A readiness to discover the size and strength of our hearts,
> Our quickness of mind, our steadiness of purpose,
> Our own authority, our love for life,
> The liveliness of our curiosity,
> The unsuspected deep well of patience and diligence,
> the keenness of our senses, and our capacity to lead.
> None of these can be discovered in an armchair or without risk.
>
> Joanna Macy & Chris Johnstone (2012: 35)

From the book *Active Hope*, © 2012 Joanna Macy and Chris Johnstone. Reprinted with permission from New World Library, Novato, CA. www.newworldlibrary.com

Learning to listen deeply

It takes two to speak the truth – one to speak and another to hear.

Henry David Thoreau

What we most need to do is to hear within us the sound of the Earth crying.

Thich Nhat Hanh

When we explore collective intelligence and wisdom, we should not make the mistake of assuming that only fellow humans can inform insights, provide evidence and support decisions. The wider community of life, the embedded intelligence of 'the pattern that connects', the practice of asking nature (*as* nature) can inform collective intelligence and wise action as well. I briefly explored the importance and relevance of traditional indigenous wisdom and knowledge in Chapter 6. When it comes to participatory decision-making, accessing collective wisdom and tuning into life's inherent intelligence, many traditional cultures offer powerful technologies of the sacred, rituals and practices that should not be dismissed as 'irrelevant' to our modern societies.

To the contrary, we need to recover these deeper forms of listening and gaining insight in order to recover the wisdom we have lost in an avalanche of information and knowledge. Our methodologies tend to be focused on (rational) thinking alone, but deep insights can be gained from processes that include and value sensing, feeling and intuiting as part of decision-support.

Three such practices have helped me personally to experience collective intelligence in action and to gain deeper insights into and through my relationship with life. All three have deeply informed and supported my work as an educator, facilitator and consultant; and have deeply affected the quality of my own interbeing with all my relations. For me, personally, the practices of *mindfulness* (connecting to the wisdom with), *council* (connecting to the wisdom of the group), and *solo time in the wild* (connecting with the wisdom of nature) offer important pathways towards regenerative cultures, as they are embodied direct experiences of our interbeing. These technologies of the sacred are more than simple practices, they are ways of walking in an ancient lineage of living the questions. They can guide our healthy participation in wholeness.

Council

Council is an ancient way and modern practice, spanning many cultures and religions. In council we listen to the whole: the people and the place, earth, water, fire, air – the living planet. The practice elicits an experience of true community, a recognition that each voice needs to be heard, that every person has a gift, a story to share, a perspective of the whole. It allows us to share our common humanity. Every time someone opens up and shares what truly moves their heart, in heartful listening we are given the opportunity to experience that beyond all our differences we care about very similar things.

Council creates space for new insights and understandings, wisdom in decision-making and the healing of differences. More than being just another communication tool, the deep practice of council allows us to access and experience collective intelligence and group wisdom, offering a way both new and ancient of guiding collaborative processes.

Council is a non-hierarchical form of deep communication where each person is empowered to speak. Its primary intentions – listening and speaking from the heart – encourage genuine self-disclosure and attentive empathic listening. The quality of deep listening extended by everyone in the circle towards the person holding the 'talking piece' contributes to creating a container of deep trust and openness.

Once this container is co-created – also helped by an attitude of ritual – it enables us to share deeply from the heart. Often people find themselves expressing a quality of insight and wisdom that they did not know they had. In these magical moments, people speak from a place that is deeply nourished by the collective intelligence and wisdom of the whole group and beyond as the guidance of the ancestors, of future generations and of all of nature is invited in at the beginning of the council.

Council encourages participants to speak from their own experience, making I-statements rather than speaking in generalities for others. As the practice deepens, participants achieve greater tolerance for different perspectives and greater understanding of the feelings of others. Council can help us to develop our ability to mediate conflict non-violently. It offers a simple but powerful contribution to the creation of a culture of peace and understanding. Council lets us experience empathy and compassion as the bedrock of our own humanity. There are many forms and lineages of council practice. In particular the work of the Ojai Foundation in the USA, the book *The Way of Council* by Jack Zimmerman and Virginia Coyle, and the European Council Network have spread this practice internationally.†

Solo time in the wild

Spending time alone in nature, with an open heart/mind, maybe holding a question or maybe simply letting one come, is also a valuable ally for evolutionary activists. Solo time in nature can generate powerful insights. It serves as an effective way of letting go of the old and inviting the new (story) into our lives.

Rites of passage ceremonies exist in all of the world's indigenous cultures. They are an important marker of transition, transformation and change in the lives of members of these cultures. The transition from childhood to adulthood, from adulthood into eldership, the transition into parenthood, the confirmation of a new role in the community, the intentional and ceremonial leaving behind of modes of thinking and acting that no longer serve us – these important moments of change and transformation can be energized and celebrated through rites of passage ceremonies. They serve to support individuals and help them to recognize their unique gifts and potential, for their own benefit, for the benefit of their community and for the benefit of the world.

In the industrial growth society we have done away with traditional rites of passage or turned them into ineffective vestiges of their ancient counterparts. Vision quest, or vision fast, is a powerful ritual that can help individuals to mark these important life stages and transitions in a meaningful and helpful way.

For most people, there comes a time in life when engaging in such a ritual could be an important act of transformative innovation at the very personal level of our own way of being in the world. Rites of passage ceremonies enable men and women of all ages, but especially young adults, to engage in an age-old ceremonial pattern: completion of an old life, movement through the threshold of the unknown and return to the world reborn. People in transition from one phase of life to another often find deep meaning and guidance in this process. It is a path that has been followed by human beings for many thousands of years. When it is time to consider such a ritual, these questions call us:

Q   Who am I?

Q   What do I have to give?

- Q How can I heal my wounds and leave behind habits that no longer serve?
- Q How can I become an effective agent of positive change?
- Q How can I love this world, every day a little bit more?
- Q What is my true calling?
- Q How can I serve?

Just as meditation connects us to our inner wisdom and intuition, and practising the way of council connects us to the collective wisdom of our people and community, nature-based rites of passage rituals – or simply spending conscious solo time in nature – connect us to nature as a profound source of insight, guidance, vision and strength.

The School of Lost Borders in California, Sacred Passages in Colorado, and the Eschwege Institute in Germany are among the many places where you can start to explore the power of modern day rites of passage for yourself and experience how these rituals can help you to step into your own full power as an agent of positive change in this world. For me, solo time in nature is an important source of insight, creativity, meaning and vitality. I have seen in workshops I co-facilitated how such immersion in wild nature, combined with council and other practices, can have a deeply transformative effect on people.

Shortly after my own first vision fast in 2008, I read Peter Senge, Otto Scharmer, Joe Jaworski, and Betty Sue Flowers' book *Presence* (2005) and was delighted to find out about John P. Milton's vision fast work with global business leaders. John's programme seemed to have had a profound effect on many of them. I met John only a few weeks later when he paid a surprise visit to Findhorn. He gave me a copy of *Sky Above, Earth Below* (2006). The book describes many useful techniques for meditation, conscious movement, and visualizations to draw strength and insight from our conscious participation in nature. It has been a treasured companion.

Mindfulness practices, council and solo time in nature can support us on our path of living the questions, individually and collectively. We *are* all making a difference, not just by what we do, also by what we say, the questions we ask, the way we think and invite others to think, but most of all by how we 'show up'. The quality of our being *in* and *through* relationships and how we help others relate to the future potential of the present moment changes outcomes. Setting an intention about who we want to be, how we want to behave, and what we want to activate in the world and affirming this intention every day in our thoughts, words and actions is a practice of personal transformation that catalyses cultural transformation. The most effective way of writing the narrative of interbeing into humanity's collective consciousness is by living it with compassion for others and our own failures on the way. If enough of us become culturally creative evolutionary activists we will contribute to the emergence of diverse regenerative communities and a thriving future. Listening more deeply is an invaluable source of insight and guidance for all who are willing to follow that call.

> My Life is a gift
> from the whole of Life
> to the whole of Life […]
>
> Tom Atlee

Inner and outer resilience

> The secret of living a meaningful and fulfilling life is to be ready – at every moment – to give up who you are for what you could become.
>
> Brian Goodwin (personal comment)

Definitions of 'resilience' vary according to what discipline the word is used in. In engineering, the resilience of a material refers to the tendency of the material to return to its original state after being stretched, bent or compressed. In psychology we can speak about emotional resilience as the ability to cope well with changes and recover after illness, misfortune and traumatic experiences. As we saw in Chapter 4, in socio-ecological systems resilience, as the persistence of existing patterns, is not necessarily always a good thing, depending on how appropriate the patterns of organization and behaviour are that we are 'bouncing back to'. The resilience of some of the outdated systems we have created can actually resist transformative innovation and prolong patterns that are destructive. This is also true for inner resilience.

On the one hand we need the ability to maintain our individual identity and recover from setbacks in a rapidly changing environment; on the other hand we have to be discerning about our own habits and mental concepts. Many have been passed on to us through cultural transmission and an education that might not reflect the deeper values we would like to live in accordance with. We were raised and educated within the cultural narrative of separation. We are therefore carrying the habit of seeing the world through the lens of scarcity and competition. Inner resilience is about becoming conscious of how our worldview influences our judgement and behaviour. If we are willing to try on other worldviews and perspectives for size, we can often see connections and opportunities that we were blind to from within a fixed point of view.

Another important aspect of inner resilience is to deal with disruptions in our own life creatively and to overcome setbacks, turning the lessons of failure into the opportunity to develop a more successful approach and adapt to changes in our living conditions. Mental and psychological health, as well as a supportive family environment and embeddedness in a community with high social cohesion, are all important contributors to high inner resilience.

It can be disempowering to be submitted to the flood of negativity and seeming hopelessness we face by simply watching the news and seeing how the multiple converging global and local crises are playing out through the suffering of humanity and the desecration of nature. Habits of mind, learned through cultural osmosis, can lock us into the separation perspective that makes us feel powerless to make a difference in the face of so much misery. We get so absorbed by this negativity and hopelessness that we forget that billions of people are in love, nurturing their children, helping their neighbours, rescuing strangers, caring for animals, nurturing plants and restoring ecosystems, saving lives, delighting their communities through art, dance and poetry, celebrating the beauty of life and contributing to the thriving of their communities.

Inner resilience is about the capacity to face the horrors and misery of the world square on, rather than trying to ignore them, but it is also about seeing the beauty, collaboration, compassion, care and love that is all around us. Finding the strength to be actively hopeful in the face of calamity; living from the conviction that abundance is all around us if we shift our narrative and live accordingly; being willing to plant an apple tree today even if others try to tell you the world will end tomorrow (as Martin Luther suggested) – all of these capacities are expressions of inner resilience.

While writing this chapter I heard about the death of the Hollywood actor Robin Williams, who inspired millions with his humour and the deep caring for others he portrayed in many of his roles. He killed himself unable to find a way to exit the spiral of depression and addiction he kept secret from the world. In conversation with a fellow writer, Jonathan Leighton (see Leighton, 2011), trying to make sense of this news, I found myself suggesting: "It seems that depression is not an illness but a symptom of and reaction to the pathological narrative of separation".

Most of the conventional psychological approaches to the treatment of depression focus on having a dialogue with the depressed person about their own perspective on their situation. These approaches tend to focus people back on the separate self. Maybe there is a point, early on in the downward spiral of depression, where the simple act of encouraging the depressed person to apply their abilities – in whatever way they can – to caring for and helping others would be enough to shift people from feeling locked into the perspective of separation to having a direct experience of interbeing. This experience of being capable of helping others and seeing the positive impact we can have on their lives inspires new hope and can trigger a transformative response to depression. By living from the narrative of interbeing we are able to propagate positive health in our eco-social systems, helping ourselves by helping others and the wider community of life.

Connecting with our innate biophilia – our love for life – and the insights and strength we can gain from being in communion with nature *as nature* are powerful sources of inner resilience. As Joanna Macy once told me: "Things change when you step into your full authority as a living being, speaking as and on behalf of life." Connecting with our 'ecological self' is a powerful source of inner resilience.

Transformative *inner* resilience is about personal development and transformation, not in order to become somebody else but to become more fully who we really are and share all our unique gifts and creative passions with our community. On the path of personal growth we are repeatedly challenged to give up who we are for who we could become. If we want to live in regenerative cultures and thriving communities we need to ask ourselves:

Q   How can I best live in accordance with the insight that by serving others and the community of life I am serving myself in both a deeper and a higher sense?

Q   What are my unique gifts and my role in co-creating thriving communities and a regenerative culture?

The dynamic relationship between inner and outer is a recurring theme that this book invites us to explore. This dynamic describes how our cultural narrative shapes our worldview and vice versa, and how both affect our perceived needs and intentions, and therefore the designs we create and solutions we propose. Working consciously with our inner resilience points us towards the deeper dynamics of transformative innovation – culture and behaviour change.

We are all co-creative and co-responsible microcosms of our culture, and therefore changing ourselves is changing our culture. Transformative resilience is also about our willingness to give up and let go of the *status quo*, questioning who we are individually and collectively, and letting go of patterns, systems and attitudes (narratives) that no longer serve so that we can transform into co-creative change agents of diverse regenerative cultures in service of all life. This process of continuous learning and transformation never stops, as it is in its very essence a reflection of our continuously transforming universe and life's continuous exploration of novelty.

> Watch your thoughts; they become words. Watch your words; they become actions. Watch your actions; they become habits. Watch your habits; they become character. Watch your character; it becomes your destiny.
>
> Lao Tzu

The Taoist sage Lao Tzu's advice paraphrases the fourth book of the *Brihadaranyaka Upanishads* (IV, 4.5) which is often translated as "You are what your deep, driving desire is. As your desire is, so is your will. As your will is, so is your deed. As your deed is, so is your destiny." Both of these versions express the same profound wisdom. They are good advice for anyone deeply committed to co-creating a regenerative culture. We will never live, act and contribute to the world in any other moment but the present moment. This is not to say that our actions cannot be informed by past insights or have formative effects on the future that lies before us. Acknowledging the future potential of the present moment we come to understand that how we relate to 'other' and behave from moment to moment *is* how we contribute to bringing forth a world.

The most culturally creative spaces we engage in are the conversations we have about where we are going and the re-telling of the narrative of who we are and what we are here to do. Such conversations create future consciousness. The vibrant and meaningful visions of diverse regenerative cultures we can co-create will inspire worldview and behaviour change, and affect what kind of future will emerge. Our ideas, thoughts and visions of the future have creative agency and contribute to bringing forth the world we will live in.

Watch your intentions, they become the way you contribute to the design of the world you live in. Watch how and what you design, it will shape the culture you live in. Watch the culture you live in; it will shape how you see the world. Watch how you see the world, it will shape your intentions. *The cycle continues.* We are bringing the world into being. We are bound to make mistakes. We learn through making mistakes. They help us to change our attitudes and responses. Being forgiving with ourselves, so we can be forgiving with others, is also a good practice for developing inner resilience.

> Come, come, whoever you are
> – wanderer, worshiper, lover of leaving.
> It doesn't matter.
> Ours is not a caravan of despair.
> Come,
> even if you have broken your vows a thousand times.
> Come, yet again, come, come.
>
> Jalaluddin Rumi (1207 – 1273)

This invitation by the Sufi sage and poet Rumi reminds me not to be too harsh with my own shortcomings and fallibility; to let go and forgive myself over and over again if I have fallen short of acting on my own higher intention to contribute not only to a fulfilled, joyful and meaningful life for myself and the communities I live and work in, but to do so while caring for all of life. Rumi reminds me: *now* is the time to act on these intentions, in every new *opportunity of the present moment*. What good is it if I miss such an opportunity because I am busy mulling over my past shortcomings?

My personal source of inner resilience is the deep knowledge that my actions and my way of being can help to create the world I would like to live in – a world in which all of life thrives and creates conditions conducive to life. In such a world, inner and outer resilience are expressions of whole-systems health. By paying attention to my own interbeing I can live the connection of inner to outer, mind to body, and self to world. In those moments I experience humanity *as* nature.

CONCLUSION

REGENERATIVE CULTURES ARE ABOUT THRIVING TOGETHER

> You never change things by fighting the existing reality. To change something, build a new model that makes the existing model obsolete.
>
> R. Buckminster Fuller

> […] the ones who are crazy enough to think that they can change the world, are the ones who do.
>
> Steve Jobs

In the end it comes down to asking ourselves: will we continue to strive to out-compete each other and in the process unravel the thread that all life depends upon? Or will we learn to collaborate in the healing of the whole through transformative innovation and regenerative design creating vibrant cultures and thriving communities for all?

In early 2010, my friend Samantha Sweetwater, an evolutionary activist in the Bay Area of San Francisco, invited me to contribute to an experiment in co-creation. Jean Russell had the inspiration to start a collective inquiry into the meaning of a word with transformative agency: *Thriving*. "What does thrivability mean to you?" Around this question Jean curated the co-creation of *Thrivability - A Collaborative Sketch*. Seventy of us from all walks of life and a diversity of places were invited to write a short reflection on the meaning of 60 words and phrases that relate like a broad map to this magnetic notion. "In the dance between the individual and humanity as a whole, there is an aliveness. In aliveness, there is a yearning for thriving", writes Jean in the introduction. "All living things strive to move beyond survival to truly flourish." A simple yet magnetic idea galvanized our enthusiasm and contributions: "that the goal of evolving our behavior should be to thrive" (Russell, 2010: 6), both individually *and* collectively.

I encourage you to look at the kaleidoscopic collage of meaning that emerged. As Jean had intended, it was a starting point for a wider conversation and inquiry. In her subsequent book, *Thrivability - Breaking Through to a World that Works*, Jean asks the question: "What would our lives and the sum of our society be like if we said they were thriving?" She describes how we can move from "breakdown thinking" to "breakthrough thinking" by inquiring into the way we see (perceive the world), understand ourselves, and can take effective transformative actions to co-create a thriving world (Russell, 2013). My contribution to the 'collaborative sketch was on 'integrity.' I found myself inspired to write:

> Integrity is all about wholeness. […] Integrity is about living in congruence with the insight that as co-creative participants in the world we live in, we can all contribute to the transition towards a sustaining, resilient and thriving culture, moving from the mess we are in, beyond sustainability, to the thrivability of the whole community of life.
>
> Daniel Wahl in Russell (2010: 15)

The short answer to why we should aim to create regenerative cultures together is simple: choosing the path of regeneration and cooperation will create a greater level of wellbeing, health, happiness and equality for everyone and all life; *and* in the process of co-creating a better future together, our lives will be more meaningful, fulfilling, creative and fun.

For too long the narrative of separation has conditioned us to the knee-jerk response of competition in the face of perceived scarcity. Local and global collaboration in the co-creation of regenerative communities, enterprises, economies and cultures can unlock a very different future for humanity. Collaboration in regenerative practices can change our experience of reality: turning a resource-constrained planet on a path to ecological collapse into a thriving patchwork of socio-ecological systems generating an abundance of renewable resources, restoring vital ecosystems functions, nurturing solidarity, community cohesion and resilience, while effectively mitigating – and adapting to – climate change.

The creation of regenerative cultures is also rooted in a shift from seeing ourselves only as separate individuals, communities, nations and species to understanding our deep interbeing as fundamentally interconnected expressions of life itself. By shifting to a relational perspective and paying attention to the ways that life creates conditions conducive to life, both the need for *and* promise of regenerative cultures become apparent.

As we recognize ourselves as participants in the evolution of life and consciousness, we come to understand ourselves as creative expressions of natural process. The path of exploitation leads via increasing separation, disintegration and competition to the early demise of our relatively young species. The path of regeneration through conscious interbeing, integration and collaboration opens up the possibility of a thriving future for humanity as a mature member in the community of life. If we choose to, we can generate abundance for all by consciously creating conditions conducive to life. Let us ask:

Q   What if we choose regeneration over exploitation?

Q   What if we choose to thrive together, rather than compete against?

The future potential of these transition times invites us to explore in community how we can co-create diverse regenerative cultures with sensitivity to place and scale. Global-local collaboration, based on knowledge and technology exchange, can help us to value diversity in the process of creating increased self-reliance and redundancies at multiple scales. Transformative innovation applied to redesigning the human presence on Earth requires global cooperation in the process of building circular and regionally focused economies in support of resilient communities and the regeneration of their ecosystems. Thriving regional economies, supported by scale-linking collaboration and global solidarity, are the basis for collaborative abundance for all.

We can all start cultural transformation and seed regenerative patterns simply by asking the kind of questions explored in this book and inviting others around us to explore them with us. Questions can initiate conversations that will lead us to re-examine the relationship between nature and culture. In these conversations, we can learn to value the importance of whole-systems health and help each other to understand our interdependence. A relational perspective of interbeing makes the objectives ahead seem quite clear: create conditions where all life can thrive by nurturing the health of communities and ecosystems functions everywhere. Sustainability is not enough. We need to do more than just sustain. We need to regenerate the vitality and bioproductivity of the planetary life support system. We need to nurture and regenerate the pattern of socio-ecological interdependencies that support human and planetary health. It is this pattern of health that allows us to stay responsive, adaptable and resilient in the face of change (see Chapter 4).

To improve the regenerative capacity of communities and ecosystems we need to pay close attention to the effect of our actions at multiple interconnected scales, developing a participatory, living-systems perspective. We also need to develop future consciousness that can guide wise action in the face of an unpredictable future and humble recognition of the limits of our knowledge and capabilities (see Chapter 2). This includes processes that help us decide more wisely which technologies to employ at what scale and in which place. Not all that is technologically possible creates conditions conducive to life.

The socio-cultural transition ahead will require a move towards participatory democracy which depends on a widespread culture of learning and radical responsibility. Co-production of vital community services can help to ensure that life-long learning enabled by ongoing, community-focused design conversations will also inform participatory governance. An 'Open source everything' approach would enable learning to take place throughout the whole system (rapidly) and offer vital decision support, education and technological capability to *all* of humanity.

Education for ecological and social literacy will play an important role in spreading the understanding that we are participants in a fundamentally interconnected physical, chemical, biological, ecological, social and psychological process. By living the questions together we can begin to educate each other in our communities and businesses about how to participate appropriately in this process – and nurture our capacity to access collective intelligence and wisdom. Since we cannot predict with certainty what kind of disruptions and unforeseen consequences of our actions might challenge us in the future, the best preparatory action is to create resilient communities at multiple scales networked for mutual support. This will create the basis for widespread collaboration as a path to increased wellbeing and meaning, solidarity and social cohesion, healthier ecosystems, more vibrant local economies and, thus, to thriving communities.

We have to re-invent education as a process that inspires everyone – regardless of their age – to keep on exploring the kind of questions asked in this book and adapt them to the unique conditions of a particular culture and place. In the 'age of information', education is about learning to ask the right questions rather than memorizing pre-formulated answers and temporary solutions. By asking the right questions we can gain a deeper understanding of systems structures and dynamics, and we can work towards synthesis and integration, learning to optimize the system as a whole.

We are drowning in information and choking on 'big data'. Our knowledge is compartmentalized and locked into silos protected by jargon and isolated communities of specialized knowledge. We long for synthesis and integration. We are starving for wisdom and thirsting for meaning. The role of education in cultures with advanced telecommunication and data processing technologies is not so much about memorizing information and accumulating knowledge. Education in the 21st century is about nurturing a general social and ecological literacy along with the capacity to collaborate in the process of asking the right questions that will guide wise action informed by future consciousness *and* readily available big data and factual knowledge.

Working together to find the appropriate questions is a more effective cultural guidance system towards a regenerative future than forcing one-size-fits-all solutions. We can unleash the culturally transformative power of collective intelligence by forming local, regional and global communities of practice that live the questions together. These communities offer the context for life-long learning and formal and informal education. To skill-up the transition we need design thinking, future consciousness and an understanding of the living systems view of life to be woven through curricula from pre-school to university and beyond to life-long learning opportunities for all.

Regenerative design, including education as regenerative meta-design driving worldview and culture change, can drastically reduce and reverse the negative human impact on the planetary life support system. Eco-social resilience and health can be restored at a local, regional and global scale. Global collaboration, based on open knowledge and technology exchange, can unite local and regional regeneration projects into a worldwide and systemic response to climate change and the converging crises we face.

Biologically and ecologically inspired design and innovation offer an opportunity to root regenerative cultures in the ground of 3.8 billion years of life's intelligence and ingenuity. The creative challenge of redesigning our material culture, our systems of production and consumption, our life-styles and economic systems, offers countless opportunities for transformative innovation and design for regenerative cultures. In weaving the multiple opportunities for synergy and symbiosis into cooperatively integrated mosaics of diverse regenerative eco-social systems we *are* designing *as* nature.

As we explored in Chapter 6, pioneers in green chemistry and material science, bio-inspired technologies, product design, architecture, industrial ecology, and community, urban and regional planning are already living the questions of regenerative design inspired by life's principles. They are actively engaging with the most important and meaningful creative challenge of the 21st century.

Q   How do we design for the emergence of regenerative cultures everywhere?

Q   How do we co-create health, wellbeing and happiness in thriving communities?

Q   How do we nurture human and planetary health by redesigning the human presence on Earth?

Pathfinders on our collective pilgrimage are already applying ecosystem mimicry to the creation of regenerative business ecologies, new financial and economic systems, as well as ecosystems restoration and regenerative agriculture. All of these communities of practice are now forming networks of active change agents (evolutionary activists) who are beginning to link up across scales and disciplines (see Chapter 7).

Social innovation, peer-to-peer collaboration, open knowledge and technology, the spread of maker culture, additive manufacturing, circular economy initiatives and diverse online and off-line community networks are all powerful enablers and catalysts in the creation of collaborative and regenerative systems structures that will nurture regenerative cultures. In many places and cultures, people are already living the questions together and transforming the world one place at a time. Another world is possible. If we pay attention, we can already see this world taking shape all around us.

Collectively envisioning a regenerative future and design conversations at the community scale about how to implement these visions *are* powerful processes of cultural transformation. Conversations like these are beginning to take place everywhere, in community groups, boardrooms, town halls, universities, government think tanks and within the UN system. Together – *as one humanity* – we are capable of responding to the converging crises and offering culturally transformative responses to them. By forming networks of collaboration we can begin to heal divisive ideologies and old habits of competition driven by the outdated narrative of separation.

Only seeing separation and therefore competition, rather than also seeing the underlying wholeness of our interbeing with all life, has caused a cultural myopia that created many of these crises in the first place. Now, we are beginning to see the relationships of our 'belonging-together' rather than seeing only isolated individuals and objects. We are overcoming modernity's 'crisis of perception'. The future possibility of thriving communities and ecosystems providing a better life for *all of* humanity is within our reach if enough of us commit to creating such a future together.

New models that make the existing ones obsolete are already taking shape. Transformative innovation and regenerative design act like viruses of infectious health, nurturing regenerative cultures everywhere. Our species can take the path to becoming a restorative and regenerative presence on Earth. Caring for Earth *is* caring for ourselves and our community. We can collaboratively create abundance in thriving communities intimately and elegantly adapted to the uniqueness of place.

Art, music, poetry, dance, story and the sciences celebrate the process of life. Through them, we can celebrate our diversity in the unity of interconnection and joyous cooperation.

By asking appropriate questions we can respond wisely to change, knowing when to persist, when to adapt and when to fundamentally transform. We can learn to appreciate disturbance and breakdown as an enabling constraint and a design opportunity for systemic transformation and breakthrough.

The very act of living the questions together is a 'presence-ing' of the future in the now. It cultivates the practice of asking 'what if' to unlock creative opportunities and inform future consciousness. Deep collective inquiry and design conversations facilitate transformative innovation in the second horizon (H2+ innovation) which seeds the future of H3 regenerative cultures in the present moment and, if successful, creates pockets of the future in the present with culturally transformative effect.

Together we can design for positive emergence and whole-systems health. Systemic thinking and nurturing future consciousness through the Three Horizons framework can help us to make wiser choices as we evaluate disruptive innovation and identify the kind of transformative innovation and design that will help us to co-create regenerative cultures. The third horizon is already here, just unevenly distributed.

Let's spread greater wellbeing, thriving community life, deeper meaning, cooperation and solidarity outwards from the already existing 'outbreaks of infectious health' in business, governance and civil society around the world. Let's continue to reconnect to our profound interbeing with each other and the community of life. Let's continue to regenerate healthy ecosystems functions and planetary health. Let's continue to co-create the regenerative communities, enterprises, economies and cultures we want to see in the world. Let's continue to live the questions together.

We are relational beings who come from cooperation, are cooperation, and can choose to co-create a thriving and regenerative future through cooperation. As beings who are blessed with the miraculous gift of a self-reflective consciousness, our greatest challenge and our greatest opportunity is not to *know* the meaning of life, but to *live* a life of meaning. That is why humanity is worth sustaining.

As life, *as* nature, *as* consciousness, *as* universe we can bring forth a world in which humanity, like the rest of life, creates conditions conducive to life. Living the questions together is the practice of doing so responsively and responsibly, using our human capacities for collective intelligence, foresight and vision to get clear about our collective intentions and to design and co-create the regenerative communities we want to live in.

Living the questions is an opportunity to connect, to yourself, to your community, to your world. By living the questions together, rather than obsessing with definitive answers and permanent solutions, we can give up the futile attempt to *know* our path into the future. We can move from prediction and control to aiming for appropriate participation. As humble pilgrims and apprentices of life, we can begin to *live* our way into an uncertain yet potentially thriving future. I am confident that increasing collaboration will unleash newfound creativity and innovation that will shape the transition towards regenerative cultures and thriving communities.

Intellectually, this seems the only viable way through the eye of the needle. Emotionally, it gives me meaning and nourishes me. Intuitively, it feels right and has opened up a path full of synchronicity. Somatically, it gives me an embodied experience of *belonging* to many communities, to life, and to an animate and intimate Earth. Spiritually, my interbeing with life's continuous exploration of novelty and the evolution of consciousness has simultaneously taken away my fear of death and increased my love for life. The intention to act as a cultural creative, a transition designer and an evolutionary activist in the co-creation of regenerative cultures is something that deeply informs my being and my doing. I am excited about the times ahead. Despite all that is still 'wrong' in the world, I am confident that we are capable of co-creating regenerative cultures everywhere. What about you?

What did you do once you knew?

What did you do once you knew?
It's 3:23 in the morning
and I'm awake... because my great great grandchildren won't let me sleep.
My great great grandchildren ask me in dreams,
What did you do while the planet was plundered?
What did you do when the earth was unraveling?
Surely you did something,
when the seasons started failing?
Surely you did something,
as the mammals, reptiles, and birds were all dying?
Surely you did something?
Did you fill the streets with protest when democracy was stolen?
What did you do once you knew?
(Excerpt from 'Hieroglyphic Stairway', a poem by Drew Dellinger)

ACKNOWLEDGEMENTS

In Deep Gratitude!

In 2002, while studying for my Masters in Holistic Science, I had a conversation with the physicist and now director of the Mind & Life Institute Arthur Zajonc in which he said "the next major shift in human affairs will be initiated by the Arts". Deeply enthusiastic about the holistic revolution in cutting edge sciences, Brian Goodwin and Stephan Harding were exposing us to, I took a while to understand what Arthur might have meant. Later, John and Nancy Todd, together with David Orr, made me see design as the art of conscious participation. Henri Bortoft introduced me to the notion of "a work that works". This high ideal has had me fascinated ever since. After Joanna Macy encouraged me to take up the offer of a funded PhD to "put another string on my harp", I wanted to write a work that works, that leaves the reader thinking and feeling differently about themselves and the world. This notion guided me through my PhD research, mentored skilfully by Seaton Baxter. The resulting thesis was over 700 pages – not very workable for a work that works, I have to admit. In 2006, David Orr challenged me to write *that* book that only I could write, yet after the doctorate I needed some time to decompress from academia and deepen in all dimensions of my being. I needed work experience with diverse constituencies. Working with Gaia Education, CIFAL Scotland (UNITAR), the Findhorn College, Bioneers, the State of the World Forum, the International Futures Forum and as a consultant to large businesses, civil society organizations, universities and local and national government provided this opportunity. The Findhorn Foundation Community will always be a home away from home and I am deeply grateful to everyone there.

In 2009 Rick Tarnas, Brian Swimme, Allan Combs and Sean Kelly encouraged me to get on with it (the book); and in 2013 my friend Goeff Oelsner taught me a profound lesson in trusting the universe and following my inner knowing. He got me writing again! The 'book that only I could write' feels less like it was written by me than written through me. So many people, experiences, conversations, fortuitous circumstances and enabling constraints, so many walks through Majorca's nurturing beauty with Alice and alone, so many hours spent by the Mediterranean Sea, all these people and places have contributed to the book you are holding. Like the sheet of paper in Thich Nhat Han's poem, this book *inter-is*.

On my own journey of personal transformation, aspiring to effective evolutionary activism, and on my own pilgrimage of learning about the *why*, the *how*, the *what* and the *what if* of regenerative design and culture, I have been blessed with a plethora of mentors, teachers and friends who have supported me on many levels. I have found insight, deep meaning and my own voice in the nourishment they provided. Invaluable guidance and support with lasting impact was offered by Seaton Baxter, Brian Goodwin, John Todd, Joanna Macy, David Orr, Tony Hodgson, May East, Gigi Coyle, Satish Kumar, Stephan

Acknowledgements

Harding, Henri Bortoft, John Clausen, Peter Harper, Pracha Huanwatr, Sybilla Sorondo and Geoffrey Oelsner.

Even if the list is large, I feel I need to mention many people who I deeply thank for providing me an opportunity to live the questions together with them. I have drawn insight, inspiration and encouragement from my conversations with: Fritjof Capra, James Lovelock, Brian Swimme, Rick Tarnas, Allan Combs, Sean Kelly, John P. Milton, Kenny Ausubel, Nina Simmons, Paul Stamets, John Seed, Rupert Sheldrake, Christopher Cooke, Paul Hawken, Frances Moore Lappé, Helena Norberg-Hodge, Jane Goodall, Roger Collis, Albert Bates, David Abram, Arthur Zajonc, Lady Angelika Cawdor, Bill and Lynne Twist, Ann Pettifor, Vera Kleinhammer, David Lorimer, Aubrey Manning, Ulrich Loening, Michael Shaw, Galen Fulford, Gill Emslie, Alberto Fraile, Tomeu Serra, Jordi Pigem, Jonathan Dawson, Declan Kennedy, Herbert Girardet, Ross and Hildur Jackson, Max Lindegger, Maddy and Tim Harland, Achim Ecker, Michel Daniek, Richard Heinberg, Win Phelps, Kosha Joubert, Giovanni Ciarlo, Peter Merry, Morel Foreman, Jim Garrison, Amory Lovins, Martin Blake, Jonathon Porritt, Jakob von Uexküll, Thomas Ermacora, Richard Douthwaite, Marcello Palazzi, Cornelius Pietzner, Antonio Marin, José Luis Escorihuela, Juan del Rio, Julio Cantos, Miquel Ramis, Chris Mare, Polly Higgins, Gonzalo Salazar, Chris Garvin, David Loy, Jeff Clearwater, Terry Irwin, Gideon Kossoff, Bryony Schwan, Teresa Millard, Taryn Mead, Paul Allen, Paul Hughs, Naresh Giangrande, Sophy Banks, Rob Hopkins, Stephen Sterling, Bryce Taylor, John Prewer, Edgar Gouveia Jùnior, Kimberley Hunn, John Dennis Liu, Louis Schwartzberg, Daniel Greenberg, Clinton and Marion Callahan, Greg Watson, Hazel Henderson, Sim Van der Ryn, David Ehrenfeld, Thomas Hübel, Ken Wilber, Barrett Brown, Frank Cook, Patricia and Reinhard Hübner, Ana Digon, John Ehrenfeld, Michel Bauwens, Xavi Villanueva, Patricia Reglero, Hanna Bonner, Mandy Merklein, Bruce Robson, Larry Hobbs, Toni Font, Miguel Payeras, Miquel Riera, Biel Torrens, Jaume Miralles Isern, Martin Stengel, Iris Kunze, Jan Martin Bang, Lara Cifre, Irene Carbó, Georgina Follett, Tom Inns, Stuart Walker, Wolfgang Jonas, John Wood, Andrew White, Aubrey Meyer, Sulak Sivaraksa, Liz Walker, Anna Warrington, Hugh Knowles, Rodrigo Bautista, Tom Domen, Paul Dickinson, Robin Alfred, Grant Abert, Stephen Busby, Paul Ray, Jean Houston, Ervin László, Lester Brown, Samantha Sweetwater, Andy Lipkis, Neil Meiklehan, Scott Spann, Wolfgang Sachs, Michael Braungart, Janine Benyus, Sean Esbjörn Hargens, Lisette Schuitemaker, Mary-Alice Arthur, Sylke Iacone, Martin Cadee, John Croft. Michael Hann, Martin Stengel, David McNamara, Craig Holdrege, Margaret Colquhoun, Jasper Sky, Graham Meltzer, Liora Adler, Brock Dolman, Mari Hollander, Karl-Henrik Robèrt, Rupert Hutchinson, Yvan Rytz, Holger Heiten, Katrin Lüth, Hartwig Spitzer, Werner Pilz, Gavin Morgan, Ruby Worth, Ana Rhodes, Rafa Giménez, Eugenia Cusi, Alexis Urusof, Heloise Buckland, Craig Gibson, Roger Doudna, Samantha Graham, John Talbott, Vance Martin, Alan Heeks, Giles Chitty, Mathis Wackernagel, Robert Costanza, Alice Jay, David Hodgeson, Christian Marx, Iris Kunze, Richard Olivier, Ed Gillespie, Robert Steele, Elisabet Sathouris, Gunter Pauli, Jane Hera, Guillem Ferrer, Pedro Barbadillo, David Suzuki, Ian Skelly, Robert Gilman, Bob Horn, Bill Sharpe, Ian Page, Napier Collyns, Noah Rafford, and Graham

Leicester. I also want to thank Nancy Roof for her encouragement at a critical point in the writing process.

Communities of learning that have deeply affected my practice and the way I think are Schumacher College, the Centre for the Study of Natural Design (University of Dundee), the Findhorn Foundation and Findhorn Fellows, the Centre for Alternative Technology, Gaia Education, the 'Learning Partnership for Creative Sustainability' (LPCS), Bioneers, the State of the World Forum, the RSA and last, but by no means least, the International Futures Forum. Time in wild nature has provided nourishment on many levels. The island of Majorca has been my muse. Special thanks to the staff of 'El Xorri', my neighbourhood café where I could write and look up at the far horizon of the Sea of Middle Earth. This book in its final form would not have been possible without the help of Andrew Carey, my editor at Triarchy Press, and Flavia Gargiulo Rosa, my illustrator. I also thank all the publishers, authors, and graphic designers who have given permissions to reproduce images or quote longer passages.

Good friends are a source of strength, confidence and joyful memories, yet they also offer a mirror for self-reflection when it is needed. Thank you Andreas Rotheimer, Bernhard Schmidt, Enrique Buchner, and Ulrich Masch for decades of nurturing friendship. May we share many more! Finally, I want to thank my parents, Adalbert and Brigitte, and my brother Constantin for their love, patience and support, my 99-year old grandmother for teaching me about tireless curiosity and the appreciation of the beauty of the small (or truly big) things in life, and my travel companion and loving partner Alice who has lent a patient ear to my trials and tribulations as an author. Teaching by example, Alice as taught me to be a better human being. All of them have made me who I am today and therefore contributed to this book in important ways. In deep gratitude, to *all* my relations! May it serve!

REFERENCES

ABC Carbon (2012) 'Profile: 100 Global Sustain Ability Leaders', bit.ly/DRC01
Abram, David (1996) *The Spell of the Sensuous*, Vintage Books
AEIDL (2013) *Europe in Transition – Local Communities Leading the Way to a Low-Carbon Society*, European Association for Information on Local Development (AEIDL), bit.ly/DRC02
Aldersey-Williams, Hugh (2003) *Zoomorphic: New Animal Architecture*, Laurence King Publishing
Alliance for Regeneration (2015) 'Inspiring Communities to Reclaim their Identities and Destinies', bit.ly/DRC03
Altieri, Miguel A. (1995) *Agroecology: The Science of Sustainable Agriculture* 2nd ed., Westview Press
Altieri, Miguel A. & Toledo, Victor M. (2011) 'The agroecological revolution in Latin America', *The Journal of Peasant Studies*, Vo.38, No.3, pp.587-612, bit.ly/DRC04
AMSilk (2015) 'Biosteel Spidersilk Fibers', bit.ly/DRC05
Anastas, Paul T. and Warner, John C. (1998) *Green Chemistry Theory and Practice*, Oxford University Press
Anbumozhi, Venkatachalam et al. (2013) *Eco-Industrial Clusters – A Prototype Training Manual*, Asian Development Bank Institute: bit.ly/DRC06
ARUP (2013) 'The Smart City Market: Opportunities for the UK', DBIS Research Paper No. 136, bit.ly/DRC239
Ashby (1962) bit.ly/DRC007
Ashoka (2012) 'Social Entrepreneurship, Empathy at the Heart of Rio+20 and the New Economy', bit.ly/DRC008
Ask Nature (2015a) 'Morphotex Structural Colored Fibers', The Biomimicry Institute, bit.ly/DRC178
_____ (2015b) 'Surface Allows Self-Cleaning: Sacred Lotus', The Biomimicry Institute, bit.ly/DRC123
_____ (2015c) 'Beak Provides Streamlining: Common Kingfisher', The Biomimicry Institute, bit.ly/DRC122
_____ (2015d) 'Zeri Coffe Farm System', bit.ly/DRC121
Assadourian, Erik (2012) 'The Path to Degrowth in Overdeveloped Countries', *State of the World 2012*, Island Press
Atlee, Tom (2012) *Empowering Public Wisdom – A Practical Vision of Citizen-Led Politics*, Evolver Editions
_____ (2010) *The Tao of Democracy*, The Writers Collective, Revised Edition
_____ (2009) *Reflections on Evolutionary Activism*, CreateSpace
_____ (2004) 'Thoughts on Wisdom and Collective Intelligence', Blog of Collective Intelligence, bit.ly/DRC09
_____ (2002) Introduction to *The Tao of Democracy*, bit.ly/DRC274
Ausubel, Kenny (2012) *Dreaming the Future*, Chelsea Green Publishing
Avaaz.org (2015) bit.ly/TPliving215
BALLE (2012) Business Alliance for Local Living Economies Local Economics, bit.ly/DRC214
Barfield, Owen (1988/1965) *Saving Appearances – A Study in Idolatry*, 2nd ed., Wesleyan Paperback
Bass, Leo (2010) 'Planning and Unfolding Eco-Industrial Parks: Reflections on Synergy', Linköping University, Department of Management & Engineering, bit.ly/DRC027
Bateson, Gregory (1972) *Steps to an Ecology of Mind*, new edition, The University of Chicago Press
Bateson, Nora (2010) 'An Ecology of Mind – A Daughter's Portrait of Gregory Bateson', bit.ly/DRC213
B-Corporation (2015) 'The B Corp Declaration', bit.ly/DRC028
Beck, Don & Cowan Chris (1996) *Spiral Dynamics: Mastering Values, Leadership and Change*, Blackwell Business
Benyus, Janine M. (2002/1997) *Biomimicry – Innovation Inspired by Nature*, 2nd ed., Perennial Publications
Berger, Warren (2014) *A More Beautiful Question: The Power of Inquiry to Spark Breakthrough Ideas*, Bloomsbury
Berry, Thomas (2006) *Evening Thoughts – Reflecting on Earth as Sacred Community*, ed. Mary Tucker, Counterpoint
_____ (2001) 'Airlie Principles' approved at the 1st Earth Jurisprudence meeting, Washington, bit.ly/DRC010
_____ (1999) *The Great Work – Our Way into the Future*, Harmony
Beyond Benign (2015) Beyond Benign Green Chemistry Education, bit.ly/DRC230
Biggs, Reinette et al. (2012) 'Towards Principles for Enhancing the Resilience of Ecosystem Services, *Annual Review of Environment and Resources*, Vol. 37, pp.421-448, bit.ly/DRC177
Biochar International (2015) 'What is Biochar?', bit.ly/DRC211

References

Biomimicry 3.8 (2014a) 'Biomimcry – A conversation with Janine', Biomimcry Group, bit.ly/DRC212

_____ (2014b) 'Architecture – Learning from Termites How to Create…', Biomimicry Group, bit.ly/DRC124

Biomimicry Group (2014) 'Life's Principles', bit.ly/DRC125

Blake, William (1802) 'Letter to Thomas Butt, 22 Nov. 1802' in Keynes, G. (ed.), *The Letters of William Blake* (1956) OUP

Bocken, N.M.P., Short, S.W., Rana, P. & Evans, S (2014) 'A literature and practice review to develop sustainable business model archetypes', *Journal of Cleaner Production*, Vol.65, pp.42-56, bit.ly/DRC012

Bollier, David (2011) 'The Commons, Short and Sweet', bit.ly/DRC210

Borgen Project (2015) 'Poverty and Overpopulation', bit.ly/DRC13

Bortoft, Henri (2012) *Taking Appearances Seriously*, Floris Books

_____ (1996) *The Wholeness of Nature – Goethe's Way of Science*, Floris Books

_____ (1971) *The Whole: Counterfeit and Authentic*, Systematics, Vol.9, No.2, (September 1971), pp.43-73

Botsman, Rachel & Rogers, Roo (2011) *What's Mine is Yours*, Harper Collins Business

Boulding, Kenneth (1966) 'The Economics of the Coming Spaceship Earth', in H. Jarrett ed., *Environmental Quality in a Growing Economy*, pp.3-14, Johns Hopkins University Press, bit.ly/DRC176

Bourriaud, Nicolas (1998) *Relational Aesthetics*, reprinted in Prigann, H. (2004) *Ecological Aesthetics: Art In Environmental Design: Theory And Practice*, Birkhäuser

Boyle, David & Harris, Michael (2009) *The Challenge of Co-Production – How equal partnerships between professionals and the public are crucial to improve public services*, New Economics Foundation & Nesta, bit.ly/DRC014

Brown, Juanita, Isaacs, David & World Café Community (2005) *The World Café*, Berrett-Koehler

Brown, Lester R. (2009) *Plan B 4.0: Mobilizing to Save Civilization (Sustainability Revised)*, W.W. Norton

Brown, Tim (2009) *Change by Design*, Harper Business

Brown, Valerie A., Grootjans, John, Ritchie, Jan, Townsend, Mardie & Verrinder, Glenda (2005) *Sustainability and Health – Supporting Global Ecological Integrity in Public Health*, Earthscan Publications

Brunckhorst, David (2002) *Bioregional Planning: Resource Management beyond the New Millennium*, Routledge

B-Team (2015) 'We, the undersigned believe that the world is at a critical crossroads', bit.ly/DRC197

Buckland, Heloise & Murillo, David (2013) *Vías hacia el cambio sistémico – Ejemplos y variables para la innovación social*, Antenna de innovación social, ESADE, Universidad Ramon Llull

Cahn, Edgar S. (2008), Foreword to *Co-production*, new economics foundation, bit.ly/DRC015

_____ (2004) *No More Throw-Away People: The Co-Production Imperative*, 2nd Edition, Essential Books

Cajete, Gregory ed. (1999) *A People's Ecology – Exploration in Sustainable Living*, Clear Light Publishers

Capra, Fritjof & Luisi, Pier Luigi (2014a) *The Systems View of Life – A Unifying Vision*, Cambridge University Press

_____ (2014b) 'The Systems View of Life', *Transition Consciousness*, 19th April, bit.ly/DRC127

Capra, Fritjof & Henderson Hazel (2013) 'Qualitative Growth', Outside Insights, ICAEW

Capra, Fritjof (1995) 'Deep Ecology', in Sessions, George (ed.) *Deep Ecology for the 21st Century*, Shambhala

Carbon Tracker (2013) *Unburnable Carbon 2013 – Wasted capital and stranded assets*, bit.ly/DRC129

Carnegie Mellon Design (2015) 'About our Research', Carnegie Mellon University, bit.ly/DRC30

Capital Institute (2015) 'Regenerative Capitalism White Paper', bit.ly/DRC031

Casey, Tina (2011) 'Growing the Business with Biomimcry', *Triple Pundit – people, planet, profit*, bit.ly/DRC130

CDP (2015) 'CDP – Driving Sustainable Economies, Catalyzing business and government action', bit.ly/DRC033

Center for Ecoliteracy (2015) 'Ecological Principles', bit.ly/DRC035

Center for Food Safety (2014) *Food & Climate – Connecting the dots, choosing the way forward*, bit.ly/DRC016

Checkland, Peter B. (1981) *Systems Thinking, Systems Practice*, John Wiley

Chertow, Marian R. (2007) 'Uncovering Industrial Symbiosis', *Journal of Industrial Symbiosis*, bit.ly/DRC017

Christensen, Clayton M. (1997) *The Innovator's Dilemma*, Harvard Business School Press

CIC (2015) 'Cooperativa Integral Catalana – General Principles', bit.ly/DRC131

Clark, J. R. et al. (1997) 'A model of Urban Forest Sustainability', *Journal of Arboriculture*, Vo. 23, #1, bit.ly/DRC126

Clear Village (2015) Creative Regeneration Specialists, bit.ly/DRC196

Cohen, David (2007) 'Earth's natural wealth: an audit', in *New Scientist*, Issue 2605, bit.ly/DRC132

Collins, Katherine (2014) *The Nature of Investing: resilient Investment Strategies through Biomimicry*, Bibliomotion

Collins, Timothy (2004) "Towards an aesthetics of diversity" in *Ecological Aesthetics – Art in Environmental Design: Theory and Practice*, Prigann & Strelow (eds.), Birkhäuser, pp.170-180

Columbia Forest Products (2014) 'Pure Bond – Formaldehyde-free Hardwood Plywood', bit.ly/DRC120
Combs, Allan (2009) *Consciousness Explained Better*, Omega Books
_____ (2002) *Radiance of Being: Understanding the Grand Integral Vision*, Omega Books
Community Planning (2015) 'Planning for Real', bit.ly/DRC119
Connor, Steve (2008) 'Educate girls to stop population soaring', *The Independent*, 4 Dec., bit.ly/DRC133
Cooper, Arnie (2009) 'A Material based on Sharkskin stops…', *Popular Science*, 29th Oct., bit.ly/DRC134
Corning, Peter (2005) *Holistic Darwinism*, University of Chicago Press
Costanza, Robert et al. (2013) 'The Future We Really Want', *Solutions Journal*, July/August 2013, bit.ly/DRC209
Costanza, Robert (1992) 'Towards an Optimal Definition of Ecosystem Health', in Costanza, Norton and Hackell eds., *Ecosystem Health*, Island Press, pp.239-256
_____ (1991) *Ecological Economics: The Science and Management of Sustainability*, Columbia University Press
Cullinan, Cormac (2011) *Wild Law: A Manifesto for Earth Justice*, 2nd ed., Chelsea Green Publishing
Curry, Andrew & Hodgson, Anthony (2008) 'Seeing in Multiple Horizons: Connecting Futures to Strategy', in *Journal of Futures Studies*, 13(1): pp.1-20
Cyclifier (2015) 'Tunweni Beer Brewery', bit.ly/DRC135
Daimler (2015) 'Taking its clues from nature – Mercedes-Benz bionic car', bit.ly/DRC036
Daimler Chrysler AG (2004) 'Examining the great potential of bionics', Daimler Crysler AG, bit.ly/DRC037
Daly, H. (2009) 'From a Failed Growth Economy to a Steady-State…', *The Encyclopaedia of Earth*, bit.ly/DRC194
_____ (1991) *Steady-State Economics*, 2nd ed., Island Press
Datschefski, Edwin (2001) *The Total Beauty of Sustainable Products*, Design Fundamentals, Rotovision
David Suzuki Foundation (1992) *The Declaration of Interdependence*, (for the UN Earth Summit, Rio) bit.ly/DRC195
Davies, Emma (2011) 'Critical Thinking – As our supply of some essential…', *Chemistry World*, Jan. 2011, pp.50-54
Dawson, Jonathan, Norberg-Hodge, Helena & Jackson, Ross (2010) *Gaian Economics – Living Well within Planetary Limits*, The Economic Key of the EDE by Gaia Education, Permanent Publications
Dawson, Jonathan (2006) *Ecovillages: New Frontiers for Sustainability*, Schumacher Briefing No.12, Green Books
Dawkins, Richard (1976) *The Selfish Gene*, Oxford University Press
DCFR (2012) 'Bright Green Fossa Region', The Development Centre of Fossa Region, bit.ly/DRC18
DeKay, Mark (2011) *Integral Sustainable Design: Transformative Perspectives*, Routledge
Dellinger, Drew (2007) 'Hieroglyphic Stairway', poem, bit.ly/DRC273
DeLuca, Denise et al. (2010) *The Firm of the Future - A Business Inspired by Nature*, BCI & Atos Origin, bit.ly/DRC275
Desai, Pooran & Riddlestone, Sue (2002) *Bioregional Solutions*, Schumacher Briefing No.8, Green Books
Design Futures (2015) *The Design Futures Program*, Griffith University, Australia, bit.ly/DRC191
DESIS (2015) Design for Social Innovation and Sustainability Network, Vision, bit.ly/DRC192
Despommier, Dickson (2011) *The Vertical Farm: Feeding the World in the 21st Century*, Picador
Dickinson, Tim (2015) 'The Logic of Divestment', *Rolling Stone*, 14th Jan, 2015, bit.ly/DRC136
Dragon Dreaming (2015) 'Dragon Dreaming International E-Book', bit.ly/DRC193
Economic Times (2012) 'WEF Davos meet', bit.ly/DRC038
Einstein, Albert (1950) Letter to a Rabbi quoted in *The New York Times* (29th March, 1972)
Eisenstein, Charles (2013) *The More Beautiful World Our Hearts Know is Possible*, North Atlantic Books
Eliot, T.S. (1943) *Four Quartets*, Harcourt
_____ (1934) 'Choruses from the Rock' in *Collected Poems 1909-62*, Faber & Faber
Ellen MacArthur Foundation eds. (2014) *A New Dynamic – Effective Business in a Circular Economy*, Ellen MacArthur Foundation
Ellen MacArthur Foundation (2013a) 'The circular model – an overview', bit.ly/DRC039
_____ (2014b) *Towards a Circular Economy Vol.3*, bit.ly/DRC065
_____ (2013b) *Towards the Circular Economy Vol.2*, bit.ly/DRC231
_____ (2012) *Towards the Circular Economy Vol.1*, bit.ly/DRC064
Equator Initiative (2012) *Equator Initiative*, UN Development Programme, bit.ly/DRC020
Erle, C. Ellis, et al. (2012) 'Used planet: A global history', *Proceedings of the National Academy of Sciences of the United States of America* (PNAS), Vol.110, No.20, pp.7978-7085, bit.ly/DRC066

References

Erzen, Jale (2004) 'Ecology, art, ecological aesthetics', in Prigann & Strelow edits. *Ecological Aesthetic – Art in Environmental Design: Theory and Practice*, Birkhäuser, pp.22-50

Esbjörn-Hargens, Sean (2005) 'Integral Ecology', in *World Futures*, Vol.61, No.1-2, pp.5-49

Esty, Daniel C. & Winston, Andrew (2009) *Green to Gold*, John Wiley

Ethical Markets (2012) 'Statement on Transforming Finance Based on Ethics and Life's Principles', Ethical Markets & Biomimcry 3.8, bit.ly/DRC019

Ewing Duncan, David (2014) 'Chemicals Within Us', republished from *National Geographic Magazine*, bit.ly/DRC67

FAO (2015) 'Can organic farming produce enough food for everybody?', FAO of the United Nations, bit.ly/DRC059

_____ (2011) *The State of Food and Agriculture 2010*, bit.ly/DRC216

Fair Coop (2014) 'Fair Coop. Target: Earth', Enric Duran's Statement, bit.ly/DRC068

Ferwerda, William (2012) *Nature Resilience*, Rotterdam School of Management, Erasmus Univ., bit.ly/DRC175

Fischer, Hermann (2012) *Stoffwechsel – Auf dem Weg zu einer solaren Chemie für das 21. Jahrhundert*, Verlag Antje Kunstmann GmbH

Fischer-Kowalski, Marina (2003) 'On the History of Industrial Metabolism', in Bourg & Erkman eds., *Perspectives on Industrial Ecology*, Greenleaf Publishing, pp.35-45

Fleming, Rob (2013) *Design Education for a Sustainable Future*, Earthscan from Routledge

Fleming, Thomas & Zils, Markus (2014) 'Toward a circular economy: Philips CEO Frans van Houten', McKinsey & Company, bit.ly/DRC040

Folke, Carl et al. (2011) 'Reconnecting to the Biosphere', *AMBIO*, 0044-7447, bit.ly/DRC041

_____ (2010) 'Resilience Thinking', *Ecology and Society*, 15(4):20, bit.ly/DRC021

Forum for the Future & Novelis (2014) 'Circular Futures – Accelerating a new economy', Booklet on Novelis new Nachtersedt aluminium recycling centre, Forum for the Future & Novelis

Fromm, Erich (1956) *The Art of Loving*, Harper & Brothers

Fry, Tony (2004) 'The Voice of Sustainment: The Dialectic" in *Design Philosophy Papers*, #01/2005

Fuller, R. Buckminster (1970) *I Seem to Be a Verb – Environment and Man's Future*, Bantam Books

Fullerton, John (2015) *Regenerative Capitalism – How Universal Principles and Patterns will shape our New Economy*, Capital Institute, bit.ly/DRC218

Fullerton, John & Lovins, Hunter (2013) 'Creating A 'Regenerative Economy' to Transform Global Finance Into a Force for Good, What if the economy protected people and the planet?', bit.ly/DRC118

GABV (2014) Global Alliance for Banking on Values – website, bit.ly/DRC190

Gardner, John (2014) 'Disruptive innovation through collaboration', Forum for the Future Blog, bit.ly/DRC189

GARN (2010) 'Global Alliance for the Rights of Nature – Founding Principles', bit.ly/DRC042

Geddes, Patrick (1915) *Cities in Evolution*, Williams & Norgate

GEN (2015) The Global Ecovillage Network – A few words about us, bit.ly/DRC022

Gilman, Robert (1991) 'The Eco-village Challenge', *Context Institute*, bit.ly/DRC137

Girardet, Herbert (2010) 'Regenerative Cities', World Future Council, bit.ly/DRC023

_____ (2015) *Creating Regenerative Cities*, Routledge

GIZ (2012) *Pathways to Eco Industrial Development in India – Concepts and Cases*, Deutsche GIZ, bit.ly/DRC043

Global Footprint Network (2013) Earth Overshoot Day 2013, bit.ly/DRC138

_____ (2008) Earth Overshoot Day 2008, bit.ly/DRC139

Glocal (2015) 'Glocal – A local circular economy experiment', Ecover and Forum for the Future, glocal.ecover.com/

Goldstein, Jeffrey (1999) 'Emergence as a Construct: History and Issues', in *Emergence*, Vol.1, No.1, pp.49-72

Goodwin, Brian (2001) 'Holistic Education in Science', *Society of Effective and Affective Learning Conference Proceedings*, pp.40-43

_____ (1999a) 'From Control to Participation via a Science of Qualities, *Revision*, Vol.21, No.4, pp.2-10

_____ (1999b) 'Reclaiming a Life of Quality', *Journal of Consciousness Studies*, Vol.6, No. 11-12, pp.229-235

Goodwin, Brian, Mills, Stephanie & Spretnak, Charlene (2001) 'Participation in a Living World', *Revision*, Vol.23, No.3, pp.26-32

Graedel, T.E. & Allenby, B.R. (1995) *Industrial Ecology*, Prentice Hall

Graves, Clare (2005) *The Never Ending Quest: Dr. Clare W. Graves Explores Human Nature*, Cowan & Todorovic (eds.), ECELT Publishing, 2nd ed.

_____ (2004) *Levels of Human Existence*, ECELT Publishing
_____ (1974) "Human Nature Prepares for a Momentous Leap", *The Futurist*, pp.72-87, bit.ly/DRC188
Gunderson, Lance H. & Holling, C.S. (2001) *Panarchy*, Island Press
Hadlington, Simon (2014) '3D printing reveals shark skin secrets', *Chemistry World*, May 14th, bit.ly/DRC061
Halweil, Brian (2006) 'Can Organic Food Feed Us All?', *World Watch Magazine*, Vol.19, No.3, bit.ly/DRC062
Hanh, Thich Nhat (2013) *Love Letter to the Earth*, Parallax Press
_____ (1988) *The Heart of Understanding*, ed. Peter Levitt, Parallax Press
_____ (1987) *Being Peace*, Rider
Hardin, G. (1968) 'The Tragedy of the Commons', *Science*, New Series, Vol.162, #3859, 13 Dec, pp.1243-48, bit.ly/DRC232
Hartman, Thom (1999) *Last Hours of Ancient Sunlight*, Three Rivers Press
Harding, Stephan ed. (2001) *Grow Small, Think Beautiful*, Floris Books
Harding, Stephan (2009) *Animate Earth: Science, Intuition and Gaia*, Green Books
Harland, Maddy & Keepin, William eds. (2012) *The Song of the Earth – A Synthesis of the Scientific & Spiritual Worldviews*, The Worldview Key of the EDE by Gaia Education, Permanent Publications
Harman, Jay (2013) *The Shark's Paintbrush*, White Cloud Press
Harman, Willis (1998) *Global Mind Change*, 2nd ed., Institute of Noetic Sciences, Berret-Koehler
Havel, Václav et al. (1985) *The Power of the Powerless*, Hutchinson
Hawken, Paul (2007) *Blessed Unrest*, Viking
_____ (1993) *The Ecology of Commerce – How Business can Save the Planet*, Weidenfeld & Nicolson
Hawken, Paul, Lovins, Amory B. & Lovins, L. Hunter (2000) *Natural Capitalism*, Earthscan Publications
Heck, Stefan & Rogers, Matt (2014) *Resource Revolution*, New Harvest
Henderson, Hazel (2014) 'Mapping the global transition to the solar age – From 'economism' to earth systems science', ICAEW & The Centre for Tomorrow's Company, bit.ly/DRC140
Higgins, Polly (2010) *Eradicating Ecocide*, Shepheard-Walwyn
Hodgson, Anthony (2012) *A Transdisciplinary World Model*, Proceedings of the 55th conf. of the ISSS, bit.ly/DRC045
_____ (2011) *Ready for Anything – Designing Resilience for a Transforming World*, Triarchy Press
Hodgson, Anthony & Sharpe, Bill (2007) 'Deepening Futures with System Structure', in *Scenarios for Success: Turing Insights Into Action*, von der Heijden & Sharpe eds. Wiley
HOK (2015a) 'Fully Integrated Thinking [FIT]', bit.ly/DRC46
_____ (2015b) 'Genius of Biome – Temperate Broadleaf Forest', bit.ly/DRC47
_____ (2015c) 'A New Community Rooted in Nature – Lavasa Hill Station Master Plan', bit.ly/DRC198
Holdrege, Craig (2000) 'Where do organisms end?', *Context Magazine*, Spring 2000, pp.14-16
Holistic Management International (2015) 'Holistic Management', bit.ly/DRC199
Holling, C.C. & Meffe, G.K. (1996) 'Command and Control and the Pathology of Natural Resource Management, *Conservation Biology*, Vol. 10, No. 2, pp.329-337
Holling, C.S. (1973) 'Resilience and Stability of Ecological Systems', in *Annual Review of Ecology and Systematics*, Volume 4, pp.1-23, Annual Reviews Inc.
Holmgren, David (2011) *Permaculture Principles & Pathways Beyond Sustainability*, Permanent Publications
_____ (2002) *Essence of Permaculture*, Holmgren Design, bit.ly/DRC116
Homer-Dixon, Thomas (2006) *The Upside of Down*, Island Press
Honeyman, Ryan (2014) *The B Corp Handbook*, bit.ly/DRC276
Hopkins, Rob (2014) *The Transition Handbook: From Oil Dependency to Local Resilience*, UIT Cambridge
_____ (2011) *The Transition Companion*, Chelsea Green Publishing
_____ (2009) 'Resilience Thinking', *Resurgence*, No.257, Nov/Dec 2009, pp.12-15
Hosey, Lance (2012) *The Shape of Green: Aesthetics, Ecology, and Design*, Island Press
Hutchins, Giles (2014) *The Illusion of Separation – Exploring the Cause of our Current Crises*, Floris Books
_____ (2012) *The Nature of Business – Redesigning for Resilience*, Green Books
_____ (2011) 'Transformational times call for transformational change', *The Guardian*, 28th July, bit.ly/DRC117
Huxley, T.H. (1869) *Goethe: Aphorisms on Nature*, Introduction to the 1st edition of *Nature*, bit.ly/DRC187
IAFN (2015) 'What is Analog Forestry?', International Analog Forestry Network, bit.ly/DRC186

References

International Futures Forum (2009) *Transformative Resilience,* bit.ly/DRC71
International Living Future Institute (2014) *Living Building Challenge 3.0,* bit.ly/DRC072
IPRN (2015) Society for Ecological Restoration – Indigenous Peoples' Restoration Network, bit.ly/DRC200
Irwin, Terry (2012) 'Transforming the Design process to Create Better Solutions', *Solutions Journal,* April 2012, bit.ly/DRC201
_____ (2011) 'Wicked Problems and the Relationship Triad', in *Grow Small, Think Beautiful,* Floris Books, bit.ly/DRC202
Jackson, Ross (2012) *Occupy World Street,* Green Books
Jackson, Tim & Victor, Peter A. (2013) *Green Economy at Community Scale,* Metcalf Foundation, bit.ly/DRC203
Jackson, Tim (2009a) *Prosperity Without Growth?,* UK Sustainable Development Commission, bit.ly/DRC073
_____ (2009b) *Prosperity Without Growth – Economics for a Finite Planet,* Earthscan
Jackson, Wes (2002) 'Natural Systems Agriculture: A radical alternative', *Agriculture, Ecosystems and Environment,* Vol.88, pp.111-117, bit.ly/DRC074
Janisch, Claire (2015) 'Abalone Inspires a Materials Revolution for Lightweight & Strong Materials, Two Oceans Aquarium & GeniusLab, South Africa, bit.ly/DRC234
Jonas, Wolfgang (2001) 'Design – Es gibt nichts theoretischeres als eine gute Praxis', *Symposium IFG Ulm,* 21-23 Sept.
Joubert, Kosha Anja & Dregger, Leila (2015) *Ecovillage: 1001 Ways to Heal the Planet,* Triarchy Press
Joubert, Kosha Anja & Alfred, Robin (2007) *Beyond You and Me – Inspiration and Wisdom for Building Community,* The Social Key of the EDE by Gaia Education, Permanent Publications
Jung, Carl (1921) *Psychologische Typen,* Rascher Verlag
Kahane, Adam (2012) *Transformative Scenario Planning,* Berrett-Koehler
_____ (2010) *Power and Love: A Theory and Practice of Social Change,* Berrett-Koehler
_____ (2004) *Solving Tough Problems,* Berrett-Koehler
Kauffman, Stuart A. (1995) *At Home in the Universe,* Oxford University Press
Kelly, Sean M. (2010) *Coming Home – The Birth & Transformation of the Planetary Era,* Lindisfarne Books
Kennedy, Margit & Kennedy, Declan *eds.* (1997) *Designing Ecological Settlements,* Dietrich Reimer Verlag
Klein, Naomi (2014) *This Changes Everything – Capitalism vs The Climate,* Simon & Schuster
Knapp, Clifford E. & Smith, Thomas E. (2005) *Exploring the Power of Solo, Silence and Solitude,* Association for Experiential Education
Koestler, Arthur (1989) *The Ghost in the Machine,* Arkana Books (first published in 1967)
Koestler, Arthur & Smythies, John R. (1969) *Beyond Reductionism – New Perspectives in the Life Sciences,* Proceedings of the Alpbach Symposium in 1968, Hutchinson
Koohafkan, Parviz & Altieri, Miguel A. (2010) *Conserving Our World's Agricultural Heritage,* Food and Agriculture Organization of the United Nations (FAO), bit.ly/DRC049
Kossoff, Gideon (2011a) *Holism and the Reconstruction of Everyday Life,* PhD Thesis, Univ. of Dundee, bit.ly/DRC050
_____ (2011b) 'Holism and the Reconstruction of Everyday Life', in *Grow Small, Think Beautiful,* Harding, Stephan *ed.,* Floris Books, bit.ly/DRC051
Kostakis, Vasilis & Bauwens, Michel (2014) *Network Society and Future Scenarios for a Collaborative Economy,* Palgrave MacMillan
Kricher, John (2009) *The Balance of Nature: Ecology's Enduring Myth,* Princeton University Press
Kumar, Satish (2002) *You Are Therefore I Am – Impressions and Inspirations,* Green Books
Land Institute (2015a) 'Vision & Mission – Transforming Agriculture, Perennially', bit.ly/DRC185
_____ (2015b) 'History & Timeline of the Land Institute', bit.ly/DRC075
_____ (2014) 'Transforming Agriculture with Perennial Polycultures', bit.ly/DRC115
László, Ervin (2006) *The Chaos Point – The World at the Crossroads,* Piatkus Books
Lawrence, D.H. (1930) 'A Propos of Lady Chatterley's Lover' in Roberts, W. & Moore, H. T. (eds), *Phoenix II: Uncollected, Unpublished, and other prose works by D.H. Lawrence,* (1968) The Viking Press
Leicester, Graham & O'Hara, Maureen (2009) *Ten Things to Do in a Conceptual Emergency,* Triarchy Press
Leighton, Jonathan (2011) *The Battle for Compassion – Ethics in an Apathetic Universe,* Algora Publishing
Leopold, Aldo (1949) *A Sand County Almanac,* Oxford University Press
Lewis, Michael & Conaty, Pat (2012) *The Resilience Imperative,* New Society Publishers

Lietaer, Bernard, Arnsperger, Christian, Goerner, Sally & Brunnhuber, Stefan (2012) *Money and Sustainability – The Missing Link*, Triarchy Press

Living Future Institute Australia (2014) 'Living Futures Challenge', bit.ly/DRC114

Liu, John D. (2014) 'Embracing Inevitable Transformational Change',17 Dec., Cusco, Peru, bit.ly/DRC204

_____ (2011) 'Finding Sustainability in Ecosystem Restoration', in *Kosmos Journal*, Fall/Winter 2011, pp.17-24, bit.ly/DRC025

Lovelock, James (2000) *Gaia: The Practical Science of Planetary Medicine*, Gaia Books

Lovins, Amory (2011) *Reinventing Fire – Bold Business Solutions for the New Energy Era*, Chelsea Green

Lovins, L. Hunter & Lovins, Amory B. (1995) 'How Not To Parachute More Cats', The Rocky Mountain Institute

Lushwala, Arkan (2012) *The Time of the Black Jaguar*, Hernan Quinones

Macy, Joanna & Young Brown, Molly (2014) *Coming Back to Life*, New Society Publishers

Macy, Joanna & Johnstone, Chris (2012) *Active Hope*, New World Library

Macy, Joanna & Young Brown, Molly (1998) *Coming Back to Life*, New Society Publishers

Macy, Joanna (1994) 'Towards a Healing of the Self and the World', in *Key Concepts in Critical Theory: Ecology*, Carolyn Merchant ed., Humanity Books

Madron, Roy & Jopling, John (2003) *Gaian Democracies – Redefining Globalisation and People Power*, Schumacher Briefing No.9, Green Books

Manzini, Ezio & Francois Jégou (2004) *Sustainable Everyday – scenarios of urban life*, Edizioni Ambiente

Marin, Colin (2004) 'Watch the Animals – Review of Zoomorphic', *ArchitectureAU*, bit.ly/DRC183

Martinez, Dennis (2010) 'The Value of Indigenous Ways of Knowing to Western Science and Environmental Sustainability', *Journal of Sustainability Education*, May 2010, bit.ly/DRC076

Mascaró, Juan (1961) *Lamps of Fire – The Spirit of Religions*, Methuen

Maturana, Humberto, Verden-Zoller, Gerda (1996) 'Biology of Love', bit.ly/DRC184

Maturana, Humberto R. & Varela, Francisco J. (1987) *The Tree of Knowledge*, New Science Library, Shambhala

Maturana, H.R., Varela, F.J., & Uribe, R. (1974). 'Autopoiesis', *Biosystems*, 5, 187-196

Mare, Christopher & Lindegger, Max eds. (2011) *Designing Ecological Habitats – Creating a Sense of Place*, The Ecological Key of the EDE by Gaia Education, Permanent Publications

Marks, Paul (2014) 'Vertical farms sprouting all over the world', *New Scientist*, 2952, Jan 2014, bit.ly/DRC052

McDonough, William & Braungart, Michael (2013) *The Upcycle – Beyond Sustainability,* North Point Press

_____ (2002) *Cradle to Cradle – Remaking the Way we Make Things*, North Point Press

McHarg, Ian L. & Steiner, Frederick R. (1998) *To Heal the Earth – Selected Writings of Ian L. McHarg*, Island Press

McHarg, Ian L. (1996) *A Quest for Life – An Autobiography*, John Wiley

_____ (1970) 'Architecture in an Ecological View of the World', in McHarg & Steiner (1998) pp.175-185

_____ (1969) *Design With Nature*, The American Museum of Natural History & Doubleday

_____ (1964) 'The Place of Nature in the City of Man', in McHarg & Steiner (1998) pp.24-38

_____ (1963) 'Man and the Environment', in McHarg & Steiner (1998) pp.10-23

Meadows, Donella (2008) *Thinking in Systems – A Primer*, Diana Wright ed., Chelsea Green

Meadows, Donella, Randers, Jorgen & Meadows, Dennis (2005) *Limits to Growth – The 30 Year Update*, Earthscan

_____ (1992) *Beyond the Limits – Global Collapse or a Sustainable Future*, Earthscan

Mehta, Nipun (2012) 'Designing for Generosity', TEDxBerkeley, bit.ly/DRC219

Millennium Ecosystem Assessment (2005) *Ecosystems and Human Well-being: Synthesis*, Island Press

Miller, Ethan (2010) *Solidarity Economy: Key Concepts and Issues'*, in Kawano, Emily, Masterson, Tom Teller-Ellsber eds., *Solidarity Economy I: Building Alternatives for People and Planet*, Center for Popular Economics

Milton, John P. (2006) *Sky Above Earth Below – Spiritual Practice in Nature*, Sentient Publications

Mollison, Bill (1988) *Permaculture – A Designer's Manual*, Tagari Publications

Mulgan, Goeff & Leadbeater, Charlie (2013) *Systems Innovation*, Discussion Paper, Nesta, bit.ly/DRC182

Mulgan, Goeff (2007) *Social Innovation – What it is, Why it matters, and How it can be accelerated*, Saïd Business School Oxford, Skoll Centre for Social Entrepreneurship, The Young Foundation

Murray, Robin, Caulier-Grice, Julie, Mulgan, Geoff (2010) *The Open Book of Social Innovation*, Nesta & The Young Foundation, bit.ly/DRC141

Naess, Arne (1988) 'Self-Realization', in Seed, John *et al.*, *Thinking Like a Mountain*, New Society Publishers, pp.19-30

References

Nature of Business (2013) 'Biomimicry for Business? 'Nature's Business Principles', bit.ly/DRC174

Nelson, Melissa K. (2011) 'Red & Green', bit.ly/DRC181

Nelson, Melissa K. ed. (2008) *Original Instructions – Indigenous Teachings for a Sustainable Future*, Bear & Co

New Economics Foundation (2015) 'About NEF: What we do', bit.ly/DRC026

New Economy Coalition (2015) 'New Economy Coalition', bit.ly/DRC173

Newman, Peter & Jennings, Isabella (2008) *Cities as Sustainable Ecosystems*, Island Press

Nguyen, H., Stuchtey, M. & Zils, M. (2014) 'Remaking the industrial economy', *McKinsey Quarterly*, bit.ly/DRC53

Norton, Brian G. (1992) 'A New Paradigm for Environmental Management' in Costanza, Norton & Haskell, eds., *Ecosystem Health*, Island Press

Oppenheimer, Leonora (2010) 'Can we use Biomimcry to Design Cities?', *Treehugger*, 3rd June, 2010, bit.ly/DRC078

Orr, David W. (2002) *The Nature of Design – Ecology, Culture, and Human Intention*, Oxford University Press

_____ (1994) *Earth in Mind – On Education, Environment, and the Human Prospect*, Island Press

_____ (1992) *Ecological Literacy*, State University of New York Press

Ostrom, Elinor (1990) *Governing the Commons*, Cambridge University Press

P2P Foundation (2014) 'Part Three: The Hypothetical Model of Mature Peer Production', in *Network Society and Future Scenarios for a Collaborative Economy*, Kostakis & Bauwens, bit.ly/DRC254

Palmer, Parker J. (2004) *A Hidden Wholeness: The Journey Toward an Undivided Life*, Jossey-Bass

Pasture Cropping (2008) 'Pasture Cropping and No Hill Cropping', bit.ly/DRC079

Pauli, Gunter (2010) *The Blue Economy – 10 Years, 100 Innovations, 100 Million Jobs*, Paradigm Publications

Pawlyn, Michael (2014) Exploration Architecture website, bit.ly/DRC278

_____ (2011) *Biomimicry in Architecture*, Paperback reprinted edition, RIBA Publishing

PAX Scientific (2015a) 'Capturing the Force of Nature', company website: bit.ly/DRC170

_____ (2015b) 'Using Biomimicry in Tank Mixing', company website: bit.ly/DRC171

_____ (2015c) 'Capturing the Force of Nature – Pax Fan', bit.ly/DRC113

PAX Pure (2012) 'Pax Pure – The Future of Desalination', company website, bit.ly/DRC172

Pearce, Fred (2013) *True Nature: Revising Ideas on What is Pristine and Wild*, Yale Environment 360, 13 May 2013, bit.ly/DRC241

Philips, April (2013) *Designing Urban Agriculture*, Wiley

Petrini, Carlo *et al.* (2012) 'The Central Role of Food', Slow Food World Congress Paper, bit.ly/DRC142

Pigem, Jordi (2009) *Buena crisis: Hacia un mundo postmaterialista*, Editorial Kairós

Plan C (2014) 'The Business Model Innovation Grid', bit.ly/DRC169

Plotkin, Bill (2008) *Nature and the Human Soul*, New World Library

Polyface (2015a) 'The Polyface Story', Joel Salatin Polyface Farm, bit.ly/DRC143

_____ (2015b) 'Polyface Guiding Principles', bit.ly/DRC220

Post Growth Institute (2015) 'About Post Growth', bit.ly/DRC056

Prigann, Hermann (2004) *Ecological Aesthetics: Art In Environmental Design: Theory And Practice*, Birkhäuser

Rawls, W.J. *et al.* (2003) 'Effects of solid organic carbon on soil water retention', *Geoderma*, Vol.116, pp.61-76

Ray, Paul & Anderson, Sherry Ruth (2000) *The Cultural Creatives*, Harmony Books

Reed, Bill (2007) 'Shifting from 'Sustainability' to Regeneration, *Building Research & Information*, 35(6), pp.674-680, Routledge, Taylor & Francis Group, bit.ly/DRC080

_____ (2006) 'Shifting our Mental Model', Integrative Design Collaborative, bit.ly/DRC280

Resilience Alliance (2015a) 'Resilience', bit.ly/DRC168

_____ (2015b) 'Key Concepts', bit.ly/DRC242

_____ (2015c) 'Panarchy', bit.ly/DRC221

Rifkin, Jeremy (2013) *The Third Industrial Revolution*, Palgrave Macmillan Trade

_____ (2009) *The Empathic Civilization – The Race to Global Consciousness in a World in Crisis*, Tarcher

Rilke, Rainer Maria (1903) *Letters to a Young Poet*, Letter number 4, bit.ly/DRC279

Robert, Karl-Henrik (2008) *The Natural Step Story*, New Catalyst Books

Robinson, Simon & Moares Robinson, Maria (2014) *Holonomics*, Floris Books

Rockefeller Foundation (2015a) *100 Resilient Cities* website, bit.ly/DRC166

_____ (2015b) *100 Resilient Cities – Selected Cities,* bit.ly/DRC167

Rockström, Johannes *et al.* (2009) "A Safe Operating Space for Humanity, *Nature,* No.461, 472-475, bit.ly/DRC207

Rodale Institute (2014) 'Regenerative Organic Agriculture and Climate Change', bit.ly/DRC112

Rogers, John (2013) *Local Money - What difference does it make?* Triarchy Press

Roland, Ethan & Landua, Gregory (2013) *Regenerative Enterprise,* Version 1.0, bit.ly/DRC206

_____ (2011) *Eight Forms of Capital – A Whole System of Economic Understanding,* bit.ly/DRC208

Rowson, Jonathan (2014) *Spiritualise – Revitalizing spirituality to address 21st century challenges,* The RSA, Dec. 2014

Russell, Jean M. (2013) *Thrivability,* Triarchy Press

Russell, Jean M. ed. (2010) *Thrivability – A Collective Sketch,* bit.ly/DRC057

Sahara Forest Project (2015) 'Restorative Growth', bit.ly/DRC222

Saikku, Laura (2006) *Eco-Industrial Parks,* Regional Council of Etelä-Davo, Finland

Salazar-Preece, Gonzalo (2011) *Co-Designing in Love,* PhD Thesis, University of Dundee, bit.ly/DRC058

Sale, Kirkpatrick (1982) *Human Scale,* Putnam Publishers

San Diego Zoo (2010) *Global Biomimcry Efforts,* San Diego Zoological Society, bit.ly/DRC145

Sathouris, Elisabet (2014) 'The Brink of Disaster… or The Brink of Maturity?', *World Future Review,* Fall 2014

Savory, Allan (2013) 'Response to request for information on the 'science' and 'methodology' underpinning Holistic Management and holistic planned grazing', bit.ly/DRC164

Savory Institute (2015) 'Empowering Caretakers of the Land', bit.ly/DRC146

_____ (2014) 'Holistic Management: Portfolio of Scientific Findings', bit.ly/DRC146

_____ (2013) 'Restoring the Climate through Capture and Storage of Soil Carbon through Holistic Planned Grazing', bit.ly/DRC59

Scharmer, C. Otto (2009) *Theory U – Leading from the future as it emerges,* Berrett Koehler

Schmidheiny, Stephan (1992) *Changing Course – A Global Business Perspective on Development and the Environment,* Business Council for Sustainable Development, MIT Press

Schmidt, Michele C. *et al.* (2011) 'Increasing farm income and local food access', *Journal of Agriculture, Food Systems, and Community Development,* Vol.1, Issue 4, pp.157-175

Schmidt-Bleek, Friedrich (1997) *Wieviel Umwelt braucht der Mensch? Faktor 10 – das Maß für ökologisches Wirtschaften,* Deutscher Taschenbuch Verlag (first edit. with Birkhäuser in 1994)

Schrödinger, Erwin (1944) *What is Life? - Mind and Matter,* Cambridge University Press

Schumacher, E. Fritz (1973) *Small is Beautiful,* Harper Perennial, bit.ly/DRC165

Schwartz, Peter (1996) *The Art of the Long View,* Currency Doubleday, reprinted edition

Science Daily (2008) 'Humans Have Ten Times More Bacteria Than Human Cells', bit.ly/DRC147

Seed, John (2002) 'Ecopsychology', bit.ly/DRC110

Senge, Peter (2008) *The Necessary Revolution – How Indiviuals and Organizations Are Working Together to Create a Sustainable World,* with Brian Smit, Nina Kruschwitz, Joe Laur, and Sara Schley, Nicholas Brealey

Senge, Peter, Scharmer, C. Otto, Jaworski, Joseph & Flowers, Betty Sue (2005) *Presence,* Nicholas Brealey

Senosiain, Javier (2003) *Bio-Architecture,* Architectural Press

Sharklet Technologies Inc (2015) 'Sharklet Products', bit.ly/DRC179

Sharpe, Bill (2013) *Three Horizons,* Triarchy Press

Shiva, Vandana (2012) *Making Peace with the Earth,* Pluto Press

_____ (2005) *Earth Democracy – Justice, Sustainability, and Peace,* South End Press

Sinek, Simon (2011) *Start with Why: How Great Leaders Inspire Everyone to Take Action,* Portfolio Trade

Smith, Sally E. & Read, David J. (2008) *Mycorrhizal Symbiosis,* 3rd edition, Academic Press

Smuts, Jan Christiaan (1927) *Holism and Evolution,* Macmillan, bit.ly/DRC148

SolidarityNYC (2015) 'The Basics', bit.ly/DRC111

Soubbotina, Tatyana P. (2000) *Beyond Economic Growth,* The IBRD / World Bank

Stahel, Walter (2014) 'The Business Angle of a Circular Economy', in Ellen MacArthur Foundation *eds., A New Dynamic – Effective Business in a Circular Economy,* Ellen MacArthur Foundation

Stamets, Paul (2005) *Mycelium Running – How Mushrooms Can Help Save the World,* Ten Speed Press

Steele, Robert David (2014a) 'UN Paper: Beyond Data Monitoring, Public Intelligence Blog, bit.ly/DRC160

_____ (2014b) 'Applied Collective Intelligence', Public Intelligence Blog, bit.ly/DRC161

References

_____ (2012) *The Open-Source Everything Manifesto: Transparency, Truth, and Trust*, Evolver Editions
Steffen, Will *et al.* (20015) 'Planetary boundaries: Guiding human development on a changing planet' in *Science*, Vol. 347, Issue 6223, bit.ly/DRC277
Steffen, Will *et al.* (2011) 'The Anthropocene', *Ambio* 0044-7447, bit.ly/DRC105
Stewart, John E. (2014) 'The Direction of Evolution', *Biosystems*, Vol.123, pp.27-36, Elsevier, bit.ly/DRC83
Stiglitz, Joseph E. (2013) *The Price of Inequality*, WW Norton & Company
Swimme, Brian & Berry, Thomas (1992) *The Universe Story*, Harper Collins
Tarnas, Richard (2007) *Cosmos and Psyche – Intimations of a New World View*, Plume Books
_____ (1996) *The Passion of the Western Mind*, Pimlico & Random House
The Work that Reconnects (2012) 'Foundations of the Work', bit.ly/DRC060
Time Banking UK, (2015) bit.ly/DRC245
Todd, John, Brown, Erica J.G. & Wells, Eric (2003) 'Ecological design applied', *Ecological Engineering*, Vol.20, pp.421-440, bit.ly/DRC149
Treanor, Jill (2014) 'Richest 1% of people own nearly half of global wealth…', *The Guardian*, 14th Oct. bit.ly/DRC84
Tullio Lieberg, Albert (2010) *The Systems Change – The Doctrine of the Commons and Demonetarisation – The Globally Renewed Society for Planet Earth,* Berlin – Barcelona
UK Government Office for Science (2011) *Foresight International Dimension of Climate Change*, Final Project Report, The Government Office for Science, UK
UNCTAD (2013) *Trade and Environment Review – Wake Up Before it is too Late,* United Nations Conference on Trade and Development, bit.ly/DRC085
UNGSP (2012) *Resilient People, Resilient Planet: A future worth choosing*, United Nations Secretary-General's High-level Panel on Global Sustainability, bit.ly/DRC107
UNISDR (2015) *Making Cities Resilient Campaign*, United Nations Office for Disaster Risk Reduction, bit.ly/DRC223
UNITAR (2012) 'Leading international thinkers call for a new social contract', bit.ly/DRC162
UNRISD (2014) *Social and Solidarity Economy – Is There a New Economy in the Making?*, Authors: Utting, Peter, van Dijk, Nadine & Matheï, Marie-Adélaïde, United Nations Research Institute for Social Development
Vanderbilt, Tom (2012) 'How Biomimcry is Inspiring Human Innovation', *Smithsonian*, Sept. 2012, bit.ly/DRC108
van der Ryn, Sim & Cowan, Stuart (1996) *Ecological Design*, Island Press
van Houten, Frans (2014) 'Are we on the cusp of the new economic revolution?', Philips, bit.ly/DRC109
Vatican (2015) 'Encyclical letter *Laudato Si*', bit.ly/DRC205
Vester, Frederic (2004) *Die Kunst vernetzt zu Denken,* Der Neue Bericht an den Club of Rome, Deutscher Taschenbuch
Via Campesina (2011) 'What is La Via Campesina? The International peasant's voice', bit.ly/DRC90
Victor, Peter (2010) 'Questioning economic growth', *Nature*, Vol. 468, pp.370-371
Village Lab (2015) 'Vision & Mission', bit.ly/DRC091
Von Weizsäcker, Ernst U., Lovins, Amory B. & Lovins, L. Hunter (1997) *Factor Four: Doubling Wealth, Halving Resource Use*, Earthscan Publications
Wahl, Daniel C. (2011) 'Transformative Resilience', in *Designing Ecological Habitats,* Mare & Lindegger *eds.,* Permanent Publications
_____ (2010) 'Integrity', in *Thrivability – A Collective Sketch* (Russell, 2010) p.16
_____ (2007) 'Scale-linking Design for Systemic Health', *Int. Jnl. of Ecodynamics*, Vol.2 No.1, pp.1-16, bit.ly/DRC93
_____ (2006a) 'Design for human and planetary health: a transdisciplinary approach to sustainability', in *Management of Natural Resources, Sustainable Development and Ecological Hazards,* Brebbia *et.al eds.*, WIT Transactions on Ecology and the Environment, Vol.99, pp.285-296, bit.ly/DRC094
_____ (2006b) *Design for Human and Planetary Health*, PhD Thesis, University of Dundee, bit.ly/DRC095
_____ (2005) 'Eco-literacy, Ethics and Aesthetics in Natural Design', *Design System Evolution*, European Academy of Design Conference 2005, bit.ly/DRC96
_____ (2002) *Exploring Participation – Holistic Science, Sustainability and the Emergence of a Healthy Whole through Appropriate Participation*, Master's Thesis, Schumacher College & Plymouth University, bit.ly/DRC97
Wahl, Daniel C. & Baxter, Seaton (2008) 'The Designer's Role in Facilitating Sustainable Solutions', *Design Issues*, Vol.24, No.2, pp.72-83, bit.ly/DRC92

Waller, Tom (2012) 'Stretching the Boundaries', *Nature Materials*, Vol.11, August 2012, bit.ly/DRC98
Walljasper, Jay (2011) 'What, Really, is the Commons?', *Terrain*, No.27, Spring/Summer, bit.ly/DRC99
Waltner-Toews, David (2004) *Ecosystem Sustainability and Health*, Cambridge University Press
Warner Babcock (2015) Warner Babcock Institute for Green Chemistry, bit.ly/DRC224
WBCSD (2010) *Vision 2050*, World Business Council for Sustainable Development, bit.ly/DRC159
WBGU (2011) *World in Transition*, German Advisory Council on Global Change, bit.ly/DRC100
Weber, Andreas (2013) *Enlivenment*, Heinrich Böll Stiftung, bit.ly/DRC158
Wenner, M. (2007) 'Humans Carry More Bacterial Cells than...', *Scientific American*, 30th Nov, bit.ly/DRC255
Westley, Frances *et.al.* (2011) 'Tipping Towards Sustainability', *Ambio* 40(7) pp.762-780, bit.ly/DRC240
Wheatley, Margaret (1999) *Leadership and the New Sciences - Discovering Order in a Chaotic World*, Berrett-Koehler
Whitman, Steve & Ferguson, Sharon (2014) 'Taking the Permaculture Path to Community Resilience', bit.ly/DRC101
Wilber, Ken & Combs, Allan (2010) 'Consciousness Explained Better', Ken Wilber's Blog, bit.ly/DRC153
Wilber, Ken (2007) *The Integral Vision*, Shambhala Publications
_____ (2001) *A Theory of Everything*, Gateway, Gill & Macmillan
Wilkinson, Richard & Pickett, Kate (2011) *The Spirit Level*, Bloomsbury Press
Wilkinson, Richard G. (2005) *The Impact of Inequality - How to make sick societies healthier*, Routledge
_____ (1996) *Unhealthy Societies - The Afflictions of Inequality*, Routledge
Wilson, Edward O. (1986) *Biophilia - The human bond with other species*, Harvard University Press
_____ (1999) *Consilience - The Unity of Knowledge*, Vintage, reprint edition
Wilson, Monte (2013) 'Bio-inspired Planning and Design', *American Architectural Foundation*, July, 2013
Wines, James (2000) *Green Architecture*, Taschen Verlag
Wingspread Statement (1998) 'The Wingspread Consensus Statement on the Precautionary Principle', Wingspread Conference, bit.ly/DRC102
Wolfe, Josh (2012) 'The Father of Green Chemistry' (Interview with Paul Anastas), *Forbes*, bit.ly/DRC154
Wonder, Stevie (1979) *Journey Through the Secret Life of Plants*, bit.ly/DRC155
World Bank (2013) *Building Resilience*, bit.ly/DRC156X
_____ (2012) *Carbon Sequestration in Agricultural Soils*, bit.ly/DRC103
World Economic Forum (2014) *Towards the Circular Economy*, WEF (with Ellen McArthur Foundation and McKinsey & Co), bit.ly/DRC157
_____ (2012) *Well-being and Global Success*, Global Agenda Council on Health & Wellbeing, bit.ly/DRC104
World Health Organization (1992) *Our planet, our health*, WHO
Worldwatch Institute (2012) *State of the World 2012*, Island Press, bit.ly/DRC86
Wright, Robert (2001) *Nonzero - The Logic of Human Destiny*, reprint edition, Vintage
Yeomansplow (2015) 'Yeomans Plows', bit.ly/DRC87
YSI (2014) 'YSI Advancing Social Innovation', Young Social Innovators Ireland
ZERI (2013) 'Beer: Making Bread and Mushrooms', bit.ly/DRC089
Zimmerman, Jack & Coyle, Virginia (2009) *The Way of Council* (Second Edition), Bramble Books
Zimmerman, Michael E. (2005) 'Integral Ecology: A Perspective, Developmental, and Coordinating Approach to Environmental Problems', in *World Futures*, Vol.61, No.1-2, Special Issue on Integral Ecology, pp.50-62

About the Author

Daniel Christian Wahl was born in Munich in 1971 and grew up in Germany. By the time he was 28 he had travelled in 35 different countries on six continents. His early career was as a marine biologist and scuba diving instructor, before he decided to focus on sustainability and sustainable communities in 1998. Originally trained as a biologist and zoologist at the University of Edinburgh and the University of California, Santa Cruz, Daniel also holds an MSc in Holistic Science (Schumacher College, 2002) and a PhD in Natural Design (University of Dundee, 2006).

Daniel has taught capacity building workshops on a wide range of sustainability issues to local authorities and businesses through the UN-affiliated training centre CIFAL Scotland. Among his consultancy clients have been the United Nations Institute of Training and Research (UNITAR), the British Government's UK Foresight (with Decision Integrity Ltd.), LEAD International, CLEAR Village, and companies like Camper, Ecover (with Forum for the Future), Lush and the tourism innovation cluster Balears.t, as well as, various universities and charities.

He was the director of Findhorn College between 2007 and 2010, during which time he helped to create the MSc in Sustainable Community Design (Heriot-Watt University), co-founded the 'Learning Partnership for Creative Sustainability' and co-organized two international Bioneers conferences in Holland and Findhorn. Daniel has been a member of Gaia Education (since 2007) and the International Futures Forum (since 2009). He is also a fellow of the RSA (Royal Society for the encouragement of Arts, Manufactures and Commerce) and the Findhorn Foundation Fellowship.

Daniel has worked closely with Gaia Education since 2006 when he participated in the first training of trainers for the 'Ecovillage Design Education' (EDE) programme. He has taught EDE courses in Scotland, Thailand, and Spain. He is a co-author of all four dimensions (social, ecological, economic, worldview) of the curriculum for Gaia Education's online course in 'Design for Sustainability' (GEDS), and is co-developing a new programme in 'Bioregional Design Education' (BDE) for Gaia Education. He also collaborates with the research working-group of the Global Ecovillage Network (GEN).

Daniel lives on Majorca, and works locally and internationally as a consultant, educator and activist. In 2012, he co-founded 'Biomimicry Iberia' and in 2015 co-organized the first practitioners camp of the 'European Biomimicry Alliance' (EBA) on Majorca. He collaborates with the Masters of Design and Innovation at the IED (European Institute of Design) in Madrid, has taught at Elisava Design School in Barcelona, and co-developed the S.M.A.R.T. UIB project of the Universidad de las Islas Baleares (Sustainable, Multi-stakeholder, Applied, Regenerative, Transformative) where he is helping to develop a series of programmes in transformative innovation. Daniel has published numerous articles and academic papers and collaborated with a number of documentary film projects. *Designing Regenerative Cultures* is his first book.

About the Publisher

Triarchy Press is an independent publisher of new alternative thinking (altThink) about organizations and society – and practical ways to apply that thinking. Where Daniel Wahl takes the broadest view of the opportunities available to us, some of our authors focus on narrower areas: education, local government, managing commercial organizations, policing, among others. Looking more widely, Triarchy Press books also consider emergent changes in fields like walking, dance, psychogeography, performance and psychotherapy. All exemplify the kind of practical hope and wise initiative pioneered by IFF (below).

- International Futures Forum (IFF) is one of Triarchy's Publishing Partners. IFF's books on designing resilience, transformative innovation in education, Three Horizons thinking and things to do in a conceptual emergency are all published by Triarchy.

- Planning for the future is also a highly technical matter and one of the longest-established approaches is Scenario Planning. *Facing the Fold* brings together a collection of the best essays on the subject by one of its leading proponents, James (Jay) Ogilvy.

- Stephen Millett's guide to forecasting and planning, *Managing the Future,* offers a straightforward approach to strategic planning in business. Alongside it, Tricia Lustig's *Strategic Foresight* offers leaders tools for navigating into an uncertain future.

- *Ecovillage* brings together an inspiring selection of ecovillage community projects from all over the world.

www.triarchypress.net/the-future

About International Futures Forum

International Futures Forum (IFF) is a centre for transformative innovation based in Scotland and working with partners in business, government and communities worldwide. Its experience and expertise covers fields related to economy, governance, sustainability and culture – notably in healthcare, education, local government, policy-making and community regeneration. The IFF Practice Centre offers a selection of resources to support any group or organization on its journey to transformative innovation – and the chance to join a community of hearts and minds engaged in similar endeavours.

The Practice Centre is a collection of micro-sites, each complete in itself and tailored either to a particular task or to a particular domain. These resources are the result of IFF's learning through practice for over a decade. They are available on open access:

www.iffpraxis.com